Media and Democracy

Media and Democracy addresses key topics and themes in relation to democratic theory, media and technology, comparative media studies, media and history, and the evolution of media research. For example:

- How does TV entertainment contribute to the democratic life of society?
- Why are Americans less informed about politics and international affairs than Europeans?
- How should new communications technology and globalisation change our understanding of the democratic role of the media?
- What does the rise of international e-zines reveal about the limits of the Internet?
- What is the future of journalism?
- Does advertising influence the media?
- Is American media independence from government a myth?
- How have the media influenced the development of modern society?

Curran's response to these questions provides both a clear introduction to media research for university undergraduates studying in different countries and an innovative analysis by one of the field's leading scholars.

James Curran is Director of the Goldsmiths Leverhulme Media Research Centre and Professor of Communications at Goldsmiths, University of London, UK. He has authored and edited numerous books, including *Power without Responsibility* (seventh edition, with Jean Seaton, 2010), *Media and Society* (fifth edition, 2010) and *Media and Power* (2002).

Communication and Society
Series Editor: James Curran

This series encompasses the broad field of media and cultural studies. Its main concerns are the media and the public sphere: whether the media empower or fail to empower popular forces in society; media organizations and public policy; political communication; and the role of media entertainment, ranging from potboilers and the human interest story to rock music and TV sport.

Media and Democracy

James Curran

Routledge
Taylor & Francis Group

LONDON AND NEW YORK

First published 2011
by Routledge
2 Park Square, Milton Park, Abingdon, Oxon, OX14 4RN

Simultaneously published in the USA and Canada
by Routledge
711 Third Avenue, New York, NY 10017 (8th Floor)

Routledge is an imprint of the Taylor & Francis Group, an informa business

© 2011 James Curran

British Library Cataloguing in Publication Data
A catalogue record for this book is available from the British Library

Library of Congress Cataloging in Publication Data
Curran, James.
    Media and democracy / James Curran.
    p. cm. – (Communication and society)
    1. Mass media–Political aspects. 2. Communication in politics.
    3. Democracy. I. Title.
    P95.8.C85 2011   302.23–dc22
    2010040384

ISBN: 978-0-415-31706-1 (hbk)
ISBN: 978-0-415-31707-8 (pbk)
ISBN: 978-0-203-40687-8 (ebk)

Typeset in Bembo
by Bookcraft Ltd, Stroud, Gloucestershire.
Printed and bound in Great Britain by
TJ International Ltd, Padstow, Cornwall

To Cassie and Kitty

Contents

PART IV
Media and history   **121**

  8 Narratives of media history revisited   123

  9 Press as an agency of social control   140

10 Advertising as a bounty system   153

PART V
Media and culture   **169**

11 Media as custodians of cultural tradition   171

12 Media and cultural theory in the age of market liberalism   191

List of tables

Acknowledgements

Chapters in this book have been published as follows:

Chapter 3: *European Journal of Communication*, 24(1), 2009 (co-authored with S. Iyengar, A. Lund and I. Salovaara-Moring);

Chapter 4: J. Curran (ed.), *Media and Society*, London: Bloomsbury Academic, 2010;

Chapter 5: N. Fenton (ed.), *New Media, Old News*, London: Sage, 2010 (co-authored with T. Witschge);

Chapter 6: N. Fenton (ed.), *New Media, Old News*, London: Sage, 2010;

Chapter 7: *Journalism Studies*, 11(4), 2010;

Chapter 8: M. Bailey (ed.), *Narrating Media History*, London: Routledge, 2009;

Chapter 9: G. Boyce, J. Curran and P. Wingate (eds), *Newspaper History*, London: Constable, 1978;

Chapter 10: H. Christian (ed.), *The Sociology of Journalism and the Press* [Sociological Review Monograph 29], 1980;

Chapter 11: J. Curran (ed.), *Media Organisations in Society*, London: Arnold, 2000;

Chapter 12: J. Curran and D. Morley (eds), *Media and Cultural Theory*, London: Routledge, 2006.

My thanks to Arnold (Chapter 11), Bloomsbury Academic (Chapter 4), Constable (Chapter 9), Routledge (Chapters 7, 8 and 12), Sage (Chapters 3, 5 and 6) and University of Keele Press (Chapter 10) for permission to republish these essays. Save for the two co-authored essays, they have been revised for publication in this book.

Introduction

This book was commissioned as a collection of case studies, to follow my first volume of overview essays reappraising bodies of literature concerned with different aspects of media and power.[1] This first volume was reprinted several times and translated into five languages. This prompted me to reconceive this book as a more ambitious project. Eight essays (Chapters 1–8) have been written for it, leaving me with the problem of deciding which of the residue of earlier published essays I should select. The ones that survive the resulting cull include two (Chapters 10 and 11) that disappeared into a black hole of obscurity, virtually unread, in preference to more obvious choices (including one anthologised in four books and another cited in over 200 publications). I thought that I would give these two disregarded essays a second chance.[2]

Since many readers will dip into this book rather than read it from beginning to end, it may be helpful to provide a brief indication of its contents and identify the threads of argument that run through it. Media and democracy is one of the most intensively ploughed areas in media studies, resulting in a number of good books.[3] There seemed no point, therefore, in going over the same ground or even synthesising what has been published, since this latter has been done a number of times – not least in an illuminating summation of media democratic theory that has taken leading scholars over a decade to complete.[4]

However, most books on media and democracy are either theoretical or grounded in the experience of one nation. So my point of departure has been to look concretely at the democratic functioning of the media in different contexts, beginning with America. The design of the American news media system is based on two assumptions. If the media are to be free from government, they have to be organised as a market, not a state, system; and if they are to serve fully democracy, they should be staffed by professionals seeking to be accurate, impartial and informative. The allure of this system, the soft power of its global attraction, is brought out in the opening chapter by contrasting the ideals and achievements of American journalism with the limitations of journalism in other countries, exemplified by cowed journalism in numerous authoritarian states, the fusion of media and political power in Italy and the irresponsibility of tabloid journalism in Britain.

This is followed by a chapter that takes a closer look at American news media. The shining city on the hill turns out to be less luminous when viewed from the inside. There is compelling evidence that American news reporting is, in some contexts, only semi-independent of government. The product of a very unequal society, American media tend to legitimate inequality, especially in their coverage of the poor. As the principal vehicle of costly, almost unregulated political advertising, American television also plays a pivotal role in sustaining the money-driven nature of American politics. These links between media and politics in America go largely unnoticed in the standard comparative map of media systems, whose validity is questioned.

The first two chapters thus laud and criticise American journalism. This leads to the third, co-authored, chapter (with Shanto Iyengar, Anker Brink Lund and Inka Salovaara-Moring), which compares the democratic performance of news media in the US, Britain, Denmark and Finland. Television in Scandinavian countries pays more attention to political and international news than does American television, which is one reason why Scandinavians are much better informed about these topics than Americans (with the British falling in between). Television in Denmark and Finland (and, to a lesser extent, Britain) also broadcasts more news at peak times than in America. This encourages greater inadvertent viewing of the news, contributing to a smaller knowledge gap between advantaged and disadvantaged groups. In short, Europeans are better informed about politics and international affairs partly because they are better briefed about these topics by their public-service television systems than are Americans by their more consumer-orientated television system (though there are additional, more important societal reasons as well).

The analysis of Chapter 3 can be challenged on the grounds that it is based on the conventional assumption that 'hard news' supports political knowledge. But surely soft news has a political dimension, once it is acknowledged that 'the personal is political'? More generally, the central argument mobilised in Chapter 3 – that hard news is being crowded out by entertainment in market-driven media – seems blind to the political meanings embedded in entertainment, which researchers in cultural and film studies take almost for granted.

Chapter 4 acknowledges the full force of the argument that media entertainment connects to the democratic life of society. It explores the way in which film and TV drama facilitate a debate about social values that underpin politics; enable an exploration of social identity (closely linked to a sense of self- and group interest central to politics); offer contrasting interpretations of society; and contribute to a normative debate about our common social processes – about how they are and how they should be. Thus, the television series *24* provided a catalyst for a national debate in the US about whether state torture was acceptable, while *Sex and the City* supported a collective conversation about the role and expectations of women at a time of rapid transition in gender relations. But although entertainment fuels democratic debate, a distinction needs to be made between fiction and journalism. This is because citizens need to be informed about important, real-life actions taken by their government – especially if this entails visiting death on another country. That more than a third of Americans thought in 2006 that Iraq had weapons of mass destruction or a major programme for developing them at the time of the 2003 invasion, or that nearly half believed that Iraq was heavily implicated in the September 11 attacks, is an indictment of a society rendered politically under-informed by its dependence on a diet of entertainment. A democracy needs to be properly briefed to be effectively self-governing.

If media democratic theory needs to take account of the rise of mass entertainment, another necessary adjustment is to come to terms with increased globalisation. Global economic forces are rendering national government less effective than it used to be, and are in this sense diminishing democratic power. This is leading to attempts to build a multi-tiered system of governance, from the nation state upwards, which is seeking in effect to repair democracy in a global age. The evolution of the news media – still very heavily centred on the nation – is lagging behind this transition and making democratic repair more difficult.

Much theorising about the democratic role of the media is conceived solely in terms of serving the needs of the individual voter. But democracy consists not just of government and citizens, but also of a large number of intermediate organisations from political parties to public-interest groups. Attention needs to be given to how media systems should best support this infrastructure of democracy. This leads logically, it is argued, to recognising that different kinds of journalism – not just the disinterested, objective, factual model upheld in American journalism schools – can usefully contribute different things to the functioning of democracy.

Media and technology is the second node of this book. One of the hopes vested in the Internet is that it is forging a 'global public sphere' empowering international citizenry. Chapter 5, co-authored with Tamara Witschge, explores this theme by investigating a distinguished e-zine, *openDemocracy*, which gained an international audience in the wake of the September 11 attacks. The development of this web-based magazine illustrates the ways in which the Internet can facilitate innovative journalism. But it also points to the way in which the web is constrained by its context and time. Most of *openDemocracy*'s contributors came from the same parts of the world because they shared the same language. Contributors were overwhelmingly men, reflecting the cultural inheritance of unequal gender participation in political life. And they were mostly from elite backgrounds, because knowledge, fluency and time are unequally distributed in the external world, though this was exacerbated by the editorial values of the magazine. And despite gaining a substantial audience (approaching half a million visits a month at its peak), the e-zine failed to generate any significant revenue. The absence of a substantial stream of advertising and subscription revenue is limiting the development of independent web-based international journalism and its capacity to build genuinely global networks of communication (without some form of subsidy).

Chapter 6 looks at what was foretold in relation to British cable television, interactive digital television, community television and the dotcom boom – and what actually transpired. Forecasts were repeatedly, wildly wrong. In most cases, they originated from the business interests promoting new technological applications, were corroborated by senior politicians and admired experts and amplified by gullible media. These forecasts were also given credence because they accorded with a widely shared technology-centred perspective little influenced by economics and sociology.

An examination of past foretelling is followed, in Chapter 7, by a look at current predictions. There are four main – and mostly inconsistent – forecasts for the future of journalism: underlying continuity in a well-managed process of transition; a crisis of journalism that threatens democracy; a liberating Schumpeterian purge;

and a renaissance of journalism based on its reinvention. Each of these forecasts is for different reasons unconvincing. What seems instead to be happening is that the Internet is contributing to the decline and increased uniformity of old media journalism. This is not being offset adequately by new web-based start-ups because, in most cases, these have been unable to generate sufficient revenue to be self-supporting. The underlying problem is that journalism as a whole – online and offline – is being partly decoupled from advertising funding.

The third node of the book is concerned with media history. Media history has not made the impact on the interdisciplinary field of media studies that it should have. This is partly because media historians tend to address only themselves and subdivide media history by medium and period. As a consequence, the potential of media history to illuminate the nature of the broad connections between media development and societal change has tended to be lost. For this reason, I had earlier attempted to summarise alternative interpretations of the role of the media in the making of modern British society (with clear parallels to other economically developed countries) as a way of illustrating how history provides a gateway to understanding the present.[5] In Chapter 8, I return to this topic by looking at recent research. The liberal interpretation – celebrating the winning of media freedom and public empowerment, linked to the democratisation of the political system – is beginning to be modified in response to radical criticism. The feminist interpretation, which argues that the development of the media empowered men at the expense of women, is responding to revisionists within its own ranks who emphasise that the media changed in response to the advance of women. The radical tradition, which views the development of the media in terms of containing working-class advance and consolidating elite domination, is urged to take account of reformist success. The anthropological interpretation centred on the role of the media in nation building is now turning to the role of the media in sustaining 'sub-national' consciousness. The libertarian interpretation charting the culture wars between moral traditionalists and liberals in the context of de-Christianisation indicates that liberals in Britain have been gaining the upper hand (though the outcome is clearly very different in some other countries). The populist interpretation that views the increased commercialisation of the media as a means of emancipation from a cultural elite, in a celebratory account of the growth of consumerism, remains influential, though perhaps not the force that it was. By contrast, the technological determinist interpretation, which sees successive new media as transforming the culture, social relations and sensibility of the age, has received a boost from the recent boom in Internet studies.[6]

The next two chapters focus on particular aspects of press history that have a wider resonance. The standard interpretation argues that the British press became free when it ceased to be subject to punitive taxation in the mid-nineteenth century and hails the politicians who campaigned for this as freedom fighters (albeit also with vested interests). Chapter 9 contests this by examining what these 'freedom fighters' actually said at the time. It shows that a major concern was to lower the price of newspapers and expand the press as a way of indoctrinating the lower orders. They were convinced that their version of enlightenment would prevail and, in some instances, that well-funded papers controlled by businesspeople and favoured by advertisers would promote moderation. Furthermore, it is argued, they were right, partly because the shift from craft to high-cost industrial production of the press, and increased dependence on advertising, made radical journalism more difficult.

The next chapter examines the impact of advertising on the press during the first two-thirds of the twentieth century. It argues that the rise of advertising agencies as intermediaries, the development of evidence-based selection of advertising media and the rising incomes and advertising worth of workers all made it easier for radical journalism to make a breakthrough in the first half of the twentieth century. This said, advertising spending across newspapers was still very unequal, save for a brief period of newsprint rationing, because some readers had more money to spend than others, generated a higher advertising bounty and were worth more to publishers to recruit. This distorted the structure of the press, and its editorial strategies, in ways that disadvantaged the left. But this outcome came about in an unsought way and was the product of an impersonal economic process rather than of political discrimination.

In advancing this argument, I was influenced at the time by contending instrumentalist and structuralist interpretations of the state in critical political theory, and advanced in effect a structuralist interpretation of the influence of advertising on the press. But in the course of researching this essay, I became fascinated by the way in which the new business disciplines of market research and advertising media planning were developed by a motley but clever group of people. They changed the operation of the market by the way in which they reinterpreted it, in the process influencing the development of the press. Essentially the same process was at work when new ways of conceptualising and measuring the television audience, and of segmenting the market, in later twentieth-century America encouraged the growth of specialist television channels.[7] These arguments accord with a new stress on the cultural construction of markets that is being developed in the sociology of the economy.[8]

The last node of the book is concerned with media and culture. Chapter 11 shows that book reviews in the British national press centre on literary fiction, history, biography, literary studies and politics. This excludes some books that are popular bestsellers and some that are important (in particular those concerned with science and social science). This idiosyncratic selection reflects the educational backgrounds of books editors, most of whom studied history or English at elite universities. Their predilections are reinforced by editorial tradition, their skewed teams of book reviewers and their social networks. Publishing executives are mostly content to anticipate books editors' preferences rather than to challenge them. The press can thus be viewed as a custodian of cultural tradition that entrenches a humanities domination of public and cultural life, while downgrading other disciplines as falling outside the core curriculum of what 'informed' people ought to know about.[9] Little has changed since this research was done. More paperbacks are reviewed, but the neglect of science has become even more pronounced.

The last chapter reviews the development of British media and cultural studies during the last twenty-five years. The conventional way in which researchers narrate the field to themselves is to identify an inner logic in which gaps are identified and new insights are recognised, producing a succession of enlightening 'turns' to a new, improved understanding. This leaves out the way in which changes in the wider context of society influence the development of research. While some contextual influences have been positive, the ascendancy of neo-liberalism has rendered a once radical field of research less critical. Now that this ascendancy is contested, after the 2008 crash, perhaps this will change.

All previously published essays have been revised for publication here. My aim has been to make them accessible to a first-year undergraduate. Two chapters (9 and 10) have each been cut by a third to fit the publisher's length requirements.

My thanks go to Stanford University, which awarded me a Visiting McClatchy Professorship, Pennsylvania University, which provided me with a visiting Annenberg-endowed post, and the Annenberg Press Commission, which invited me to join its ranks (and produced an inquest volume on the American media).[10] This prompted me to learn more about the American media and embark on comparative survey research – something reflected in the first third of this book.

My thanks go also to the Leverhulme Trust, which awarded me and my colleagues a grant of £1.25 million to investigate new media. Early fruits of this are presented in the middle part of this book. As part of this, I would like to express my thanks to Joanna Redden, who won a Leverhulme scholarship from a crowded field and provided research assistance for Chapters 2, 6 and 7. My thanks go also to Justin Schlosberg, who rendered consistent the presentation of footnotes. All other acknowledgements are gratefully expressed at the beginning of chapters.

Part I

Comparing media

1   Shining city on a hill

The United States is the principal originator and exporter of a great media experiment. Its starting point is that the media should be organised as a free-market system on the grounds that any form of public ownership or legal regulation (beyond the barest minimum) endangers media freedom. However, this approach differs from neo-liberalism in that it also argues that the free market can have debilitating effects on the media. Its solution to this double bind – the need to have a free market and to negate its adverse effects without involving the state – is to develop a tradition of professionalism among journalists. In this way, the media can remain free, yet serve the people.

This general thesis is set out in the Hutchins Commission report, still perhaps the most cogent and elegant report on media policy ever published in the English language.[1] The report directly confronts First Amendment fundamentalism by arguing that the aim of public media policy should not be *confined* to securing media freedom from government control. The media have also a duty, it argues, to serve the public good – something that cannot be fulfilled automatically through the free play of the market. This is because the effort to attract the largest audience can sometimes undermine accuracy and encourage a preoccupation with the exceptional rather than the representative, the sensational rather than the significant. Free-market processes have also given rise to plutocratic ownership of newspapers and their concentration into chains, creating the potential for abuse.

Yet, the report recoils from the idea of advocating 'more laws and government action'[2] since this poses a threat to media freedom. What, then, should be done? The answer, according to the report, is to promote an overriding commitment to the common good among media controllers and staff, foster 'professional ideals and attitudes'[3] and a tradition of 'competence, independence and effectiveness'.[4] In short, the media can be best improved not through laws but through leadership and the entrenchment of a public-interest culture in its staff.

The Hutchins report was written by leading American public intellectuals and published in 1947. It came out of a reform movement that had not only public support but perhaps more importantly the backing of major media controllers,[5] leading journalists and also journalism educators.[6] This movement had also a long history extending back to the nineteenth century. And its championship of journalistic autonomy, standards and public service was *anchored* by adherence to the codes and procedures of 'objective' reporting. This demanded 'detachment, nonpartisanship, inverted pyramid writing, reverence for facts and balance'.[7]

This reformist tradition was also nurtured by the oligopolistic structure of the American media. During the reformist 'golden age', in the third quarter of the twentieth century, just three networks dominated television, two news magazines loomed large in the underdeveloped national printed press and most metropolitan dailies enjoyed a local monopoly. It was much easier to be high-minded when competition was limited and profitability was assured by a rising volume of advertising.

This high tide of professional media reformism is memorialised in Herbert Gans' classic ethnography of the three commercial TV networks and the two principal news magazines during the 1960s and 1970s. The growth of conglomerate media ownership had resulted, he argued, in the devolution of shareholder power to managers, who delegated, in turn, considerable decision-making authority to journalists. This was, he argued, partly an operational consequence of the specialisation of function within news organisations, but it was also a response to the high degree of professional consciousness among journalists. 'Delegation of power', Herbert Gans writes, 'also takes place because the news organisation consists of professionals who insist on individual autonomy'.[8] Thus while large business corporations were 'nominal managers' of leading media, the people working in them were effectively in control and did not shrink from carrying news detrimental to their parent companies' interests.[9] Managerial pressure to make profits was also offset by journalists' commitment to professional goals. This could result in journalists deliberately shunning information about audience preferences, particularly if they feared that viewers and readers are 'not particularly interested in the news they now receive'.[10]

Gans' overall conclusion was thus that America's flagship media were strongly influenced by the professional values of their staff and their desire for autonomy. It now reads as an elegiac rendering of how America's top media used to be.

Responsible media capitalism

This influential account acknowledged that news media were influenced by the underlying belief systems of society and recognised the subtle ways in which journalistic autonomy was in fact constrained. The book is far from being uncritical. Yet, it failed to engage fully with the way in which the underlying conservatism of American society left a gelatinous imprint on American journalism. This is something to which we shall return in the next chapter.

American iconoclasts have also pointed to the limitations of the professional reformist tradition. Thus, some media historians argue that the development of a commitment to objectivity masked a pragmatic, marketing concern to appeal to readers with different politics; the growing stress on factuality reflected the naïve empiricism of high modernism; and the high-mindedness of this reformist tradition perhaps cloaked, at some level, an accommodation to power.[11] Similarly, a number of media sociologists argue that the procedures of 'objective reporting' privileged the powerful in sourcing and framing the news; and that balancing authorities' truth claims became a sorry substitute for truth-seeking. These limitations were a response, it is argued, to deadline pressure, lack of relevant expertise and sometimes concern to avoid a running battle with authority.[12]

While all these criticisms have some validity, they should not obscure the enormous achievements of the American experiment. In particular, the standard leftwing accusation that American journalism reproduces a news script written by established authority fails to register the multiple conditions in which this is not true.[13] When powerful actors have transgressed shared norms, when elite groups have strongly differed with each other or when there has been an effectively organised popular mobilisation of dissent (as in the civil rights movement), the American media have hosted or expressed strong criticism of established power.

The classic illustration of this is the 1972–4 Watergate scandal.[14] In this often-narrated saga, a group of men linked to the re-election campaign for President Nixon illegally broke into the National Democratic headquarters in the Watergate complex, and were caught in the act. Subsequent investigations revealed the high-level connections of those involved, and the attempt of President Nixon and his closest advisers to cover this up. Leading media, most notably the *Washington Post*, played a significant part in this disclosure. The ensuing outcry generated pressure for President Nixon's forced resignation in 1974 and paved the way for the pros-ecution and imprisonment of a number of his senior aides.

Of course, press revelations did not occur in a vacuum. They were fuelled by leaks, press releases, official investigations and public protests from a variety of powerful actors – a judge, a Deputy Director of the FBI, federal prosecutors, a powerful Senate committee, an Attorney and Deputy Attorney General, among others. Political insiders within the American establishment were especially impor-tant in signifying Watergate as being part of a bigger problem – the systematic abuse of government authority – in the immediate aftermath of Nixon's landslide 1972 re-election, when the press seemed ready to downgrade Watergate as a 'sour grapes' Democratic Party issue. But none of this should detract from the record of professionally orientated journalists in tenaciously seeking and publishing revela-tions about Watergate, contributing to the downfall of the most powerful man in the world.

American local television could also mount exemplary investigations during this reformist professional era. This is perhaps best illustrated by a remarkable series of reports, under the title 'Beating Justice', broadcast by the NBC affiliate in Chicago, Channel 5, in 1983.[15] Their origin lay in a conversation between a recently arrived reporter, Peter Karl, and a local lawyer who complained that the police had thrust an electric cattle rod down his client's throat and applied it to his genitals. Shocked, the reporter dug further and discovered, with his colleagues (and, crucially, with the help of concerned lawyers and hospital staff) a pattern of systematic abuse in which the same police officers were repeatedly involved in beating up people, most of whom were black. The series reported extreme levels of violence, including the transformation of a once healthy 21-year-old man into a quadriplegic following a short ride in a police 'paddy' wagon. Nothing effective was being done, the TV series suggested, to supervise an out-of-control group of Chicago police officers, even though the City of Chicago had been forced to pay out, over five years, some $5 million to settle (and hush up) police brutality complaints.

Perhaps the most admirable thing about this series is how much investment the local TV station was *then* willing to commit to serious, investigative journalism. It assigned a producer, assistant producer, a reporter (also working on other stories) and a group of three (changing) student interns to investigate police brutality for *six months*. The names of police officers repeatedly accused of brutality, as well as relevant witnesses, were identified by painstakingly combing federal and county court records and even arrest logs. The editorial budget was generous, with a camera crew spending no less than fifteen evenings in an unmarked van in a vain attempt to capture 'live' a police beating.

Chicago's Channel 5 also backed the investigation with its most precious resource – airtime. It ran the 'Beating Justice' series of news reports on five consecutive evenings on its ten o'clock local news, and repeated an expanded version of each item the next day on the late afternoon local newscast. This enabled a detailed and fully documented presentation of its evidence of wrongdoing. The prominence given to the news reports also helped to ensure that they influenced the political process. Congressman Harold Washington capitalised on their impact in his 1983 mayoral election campaign, promising police reform and mounting a sensational press conference in which he featured fifty alleged victims of police brutality. Washington was elected as the first black Mayor of Chicago. Under his short-lived regime (cut short by his early death), the police superintendent, Richard Brzeczek, was forced to resign, and internal supervision and control of the police was tightened. However, the police commander of the notorious 'midnight crew' was not fired until 1993.[16]

Even when the professional power of journalists was weakened during the subsequent period, for reasons that we will come to, an impressive legacy lingered on. A professional culture had been created; talented people had been recruited to journalism and, in the upper reaches, American news media had enormous staffs and budgets. This could still result in remarkable journalism, something that will be illustrated by an unsung series of articles that appeared in the *New York Times* in 2005. Unlike the exceptional 'Beating Justice' series that garnered numerous awards, or the Watergate revelations that were immortalised in a celebrated film,[17] this series attracted little acclaim. But it nevertheless exemplifies the industry, intelligence and public purpose of well-resourced American journalism, even during its period of decline.

In February and March 2005, the *New York Times* published three articles, written by Paul von Zielbauer, under the general title 'Harsh Health'.[18] The first of these presented a Dickensian chronicle of poor medical care in New York State prisons, leading to avoidable deaths. The second article centred on neglect of mentally ill prisoners leading to a spike of suicides, and the third concentrated on failures of care in juvenile detention centres.

The articles were memorable partly because they provided dramatic human-interest cameos. One inmate, Brian Tetrault, had his medication drastically reduced on admission to prison. Over the next ten days, he slid into a stupor, soaked in his own sweat and urine. Dismissed as a fake (one prison nurse noted tartly that Tetrault 'continues to be manipulative'), he died on the tenth day. His records were then doctored to make it appear that he had been released before dying.

Another inmate, Carina Montes, was admitted to gaol after a long history of mental illness and a suicide attempt as early as thirteen years old. Her records went missing, and she never saw a psychiatrist in her five months in gaol. Despite clear warning signals that were ignored, she hanged herself – joining what inmates call, with black humour, the other 'hang-ups'.

Tiffany S., aged fourteen, was another troubled inmate. She had been removed from her drug-addicted parents at the age of three, and moved again when her sister was sexually molested by her brother. She had a long history of suicide threats and psychological disorder, and had been given powerful medication by her hospital. When she was admitted to a detention centre after a minor infringement, this medication was stopped by the doctor and replaced by a drug for hyperactivity. The doctor, responsible for health care in nineteen juvenile centres, had been widely criticised for replacing expensive drugs with cheaper, inappropriate prescriptions. Tiffany S. went into sharp decline, started hallucinating and behaved in a strange and distressed way. At this point a redoubtable family court judge, Paula Hepner, stepped in and ordered that Tiffany receive proper medical treatment.

At the centre of the problem, argued the three articles, was Prison Hospital Services, the leading company in the $2 billion prison health-care industry. It had been found officially wanting in relation to 23 recent inmate deaths. A third of its full-time psychiatric positions were unfilled; fourteen of its doctors had state or federal disciplinary records. It had a controversial record not merely in New York State but in other parts of the United States, where its failures had been repeatedly criticised.

However, the article series transcended the standard narrative of investigative journalism that features wrongdoers doing wrong (with the simplifying implication that evil must be confounded). While pointing an accusing finger at Prison Health Services, and some of its employees, it also offered an intelligent, contextualising account. Prison health care has always been beset with difficulties, because numerous inmates have mental health or addiction problems, making them both difficult and vulnerable. Prison health is unglamorous work, making good staff difficult to recruit and retain. Above all, the series emphasised, there has also been a sustained drive to limit spending on prisons. Forty per cent of inmate health care in the United States is contracted to private companies. Competitive underbidding to secure contracts has led to economies and skeletal staffs, leading to mismanagement and neglect. Little information about prison health care is publicly available, and it is not a topic that people are disposed to worry about. In this situation, 'businesses with the most dubious track records can survive, and thrive'. But the ultimate responsibility, the articles suggested, lies with the wider community, which wants to save money. This uncomfortable conclusion was rammed home explicitly by an editorial arguing that 'the root problem is that the country has tacitly decided to starve the prison system of medical care'.[19]

The series was triggered in 2003 when Paul von Zielbauer, then a specialist reporter covering local prisons and gaols on the metropolitan desk of the *New York Times*, noticed that there had been six suicides, in as many months, in one prison and decided to check out Prison Hospital Services, responsible for health care in the prison.[20] He filed Freedom of Information Act requests for reports of all deaths in gaols for which the company had a contract in New York State and found that it was repeatedly criticised. This led subsequently to a year-long investigation, which included a trawl through the company's record in other states and thirty interviews with current and former prison health employees, as well as examining numerous court and regulatory agency reports.

What made the series good, apart from the evident ability of Zielbauer (who subsequently wrote memorable articles about the abuse of power in post-Saddam Iraq), were three things. First, the *New York Times* committed significant resources to the investigative project, not only assigning Zielbauer for an extended period, but also Joseph Plambeck to assist him with research and reporting. It also gave prominence to the series: the opening article, for example, was the joint lead story on the first page even though it was not reporting yesterday's news. The second thing that lifted the series was that it was able to draw upon the work of the democratic state in investigating itself: key sources for the series were the sharply critical reports of regulatory authorities, both inside and outside New York State, and also court cases. This documented record helped to build up a compelling picture of a bad situation in need of reform. The third thing that made the series impressive was its straining to achieve balance. Prison Health Services was rightly given the opportunity to defend itself, and its record was contextualised in a way that made for critical understanding rather than facile indignation.

But while exemplary, the series also had defects characteristic of American prestige journalism. Its central weakness was that it was excessively over-long, with the three articles running respectively to 8,624, 6,510 and 3,020 words. It was also artlessly presented, with infrequent subheadings, mostly dull pictures and, in the case of the third article, a dire headline ('A spotty record of health care at juvenile sites in New York'). However, the articles themselves were very skilfully written. They alternated dramatic human-interest stories with analysis, with the reporter enlisting the horror engendered by individual tragedies to motivate the reader to find out more about what was going wrong. The series also shrewdly anticipated reader resistance, not least by concentrating attention on sympathetic inmates, some with minor infractions, with whom sceptical readers of the *New York Times* might be more disposed to care about.

Thus, these three articles – despite their flaws – are a testament to the disciplined moral passion, hard work and intelligence of good American journalism. They were enabled by the enormous resources of a paper,[21] stuffed with advertising generated by a wealthy readership in one of the richest places in the world. And all these assets were deployed in an attempt to protect one of the most despised pariah-groups in the community – gaoled felons – in a country then without universal health care.[22] It is journalism like this that explains why the American model of responsible media capitalism has admirers around the world.

Shining city on a hill

The three examples of American journalism that have just been featured are all exposés of the abuse of official power by, respectively, the US President, police and prison administration. The robust independence of this journalism contrasts with the overt ways in which the media are still controlled in most parts of the world.

The principal way control is exercised is through repressive legislation. For example, in Mugabe's Zimbabwe, the law provides for a maximum of seven years' imprisonment for the publication of (allegedly) 'false' stories that are likely to cause 'fear, alarm or despondency among the public'.[23] Still more restrictive legislation exists in Saudi Arabia, resulting in the lengthy imprisonment of the Saudi Arabian journalist Saleh Al-Harith for phoning through news in April 2000 to al-Jazeera TV that there had been clashes between the police and the Ismaeli minority in Nijran.[24] Repressive laws also enable the banning of troublesome publications, as in Indonesia in 1994, when three leading weeklies were closed down by official fiat.[25]

Second, control can be exerted through public ownership, licensing and regulation of the media. In most authoritarian states, from Albania to Morocco, publicly owned television follows the official line of the government.[26] An effective way of muzzling commercial television has been to allocate licensed franchises to allies of the government and governing party or coalition. For example, this is what happened in much of Eastern Europe, following the collapse of communism.[27] Most restrictive regimes, from China to Syria, also require internet service providers, licensed within their jurisdictions, to filter out critical or dissident websites.[28] Some, as in Saudi Arabia, seek to jam 'undesirable' TV broadcasts from abroad.[29] Overlying this system of regulatory control can be the routine issuing of editorial guidelines to the media. For example, the Chinese government, headed by Deng Xiaoping, instructed that there should be no media debate about whether the introduction of pro-market reform policies endangered social relations. This had the desired effect of marginalising leftwing criticism and restricting the reporting of grassroots protests in the immediate post-1989 period.[30]

Third, control can be exercised through a second party – in particular, the owners of private media – operating in collusion with government. Throughout Latin America, there was an informal coalition between the principal media conglomerates and the dictatorships,[31] as there was also in pre-democratic Taiwan[32] and South Korea.[33] These partnerships were founded primarily on shared interests and outlooks: a common desire to defeat communism/terrorism, maintain order and stability and sustain free enterprise. But narrowly instrumental pragmatism on the part of media controllers can also play a part in securing compliant media. Thus, the desire of press owners to expand their wider commercial interests in mainland China, with the approval of the Beijing government, was a significant factor in the increased taming of the Hong Kong press in the post-1997 period.[34] More generally, the flow of advertising tends to be politicised in authoritarian regimes. Thus, throughout the Middle East, commercial advertising is often withheld from media that have lost favour with the government,[35] a recurring problem for the pan-Arab TV enterprise, al-Jazeera.[36]

Fourth, media can also be intimidated through vigilantism. Especially in countries where crime is highly organised and has links to the state, and where the rule of law is weak, journalists are vulnerable to physical intimidation. In Russia, for example, outspoken media workers can be exposed to an escalating scale of violence, beginning with a threatening phone call and progressing to systematic beating up, arson attack and assassination. According to Olessia Koltsova, it is often difficult to distinguish analytically between state and non-state agents of violence in Russia because the two tend to overlap.[37]

Lastly, an indirect system of control can be established through the invisible threads of domination. While all governments seek to 'manage' their media through public relations and other means, this is more intimidating in authoritarian than in non-authoritarian societies. This distinction is perhaps best exemplified by Singapore's authoritarian democracy, where the media are not controlled through formal censorship and are in a formal sense 'free', yet are strongly subordinated to government.[38] This is achieved through an all-encompassing hegemony within this small city state. An integrated elite monopolises political power through its control of the People's Action Party, which has won every election since national independence in 1965, and through annual licensing of civil-society organisations by the state. The ruling elite also dominates local businesses. Above all, it enjoys an almost unchallenged cultural ascendancy, through popular acceptance of its governing ideology of national development, Asian values and ethnic harmony, through its control of public institutions (including the educational system) and through the prestige it has garnered as a consequence of Singapore's remarkable economic success. For an editor to incur the wrath of the Singaporean government, in the context of a strongly authoritarian, conformist culture, requires courage and independence of a different order from that required in an open, pluralistic society.

So from the vantage point of numerous countries around the world, the independence of American media from government control, and the fearless way in which American journalists are able to criticise authority, is a source of admiration and inspiration. American media – viewed from a distance – seem like a shining city on a hill.

Fact–checking responsibility

It is not only in countries lacking free media that American media reformism commands respect. The fact-checking responsibility of American journalism, its commitment to reporting important news, even its tendency towards bland worthiness, can seem a refreshing contrast to what is available in some other countries. This is especially true in countries with a tradition of irresponsible tabloid journalism.

Few countries have a more irresponsible tabloid press than Britain. It is unusual in having a dominant national press, with ten competing daily newspapers. Five of these are strongly orientated towards the mass market because they derive the greater part of their income from sales. They are also locked into a Darwinian struggle for survival because popular newspaper sales have been in decline since the late 1950s and are now almost in freefall. There is little counterweight to this commercial pressure, since British tabloids are dominated by an entertainment-orientated rather than professional staff culture.[39]

British tabloids have responded to their deteriorating economic situation by searching with increasing urgency for news that grabs readers' attention. One time-honoured way of achieving this is to find stories that make readers angry. As a memo to *Sunday Express* journalists enjoined in 2003, 'we must make the readers cross'.[40] This strategy led to a spate of anti-immigrant stories during the 2000s, when anti-immigrant attitudes became more widespread. However, tabloid demand for these stories outstripped supply, leading not just to distortion but outright invention.

Thus, in 2003, the tabloid press ran a number of stories about immigrant eating habits. Immigrants were reported to be eating donkeys, guzzling fish ('Now They Are Eating Our Fish!')[41] and devouring swans. This last story connected to a national taboo because swans are a symbol of British heritage, protected by law from Norman times. To eat swans was therefore to invite strong disapproval. The story was judged to be so important that the *Sun* (July 4, 2003) cleared its front page to reveal that 'Callous asylum seekers are barbecuing the Queen's swans', under the banner headline, 'SWAN BAKE'. 'East European poachers', the paper reported, 'lure the protected Royal birds into baited traps, an official Metropolitan Police Report says.' Its continuation story inside the paper recorded unambiguously: 'Police swooped on a gang of East Europeans and caught them red-handed about to cook a pair of swans.'

Although the story was well judged to raise readers' blood pressure, it had one demerit. It was not true. There was in fact no Metropolitan Police report about East Europeans eating swans, merely an internal, one-page memo clarifying the nature of the law in relation to poaching. There were no police arrests of any immigrant 'gang' laying traps for or barbecuing swans.[42] The *Sun*, concluded the official Press Complaints Commission, 'was unable to provide any evidence for the story'.[43]

In a similar vein, the *Daily Express* (July 27, 2005) revealed on its front page that 'Bombers are all spongeing asylum seekers', a reference to bombers who had attempted to set off bombs in London on July 21. Although calculated to produce outrage, the accusation was inaccurate – as subsequent investigation revealed.[44] Still, it made a good cue to the poll, published in the same issue, inviting readers to answer the question: 'Should all asylum seekers now be turned back?'

If one attention-seeking strategy is to make readers indignant, another is to make them scared. This is typified by a campaign led by the *Daily Mail* and *Sun* – Britain's two best-selling dailies – alerting readers to the alleged dangers of the 'three-in-one' mumps, measles and rubella (MMR) vaccine. The trigger for the campaign was a press conference, in 1998, in which Dr Andrew Wakefield, the co-author of a medical article, suggested that it was possible that the triple vaccine could cause bowel disorder, leading to autism.[45] The article was methodologically weak, being based on just twelve, non-randomly selected subjects, and did not even claim to have demonstrated the existence of a connection between the triple vaccine and autism. It was subsequently disowned by the journal which published it.[46] Dr Wakefield was censured in 2010 for, among other things, failing to declare a financial interest in the outcome of his research (which received funding from litigants against the vaccine),[47] and was struck off the British General Medical Council register. His suggestion that the MMR jab was hazardous was also refuted by major, scientifically conducted studies in the US, Japan and Finland, as well as research elsewhere.[48]

But this did not prevent leading British tabloid papers from championing an unsubstantiated, maverick view. It was, after all, a story guaranteed to win the attention of parents, and grandparents, of young children. At the height of the MMR scare, in January 2001, the *Sun* published an anxiety-inducing article about the vaccine, on average, every other day for the entire month.[49] This is typified by its report that 'anguished mother Mary Robinson' is 'convinced' that the MMR jab 'caused autism in four of her kids and behaviour problems in another'.[50] The article offered no medical support to back up Mary Robinson's conviction, but quoted her as saying that 'they withdraw a hairdryer if there is a problem – why aren't they withdrawing this drug' (by which she meant the MMR vaccine). Celebrities were also mobilised in the cause. 'TV star Carol Vorderman led calls for a safe measles jab last night', reported the *Sun*, adding that the *Countdown* star had 'talked to many people' with children who had been damaged by the MMR vaccine.[51]

The problem with these unqualified diagnoses is that autism often becomes apparent at around the age of two, when children are given the first dose of the triple MMR vaccine. This is coincidental, not causally connected. But leading British tabloids gave the impression that to allow one's children to receive the triple vaccine was to play Russian roulette with their health. This view was seemingly legitimated when the prime minister, Tony Blair, declined to say in 2002 whether his youngest son, Leo, had received the vaccine. This gave the story a new lease of life, only for it to begin to peter out in 2003 – some five years after the initial scare.

However, the damage had been done. There was a marked decrease in those taking the MMR vaccine in 1998 that was only partly reversed from 2004 onwards.[52] Even in 2009, the MMR uptake had not recovered to the pre-scare level before 1998.[53] There were also enormous variations of take-up, with London remaining a black spot. This increased children's exposure to illness, and reduced collective 'herd' immunity, with the result that cases of measles increased from 2001 onwards and were still rising in 2009.[54] Whereas there were only 70 reported cases of measles in England and Wales in 2001, this had risen to 1,143 by 2009.[55] Measles can give rise to serious complications, including encephalitis, brain damage and even death (with one British child dying in 2005). The MMR story sold newspapers: it also revived an avoidable disease.

The British press is the least trusted in Western Europe because of the excesses of its tabloid newspapers.[56] But tabloid excess is to be found elsewhere, from Germany to Hong Kong. Viewed from these countries, the professional orientation of mainstream American journalists – their reluctance to lace stories with artificial flavouring and additives, their general adherence to journalistic ethics and their loud protests when these are cynically breached – can seem worth transplanting.

Hazards of partisanship

Another aspect of the American journalistic tradition inspires envy in some places. Its stress on editorial neutrality and detachment from politics can seem immensely appealing to some with first-hand experience of journalistic partisanship. Partisan media systems tend to generate an alliance between a section of the media and government. This can have negative results when there is a high degree of media concentration and the media are lopsidedly partisan in one direction. The prime illustration of this problem is Berlusconi's Italy.[57]

Silvio Berlusconi, Italy's foremost TV mogul, was the first person in Western Europe to be allowed to effectively control the terrestrial commercial television system of an entire nation, albeit one which has popular public television. By 1992, Berlusconi's TV channels accounted for 43 per cent[58] and by the early 2000s 45 per cent of total viewing time (and 90 per cent of commercial television viewing time) in Italy.[59] In addition, Berlusconi possessed or acquired substantial interests in publishing, advertising, construction, insurance and food.

Berlusconi's media and business empires became the launch pad for his political rise. During the early 1990s, the governing political class was discredited by public corruption scandals. Berlusconi filled the resulting political vacuum by creating in 1993 a 'plastic' political party, with few members, many of whom were his employees and their friends. The party's launch was meticulously planned, with careful market research and sustained promotion, almost as if the electorate was a new market to conquer. The new political party was named after the football chant 'Go Italy' – Forza Italia – and teamed up with two other rightwing parties, with regional bases respectively in the north and south. In 1994, they won the general election, with strong support from Berlusconi's television channels. Around fifty of Berlusconi's employees were elected to parliament, and Berlusconi himself became prime minister without ever holding public office before. Although Berlusconi's first administration lasted only seven months, Berlusconi again won power in 2001 at the head of essentially the same rightwing coalition. This time his administration proved to be the longest-serving in post-war Italian history. After being defeated in 2006, Berlusconi was elected in 2008 to head a new government, with a majority in both houses of parliament. Berlusconi thus parlayed his position as media tycoon to become the dominant figure in Italy's notoriously fissile politics.

However, it would be too simplistic to suggest that Berlusconi achieved political pre-eminence only because of his media power. In 1992–4, the implosion of the political class (to which, ironically, Berlusconi was closely linked) presented him with the opportunity to make a breakthrough as a 'clean hands' outsider. Berlusconi then consolidated his position partly because he was a media-savvy politician, with a shrewd instinct for headlines, populist policies and projection of personality. He was a man at ease with the new style of politics. But he was also adept in the old political arts: an astute mediator, with great charm, he held together the sparring partners of his political coalition and restructured its main bloc in a more stable form in 2007. Above all, he reconstituted the dominant centre–right coalition in a new form by articulating the central themes of Christian Democracy (patriotism, family values, law and order and the perils of socialism) to an Italian version of neo-liberalism (individualism, consumerism, hedonism and low-tax anti-statism), underpinned increasingly by a virulent hatred of immigrants. This rebuilding of the centre-right was helped by the failures of the left,[60] and received its due reward in an inherently conservative country. Italy had voted for the right or centre-right in every election between 1948 and 1992. In effect, Berlusconi assisted the country to return to its natural political home after an interim period of turbulence.

However, the interaction between media and political power in Italy proved to be neither good for government nor the media. Thus, Berlusconi used state office to consolidate and extend his media power base. When the Constitutional Court ruled that one of Berlusconi's television channels (Rete 4) should be moved to cable or satellite TV in order to reduce Berlusconi's domination of terrestrial commercial television, Berlusconi's government promptly passed, in 2003, a law to overturn the court's judgment. The new law both legitimated Berlusconi's continued domination of commercial TV and also facilitated a further expansion of his media empire.

Berlusconi further abused his office to extend his influence over RAI, the public broadcaster. Its three channels had been orientated respectively towards the right, centre and left. However, following the corruption scandals of the early 1990s, RAI had gravitated towards an 'above politics', neutral orientation, something that Berlusconi set out to change. His minister of communications, Maurizio Gasparri, publicly declared in 2002 that it was time to 'stop flying and come down to earth. Let's forget the "above faction" journalists: we prefer the ones who are loyal'.[61] Loyalists were shoehorned into top managerial posts, people like Fabrizio Del Noce – a former Forza Italia senator – who was appointed as the new director of RAI 1. Under the new regime, episodes of a satire programme poking fun at Berlusconi were cancelled abruptly in late 2002. When a camera shot lingered on a protester standing outside a tribunal where the prime minister was accused of corruption in May 2003, RAI's director general ordered an official investigation of RAI 3 news, leading to abrasive interviews with its staff. Berlusconi was directly involved in this campaign of intimidation. He publicly accused in 2003 two critical broadcasters – Enzio Biagi, the presenter of a celebrated public affairs programme on RAI 1, and Michele Santaro, a top journalist on RAI 1 and 2 – of making 'criminal use of television', adding that 'I believe that RAI's new management has a definite duty to stop this from happening'.[62] The two journalists' contracts were not renewed for the next season, 2003/4, in a move that was plainly intended to foster self-censorship by other journalists. This relentless pressure continued with, for example, RAI 3's Lucia Annunziata being threatened with disciplinary action after asking Berlusconi tough questions in March 2006.

Berlusconi never in fact 'captured' the public broadcasting system, which continued to provide airtime for opposition viewpoints. But Berlusconi's assured control of commercial television, and subsequent intimidation of RAI, had two important consequences. It gave Berlusconi a built-in political advantage in that he appeared more frequently on television than his opponents, was cited more often and tended to be portrayed more favourably.[63] It also affected the tone and frame of reference of news reporting in general, especially in relation to corruption.

As a businessman, Berlusconi had sailed close to the wind, causing him to be pursued by legal furies for almost two decades. Among other things, he was arraigned for false accounting, tax fraud, bribing the financial police, corrupting judges, making illegal contributions to political parties, money laundering, having illegal ties with the Mafia, anti-trust violations and bribing a witness to commit perjury. Indeed, Berlusconi was sentenced in 1998 to two years in gaol for bribing the financial police – a verdict overturned on appeal, though his lawyer, Massimo Berruti, was sent down for the offence in 2001. Another of Berlusconi's lawyers (and a close friend and former member of his cabinet), Cesare Previti, was also found guilty of corruption charges in 2003. Berlusconi's response to the pressing attentions of the judiciary was to rewrite the law. In 2001–6, Berlusconi's government decriminalised false accounts statements; made it easier to transfer court cases to another part of Italy (in order to facilitate acquittal); introduced a much shorter statute of limitation for white-collar crime; and suspended trials against senior officers of state (this last was struck down as unconstitutional). Berlusconi's first priority, comments David Lane, 'was the enactment of bespoke laws to get the prime minister off his legal hooks'.[64]

This use of public office to deflect prosecution continued into Berlusconi's third term, when he faced charges for tax fraud and for suborning a witness, the British lawyer David Mills, who was found guilty of giving false testimony on his behalf. In 2008, a bill was passed which gave Berlusconi legal immunity in order that he should not be distracted from affairs of state. In 2009, this bill was thrown out by the Constitutional Court.

Berlusconi's influence over the media resulted in its failure to scrutinise government effectively. Corruption prosecutions could have been reported with evangelical zeal, as a continuation of the 'clean hands' campaign in which the public *demanded* an end to government abuse. Instead, prosecutions and court cases tended to be reported in a different register, as being 'controversial', because government ministers accused judges and prosecutors of leftwing bias; or as being 'inconclusive', just another episode in Italy's byzantine legal process; and, by the time of the third Berlusconi administration, simply received less media attention.

Berlusconi also emerged as a Teflon-coated politician, partly because the absence of aggressive media scrutiny (save by leftwing newspapers and magazines, with obvious axes to grind) gave him an unusual degree of leeway. There were tensions between the ideas he represented; fractures in the image he projected; and contradictions between what he said and did. It was only when the incongruity between his political championship of family values and his consorting with prostitutes became too great in 2009 to overlook that his qualified media 'protection' was lifted (with the help of the Internet).

In brief, the recent political history of Italy represents a cautionary experience. It highlights the dangers inherent in the fusion of media and political power, which encourages bad government and compromised reporting. It is no wonder that reflective Italians began to speculate in the Berlusconi era whether America offered a better way of doing journalism.

World triumph and domestic decline

Thus, large numbers of people around the world came to admire the independence, sense of public purpose and political neutrality of American journalism. For example, numerous journalists in Malta,[65] Mexico,[66] Brazil[67] and Latin America more generally[68] espoused American journalistic norms as a way of 'reforming' their media. These norms were tacitly championed by the US-dominated World Association of Newspapers, which expanded its membership both during and after the Cold War.[69] They also tended to be championed by new schools of journalism that emerged in Africa, Asia and elsewhere.[70]

Yet, during this period of international triumph, when American journalists basked in the admiration of a growing number of their peers around the world, American journalism went into decline. This was because the foundation of the American experiment − its partially successful attempt to separate business from journalism − was undermined by increased commercialisation.

The American TV networks were all bought or merged during the 1980s. Their new controllers refused to tolerate the losses incurred by their news divisions. This had perhaps something to do with the revocation of residual FCC regulation during the 1980s which clarified the status of TV licences as, in effect, private properties rather than as renewable trusts with quantifiable public obligations.[71] But it was also fuelled by the demand for rising returns on publicly traded shares, often with linked remuneration packages for senior executives. This pressure to optimise dividends and stock values also strongly influenced American newspapers during this period.[72] They were required to deliver much higher profits in the 1980s compared with two decades earlier,[73] and this pressure was maintained in the subsequent period.[74]

At the same time, it became increasingly difficult to deliver what shareholders demanded. American newspapers entered an accelerated phase of decline from the 1970s onwards. The TV networks experienced falling ratings as a result of the rise of cable and satellite TV. Between 1970 and 2001, the number of television channels received in the average American household increased from seven to seventy-one.[75] And in the 2000s, both American newspapers and television had to fend off competition from the Internet, which had become by then a 'mass' medium available in most homes.

This conjunction of increased stockholder pressure and greater competition weakened the autonomy of American journalists. This was reflected in successive surveys in 1982, 1992 and 2002 registering decreases in the proportion of American journalists who said that they were free to select their own stories, determine the emphasis of their stories or get important stories covered in the news.[76] This weakening of professional power resulted in a greater drive towards simplicity and entertainment, reflected in an increase in soft-news stories on network TV news in 1994–8 compared with 1974–8.[77] It also contributed to a reduction of foreign news coverage by American newspapers in the 1970s and 1990s,[78] and a reduction of TV news investment in foreign newsgathering.[79] Increased commercialisation also contributed to the growth of low-cost, 'magazine' and virtual reality shows, both strongly influenced by entertainment values.

These developments threw into sharp relief the nature of the settlement between commerce and professionalism that had been struck earlier. While American TV network news journalists had been given considerable freedom and large resources to report the news, they had also been sidelined. Their news programmes were transmitted at the edge of prime time, at 6.30 p.m. (and in some time zones earlier) in order to create space for uninterrupted entertainment at peak viewing times. This marginalisation reflected the underlying commercial logic of the American television system, which was driven by profit seeking rather than the desire to serve democracy.

This said, change brought some positive outcomes, partly because it was accompanied by more channels and increased provision. The drive to convert occasional network news viewers into regular ones increased coverage of some relatively neglected issues, like education and health, of greater concern to women.[80] The growth of virtual reality shows created space for minority voices to be expressed,[81] although they were also arenas where the vulnerable were bullied and the disadvantaged were rebuked rather than heard.[82] New television channels, which reported national and international news in prime time, also came into being, though they generally attracted low audiences.[83] By far the greatest gain of TV expansion was the development of a new economic model for television fiction production, based on premier subscription rather than advertising, that gave rise to high-quality drama (associated with HBO).[84] But as far as news reporting was concerned, increased commercialisation encouraged the growth of soft news at the expense of hard news, the reporting of elections more in terms of horse races than in terms of policy difference and declining coverage of the outside world, save where American troops were engaged in military action.[85]

Subversion of an ideal

This was partly also because the core values of American journalism came under attack in their heartland. The norm of journalistic neutrality had been upheld not just by professional values but also by the 'fairness doctrine' introduced by the Federal Communications Commission (FCC) in 1949, which required broadcasters to present contrasting views on controversial issues. This regulation was revoked in 1987, opening the way for partisan journalism on the airwaves. One year later, Rush Limbaud started an unabashedly rightwing radio show in New York. With the help of a growing number of local radio stations (most notably the giant Clear Channel Communications group) that syndicated his show, Limbaud built − for radio − a large national audience. His success led to imitation, including a 'Liberal Radio' alternative that attracted many fewer listeners. A distinctive genre of partisan radio journalism became part of the media landscape.

This was followed by the launch of the Fox News Channel in 1996. Although claiming to be fair and balanced, it developed a rightwing news agenda and introduced ferociously conservative political commentators. This new style of journalism attracted a substantial audience, for a cable/satellite TV channel. This encouraged a rival channel, MSNBC (also launched in 1996), to develop a liberal-leaning style of journalistic commentary. Partisan journalism thus came to occupy a substantial niche in both American television and radio journalism.

The rise of Fox News, in particular, signified not just a rejection of political neutrality, but something that seemed 'foreign'. The devolution of control within American news organisations had helped to neutralise the big business ownership of the media. But Rupert Murdoch, the principal owner of the Fox News Channel, was a wealthy businessman with strongly held conservative, pro-free-market, small government views. He had foisted these views on other parts of his global media empire through the exercise of shareholder power.[86] In the 1990s, he did the same thing in America. Conservative senior executives and journalists were put in place to orientate Fox News so that it echoed the political prejudices of its principal owner. The rise of this new style of journalism thus marked the compromising entanglement of American journalism with vested economic power.

Another source of subversion took the form of the rise of tabloid journalism. . During the Hutchins reformist era, tabloid journalism had existed at the margins, primarily in the form of supermarket magazines like the *National Enquirer*. These last concentrated on news about celebrity, sex, crime and gossip, though occasionally breaking stories about erring politicians. They were regularly accused of distorting and even fabricating stories,[87] in a way that emphasised their 'otherness', their transgression from the norms of ethical mainstream American journalism.

But from the 1970s onwards, local television channels discovered that they could make money by developing a cheap form of local sensational journalism. As one pioneering study argued, their evolving formula emphasised images over ideas, emotion over analysis, simplification over complexity, driven by what was cheap to report and generated good ratings.[88] This led to supplementing the staples of local journalism – weather, sport, accidents and so on – with an increasing volume of stories featuring violent crime that conveyed drama and emotion, and was accompanied by strong visual material. By the 1990s, local television news in the major conurbations projected an alarming image of a broken society, characterised by wave after wave of robberies, murders, carjackings, gang wars and police chases.[89] Local TV news became, as Iyengar and McGrady tartly observe, 'essentially a televised police blotter'.[90] This proved to be very successful in market terms: local TV news built very large audiences, even overtaking national network news (despite the fact that local TV ratings began to decline during the 1990s).[91] Its success resulted in tabloid norms finding a prominent place in the mainstream of American journalism.

The revival of partisan and tabloid styles of journalism – once prominent in the nineteenth century – represented a reverse for the social responsibility tradition. It also meant that American journalism ceased to be as distinctive as it once was. The US media now exhibit features that are to be found in other parts of the world.

Setbacks

Traditional news professionalism is threatened by the take-off of the Internet as a mass medium. This has such profound implications for the development of journalism that it needs a separate chapter (Chapter 7) to be addressed properly. But anticipating a little, the migration of 'old media' advertising to the web led to the closure of some American newspapers, editorial budget cuts and a 20 per cent reduction in the number of American journalists employed in the eight years up to 2009. The rise of bloggers and web-based media start-ups did not compensate for this decline, because they failed to secure an adequate revenue stream to sustain them.

Over the long term the Internet may well rejuvenate journalism, especially if it is accompanied by constructive public policies. But the cumulative decoupling of advertising from news production which brought about the rise of the Internet also poses a major problem that is likely to endure. The great triumphs of American journalism – such as investigations into the abuse of power by President Nixon, Chicago police and a prison health corporation cited earlier – have usually come about as a consequence of the secondment of a skilled journalist or journalists for months to track down an important story. It is precisely this kind of *high-cost* journalism which is endangered by the economic crisis enveloping traditional news media in the United States.

American journalism also became subject to sustained criticism in the aftermath of the 2003 Iraq War. The Bush administration 'sold' the war to the American people partly on the basis of a false prospectus. The government repeatedly claimed that Saddam Hussein had weapons of mass destruction and significant links to the terrorists behind the 9/11 attacks on America. In fact, no weapons of mass destruction or an advanced programme for making them were found in Iraq after its occupation. It was also acknowledged subsequently by government agencies that the secular Ba'athist regime in Iraq did not have close ties to the Islamic fundamentalist group al-Qaida, who were behind the 9/11 attacks.

These revelations gave rise to the accusation that the American media had failed the public by reporting prominently the government's case for invading Iraq without adequately scrutinising its validity. This indictment was conceded by some leading journalists. For example, the *New York Times* criticised its own performance in the run-up to the 2003 Iraq War:

> Editors at several levels who should have been challenging reporters and pressing for more scepticism were perhaps too intent on rushing scoops into the paper ... Articles based on dire claims about Iraq tended to get prominent display, while follow-up articles that called the original ones into question were sometimes buried. In some cases, there was no follow-up at all.[92]

Academic scrutiny has tended also to find American news media to be wanting.[93] Thus Hayes and Guardino undertook a quantitative analysis of all Iraq-related evening news stories – totalling 1,434 – transmitted by the three TV networks in the eight months before the invasion.[94] They found that Bush administration officials were the most frequently quoted sources, while scant attention was given to domestic opposition to the war. Indeed, anti-war groups accounted for a mere 1 per cent of quotations, while Democratic representatives (including some who were anti-war) accounted for only 4 per cent.

But while domestic anti-war voices were almost inaudible on network news, Bush administration claims were counterposed by those from the Hussein administration. Perhaps more significantly, since the Hussein administration was portrayed in a strongly negative light that undermined its credibility, network television news also quoted leaders of the French, German and Russian governments and UN officials, all of whom tended to take a different line from that of the Bush administration. This attempt to achieve neutrality was flawed, since 'a plurality of news stories focused on Iraq's alleged weapons of mass destruction ... and TV news reports cast a possible invasion in a more positive than negative light'.[95] The networks also offered a heavily establishment perspective: 79 per cent of all sources quoted were official ones. But at least the networks' under-representation of domestic opposition to the war was partly offset by their reporting of foreign opposition.

There was also something admirable about the way in which American journalists collectively reflected upon their performance after the dust of war had died down. Thus, the much-denigrated senior *New York Times* journalist Judith Miller answered her critics by saying that it was not her fault if government sources got it wrong. 'My job isn't to assess the government's information and be an independent intelligence analyst myself', she declared. 'My job is to tell readers of the *New York Times* what the government thought about Iraq's arsenal.'[96] This drew the acid reply from *New York Times* columnist Maureen Dowd that investigative journalism is not the same as the stenography of power, something that she implied might be lost on Judith Miller, 'the Fourth Estate's Becky Sharp', with her 'tropism toward powerful men'.[97] Despite the personal undercurrents of this exchange, this debate – and the wider dialogue of which it was a part – reflected a serious engagement with a thorny issue: the perennial tension between rival conceptions of journalism as a witness and as a watchdog, between factual dispassion and interpretative truth telling, at the heart of the professional tradition. It also reflected an attempt by a public-minded group of journalists to address its collective failure, learn from past mistakes and do better next time.

It is precisely this public consciousness, this willingness to engage in critical self-reflection, which enables the American professional tradition to renew itself, and which has resulted in a long record of distinguished journalism. But this tradition is now beset by multiple problems – an economic crisis, deepening commercialisation, a reduction of journalistic autonomy, a revival of rival journalistic traditions and public criticism that journalists themselves partly endorsed. In brief, the shining city on the hill does not seem quite so luminous to those who actually live there.

Relativising American achievement

The American cultural strategy of media reformism is not the only one available. Indeed, a very similar conception of media professionalism holds sway in British broadcasting, which has also adopted an independent, 'above politics', neutral mode of news reporting. But this shared approach is pursued in different ways. Whereas the American strategy is based on developing a 'voluntaristic' culture of professionalism within market institutions, the British approach seeks to actively support a professional culture through institutional arrangements. This includes the creation of two buffers – one against market censorship and the other against government censorship. Thus, Britain's principal broadcasting organisation, the BBC, is generously funded by the public through an obligatory TV licence fee in order to create a space for journalists to be independent of market pressure. Checks and balances – a BBC governing trust composed of people of different views and connections, *ad hoc* independent panels advising on the appointment of the BBC director general, parliamentary select committee and regulator scrutiny, all underpinned *crucially* by broadcasting staff and public support for television independence – create a shield against government control. And the autonomy of the broadcasting system as a whole is further supported by a legal obligation to display due impartiality in reporting controversial issues.

This resulted in British television reporting the build-up to the Iraq War in a more independent way than its American counterpart. Indeed, the head of government communications, Alastair Campbell, publicly accused the BBC of having 'an anti-war agenda',[98] while a controversial report by a leading judge argued that the BBC went too far in impugning the integrity of the government's 'sexed-up' case for war.[99] The government's claims that Iraq's weapons of mass destruction posed an external threat, that the Iraqi people should be rescued from a tyrant, that invasion was sanctioned by a prior UN resolution and that it would make Britain safer from terrorism were widely aired on television news and current affairs programmes. But so too were a number of counter-arguments: namely, that the weapons-inspection process should be completed and diplomacy given a chance to succeed; that there was no hard evidence that weapons of mass destruction existed; that invasion would be illegal without a fresh UN mandate; that it would lead to death and destruction, and in the long term civil war and destabilisation of the region; and that the effect of invasion would be to increase rather contain global terrorism.

However, perhaps the main reason why American and British television coverage in the run-up to war differed was because they were responding to different political environments. Unlike Britain, the US had been exposed to a major terrorist attack in 2001, giving rise to a bellicose climate of public opinion. While some Democratic politicians opposed the war, their leaders were in favour, and the Democratic Party as a whole tended to hedge its bets in the patriotic context of post-9/11.[100] By contrast, there was a cumulative build-up of opposition to the war within the governing Labour Party in Britain. As early as September 2002, the BBC reported that the majority of Labour backbench MPs, in its survey, were anti-war.[101] Despite enormous pressure from the Whips' office, about half of Labour MPs not on the government payroll voted against the Iraq invasion in parliament,[102] and two Labour cabinet ministers (including former foreign secretary, Robin Cook) resigned over the issue. Dissenting Labour MPs were joined by some senior Conservatives (including Kenneth Clarke, former chancellor of the exchequer, and John Gummer, former Conservative Party chairman), as well as by all Liberal MPs. This highlights a further key difference between the political context in the US and the UK: the opposition to the war was more broadly based in Britain. This was reflected in the press, with for example the pro-Conservative *Daily Mail* joining the pro-Labour *Daily Mirror* in opposing the war.[103] This opposition (including prominent church leaders) was galvanised by an anti-war coalition that staged in February 2003 the biggest national demonstration in Britain's political history. This surpassed the Kennington Chartist demonstration for the vote, and was very much larger than the equivalent demonstration in the US, despite the latter's larger population. This in turn reflected greater public disapproval of war in Britain compared to the US, registered in pre-invasion opinion polls.[104]

The importance of the wider political environment is further corroborated by the way in which British and American television reporting, and media reporting more generally, became more similar when their troops invaded Iraq. Journalists in both countries responded to convergent influences to rally behind their country's troops when they were engaged in actual military action.[105]

In short, the culture of news production matters,[106] as the achievements of American professionalism testify. The institutional arrangements of news media – influencing how they are financed and managed, their cultures and organisational goals – also affect news output.[107] But the wider context of society also strongly influences the news, not least through the cultural air that journalists breathe and what news sources say to them. To understand more fully what shapes American journalism, and influences its performance, it is necessary therefore to take a closer look at American society. This we will do by linking it to an appraisal of a commanding new orthodoxy in media research.

2　Questioning a new orthodoxy

A central weakness of media studies is that it tends to focus narrowly on the media in the foreground, leaving the rest of society in deep shadow. So any book that offers to explain the relationship between political and media systems is assured a respectful welcome. This has turned into acclaim in the case of Daniel Hallin and Paolo Mancini's *Comparing Media Systems*. Published in 2004, it has appeared in multiple translations. It has also been cited – at the time of writing – in 736 publications.[1] This is a very large number in a field where citation is relatively low by comparison with science and medicine, and attests to the magnitude of the book's impact.

Yet, Hallin and Mancini are becomingly modest, stressing how much they welcome future revision. They are also fastidious, emphasising variation between and within nations. Beneath their seeming self-effacement and scholarly qualification, however, a certain magisterial *hauteur* can also be detected. Much journalism research, they argue, is linked to professional education and makes evaluative judgements designed to foster the improvement of journalism. By contrast, they see themselves as detached scholars 'eschewing the normatively centred approach that … has held back comparative analysis in communication'.[2] Their scholarly mission is to determine not whether a media system is good or bad, but to describe what it is, and how it is. They are advancing, they stress, 'empirical, not normative models'.[3]

Here, then, is a book that has been saluted from all directions, and is driven – we are told – by evidence rather than by a point of view. Only a few years old, it seems set to assume the place once occupied by *Four Theories of the Press* as the bible of comparative media studies.[4]

Central arguments

Before evaluating this new orthodoxy, let us begin by summarising its key arguments. Hallin and Mancini's starting point is that there is a systemic connection between, on the one hand, political structures and cultures and, on the other, ways of organising the media and doing journalism. This is manifested, they argue, in three different 'models of media and politics', each of which is rooted in a physical heartland. While there are national differences within each model, these are presented as being less significant than their similarities.

The 'Liberal Model', according to Hallin and Mancini, is located in the United States, Canada, Ireland and Britain. To varying degrees, these four countries are characterised by limited government, a strong market orientation, an entrenched rational-legal basis of authority, majoritarian politics (typified by catch-all parties, first-past-the-post electoral systems and media-centred, consensual politics) and 'moderate or individualised pluralism' (meaning fragmented interests, individualised representation and a strong sense of the common good). These four countries, with variants, tend to have market-dominant media, professionally orientated journalists, fact-centred journalism guided by the norm of objectivity and autonomous systems of broadcast governance.

The 'Democratic Corporatist Model' is located in Belgium, the Netherlands, Denmark, Sweden, Norway, Finland, Germany, Austria and Switzerland. Although they have much in common with 'Liberal Model' countries, they differ in having highly organised social groups which are integrated into a corporatist system of governance, underpinned by consensual politics, proportional electoral systems and coalition governments; and these governments tend to be 'activist', with extensive involvement in the economy and provision of public services. Democratic Corporatist countries also tend to be associated with substantial media regulation and subsidy, a 'politics-in-broadcasting' form of governance, residual advocacy journalism (reflecting the legacy of a once strong party press) but a tradition of journalistic professionalism.

The 'Polarized Pluralist Model' is found in Greece, Italy, Portugal, Spain and France. With the exception of France, these are relatively 'new' democracies, and have a weak basis of rational-legal authority. They have sharp political and ideological divisions, dirigiste governments, clientelist forms of political patronage, strong political parties and highly organised social groups. This mode of politics gives rise to an instrumental use of media power, the close alignment of media and political parties ('parallelism'), small-circulation newspapers, a 'politics-over-broadcasting' television system and politically diverse, commentary-orientated journalism.

Hallin and Mancini then go on to argue that although different political structures and cultures have given rise to different media systems and styles of journalism, this is being modified by increasing international convergence. 'In many ways, the global focus on the Liberal Model', write Hallin and Mancini, 'as an ideal is understandable',[5] and in their view the Liberal Model represents 'the wave of the future'.[6] But perhaps recalling their own cautionary words against championing one media system, they draw back from offering a triumphalist account of what they call 'the triumph of the Liberal Model'.[7] While the Liberal Model promotes media autonomy from the political system, it may result, they warn, in harmful media dependence on the economic system.

The impact of *Comparing Media Systems* derives partly from the architectonic harmony of its structure and design. Like a Harry Potter novel, it projects a fully imagined universe, in which each part is described in detail and all parts come together to constitute a coherent whole. However, closer examination will reveal that the 'Liberal Model' is as much an elegant construct, as much a work of creative intelligence, as the Hogwarts academy for young wizards.

Imperial state

When describing different political contexts, Hallin and Mancini delve far and wide. They draw upon history, examine broad-based sociological change and depict significant power relationships. Given the panoramic sweep of their analysis, it is surprising therefore that they omit one salient fact about America, namely that it is an imperial state.

The nearest that Hallin and Mancini get to acknowledging this is by referring to the US and Britain as 'national security states', with nuclear weapons and 'considerable involvement in international conflict'.[8] This point is made in passing, with the suggestion that this is a further basis of affinity between two countries in the Liberal Model camp. It is not something that is developed or given any prominence.

This bracketing of US and Britain is misleading. Unlike Britain, the US is a global superpower. In 2008, US military expenditure amounted to an estimated $607 billion, more than the total spending of the next fourteen highest military budgets in the world.[9] This sustains US military installations and bases in at least 46 countries and territories extending from Bulgaria to Bahrain, Greenland to Guam, and Afghanistan to Japan.[10] This gives the US an extensive dominion over sea and sky and a formidable armed presence on the ground.

While the US does not have a conventional empire in the sense of possessing multiple colonies, it has an *informal empire* based partly on its military hegemony. The US has invaded a succession of countries – something that we will consider shortly – in order to be rid of hostile governments. It has supported military uprisings against unfriendly democratic regimes, as in Chile (1973) and Nicaragua (during the 1980s). It has also engaged in 'gunboat diplomacy', as when it attacked an anti-US faction in Somalia (1992). In addition, it has befriended and supplied military hardware to foreign dictators, from El Salvador to Saudi Arabia, which have supported American national interests.

Hallin and Mancini make much of the way in which America's liberal political system is founded on rational-legal authority and adheres strictly to formal rules and procedures. What they omit to mention is that the US is one of a tiny minority of countries (including North Korea, Burma and China) that refuse to abide by a regime of international law.[11] The US's willingness to deploy its military muscle, irrespective of international law, is partly what makes it an 'informal empire'.

The US also exerts a global influence through its soft power based on the appeal of its values and culture, and perhaps more importantly as a consequence of its pivotal position in the global economy.[12] The US was a leading architect of the Bretton Woods system of international economic regulation, introduced in the 1940s, which benefited the world in general, and the US in particular, since it established the dollar as the international reserve currency. This was superseded by a neo-liberal global order established from the 1970s onwards, based on privatisation, deregulation, expanded free trade and the increased primacy of international financial markets. This rendered American Treasury Bills the world's monetary reserve, and enabled America to gain privileged access to the world's savings and cheap imports. This *imperium* proved difficult to evade because it was policed by financial markets and international regulatory agencies. In effect, the new global economic regime conferred on America economic advantages normally associated with empire without incurring some of the costs and hazards of direct imperial rule.[13]

How independent?

Whether American media support the maintenance of the US's informal empire is not something that Hallin and Mancini discuss. They merely note that 'national security states' can seek to restrict media and co-opt journalists.[14] This is then qualified by reassuring references to recurring tensions between government and media, and to America's constitutional protection against media censorship.[15]

Instead, Hallin and Mancini develop a more general argument that embraces all Liberal countries. The development of journalistic professionalism promoted, they tell us, media independence not merely from government but also from 'parties and other political actors'.[16] Liberal media increasingly followed a 'media logic' based on commercial and professional conceptions of what constituted a good story, rather than a 'political logic' subordinated to the needs of politicians and governments.[17] This reflected the positive dynamic of a market system in which market revenue replaced political subsidy, and economic incentives encouraged the prioritisation of consumer concerns over those of politicians. The conjunction of market freedom and professional responsibility thus led to media 'differentiation' from political power.

Hallin and Mancini also attribute increasing media independence to wider changes in Liberal societies. Growing secularisation, they argue, eroded the power of political as well as religious faith; new social groups excluded from power demanded untainted media information, something reinforced by the tug of universalism in societies based on rational-legal authority; and a media system was needed that functioned as an effective co-ordinating agency within a more differentiated society (this last argument reflecting Hallin and Mancini's debt to structural functionalism).[18]

We are thus presented with a persuasive *theoretical* account of how the media in Liberal countries like America became increasingly autonomous. So while Hallin and Mancini do not refer explicitly to how American media report American foreign policy, we are primed to expect that it would be with due detachment and impartiality. But what does the actual evidence reveal? We will enquire further by examining how seven American military incursions into foreign countries were reported in American media,[19] beginning with the Vietnam War, when it is claimed American media were so critically independent as to have been almost subversive.

Contrary to expectation, leading US media strongly supported military engagement in Vietnam during the initial period (1962–4), reflecting the influence of government and the bi-partisan consensus of the time.[20] There followed a transitional phase (1964–7) in which network news reported differing opinions about how best to conduct the war, reflecting growing tensions between the US government and the military. However, outright opponents of the war still tended to get short shrift, at this time. For example, ABC news reported an anti-war protest in 1965 with the comment: 'While Americans fight and die in Vietnam, there are those in this country who sympathise with the Vietcong.'[21] In the final phase (post-March

1968), network news broadened to include growing criticism of the South Vietnam government and American military mismanagement, as well as asking whether the US should continue with the war. But this discussion debated execution and strategy rather than the underlying objective of Cold War containment. Critical views reported on network news came more from public officials, past and present, than from any other quarter. By contrast, the popular anti-war movement remained relatively marginalised, tending to be reported more in terms of the threat it posed to public order/military morale and the deviant lifestyle of protesters than in terms of their political views.[22] Negative statements about anti-war movements outnumbered positive ones by a ratio of 2 to 1 even in this post-March 1968 critical phase of TV news reporting.[23] In brief, TV news was only critical of the Vietnam War for part of the time, and then in a constrained, elite-driven way.

Before America faced defeat in Vietnam, it had invaded in 1965 the Dominican Republic in order to remove a leftwing government hostile to the US and contain the advance of communist influence. In the run-up to the invasion, sources in favour of invading the Dominican Republic outnumbered those opposed by a ratio of over 10 to 1 in three leading newspapers, reflecting the strong influence exerted by the Democrat government (backed on this issue by the Republican Party).[24] What criticism there was in the American press during the invasion and immediate aftermath came mainly from foreign sources, primarily communist governments.[25]

In 1983, America invaded Grenada in order to remove another leftwing government and limit the spread of communist influence. But this was in the aftermath of Vietnam, and some prominent Democrat politicians criticised the build-up to war. This was the main reason why there was more media criticism in the run-up to the Grenada invasion than in the case of the Dominican Republic.[26] But when the invasion of Grenada took place, there was the familiar political and media rallying behind American troops. The success of the invasion then caused some Democrat politicians to backtrack or fall silent. The result was a sustained consolidation of support for military action in the American media. In three leading newspapers, during the post-invasion phase, domestic sources opposed to the invasion accounted for between 5 per cent and 14 per cent of total sources cited, whereas pro-invasion domestic sources accounted for between 50 per cent and 51 per cent.[27] The one-sided nature of American reporting is corroborated by another study, which found that, over the full period, only 8 per cent of the perspectives expressed in *New York Times* news stories, and 9 per cent of ABC network TV news, were critical of the Grenada invasion, though criticism was greater on the public broadcasting (PBS) current affairs programme, *Newshour*.[28] It also found that little concern was expressed in American media about legal niceties. Just 1 per cent of relevant media content addressed the question of whether the US's invasion of Grenada violated international law.[29]

In 1986, America bombed Libya, following a number of terrorist incidents. This had strong approval from the American media and the political establishment. Less than 2 per cent of news in leading media was judged to be critical of American bombing.[30] Strong opposition from most NATO allies and France's denial of airspace to American war planes received relatively little attention in news reports, although it was noted with concern in some elite media comment.[31]

In 1988, the United States invaded Panama, ostensibly in order to rid the country of a tyrant, and close down a key source in the supply of drugs. The invasion enjoyed bi-partisan support in Congress, and was again strongly supported in the American media. Perspectives critical of the invasion accounted for just 2 per cent of *New York Times* news and 1 per cent of ABC TV news.[32] What criticism there was tended to focus on alleged mismanagement of the military occupation of Panama. Almost entirely absent from leading American media was the oppositional view that America was violating international law in order to punish a disloyal client government.[33]

Further insight into the reporting of the Grenada and Panama invasions, and the Libya bombing, is provided by another study. This draws more heavily on textual analysis than these other more quantitatively orientated studies do, and subtly illuminates rather than contradicts their conclusions. Robert Entman argues that some journalists expressed reservations in a veiled form, supported by critical quotations. But in a context where domestic elite opposition was 'disorganised and timid', this scepticism generated 'floating bits of data lacking narrative glue'.[34] By contrast, 'coherence characterised only the Administration line'.[35] The clear suggestion of this analysis is that some journalists wanted to be more independent than they were able to be, because they were forced to operate within the conventions of US fact-based journalism and source hierarchies, in the context of a largely pro-war, elite consensus.

The reporting of the Gulf War deviated to some degree from the pattern of preceding American wars. The build-up to military action began in August 1990, when American troops were deployed in Saudi Arabia, in response to Hussein's invasion of Kuwait. This had bi-partisan support and was reported with limited criticism in American media. War preparations then escalated, with the doubling of American troops in Saudi Arabia in November 1990. At this point, some senior Democrat politicians and prestigious foreign policy experts expressed misgivings about the drive to war, with polls registering deep public division. The American media reported these misgivings and gave space for critical reflection about how best to proceed, as well as to more trivial speculation about how developments would affect the standing of the Bush administration.

The period November–December 1990 was perhaps the closest the American media have ever come during the last fifty years to debating in an open way whether to go to war. But although estimates of the volume of critical coverage in leading media differ during this period,[36] it would appear nonetheless that pro-war perspectives received more attention, gained greater prominence and shaped the dominant news frame of leading news media.[37] Furthermore, criticism was overwhelmingly 'procedural rather than substantive', that is to say it debated the execution of policy within a framework that largely accepted the government's definition of the problem, and its remedy.[38]

When American and allied troops invaded and crushed the Iraqi army, there was a political and media closing of ranks. In January–February 1991, critical Democrats – in some cases concerned about the Democratic Party acquiring the public image of being 'weak' – rallied behind the flag. This encouraged TV reporting of the actual war in a form that, according to David Paletz, 'was nationalistic (if not jingoistic), overwhelmingly relayed the Bush administration and Pentagon perspectives, relied on US sources, adopted the military's sanitized lexicon of war, and transmitted US military disinformation'.[39] Anti-war protests in January 1991 received some attention but in ways that tended to subvert their message.[40]

Thus, when viewed from the perspective of half a century, American media reporting of the build-up to the 2003 Iraq War – described earlier[41] – was not an exceptional abrogation of media independence. Rather it followed a well-established pattern. All that was different was that the official case for the Iraq War rested heavily on specific claims which were revealed subsequently to be untrue. This made the media's closeness to official Washington embarrassingly transparent.

Three general conclusions can be derived from these case studies, which have been presented here in a necessarily summary form. The first is that American media have generally supported American invasions of foreign countries. Critical perspectives have generally accounted for a very small proportion of media coverage. These have usually come from foreign governments or, if they originate domestically, generally take a qualified form in which the fundamental objectives of military action are not questioned. And once an invasion is under way, American media usually rally behind the flag.

The second conclusion is that American news media are strongly influenced by the White House, Pentagon, Department of State, Congress and experts in the foreign policy establishment (including numerous former public officials). American media tend not to report extensively, and draw discursively upon, civil-society organisations, protest groups or dissenting experts outside the Washington orbit.

The third conclusion is that American news media are not autonomous. When the American government, political and state elites have a common view about the desirability of military action, there is minimal media debate. But when there are significant differences between these actors, these tend to get a media hearing. That is to say, the spectrum of views represented in the media is closely linked to the arc of opinion in the government and Congress. The relationship between the two, suggests Lance Bennet, is index-linked.[42] A looser formulation, proposed by Robert Entman, is more persuasive because it takes account of journalists' desire for autonomy, varied elite interactions, the changing ideological climate and public feedback.[43] Even so, the accumulated evidence of these case studies leaves no doubt that Hallin and Mancini greatly overstate the political independence of the American media system. American media may be independent of political parties, but they are still tethered to America's political class (and are sometimes strongly influenced by government).

So, the question that needs to be asked is almost the exact opposite of that posed by Hallin and Mancini: why are American media not more independent? The answer, in relation to reporting the build-up to foreign wars, has partly to do with the organisation of newsgathering into regular beats, which encourages the overrepresentation of administration views.[44] Partly, it arises from the culture of American journalism, which accords more importance to state actors and less to civil-society groups and independent public intellectuals than its counterparts in Europe. Partly, it is be explained by increased investment in government public relations and greater sophistication in news management (registered for example in the controlled embedding of journalists in the armed forces).[45] Above all, it is to be explained by the political and ideological context of the American political system.

America has a strongly embedded imperial culture that conditions both politicians and journalists. Within this culture, there are of course differences. In a contemporary context, there are at one end of the spectrum neo-conservatives whose sense of moral purpose is, as David Cannadine notes, remarkably similar to that of nineteenth-century British imperialists,[46] though American neo-conservatives differ in emphasising the need to export market-based democracy.[47] They are openly imperialist, calling, in the words of Richard Haas (the State Department's director of policy planning in the George W. Bush administration), for a reconception of America's 'global role from one of a traditional nation state to an imperial power'.[48] Alongside them are liberal imperialists, typified by the *New York Times* columnist Thomas Friedman, who see US armed forces as the ultimate enforcer of a global capitalist order.[49] In the centre, there is an amorphous group with a strong sense of America's destiny in upholding *pax Americana*. This is exemplified by Madeleine Albright, President Clinton's secretary of state, who declared: 'If we have to use force, it is because we are America. We are the indispensable nation.'[50] At the other end of the spectrum are the amnesiacs – perhaps the majority – who, as Niall Ferguson observes, live in 'an empire in denial'.[51] Between these polarities, and occupying the more rarefied space of foreign-policy expertise, are different views about the limitations that should be placed on the exercise of America's global power, couched in terms of the relative balance between legitimacy, acceptability and pragmatic gain.[52]

This imperial culture, extending across the two parties, has been sustained by two mobilising narratives: the global struggles led by America against communism (Cold War) and against Islamic militancy (War on Terror). The first provided the discursive frame informing the build-up to war in Vietnam, Grenada and the Dominican Republic, as well as support for South American dictators; the second framed the response to 9/11 and the Afghanistan War (2001–). But there was an aporia between the ending of the Cold War (*c.* 1989) and the beginning of the War on Terror (*c.* 2001). It is no coincidence that the most open pre-war media debate – over the Gulf War (1990) – occurred during this ideological intermission. More generally, there have been shifts and even cracks appearing in the discursive framing of foreign policy. Thus, a stress on human rights in the Carter era (1977–81) and the determined opposition to clandestine funding of the civil war in Nicaragua during the Reagan era (1981–9) were notable 'moments' when a Cold War, bi-polar view of the world was successfully contested and revised, with significant consequences for media reporting.

American media are thus not controlled by a monolithic culture of imperialism, but one that has different and contending currents within it. The media can also discomfit authority by exposing imperial wrongdoing. In 2004, CBS's *60 Minutes* obtained pictures taken by soldiers revealing graphic pictures of sexual humiliation, hooding, coerced stress positions and the use of unmuzzled dogs in the US-run Abu Ghraib detention centre in Iraq. Other American media (most notably, the *New Yorker*) followed up the CBS story, which commanded headlines around the world. However, American media differed from foreign media in that they were much more likely to use the word 'abuse' – favoured by the Bush administration – than 'torture' (or its foreign-language equivalents).[53] American media also largely accepted the official line that Abu Ghraib was an 'isolated' instance of things going wrong, in the absence of a counter-story from the Democratic Party or the judiciary. The Abu Ghraib story then subsided in the American media after about two weeks. In fact, we know now from subsequent official reports and judicial investigations that techniques used in Abu Ghraib had migrated from Afghanistan and Guantánamo Bay, and that the use of cruelty in interrogation had been sanctioned by high officials in Washington.[54] But this was not the story that was reported at the time, when its impact was skilfully contained. As Bennett, Lawrence and Livingston wryly comment: 'The photos may have driven the story, but the White House communications staff ultimately wrote the captions.'[55]

Of course, there have been other occasions when the American media have been more effectively vigilant. The last chapter brought out the very real achievements of American media reformism in promoting a public-interest culture among journalists. And a strong case can be made that American media reporting of foreign affairs is less robust than that of domestic affairs because the former is less often politically contested.

Even so, the seven case studies that have been reviewed here highlight two things. American media are not fully independent of government and political power, and they have a long history of supporting America's informal empire, even when this empire bares its teeth.

Unequal society

Another omission in Hallin and Mancini's account is that they fail to point out that America is exceptionally unequal. This is a further feature of American distinctiveness that is overlooked in their spurious catch-all category of the 'Liberal Model'.

Thus, in the OECD's survey of inequality (based on the Gini coefficient ranking of disposable household income), the US emerged as the most unequal of all the major economies.[56] Inequality in the US has been increasing since 1970, with the distribution of earnings – already very unequal – widening by 20 per cent between the mid-1980s and 2008. This was a higher rate of increase than in most other OECD countries.[57]

Yet, if income distribution is very unequal in the US, this is even more the case in relation to wealth. The top 1 per cent control some 25–33 per cent of total net worth, while the top 10 per cent possess 71 per cent of the nation's wealth.[58] By contrast, the lowest 60 per cent possess just 4 per cent.[59] Indeed, extreme concentration of wealth at the top of America society is combined with indigence at the bottom. The US has the highest poverty rate among rich nations.[60] Nearly 22 per cent of American children live in poverty, a rate second only to Mexico among OECD countries.[61] The US has the third-highest infant mortality rate among the 31 OECD countries, a record surpassed only by Mexico and Turkey.[62]

Poverty is measured usually either in absolute terms or in relation to median income.[63] On either scale, the US emerges as a country exceptionally and deliberately neglectful of its poor – something spelled out in a 2009 US Department of Agriculture report based on a very large, representative sample. The report's bureaucratic language (with phrases like 'food security' and 'disrupted food patterns') and its careful assessment of the cost of sustaining health and human activity through a 'Thrifty Food Plan' (carefully adjusted according to household size and the age and gender of household members) fails to deaden the shock of what it reveals.[64] In 2008, 17 million households (14.6 per cent of all US households) were 'food insecure', meaning that at some time during the year they went without sufficient food to sustain active, healthy living as a result of shortage of money.[65] Of these, 6.7 million households (5.7 per cent of the total) fell into the acute category: people who frequently suffered 'very low food security'.[66] In 2008, 27 per cent did not eat for a whole day because they could not afford to; 68 per cent went hungry because they had insufficient food to eat; and 97 per cent skipped a meal or reduced intake to make ends meet.[67] In this land of abundance, food insecurity was greater in 2008 than in any year since records began in 1995.[68]

America is also a high-risk society in which actuarial calculations suggest that 31 per cent will experience poverty by the age of thirty-five and 59 per cent will experience a year or more of poverty by the age of seventy-five.[69] However, these different facets of America – its inequality, poverty and acceptance of risk – have all been willed by its political system. Redistribution through government taxation and spending is lower in America than in any OECD country apart from South Korea.[70] The US's relative level of outlay on social benefits, such as unemployment and family support, is well under half the OECD average.[71] In a study of eleven rich nations, the US emerged as making the least anti-poverty effort.[72] However, the US state is 'inactive' only in some areas. It is estimated that the US has 5 per cent of the world's population, yet accounts for 24 per cent of its gaol inmates.[73]

The United States, Ireland, Canada and Britain are all countries with high income inequality[74] – something that they have in common, incidentally, with Portugal and Italy,[75] which Hallin and Mancini do not include in the 'Liberal' category. However, the United States is distinctive in that it is a *market democracy* with low social spending and limited redistribution, whereas Britain, Ireland and Canada are *welfare democracies*, with cradle-to-grave state protection and higher levels of 'social transfer' between rich and poor than in the US. In other words, the latter are societies whose market-generated inequalities are significantly reduced through the operation of their democratic systems.

Legitimating inequality

Do American media contribute to political acceptance of inequality and poverty? This is not a question that Hallin and Mancini address, though it is relevant to a review of the relationship between media and politics. Fortunately, the wider media research and social science literature offers some answers.

The first key point that relevant research makes is that, in the US, there is relatively little media coverage of poverty as a general public issue. Instead, poverty tends to be depicted in terms of *poor people*. This argument is advanced in two ways. First, news reports about poverty are very much more likely to focus on instances of poor people than the causes of poverty or public policy in relation to this.[76] Second, the relatively small media coverage of poverty as a topic is dwarfed by a multitude of stories that feature poor people.[77] The American media thus have very little to say about what gives rise to poverty and inequality, yet they provide – especially in virtual reality shows and crime drama/news – vivid images of low-income individuals.

The second key point advanced by the relevant literature is that the media regularly misrepresent who the poor are in America. In a pioneering study, Martin Gilens found that although African Americans accounted for 29 per cent of the poor in 1990, they constituted 62 per cent of poor people featured in news magazines and 65 per cent on network TV news during 1988–92.[78] Clawson and Trice updated this study for the period 1993–8, finding continuing black overrepresentation. They also demonstrated that African Americans were particularly overrepresented in negative stories in which the poor were portrayed in stereotypical ways.[79] However, black overrepresentation decreased in the subsequent period, though it was still greatly overstated. Dyck and Hussey found that, in 1999–2004, 43 per cent of poor people were depicted as black, although the true figure was roughly one in four.[80]

The media also encourage an association between poverty and crime. Entman and Rojecki examined TV representations of 'poverty symptoms' during the 1990s. They discovered that 40 per cent of TV news stories featuring poor people depicted poverty as a source of threat in the form of crimes, drugs and gangs.[81] This association was sometimes given a racial coding, a point made in a notable study by Gilliam *et al*. They found that crime accounted for 51 per cent of lead stories and 25 per cent of total local news broadcast by the ABC affiliate TV station in Los Angeles in 1993–4 on its main local newscast programme. This news focus concentrated on violent crime, even though most crime was non-violent. Local TV news also greatly distorted the perpetrators of these crimes. After comparing TV images with local crime statistics, Gilliam *et al*. concluded that local TV news 'overrepresents black violent criminals significantly … and underrepresents white violent crime dramatically'.[82] Likewise, a subsequent study of TV news during the 1990s documented the pervasive 'visualisation' of crime in terms of African American perpetrators.[83] In other words, American television – especially its local news – encourages fear of the poor, in the form of 'black criminals'.

American media also foster antipathy towards poor people in other ways. While some media coverage of low-income households is sympathetic and draws attention to their difficulties,[84] this tends to reflect a distinction, deeply embedded in American culture, between the deserving and undeserving poor. It is the 'undeserving' or 'less deserving' that tend to be given prominence in American media. Gilens discovered that the most sympathetic subgroups of the poor, such as the elderly and working poor, were underrepresented, while the least sympathetic group – unemployed working people – were overrepresented in reports of poverty in news magazines.[85] Subsequent research, mostly based on textual analysis of American media, finds that considerable attention is given to poor people with deviant lifestyles (entailing extreme indolence, 'substance abuse', crime, promiscuity or violence). Looming large among these are unmarried mothers, depicted as lazy, uninterested in education and sexually available; and 'Welfare Queens' leading lives of leisure supported by government handouts.[86] Since welfare recipients are funded by the taxpayer, these negative images are likely to fuel resentment.

In general, American media encourage disdain for the poor. By frequently depicting poverty in terms of negatively portrayed individuals, the media offer a tacit explanation of poverty: it is because poor people have personal failings. In reality, the causes of poverty in the US are varied. Over the last thirty years, the US has produced an increasing number of low-paying jobs that lock people into poverty.[87] Vertical social mobility has decreased in the US, and is now lower than in many other economically advanced countries from Sweden to Australia.[88] Further reasons have to do with racial discrimination, inadequate child care, an erosion of public benefits, weakened trade unions, the social demoralisation of communities faced with structural unemployment, and so on. But these wider explanations are often bracketed out by the media, which tend to personalise rather than contextualise poverty.

The consequences of this were highlighted in a classic experimental study, in which TV depictions were edited. Shanto Iyengar found that how people think about poverty is dependent on how the issue is framed.[89] When poverty is presented as a general outcome, responsibility for poverty tends to be assigned to society at large. But when poverty is depicted in terms of particular instances of poor people, responsibility is more often assigned to the individual. Since poverty tends to be presented on network news in a person-centred way, this partly explains, according to Iyengar, why so many Americans consider poor people responsible for their poverty. This has political consequences, because those assigning personal responsibility for poverty tend to be hostile to government welfare.[90] Iyengar found also that black people were more often held personally responsible for poverty than white people, reflecting racial prejudice. The overrepresentation of African Americans in news portrayals of poverty, noted earlier, thus encourages anti-welfarism.

Hostility towards welfare recipients was also fostered more directly, especially during what Herbert Gans calls 'the war against the poor' during the early 1990s,[91] leading to the introduction of the 1996 Personal Responsibility and Work Opportunity Reconciliation Act, which introduced strict time limits and 'workfare' requirements for welfare benefits. A content analysis of five leading American dailies between 1989 and 1993 found that welfare dependency was commonly depicted as a voluntary, self-imposed form of poverty that operates as a disincentive to work: 63 per cent of articles on welfare during this period omitted any reference to structural factors such as diminished job opportunities.[92]

American media tend also to project those on low incomes as 'other'. American television lacks the European tradition of popular TV soap opera centred on working-class communities, which encourages viewers to see the world in terms of their concerns and experiences.[93] By contrast, most American TV drama entertainment features affluent protagonists and encourages the view that, in the words of Diane Kendall, the 'core values held by the middle class should be the norm for this country'.[94] The working class, she argues, are sometimes portrayed in TV drama sympathetically, sometimes negatively (in particular, as oafish, buffoonish or reactionary) or more often not at all. But whatever these differences, they tend to be depicted symbolically as being not at the centre but at the margins of society.

American public culture is, in any case, disposed to be ungenerous to those on low incomes. By stressing achievement, it assigns low status to 'low achievers'. And by emphasising individual responsibility in a land of opportunity – a place where, supposedly, all are free to escape from poverty – American culture encourages a focus on 'personal' solutions to poverty. This finds expression in a genre of virtual reality programmes which, as Anna McCarthy and others argue, are designed to re-educate the poor into assuming responsibility for their destiny, without depending on the state.[95] More generally, America's individualistic culture is supported in numerous lifestyle programmes such as *What Not to Wear, Extreme Makeover, Queer Eye for the Straight Guy* or *How to Look Good Naked*. These proclaim that individuals, by remaking and disciplining their bodies, or by repackaging themselves in appealing clothes, can take personal control and follow a regime of self-improvement that will change their lives.[96]

However, media representations of poverty have changed in some respects over time. The 'war against the poor' in the 1980s and early 1990s gave way to a greater stress on reforming the poor in the later 1990s and early 2000s. This was followed by media reporting of Hurricane Katrina in 2005, in which the American news media awakened to the scale of US poverty and were strongly critical of the US government's failure to provide sufficient help to the hurricane's stranded victims.[97] But this sympathetic coverage largely focused on the plight of individuals and beleaguered communities in a natural disaster, without illuminating the structural causes of poverty. Perhaps for this reason, argues Deborah Belle, this short-term awakening of media concern made very little impression on public attitudes towards poverty and poverty relief.[98]

Compared with similar societies, America is more ready to endorse inequality[99] and to think that effort determines incomes.[100] Americans also have a very critical orientation towards welfare recipients.[101] While these attitudes are encouraged by America's political culture, they have also been nourished by the American media system. For years, American media have fostered hostility towards the poor by linking poverty to black people, black crime and a deviant lifestyle. By failing to illuminate the causes of poverty, American media have long encouraged the view that poverty arises from personal deficiency. More generally, the culture of individualism and neo-liberalism finds support in virtual reality and lifestyle programmes that preach the virtues of self-management and castigate those that fail to assume individual responsibility for shaping their lives. This legacy continues to stand in the way of mounting a sustained national government effort to relieve poverty.

Money-driven politics

The third major omission of Hallin and Mancini's account is that they do not recognise the money-driven nature of American politics and the pivotal role of the American media system in sustaining this. Thus, they write blandly that in the US, 'business is active in attempting to influence political decisions that affect their interests mainly through lobbying and campaign contributions'.[102] They also note that the United States has a laissez-faire approach to television political advertising.[103] However, they fail to register the connection between these two things and the toxic consequences that arise from it.

The US has witnessed a phenomenal increase in the money spent on wooing voters. Between 1980 and 2000, congressional campaign expenditure more than

doubled at constant prices.[104] By 2008, over \$5.3 billion was spent on federal elec-
toral contests.[105] This increase was fuelled by rising spending on television political
advertising, and also on campaign consultancy, public relations, fund-raising, electoral research and political marketing.

But television political advertising remains the biggest item of campaign expenditure. It accounts for over half of spending on election campaigns,[106] and a very high
proportion in close contests.[107] This reflects the effectiveness of well-judged political advertising in influencing both voters' views of rival candidates and electoral
choices.[108] In particular, television advertising can be especially effective in relation to voters with limited interest in the election campaign.[109] American political
advertising – which emerged as being the most negative in a comparative study
of twelve nations[110] – is also especially adept at 'attack ads' designed to undermine
the reputation of political opponents. Television political advertising is thus a key
political weapon that has become a central – and very expensive – component of
electioneering in the US.

This profoundly affects the nature of American politics. In order to get elected
to Congress, or to win a primary for party nomination, a candidate must raise a
large amount of money. In 2008, the average cost of winning a House race was \$1.4
million and \$8.5 million for a Senate seat.[111] In 2000, no successful challenger for a
House seat spent less than \$850,000.[112]

This means that congressional candidates must turn to business corporations and
affluent individuals in order to have a chance of winning, unless they are enormously rich in their own right. In 2000, close to 80 per cent of financial contributions to congressional candidates came from Political Action Committees (PACs),
contributions of \$200 or more, and the private funds of wealthy candidates.[113]
Business organisations account for most PAC campaign donations, contributing
about eleven times more than trade unions.[114] Business also heavily outguns public-
interest groups. In 1996, corporate energy groups gave over ten times more to
congressional candidates than environmental interest groups.[115] Individuals giving
campaign donations have traditionally been drawn from affluent households. Thus,
in the 2000 election cycle, 81 per cent of donations came from households with
\$100,000 or more annual income.[116]

This means that national politicians, whether Republican or Democrat, are
beholden to the powerful and affluent in order to get elected. They also have to
carry on being beholden because they need to replenish their campaign funds in
order to be re-elected. Case studies show that corporate campaign contributions,
especially at state level, can influence specific legislative behaviour and regulatory
outcomes.[117] In addition, business special interests allocate large sums to lobbying
legislators and influentials in Washington.[118] This buying of access to power is reinforced by the regular interchange between public office and corporate employment
that has become an accepted feature of American public life. Business influence,
exerted in different ways, encourages low corporate tax, limited social welfare and
business-friendly policies to become the default position of the American political
system.

High campaign expenditure also reduces the responsiveness of the political system.
It imposes a two-party lock on American politics, since the cost of competing

against well-funded Democrat and Republican candidates is prohibitive, something reinforced by the country's first-past-the-post electoral system. High electoral entry costs also limit competition. Incumbents (already with prior advantages) are in the best position to raise large war chests, and this makes them very difficult to defeat, since big spenders in American politics tend to win. Some American politicians are elected unopposed, while others crush their insufficiently funded opponents in 'wealth primaries'. Abramowitz and colleagues found that there has been a cumulative decline in House election competition between 1946 and 2004, which they attribute to rising campaign costs, incumbent advantage and increasing district polarisation.[119] In 2008, 94 per cent of House incumbents were returned.[120]

Attempts have been made to regulate campaign funding from 1971 onwards, with a major revision in the wake of the Enron scandal. These have taken the form of limiting the size of contributions, amount of spending and public funding. However, the intentions of reformers were largely frustrated by the rise of corporate PACs from the 1970s onwards, the take-off of 'soft money' donations in 1996 and the growth of big-donor 527 groups (named after an Internal Revenue classification) in the 2000s. A political system sustained by gifts from business and the wealthy remained dependent on its life-support machine.

Some reformers now look to the Internet as an antidote to corporate influence. Their hope is that internet networking will supplant television advertising as the principal campaign weapon; a legion of volunteers recruited through the web will lower campaign costs; and donors from Main Street, making small contributions, will provide an alternative to corporate and elite funding. These hopes found a focus in Barack Obama's skilful use of the Internet in his successful 2008 presidential bid. But Obama merely used the Internet to supplement traditional methods of campaigning. He obtained substantial corporate funding in addition to tapping significant small contributions from ordinary households.[121] His team spent $235.9 million on television advertising.[122] His election campaign was guided by professionals and duly won the Marketer of the Year award in 2008. And spending on the 2008 federal elections as a whole was up by $1.1 billion on 2004.[123]

American politics is driven by money because America has set its face against imposing democratic rules that limit the power of money over elections. Thus, in a study of 28 nations America emerged as the only nation that did not impose any limit on the amount of television political advertising expenditure.[124] By contrast, all other countries in the study applied some kind of restriction. In some, political advertising is banned; in others, it is excluded from public channels; in yet others, free broadcast time to communicate (i.e. advertise) to voters is allocated to political parties in relation to their electoral support.[125] The practice in much of Western Europe is to give political parties free airtime to advertise. But, as Kaid and Holtz-Bacha point out, there is a large difference between a free-time system that allocates commonly three or five or ten election broadcasts per candidate or party in an election campaign, and the roughly 300 advertising spots purchased in the US 2004 election on behalf of the presidential candidates.[126] Many democratic countries also have more effective restrictions on political donations and campaign spending than the US.

These differences will be illustrated by a comparison between the US and Britain, two countries that Hallin and Mancini portray as having similar political systems. In Britain, television political advertising is banned, while free party polit-ical broadcasts are few in number, limited in impact and of declining significance.[127] There are also strict limits on constituency expenditure by individual parliamen-tary candidates, though there were no controls on national political expenditure until 2000.[128] This produces big differences between the two countries in terms of campaign spending. Gerald Sussman reports that parliamentary candidature expenditure was not allowed to exceed $13,000 in Britain in 1997, compared with an average of almost $1.1 million candidate expenditure in House elections in the US one year earlier.[129] He also estimates that total campaign spending in the 2001 parliamentary elections in the UK was $60 million, compared with $4 billion in the 2000 US elections.[130] The difference in size between the two countries only partly accounts for this great disparity. Spending on Michael Bloomberg's mayoral campaign in New York in 2001 actually exceeded that of the 2001 national general election campaign in Britain.[131] A closer comparison is afforded by the mayoralty campaigns in New York and London in 2001, controlling for population difference. Bloomberg spent $92.60 per vote to become mayor of New York, whereas Ken Livingstone spent 80 cents per vote to become mayor of London.[132]

While there are similarities between American and British politics, there are also important differences. One of these is that Britain's political class is less beholden to business and affluent donors than its counterpart in the United States. Indeed, trade unions still contribute over half the total funds of the Labour Party, one of the two leading political parties in Britain.

Main limitations

In brief, Hallin and Mancini exclude salient features of the American media system and political context. They overlook the fact that America is an imperial, deeply unequal society whose politics is driven by money. They also ignore the role of its media system in supporting its informal empire, tacitly endorsing its social inequality and contributing to its money-fuelled politics.

This changes how the Liberal Model should be viewed. Hallin and Mancini argue that four North Atlantic countries – the US, Canada, Britain and Ireland – have a shared system of media and politics, the 'Liberal Model'. But this relies on a misleading and selective account of America that smoothes out differences between America and other countries in the 'Liberal' group. There are also other significant differences between the four countries, some unnoticed by Hallin and Mancini. To accept the Liberal Model at face value requires us to overlook the fact that the North Atlantic group of four nations includes different geo-political entities (a world superpower and a former colony (Ireland), whose party system and political culture are still profoundly influenced by the events surrounding its struggle for national independence), different types of state (federal, multinational and unitary), different political systems (presidential and parliamentary), different electoral systems (proportional and majoritarian), different political structures (where the political party is central and where it is not), different television systems (in 2008, public channels accounted for 38 per cent of viewing time in Britain and less than 2 per cent in the United States)[133] and strong and weak tabloid newspaper traditions. If the Liberal Model is projected as an 'identikit' picture, it would look like a Cubist portrait with clashing, disjointed features.

The Liberal Model perhaps works as a point of gravitation. But as a description of the common features of four countries, it becomes a bulging portmanteau concept of doubtful value. An alternative case could perhaps be mooted that the four North Atlantic countries constitute a 'Neo-Liberal Model', on the grounds that they have been especially affected by market influences. But the difficulty with this suggestion is that the primacy of the market is greater in the US than in the other three countries. And numerous other countries have also been influenced by market influences. So instead of a clear grouping of nations, we have instead a continuum that covers much of the world.

While this is not the place to develop a secondary argument, the two other groupings proposed by Hallin and Mancini also include dissimilar nations: none more so than cohesive Sweden and Belgium, a country divided into two antagonistic communities with different languages, religious traditions and political affiliations, that are both said to belong to the 'Democratic Corporatist' camp.

If one problem has to do the validity of Hallin and Mancini's three models, a second limitation is that they fail to recognise the underlying commonality between Western European countries (and part of Eastern Europe).[134] Although these have internal differences, they have also certain things in common with one another. This point is brought into sharp relief if a comparison is made between them and the US. Thus, Western European countries do not constitute a superpower. To a greater extent than the US, they are welfare democracies that redress inequality through redistributive politics. They mostly impose stricter democratic rules that curtail the power of money over elections. Nearly all share sovereignty through the law-making and law-enforcing European state. They also have media systems shaped by a conception of the public interest realised through the state. Thus, apart from Luxembourg, all Western European countries have significant public TV and radio channels, charged with serving the public interest.[135] Most regulate major commercial TV channels for the public good much more extensively than the USA.[136] In addition, they have a cat's cradle of subsidies for film, television and, in some countries, press production designed to promote media diversity and employment.[137]

The third major limitation is that Hallin and Mancini are weak on some aspects of globalisation. They ignore the evolution of governance as a multi-level system, only partly rooted in the nation.[138] Understandably, given the date of their publication, they pay no attention to attempts to reassert public control over global market forces through the reform of international agencies and inter-government agreement. Supporting these and other global initiatives are the growing ranks of those participating in international civil-society organisations.[139] These find some support in globalising tendencies in media production, distribution and consumption, though this is a subject of much mythologising.[140]

In brief, it would be a mistake to reproduce uncritically the new orthodoxy, as if it represented a definitive account of media and political systems, only awaiting export to the rest of the world. This is because it leaves out too much, and, as Hallin and Mancini acknowledge, is too anchored to one part of the world.

Innovative insights

These limitations raise a more general question about Hallin and Mancini's approach. It is a commonplace of historiography that there is a recurring battle between 'lumpers', who generalise and identify similarities, and 'splitters', who particularise and stress difference.[141] Hallin and Mancini are at times arch-lumpers, not averse to occasional simplification. For example, they make no reference to the Internet, which is a surprising omission, given that their book was published in 2004, when the importance of the Internet was widely recognised. But the inclusion of the Internet, an international medium, would have unsettled an analysis based on a national perspective of media and politics. Perhaps for this reason, the Internet's existence was overlooked. Similarly, Hallin and Mancini pay minimal attention to drama and factual entertainment, even though these are the largest and most-consumed categories of TV content, which, it will be argued later in this book, are politically important.[142] However, drama and entertainment do not fit readily into Hallin and Mancini's tripartite zoning of North America and Western Europe into three distinct regions, each dominated by a distinct model of media and politics. So, like the Internet, this complication was sidelined.

But if Hallin and Mancini seek narrative clarity by omitting things with the potential to destabilise their thesis, some of their exclusions are probably unconscious. They clearly believe that their work is driven by evidence rather than normative preconception. Yet, in reality it comes out of an identifiable academic tradition that is so dominant, and so little challenged, that it is largely unaware of its own partiality. Concepts like informal empire and economic inequality do not loom large in the comparative political science literature, typified by Arend Lijphart.[143] Their downplaying in Hallin and Mancini perhaps reflects the blind spots of an intellectual tradition.

But if *Comparing Media Systems* has flaws, and its central argument is not entirely persuasive, it is still a brilliant book. It draws on scholarship in different languages and has breathed new life into comparative media research. It integrates political studies and media studies in an original synthesis, counteracting the overspecialisation of media research. And it offers a stimulating and productive way of thinking about comparative difference.

Its key insight is that modes of journalism, ways of organising the media and political systems are interconnected. *Comparing Media Systems* makes also a strong case that there are uneven tendencies – if not 'Models' – at work in the part of the world they map. And they also point to the way in which these different tendencies are being diminished as a consequence of the increasing influence of market forces, not least in the development of a personalised, media-centred, professionally driven mode of politics that imports techniques from the business world. Unlike *Four Theories of the Press*, this book deserves its eminence.

Denouement

Before closing, we will comment briefly on Hallin and Mancini's final denouement. The Liberal Model, they proclaim, is gaining ground around the world. On the one hand, this is said to be positive, because commercialisation has aided the media's separation from the political sphere. On the other hand, commercialisation has also encouraged greater media integration into the economic sphere, which may be harmful. The triumph of the Liberal Model 'raises important questions', they conclude, 'about power and democracy that we cannot answer adequately here'.[144]

Some may think that this lack of a conclusion is too easy. The market has a positive role to play in the organisation of the media, not least in making the media more responsive to the public. But Hallin and Mancini overstate the benefits of commercialisation, not least by exaggerating the way it has encouraged media independence from political power. As we have seen, American media – the pre-eminent example of a market-based system – have been only semi-independent from government when reporting American military incursions into foreign countries. American media have also been, at times, very closely aligned to powerful social groups. If American media sometimes function as watchdogs scrutinising official power, they can also be guard dogs barking at the poor.

Hallin and Mancini also downplay the negative consequences of media commercialisation. This is a topic that has been investigated and debated in an extensive literature;[145] it is not something that should be opened up here – especially since it was a focus of a previous book.[146] Instead, we will concentrate on just one issue that Hallin and Mancini make prominent in their overview – the question of whether media commercialisation has increased or decreased the flow of political information or discussion. Their verdict is that it is impossible to reach a conclusion either way on the basis of the available evidence.[147]

However, new evidence has come to light since this judgement. There has been an enormous increase in the supply of political information as a consequence of the rise of the Internet and new TV channels, both made possible by new communications technology. But many new websites and TV channels have very small audiences. Television still remains the primary source of news in many countries,[148] so what is happening on leading TV channels is especially significant.

A recent study, undertaken by Toril Aalberg and her associates, found that the volume of news and current affairs on the leading TV channels during peak time in six nations had changed very little between 1987 and 2007. But they also found enormous differences between American and North European television in terms of the amount of peak-time provision. For example, the UK's leading channels offered six times more peak-time and evening news and current affairs than its American counterparts.[149] This continental difference was due to the contrast between US commercial and European public-service TV priorities. Aalberg *et al.* also found that news and current affairs programming was greater on public TV than on commercial TV in all six countries. Hallin and Mancini's agnosticism about the effect of commercialisation on the provision of public affairs information is misplaced.

3 Media system, public knowledge and democracy: a comparative study

James Curran, Shanto Iyengar, Anker Brink Lund and Inka Salovaara-Moring

Introduction

In most parts of the world, the news media are becoming more market-orientated and entertainment-centred.[1] This is the consequence of three trends that have gathered pace since the 1980s: the multiplication of privately owned television channels, the weakening of programme requirements on commercial broadcasters ('deregulation') and a contraction in the audience size and influence of public broadcasters.

Our interest lies in addressing the consequences of the movement towards market-based media for informed citizenship. The democratic process assumes that individual citizens have the capacity to hold elected officials accountable. In practice, political accountability requires a variety of institutional arrangements including free and frequent elections, the presence of strong political parties and, of particular importance to this inquiry, a media system that delivers a sufficient supply of meaningful public affairs information to catch the eye of relatively inattentive citizens. Thus, we are interested in tracing the connections between the architecture of media systems, the delivery of news and citizens' awareness of public affairs. In particular, we test the hypothesis that market-based systems, by delivering more soft than hard news, impede the exercise of informed citizenship.

Media systems in cross-national perspective

There is considerable cross-national variation in the movement towards the American model. We take advantage of this variation by focusing on four economically advanced liberal democracies that represent three distinct media systems: an unreconstructed public-service model in which the programming principles of public service still largely dominate (exemplified by Finland and Denmark), a dual system that combines increasingly deregulated commercial media with strong public-service broadcasting organisations (Britain) and the exemplar market model of the US. This sample enables us to investigate whether variations in media organisation affect the quality of citizenship by giving rise to different kinds of reporting and patterns of public knowledge.[2]

The American model is based on market forces with minimal interference by the state. America's media are overwhelmingly in private hands: its public-service television (PBS) is under-resourced and accounts for less than 2 per cent of audience share.[3] Regulation of commercial broadcasting by the Federal Communications Commission (FCC) has become increasingly 'light touch', meaning that American media are essentially entrepreneurial actors striving to satisfy consumer demand.

Yet, running counter to the increasing importance of market forces, American journalism continues to reflect a 'social responsibility' tradition. News coverage is expected to inform the public by providing objective reporting on current issues. In recent years, however, the rise of satellite and cable television and web-based journalism has weakened social responsibility norms. Increased competition resulted in smaller market shares for traditional news organisations; the inevitable decline in revenue led to significant budget cuts. One consequence was the closure of a large number of foreign news bureaux[4] and a sharp reduction in foreign news coverage during the post-Cold War era.[5] News organisations increasingly turned to soft journalism, exemplified by the rise of local TV news programmes, centred on crime, calamities and accidents.[6]

In sum, the American market model is more nuanced than it appears to be at first glance. Market pressures coexist with a commitment to social responsibility journalism. However, intensified competition during the last twenty years has compelled news organisations to be more responsive to audience demand in a society which has a long history of lack of interest in foreign affairs[7] and in which a large section of the population is disconnected from public life.[8]

In stark contrast to the US system, the traditional public-service model – exemplified by Finland and Denmark – deliberately seeks to influence audience behaviour through a framework of public law and subsidy.[9] The core assumption is that citizens must be adequately exposed to public affairs programming if they are to cast informed votes, hold government to account and be properly empowered. This argument is the basis for the generous subsidies provided public broadcasters, which helps to ensure that they secure large audiences. In Finland, the two main public television channels had a 44 per cent share of viewing time in 2005;[10] in Denmark, their equivalents had an even higher share of 64 per cent in 2006.[11] The public-interest argument is also invoked to justify the requirement that major commercial channels offer programming that informs the electorate. This requirement is enforced by independent regulatory agencies. The public-service model thus embraces both the public and commercial broadcast sectors.

Britain represents a media system somewhere in-between the pure market (US) and public-service (Denmark and Finland) models. On the one hand, Britain's flagship broadcasting organisation, the BBC, is the largest, best-resourced public broadcaster in the world and retains a large audience. The BBC's two principal channels, along with publicly owned Channel 4, accounted for 43 per cent of viewing time in Britain in 2006.[12] On the other hand, the principal satellite broadcaster, BSkyB, was allowed to develop in a largely unregulated form, and the principal terrestrial commercial channel, ITV, was sold in a public auction during the 1990s, and its public obligations – though still significant – were lightened. This move towards the deregulation of commercial television had major consequences, some of which are only now becoming apparent. Between 1988 and 1998, the foreign coverage of ITV's current affairs programmes was cut in half.[13] By 2005, its factual international programming had dropped below that of any other terrestrial channel.[14] This had a knock-on effect on other broadcasters, most notably Channel 4, whose foreign coverage in 2005 was almost a third less than in 2000–1,[15] but also on the BBC, where there was a softening of news values. Indeed, on both BBC and ITV news, crime reporting increased at the expense of political coverage.[16]

By contrast with broadcasting, there is a greater affinity between the newspapers of the four countries since these are unregulated and overwhelmingly commercial enterprises. In the US, newspaper circulation has been declining steadily for several years, contributing to a significant reduction in the number of daily papers; in fact, there are hardly any American cities with more than one daily paper.

Denmark has three directly competing national dailies, while in Finland the backbone of the press system consists of regional papers, though it has also competitive national papers. The rise of the *Metro* phenomenon of free-distribution daily papers has fuelled additional competition in both countries.

The British press is somewhat distinctive in that its national newspapers greatly outsell the local press. This gives rise to intense competition between ten directly competing national dailies. Five of these serve relatively small affluent markets, rely heavily on advertising and are orientated towards public affairs, while the other five are directed towards a mass market and focus on entertainment. The latter group, which accounts for over three-quarters of national newspaper circulation, has become increasingly frenetic in the pursuit of readers in response to a steady but now accelerating decline of newspaper sales.[17]

Overall, the differences between the media systems of the four countries are now less pronounced than they once were. But there remains, nonetheless, a significant contrast between the American television model, which is geared primarily towards satisfying consumer demand, and the public-service television systems in Finland, Denmark and, to a lesser degree, Britain, which give greater priority to satisfying informed citizenship.

Research design

In order to investigate the hypothesis that more market-orientated media systems foster less 'serious' kinds of journalism that limits citizens' knowledge of public affairs, we combined a quantitative content analysis of broadcast and print sources in each country with a survey measuring public awareness of various events, issues and individuals in the news.

Content analysis

Our media sources were the two principal television channels in each country (ABC and NBC News in the US; BBC1 and ITV in the UK; DR 1 and TV2 in Denmark; and YLE1 and MTV3 in Finland) and a representative group of daily newspapers. The US press sample consisted of an 'elite' daily (*New York Times*), a more popular-orientated national daily (*USA Today*), as well as a regional newspaper heavily dependent upon the wire services (*Akron Beacon Journal*). The Danish press was represented by the national broadsheet *Jyllands-Posten*, the national tabloid *Ekstra Bladet*, the national freesheet *Nyhedsavisen* and the regional daily

Jyske Vestkysten. The Finnish press sample was constituted by the national broadsheet *Helsingin Sanomat*, a big regional daily *Aamulehti*, the national tabloid *Ilta-Sanomat* and a national freesheet, *Metro*. Finally, the British press was represented by the circulation leaders of the upscale, mid-scale and downscale sectors of the national daily press (respectively, *Daily Telegraph*, *Daily Mail* and *Sun*),[18] and one local daily (*Manchester Metro*).

Each news source was monitored for a period of four (non-sequential) weeks in February–April, 2007. The main evening news programme on each television channel was analysed. In the case of newspapers, scrutiny was limited to the main news sections of American newspapers, which we compared to the main or general sections of their European counterparts.

The news sources were classified by trained student or research assistant coders in each country. The classification scheme consisted of a common set of content categories developed in advance by the researchers. Hard news was defined as reports about politics, public administration, the economy, science, technology and related topics, while soft news consisted of reports about celebrities, human interest, sport and other entertainment-centred stories. However, in the particular case of crime, predetermining news coverage as either soft or hard proved to be misleading, prompting us to distinguish between different types of news stories. If a crime story was reported in a way that contextualised and linked the issue to the public good – for example, if the report referred to penal policies or to the general causes or consequences of crime – it was judged to be a hard-news story assimilated to public affairs. If, however, the main focus of the report was the crime itself, with details concerning the perpetrators and victims, but with no reference to the larger context or implications for public policies, the news item was judged to be soft.

In addition to coding news reports as hard or soft, we classified news as reflecting either domestic or overseas events. Here we used a simple enumeration of nation states. Each news report was classified according to the country or countries referenced in the report. We also coded the news for the presence of international or regional organisations (e.g. the UN or EU).[19]

Survey design

We designed a survey instrument (consisting of 28 multiple-choice questions) to reflect citizens' awareness of both hard and soft news as well as their familiarity with domestic versus international subject matter. Fourteen questions tapping awareness of international events (both hard and soft) were common to all four countries. This common set included an equal number of relatively 'easy' (international news subjects that received extensive reporting within each country) and 'difficult' (those that received relatively infrequent coverage) questions. For example, questions asking American respondents to identify 'Taliban' and the incoming President of France (Sarkozy) were deemed easy, while questions asking respondents to identify the location of the Tamil Tigers separatist movement and the former ruler of Serbia were considered difficult. In the arena of soft news, easy questions provided highly visible targets such as the popular video-sharing website YouTube and the French footballer Zinedine Zidane; more difficult questions focused on the site of the 2008 summer Olympics and the Russian tennis star Maria Sharapova.

In the case of domestic news, hard–news questions included recognition of public officials and current political controversies. Soft–news questions focused primarily on celebrities, either entertainers or professional athletes. We supplemented the domestic questions with a set of country-specific questions related to the particular geo–political zone in which each country is situated. Americans, for example, were asked to identify Hugo Chavez (President of Venezuela), the British and Finnish respondents were asked to identify Angela Merkel (Chancellor of Germany), while Danes were asked about the incoming British premier, Gordon Brown. Once again, we took care to vary the difficulty level of the questions.

The survey was administered online, shortly after the period of media monitoring.[20] As internet access has diffused, web-based surveys have become increasingly cost-effective competitors to conventional telephone surveys. Initially plagued by serious concerns over sampling bias (arising from the digital divide), online survey methodology has developed to the point where it is now possible to reach representative samples. Our survey design minimises sampling bias through the use of sample matching, a methodology that features dual samples – one that is strictly probabilistic and based on an offline population, and a second that is non-probabilistic and based on a large panel of online respondents. The key is that each of the online respondents was selected to provide a mirror image of the corresponding respondent selected by conventional RDD methods. In essence, sample matching delivers a sample that is equivalent to a conventional probability sample on the demographic attributes that have been matched.[21]

From each online panel, a sample of 1,000 was surveyed. In the US, the sample was limited to registered voters; in Denmark, Finland and the UK, all citizens over the age of eighteen. In the US, UK and Finland, online sample respondents were matched to national samples on education, gender and age (and, additionally, in the US, in relation to race). In Denmark, the sample was drawn from a representative panel, on the basis of controlled recruitment procedures ensuring a close correlation to the demographics of the total society. The results were later weighted on age and gender.[22]

The format and appearance of the online surveys were identical in each country. Question order and the multiple-choice options (each question had five possible answers) were randomised, and in order to minimise the possibility of respondents attempting to 'cheat' by searching the web, each question remained on the screen for a maximum of thirty seconds before being replaced by the next question. In addition, the survey link had the effect of disabling the 'back' button on the respondent's browser.

Differences in news content

Our content data show that the market-driven television system of the US is overwhelmingly preoccupied with domestic news. American network news allocates only 20 per cent of programming time to reporting foreign news (47 per cent of which, incidentally, is about Iraq). Whole areas of the world receive very little coverage and, indeed, for much of the time are virtually blacked out in American network news. By contrast, the European public-service television channels represented in our study devote significantly more attention to overseas events. As a proportion of news programming time, foreign coverage on the main news channels in Britain and Finland is nearly 50 per cent more than that in the US (see Table 3.1). However, part of British TV's joint lead in this area is due to its greater coverage of international soft news. If international soft news is excluded, the rank ordering of 'internationalist' television coverage changes to Finland (27 per cent) at the top, followed in descending order by Denmark (24 per cent), Britain (23 per cent) and the US (15 per cent).

The view of the world offered by British and American television is significantly different from that of the two Scandinavian countries. Both Finnish and Danish television distribute their coverage of foreign news very evenly between three sets of nations: those from their continent (Europe), their wider geo-political zone (in the case of Denmark, for example, this is US, Iraq and Afghanistan) and the rest of the world. By contrast, both American and British television channels devote a much smaller proportion of their foreign-news time (respectively 5 per cent and 8 per cent) to other countries in their continent; and in Britain's case much less attention to the rest of the world. Their main focus (accounting for between over half and over two-thirds of their foreign news coverage) is overwhelmingly on their geo-political attachments, in which Iraq and Afghanistan loom large.

Ratings-conscious American networks also allocate significant time to soft news, both foreign and domestic (37 per cent), as does British television news (40 per cent). This compares with much lower proportions in Finland and Denmark. Indeed, the Anglo-American daily quota of soft news is more than double that in

Table 3.1 Distribution of content in television and newspapers in four countries

	US	UK	FIN	DK
Television				
Hard/soft news				
Hard news	63	60	83	71
Soft news	37	40	17	29
Domestic/international news				
Domestic	80	71	71	73
International	20	29	29	27
Newspapers				
Hard/soft news				
Hard news	77	40	54	44.5
Soft news	23	60	46	55.5
Domestic/international news				
Domestic	66	83	62	71
International	34	17	38	29

Total sample: 19,641 newspaper and 2,751 television news stories.

Finland. The difference is partly due to the fact that both American and British television news allocates a significant amount of time (14 per cent and 11 per cent respectively) to entertainment, celebrities and gossip, unlike Danish and Finnish news (less than 5 per cent).

In the case of newspapers, the preoccupation with soft news is no longer an American prerogative. In fact, our sample of American newspapers was more orientated towards hard news than their counterparts in the European countries. This finding may be attributable, in part, to the inclusion of the *New York Times*, arguably the most 'elite' of American dailies and to the fact that the US press lacks a tabloid tradition.

Among the European countries studied, the Finnish press proved more orientated towards hard news and international news than the press in Denmark and Britain. As expected, the British press, with its significant tabloid tradition, is preoccupied with domestic stories (83 per cent), soft news (60 per cent) and devotes more space to sport (25 per cent) than even the Danish press (13 per cent).

In short, Finnish and Danish public–service television is more hard-news orientated and outward-looking than American commercial television, with British television occupying an orbit closer to the American than Scandinavian models. This pattern is modified when it comes to newspapers, a less important source of information about public affairs than television.[23] The British and Danish press prioritise soft and domestic news more than the American and Finnish press.

Differences in public knowledge

The survey results revealed Americans to be especially uninformed about international public affairs. For example, 67 per cent of American respondents were unable to identify Nicolas Sarkozy as the president of France, even though they were tipped the correct answer in one of their five responses. Americans did much worse than Europeans in response to seven of the eight common international hard-news questions (the sole exception being a question about the identity of the Iraqi prime minister). The contrast between Americans and others was especially pronounced in relation to some topics: for example, 62 per cent of Americans were unable to identify the Kyoto Accords as a treaty on climate change, compared with a mere 20 per cent in Finland and Denmark and 39 per cent in Britain. Overall, the Scandinavians emerged as the best informed, averaging 62–67 per cent correct responses, the British were relatively close behind with 59 per cent and the Americans lagged in the rear with 40 per cent (see Table 3.2).

American respondents also underperformed in relation to domestic-related hard-news stories. Overall, Denmark and Finland scored highest in the area of domestic news knowledge, with an average of 78 per cent correct answers, followed again by Britain with 67 per cent and the US with 57 per cent (see Table 3.3).

Turning to awareness of international soft news, Americans were again the least informed. Thus, only 50 per cent of Americans knew that Beijing was the site of the forthcoming Olympic Games, compared with 68–77 per cent in the three other countries. Overall, the British were best able to give correct answers in this area (79 per cent), followed by the Scandinavians (69 per cent) and the Americans

Table 3.2 Percentage of correct answers to international hard-news questions across nations

International/hard-news items	US	UK	FIN	DEN
Kyoto	37	60	84	81
Taliban	58	75	76	68
Darfur	46	57	41	68
Sri Lanka	24	61	46	42
Maliki	30	21	13	20
Annan	49	82	95	91
Sarkozy	33	58	73	79
Milosevic	33	58	72	78

Table 3.3 Average percentage of correct answers to hard- and soft-news questions in domestic and international domains[a]

	US	UK	FIN	DK	Total
International hard news	40	59	62	67	58
Domestic hard news	57	67	78	78	70
International soft news	54	79	70	68	68
Domestic soft news	80	82	91	85	84

Note

a   An ANOVA 4 (nation: Finland, UK, US, Denmark) × 2 (type of news: hard vs soft) × 2 (domain: domestic vs international) with repeated measures on the last two factors confirms the systematic cross-national differences in the proportion of national, international, hard and soft news correctly identified by our respondents, as shown by the reliable three-way interaction nation × type of news × domain, $F(3.4444) = 45.27$, $p<.001$, *Partial η^2* = .03.

(53 per cent).

The one area where Americans held their own was domestic soft news. Thus over 90 per cent of Americans were able to identify the celebrities Mel Gibson, Donald Trump and Britney Spears. However, citizens of the other countries proved just as attentive to soft news; hence, the average American score for domestic soft news was no different from that in Britain and Denmark and significantly below that of Finland.

There are perhaps two surprises in these results. The first is that Finns and Danes have extensive knowledge of soft as well as hard news, something that is perhaps assisted by their popular press. The second is that American respondents seemed to know less in general about the world around them than Europeans (for which there is, as we shall see, an explanation).

Media visibility and public knowledge

To further pursue the connection between news coverage and public knowledge we next examined whether greater media visibility of the topics and people we asked about, in a sample of newspapers in the four countries, one month and six months prior to our survey, was associated with higher levels of knowledge, and conversely whether reduced media prominence of topics/persons was associated with lower levels of knowledge. There were two limitations to this exercise. First, the availability of longitudinal data on news coverage limited the analysis to the print media, and did not include the more important medium of television. Second, there is an element of ambiguity about our understanding of visibility: a person who receives only limited press coverage in the six months leading up to the survey may have obtained extensive coverage before then, generating accumulated knowledge that is carried forward to the survey. Yet, despite these potentially distorting influences, the analysis suggests a clear statistical relationship between extended press visibility and public knowledge: visibility scores in the long period (in the six months preceding the survey) were good predictors of the percentage of correct answers given by our participants in the US, UK and Denmark, though not in Finland. Visibility in the short term (during the preceding month) was a strong predictor in Denmark, a weak predictor in the UK but could not predict knowledge in Finland and the US.

This analysis thus corroborates our assertion that what the media report – or fail to report – affects what is known. The sustained lack of attention given to international news on American television and the lack of knowledge of international public affairs in America is no coincidence.[24]

Table 3.4 Regression model: visibility as a predictor of knowledge across countries[a]

		R^2	$F (1, 26)^2$	*Sig.*
Coverage over 6 months[b]				
US	$\beta = .48$	.23	7.62	$p<.05$
UK	$\beta = .42$	.17	5.07	$p<.05$
Finland	$\beta = .24$	.06	1.60	$p = .22$
Denmark	$\beta = .39$	.15	4.56	$p<.05$
Coverage over 1 month				
US	$\beta = .24$	.06	1.64	$p = .21$
UK	$\beta = .35$	.12	3.39	$p = .08$
Finland	$\beta = .28$	.08	2.14	$p = .16$
Denmark	$\beta = .51$	.51	9.17	$p<.01$

Notes

a The sample of newspapers in the US was one tabloid (*NY Daily News*), one popular daily (*USA Today*) and three prestige dailies (*New York Times, Los Angeles Times, Washington Post*); in the UK, two popular dailies (*Daily Mail* and the *Sun*) and two prestige dailies (*Guardian* and *Daily Telegraph*); in Finland, the biggest national daily (*Helsingin Sanomat*), biggest regional daily (*Aamulehti*) and the biggest tabloid (*Ilta-Sanomat*); and in Denmark, a national broadsheet (*Jyllands-Posten*), a national tabloid (*Ekstra Bladet*) and a regional daily (*Jyske Vestkysten*). The sampled periods for the six-month and one-month periods were January 7 to June 7, 2007 and May 7 to June 7, 2007, respectively. The search criteria required the item to appear anywhere in the text. Names were searched using both first and family name; places were searched in association with the specific event (e.g. Sri Lanka + Tamil Tigers; Sudan + Darfur).

b In the UK two items – McCann and Mourinho – were excluded from this analysis as they resulted in outliers (>3sd).

Cross-national differences in media exposure

To this point, we have examined the relationship between the supply of news and the level of public knowledge. But knowledge is obviously also contingent on individuals' motivation to know – their interest in current events and attentiveness to the news media.[25] We asked survey respondents to indicate the frequency with which they used various media sources. The results showed substantial cross-national differences: Americans consume relatively little news from conventional media by comparison with populations elsewhere. Just 39 per cent of American respondents report that they look at national TV news more than four days a week. This contrasts with 78 per cent in Denmark, 76 per cent in Finland and 73 per cent in Britain.

One reason for this contrast is that significant numbers of citizens in the US – a vast country with different time zones and a politically devolved form of government – are orientated towards local rather than national news. A higher proportion in the US (51 per cent) say that they regularly watch local television news than in Denmark (43 per cent) and Finland (29 per cent), though not in Britain (56 per cent). But low consumption of national television news in the US is also symptomatic of the traditionally light American news diet. Only 37 per cent of American respondents say that they read newspapers more than four days a week, against 71 per cent in Finland, 58 per cent in Denmark and 44 per cent in the UK. Just 39 per cent of Americans listen to radio news more than four days a week, compared to significantly higher levels elsewhere (51 per cent Finland, 56 per cent UK and 65 per cent in Denmark).

In short, one reason why Americans know less about the world around them than Finns, Danes and the British is that Americans consume relatively little news in comparison with populations elsewhere. It is possible that Americans make up for their deficit in 'old' media consumption with greater use of the Internet. But the available evidence casts doubt on this possibility. Research by the Pew Center, for instance, demonstrates that total consumption of news across all outlets in the US actually declined between 1994 and 2004.[26] Moreover, the greatest decline in news consumption occurred among young adults, the most internet-oriented cohort of the electorate.[27]

Within-nation knowledge gaps

Another factor contributing significantly to American underperformance is that the knowledge gap between social groups is greater in America than in the three European countries we studied. Disadvantaged groups in the US perform especially poorly in our knowledge tests, lowering the national average. But disadvantaged groups in Finland, Denmark and Britain know just as much as their more privileged counterparts, thus raising the national averages in these countries.

The contrast is especially notable in relation to education. We divided the populations of the four countries into three comparable educational groups – those with limited education, moderate education (including significant post-school qualifications or some university education) and the highly educated (graduates and post-graduates). Those with limited education in the US score very much lower in relation to hard-news questions than those with higher education. The difference between these groups is a massive 40 percentage points. By contrast, the difference between the same two groups is 14 percentage points in Britain, 13 percentage points in Finland and in effect zero in Denmark (see Table 3.5).

A similar pattern recurs in relation to income (though income data were not collected in Denmark). In the US, an average of only 29 per cent of the low-income group could give correct answers to hard-news questions, compared with 61 per cent of the high-income group – a difference of 32 percentage points. The comparable difference is less than half this in Britain, and is actually inverted in Finland.

There is also a significant hard-news knowledge gap between the ethnic majority and ethnic minorities in the US of 15 percentage points. But in Britain, there is none. Data were not analysed for ethnic minorities in Denmark and Finland, where they are a very small proportion of the population.

These findings fit a general pattern of higher variance in the distribution of knowledge in the US compared with elsewhere. The difference, for example, in the hard-news scores of men and women, and of young and old, is more pronounced in the US than in the three European countries. Thus, 24 per cent more correct answers to hard-news questions were given by men compared with women in the US, compared with a 16 per cent difference in the UK and 12 per cent in Finland. In Denmark the gender gap was reversed, with 9 per cent more correct answers being given by women than by men. Thus, there appears to be a significantly higher minimum information threshold in the three European countries compared with the US.

Table 3.5 Distribution of hard-news knowledge between social groups[a]

		US	UK	Finland	Denmark
Education					
Hard news	Low	31.4	57.4	65.0	71.1
	Medium	52.0	59.7	67.6	73.0
	High	71.0	70.9	78.4	70.3
Income					
Hard news	Low	28.9	54.5	79.5	–
	Medium	45.0	66.0	76.4	–
	High	61.5	67.6	67.0	–
Ethnicity					
Hard news	Minority	36.1	63.0	–	–
	Majority	51.5	62.9	–	–

Note

a Average percentage of knowledge in hard news across different levels of income, education and social status. As for education, we built a three-level index, with the first level indicating low education (up to high-school qualification), a second level indicating medium level of education (university diplomas, some university education) and a third level representing higher education (graduates and postgraduates). We grouped the income answers in three macro categories: low (US: income below $24,999; UK: income below £19,999, Finland: income below €35,000); medium (US: $25,000–$69,999; UK: £20,000–£29,999; Finland €35,001–€65,000) and high (incomes higher than the medium bracket in the three countries). Finally, majority group members are white British/EU/US citizens, whereas minority group members are citizens belonging to other ethnic background.

Media systems and social inclusion

National television in European countries is more successful in reaching disadvantaged groups (defined here in terms of income, education and ethnicity), partly as a consequence of its public-service tradition. Public broadcasters, financed by a licence fee or public grant, are under enormous pressure to connect to all sections of society in order to justify their continued public funding. Any evidence that they are losing their appeal to a section of the audience usually results in urgent internal inquests and demands for remedial action.[28] By contrast, commercial media tend to be exposed to pressure to prioritise high-spending audiences in order to maximise advertising revenue. This can result in low-income groups receiving less attention and, even in exceptional cases, being deliberately shunned.[29]

The central objectives of public-service and commercial media are also different. The primary goal of commercial media is to make money, while that of public-service organisations is to 'serve society' in ways that are defined in law and regulation. One of their principal public obligations is to inform the public, which influences when news programmes are transmitted.

The three American television networks transmit their main news programmes in the early and late evening. They reserve the hours between 7 p.m. and 11 p.m. for entertainment in order to maximise ratings and revenue. By contrast, the top three television channels in Finland transmit their main news programmes at different times throughout the evening: at 6 p.m., 7 p.m., 8.30 p.m. and 10 p.m. (and, on one of these principal channels, a daily current affairs programme at 9.30 p.m.). In Denmark, the two leading television channels transmit their main news programmes at 6 p.m., 7 p.m. and 10 p.m., spliced by a current affairs programme on one of these channels at 9.30 p.m. In both countries, the top television channels (including Finland's commercial MTV3 channel) offer a steady drip-feed of public information during prime time in contrast to the intensive entertainment diet of America's market-driven television. British television balances uncertainly between these two models. In 1999, the principal commercial television channel (ITV) adopted the American scheduling strategy of an early and late evening news slot, something made possible by its increased deregulation. This exerted ratings pressure on BBC1, which then moved its 9 p.m. news programme to 10 p.m. Public pressure then forced ITV to bring forward its main news programme to the earlier time of 10.30 p.m. in 2004 and to 10 p.m. in 2008. The main news inputs from Britain's top three channels in 2007 (when our survey was carried out) were 6 p.m., 6.30 p.m., 7 p.m., 10 p.m. and 10.30 p.m.

As a consequence of their social inclusion and information commitments, public-service broadcasters in Finland, Denmark and even Britain have been relatively successful in getting disadvantaged groups to join in the national ritual of watching the evening news. Much higher proportions of the less educated and those with low incomes watch television news on a regular basis there than in the US (see Table 3.6). This is not just a function of the higher levels of national TV news consumption in these three countries. The difference between the proportion of those with limited education and the national average in regular exposure to television news is smaller in the UK and Finland than in the US; and the same is true for low-income groups in the UK and Denmark. Similarly, ethnic minorities'

Table 3.6 Exposure to national TV news[a]

		US	UK	Finland	Denmark
TV	Low education	34	75	73	72
	Low income	30	69	82	–
	Ethnic minorities	35	73	–	–
National average		40	73	77	75.5

Note

a Proportion of low-education (up to high-school diploma), low-income (US: income below $24,999; UK: income below £19,999, Finland: income below €35,000) and minority-group (non-white) participants who watch national TV news more than four days a week.

exposure to national TV news is below the national average in the US, but the same as the national average in the UK.

The greater degree of economic inequality in the US, compared with Europe, is probably the main cause of the large knowledge disparity in the US. But one reason why the low-income and low-education groups in the US are less informed about hard news is that they are much less inclined to watch national television news than their counterparts in the three European countries. Moreover, because American television news is limited to a single time slot, there are fewer opportunities to reach the inattentive.

Hierarchy of influence

But although cross-national differences in the organisation of media, and how and when news is reported, are significant influences on levels of public knowledge, they are less important than deep-seated societal factors. This is highlighted by the regression model that we constructed for predicting knowledge of hard-news topics in the four countries (see Table 3.7). The model accounts for a good deal of variance, approaching half in the pooled dataset. It shows that gender and education are strong predictors of knowledge, more so than media exposure. But what is very much more important (and whose mediation also diminishes these other factors as autonomous influences) is interest in politics. Respondents who say that they want to be up to date with what happens in government, are interested in politics and talk about politics are considerably more knowledgeable than those who express lack of interest. Indeed, being interested is the single most important correlate of hard-news knowledge in all four countries.

Retrospect

As a determinant of knowledge about public life, how the media are organised is less important than the widespread cultural processes in a society that stimulate interest in public affairs. But this does not mean that the architecture of media systems is unimportant. Our evidence suggests that the public-service model of broadcasting

Table 3.7 Regression model for predicting hard-news knowledge[a]

	Beta	T	Sig
US	−0.27	−19.41	p<.001
Finland	0.19	13.96	p<.001
Denmark	0.15	10.59	p<.001
Gender	0.11	9.58	p<.001
Education	0.13	11.28	p<.001
Media exposure	0.09	8.01	p<.001
Interest	0.49	40.08	p<.001

Note
a   Regression model keeping UK as a baseline and adding the three nations (coded as dummy variables 1–0) and moderator variables as predictors of knowledge of hard issues. The overall model is reliable, $F(7.4172) = 554.51, p<.001, R^2 = .48$.

gives greater attention to public affairs and international news, and thereby fosters greater knowledge in these areas, than the market model. The public-service model makes television news more accessible on leading channels and fosters higher levels of TV news consumption. It also tends to shrink the knowledge gap between the advantaged and disadvantaged and therefore contributes to a more egalitarian pattern of citizenship. Indeed, we suspect that a critical difference between the public-service and market models is the greater ability of the former to engage an 'inadvertent' audience: people who might be generally disinclined to follow the course of public affairs, but who cannot help encountering news while awaiting delivery of their favourite entertainment programmes. The fact that public-service television intersperses news with entertainment increases the size of the inadvertent audience.

But perhaps the most significant result to emerge from this study is the low level of attention that the market-driven television system of the US gives to the world outside America and, to a lesser extent, to hard news generally. This lack of attention contributes to the relatively high level of public ignorance in America about the wider world and about public life in general. Yet, a growing number of countries are converging towards the entertainment-centred model of American television. This trend seems set to foster an impoverished public life characterised by declining exposure to serious journalism and by reduced levels of public knowledge.

In closing, we would note that the impact of media system attributes (e.g. the scope of television deregulation) on public knowledge will inevitably vary across nations because of existing differences in civic education and the acquisition of cultural norms known to increase knowledge (i.e. interest in politics and the sense of civic duty). Similarly, we expect deregulation to have more powerful conse-quences for nations characterised by relatively higher levels of economic inequality. Nonetheless, even after taking these structural differences into account, media provision of public information does matter, and continued deregulation of the broadcast media is likely, on balance, to lead to lower levels of civic knowledge.

Part II

Media and democratic theory

4 Entertaining democracy

Much of our thinking about the democratic role of the media dates from the eighteenth and early nineteenth centuries, when the press consisted primarily of highly politicised newspapers and journals. Since that time, the media have been transformed. The great bulk of content produced by contemporary media systems – including television drama, computer games, social networking websites, films, music videos and popular novels – has nothing to do with public affairs. Indeed, even *news* media devote increasing proportions of their output to soft news and entertainment (in the extreme case of the British tabloid press over three-quarters of its editorial content).[1] In other words, most media output consumed most of the time is unrelated to conventional understandings of politics. Any reconception of the democratic role of the media needs to think through the implication of this transformation.

There are three standard responses to the rise of media entertainment. The first is to deplore it as a diversion from the serious democratic role of the media, the principal response of late nineteenth-century liberals.[2] The second is to view entertainment as a separate category from public affairs coverage – basically, the reaction of the American political communications academic community. The third approach is to point to a cross-over between public affairs coverage and entertainment.[3] This draws attention to entertainment with explicitly political content, such as the TV series *The West Wing* (1990–2006), about the lives of staffers in the White House, or the satirist Jon Stewart's *Daily Show*. It also notes the growing tendency to report politics as a branch of entertainment, in terms of unfolding scandals and electoral 'horse races' devoid of policy difference.[4]

Each of these responses is inadequate as a basis for assessing the democratic role of the media. The first approach, dismissing entertainment as only a distraction from politics, ignores the political meaning of entertainment. The second approach, viewing entertainment as a separate category unrelated to politics, is a convenient way of pretending that nothing has changed. It is a methodological ruse for viewing contemporary media systems as if they were early nineteenth-century newspapers – a procedure that makes sense only if it is assumed that media entertainment has no political meaning or importance. The third response suffers from looking only at the segment of media content that very explicitly fuses politics and entertainment.

All three approaches step gingerly around an uncharted minefield: the democratic meaning of entertainment.[5] Perhaps the best way to start mapping this terrain is to suggest that entertainment relates to politics in four principal ways: in terms of values, identities, cognitions and norms. There is of course some overlap between these different categories, and they are presented here only as a convenient way of demarcating broad dominions of political meaning.

Debate about values

The totality of TV drama, film and factual entertainment affords a debate about the values that underpin politics. This matters because values have assumed an increasing significance in contemporary politics and motivate some people to vote idealistically against their ostensible economic self-interest in the US and elsewhere.[6] Nations also differ in terms of the values that shape their political cultures,[7] which contribute in turn to differences in public policy and the allocation of resources and rewards.[8] And shifts in values give rise to political change, exemplified by the way in which increased individualism sustained the rise of neo-liberal regimes in the later twentieth century.[9] So when 'entertainments' uphold different values, and implicitly invite audiences to choose between them, their function is not simply to entertain. They are potentially contributing to the political process.

To illustrate the ways in which drama can express different values, and sustain different politics, we will consider three contrasting examples. The first is the internationally successful magical-realist film *Chocolat* (2000), directed by the Swedish film director, Lasse Hallström. The film begins with a mysterious woman and her daughter arriving in a sleepy French village and opening a chocolate shop during Lent. The mayor and the priest urge local people to boycott the shop because it is encouraging people to transgress Lenten vows of abstinence. A battle ensues between the shopkeeper and the leadership of the local community which the shopkeeper gradually wins. Her shop, serving chocolates and hot cocoa with magical properties, radiates a widening gyre of social healing and happiness. Regular customers are transformed: a sour grandmother establishes a rapport with her grandson; a battered wife is rescued from her husband; an elderly man gains the courage to make welcomed overtures to a widow; a shunned Irish Traveller acquires local friends; and so on.

A new spirit of fun enters the life of the village, as when the shopkeeper (Vianne) gives away a freebie:

Shopkeeper: And these are for your husband to awaken his passion.
Customer [Yvette]:   You've obviously never met my husband.
Shopkeeper: You've obviously not tried these.

And then after the cocoa beans have had the desired effect, the customer reappears:

Customer: Do you have any more of those thingies please?
Shopkeeper: How many do you want?
Customer: How many have you got?

The village gradually sloughs off its inherited culture of tradition, hierarchy and repression, and embraces a new spirit of generosity and hedonism. The forces of reaction are triumphantly defeated. The mayor gorges himself on pagan chocolate, in a symbolic act of surrender, and is transformed into a warm, giving person. He comes to terms with the fact that his wife has left him, never to return, and makes advances to his secretary, who loves him. The priest relents and, warming to the new mood in the village, delivers a sermon that repudiates the old values of censoriousness and abstinence in favour of tolerance and good will. 'I think', he declares, 'that we can't go round measuring our goodness by what we don't do – by what we deny ourselves, what we resist and who we exclude.'

Although the film does not concern itself with the political realm, it is nonetheless a profoundly political film. Its characterisation of the conservative mayor as a stiff, authoritarian aristocrat and of the priest as his weak, callow mouthpiece, its identification of 'tradition' with a gendered, class-based hierarchy and its association of Catholicism with cruelty and hypocrisy make it a sustained onslaught on the culture that supports faith-based parties of the right in Catholic Europe. Indeed, the film's unwillingness to acknowledge any positive aspect of the tradition that it attacks – the priest and the mayor, for example, are portrayed in a partly sympathetic light only when they recognise the error of their ways and embrace their opponents' values – makes it a dramaturgic manifesto for an anti-clerical, left politics that is immediately recognisable in the context of mainland Europe.

However, it also expresses a political meaning within an Anglo-American orbit that is not dependent on local contextual references. The film embraces progressive liberal values in being overtly anti-racist (with 'decent' people recoiling in horror at an arson attack on an Irish Traveller's boat). It is also overtly opposed to patriarchy: the old order in which 'if you don't go to confession … or if you don't pretend … that you want nothing more in your life than to serve your husband three meals a day, and give him children, and vacuum under his ass' is openly derided. Its core value is the expression of liberal individualism as a moral code. Characters in the film discover both happiness and tolerance by rebelling against the conformity, sexual repression and bigotry of an authoritarian *collectivist* culture. In this way, they learn to be true to themselves, to respect difference in others and to find fulfilment. Thus, a grandmother is applauded for electing not to go into a nursing home to be 'caged', monitored and controlled. Instead, she chooses to lead a full, if shortened, life, and in the process gains friends and reciprocated love that she did not have before. This is revealed to be right for her, unlike the 'sensible' course of institutional care urged by her daughter (who really wants to be rid of her). Doing your own thing, the film tells us, makes for happiness; and respecting other people's right to do their own thing makes for all-round serendipity.

If the values of this film have a strong political resonance in a European continental context, they also have a political history in Britain. The growth of progressive individualism, reacting against an authoritarian culture, gave rise to liberalising legislation in 1960s Britain, leading to easier divorce and the legalisation of abortion and adult gay sex.[10] It was an important current also in the adoption of anti-racist, anti-homophobic and feminist policies in radical town halls in the 1980s, and culminated in liberalising social reforms during the Blair era.[11]

But if the individualism extolled in *Chocolat* is progressive, it can also take a more conservative form. This is illustrated by the American television reality show

Random 1, insightfully dissected by Anna McCarthy.[12] Transmitted on the Arts and Entertainment network in 2005, it is an extreme makeover programme where a TV 'tracker' and 'case worker' befriend at random someone in need and enhance his or her life. Thus, one programme features Bruce, a 'drifter', with a stunned, palsied face, who is missing a leg as a result of a childhood accident. He is currently sober and in need of considerable help, not least because his artificial leg is falling apart. The TV case worker gets to work and raises cash from well-wishers for a new artificial leg. The implication is that Bruce can now confront his inner demons and make something of his life. He has been given a new start; it is up to him to avail himself of the opportunity created by warm-hearted charity. The TV case worker concludes the show: 'With the leg no longer an obstacle, Bruce can decide if and when to rebuild his life.' Bruce seems to agree, saying 'I got my freedom.'

The programme proclaims more generally the value of self-help, apostrophising in the trailer '*Random 1* … asks the question, "What can we do to help you to help yourself?".' But as Anna McCarthy points out, 'the program is not, ultimately, a makeover but rather an extended meditation on the nature of making over'.[13] Thus, Bruce remains seemingly homeless and jobless, and his life is visibly not remade. But the programme's point is that he has been given the cue to assume responsibility – the rest is up to him. The same neo-liberal gospel of individual self-help is transmitted by other American entertainments such as the successful CBS courtroom show *Judge Judy*, in which the troubled, disadvantaged 'other' are regularly cajoled and humiliated. In essence, argues Laurie Ouellette, this top-rating show functions as a civics lesson in which TV viewers are encouraged 'to function without state assistance or supervision as self-disciplining, self-sufficient, responsible, and risk-averting individuals'.[14]

Standing in opposition to the values expressed in these shows are the progressive collectivist values of a successful TV hospital drama series, *Casualty*, which started in 1986 and was still among the BBC's most popular programmes in 2010. Patients are more prominent in *Casualty* than in most hospital soap operas. They come from enormously varied backgrounds: for example, a restaurant manager with a missing finger (left in the strawberry sundae), a doctor who is seriously ill (and asks to die), an alcoholic tramp infested with fleas, teenagers with dodgy DIY piercings, a woman whose stomach is full of condoms containing heroin, a suicidal Catholic woman made pregnant by her brother-in-law, a Jehovah's Witness who refuses treatment, a bald man with a wig glued to his head, a badly beaten prostitute, and so on. In the accident and emergency department where the show is set, these patients are well cared for, with priority going to the most desperately ill. The way in which Britain's health is organised as a state-funded comprehensive care system available to all, with priority determined by need, is implicitly presented as the way it should be. Indeed, the political meaning of the show is conveyed partly through its effacement of politics. Britain's collectivist state organisation of health care is *naturalised*: it is made to seem outside of politics, the expression of a shared way of doing things and looking after one another.

Casualty is also a soap opera, with a weekly dose of trouble. Some hospital staff become jealous, clash, fall in and out of love and have troubled home lives. Awful things can happen, as when a MP's son dies in the corridor and a desperate asylum seeker commits suicide by hanging himself from the hospital roof. But the impression is still conveyed that Britain's public health system is fundamentally effective, and that front-line hospital staff – whatever their human flaws – are motivated by a strong sense of public service.

This is the central theme, for example, of a 2001 episode, featuring a hospital paramedic, Josh Griffiths, who has resigned and returns to the hospital to hand in his kit.[15] He is unable to cope with the human suffering he encounters regularly in his work. 'I can't go on seeing the things we see', he tells a colleague, 'and then seeing them again when I shut my eyes.' However, Josh has no firm plans to do anything else, apart from the vague aspiration 'to get a life'. He is persuaded very reluctantly to go out one last time to a car crash because there is a staff shortage. He finds a young woman, whom he has met briefly before, trapped in her car. The medical team realise that she is dying and beyond help. She complains that 'it hurts everywhere' and is terrified. Josh dulls the pain, and with a perfect choice of words – expressing warmth and human understanding, but also offering distraction and hope – comforts the woman before she dies. Afterwards, Josh laments that he was unable to help her. 'You were there', replies his colleague, 'you made her feel safe. You cared. And she knew.' Another colleague commented, 'If that were me, I would want someone to talk to … He was the last person for her.' Inevitably, the episode ends with Josh withdrawing his resignation. He is good at his job, and it gives meaning to his life. 'I'm a paramedic, me. Nothing else makes sense', he declares. 'Course I am coming back!' The implication is clear. Josh can no more walk away from his job than a priest can leave his vocation.

Thus, each of these dramas has a different political resonance. *Casualty* affirms a progressive collectivism supporting a tax-and-spend welfare state; *Random 1* endorses a conservative individualism, in which private charity nurtures self-reliance; and *Chocolat* champions a progressive social individualism that has been politically seminal. Of course, extensive audience research demonstrates that people respond differently to the same communication, reflecting their different beliefs and dispositions. However, divergent responses to drama, and the discussion that this promotes (something that can be observed on fans' websites), merely extend the democratic function of entertainment in facilitating a debate over contending values.

Indeed, entertainment can sometimes provide a less constrained way of engaging with the values informing politics than the official discourse of politics itself. Through entertainment, it is possible to glimpse that conservative collectivism (stressing patriotism and moral order) has something in common with progressive collectivism (stressing solidarity and collective provision); and that conservative individualism (emphasising slimline welfarism and self-help) has something in common with liberal individualism (emphasising freedom from government and individual tolerance).

But politics in much of the West has been organised along different lines, based on an alliance between fiscal and social conservatism (low taxes and traditional morality) pitted against an opposing alliance of state collectivism and progressive individualism (welfare spending and liberal reform). Political parties have to aggregate both economically based and value-based groups in order to optimise votes and then contain their differences in order to appear fit to govern. But entertainment is not subject to the dragooned disciplines of public life and can offer a flexible exploration of the emotional deep structures that underpin politics.

Entertainment and identity politics

The second way in which entertainment supports the democratic process is by contributing to the formation, maintenance and (sometimes) reformation of social identity. Politics is partly about the pursuit of self-interest. However, what people think is in their best interest can depend not merely on their 'objective' situation, but also on which group they identify with and also whom they feel threatened by. Most people have multiple social identities, so what is politically important is which identity from a pack of available identities (linked to nationality, ethnicity, class, gender, sexuality, religion, age or region) they judge to be salient. Social identity is a strong influence on how large numbers of people vote.[16] More generally, shifts of social identity can have a profound impact on politics. For example, one major change in Europe has been the decline of class identity, forged in the crucible of mass industrialisation, in favour of other identities shaped by the culture of leisure and consumption. This has contributed to a shift in the structure of politics, reflected in the decline of traditional political parties appealing to class identity, and the rise of new social movements appealing to identities based on gender, sexuality and ethnicity. It has led also to attempts by political parties – especially declining European social democratic parties – to connect to changed social identities as a way of renewing their electoral appeal, something that has led also to a shift in their politics.

So, media consumption that influences people's understanding of who they are, where they fit in and whom they are against is central to the dynamics of contemporary politics. This confers particular significance on the media, and the related fields of style and fashion, that are consumed by young people. Subcultural style can be like an experimental laboratory for the production of self: a means of exploring and realising a satisfying social identity and of joining a desired group and excluding others, though within the constraints of specific contexts.[17] This can subsume an implied or explicit politics. Dick Hebdige gives as an example the way in which 'skinheads' in early 1980s Britain responded to their low social status as young working-class men, and the dislocation of their neighbourhood communities, by developing a subcultural style that invoked an exaggerated, nostalgic evocation of traditional 'lumpen' working-class life. To this were added two further elements – a stress on masculinity and white Britishness – that offered compensation for their low status and sense of loss. Style, in this case, was associated with angry working-class conservatism.[18] But this association between media consumption, cultural identity and implied politics need not be confined to exotic groups or young people – the hunting ground of the Birmingham school of cultural studies. Thus a number of researchers have pointed to the way in which certain lifestyle magazines and popular TV series have fostered the conviction that women can through self-monitoring, self-discipline and self-determination take control of their lives and shape their destinies.[19] The 'fiction of autonomous selfhood', they argue, is incubating a new strain of conservatism, centred on a strong sense of feminine identity.

Popular music is especially important, both as a component of subcultural identity and as a vehicle of political protest. This can be registered explicitly in lyrics and
tone, as in the radical African American rap music of the early 1990s that protested
against urban and industrial decline.[20] More often, it is the conjunction of one or
more elements – lyrics, rhythm, genre, artists (and their known views), audience
appropriation, context and time – that turns particular forms of music, or particular
songs, into a 'statement' that can acquire political significance.[21]

Cognitive maps

The third way in which popular entertainment impinges on politics is by offering
ways of making sense of reality. Entertainment offers images of society and its component parts, helping us to visualise its totality in a way that goes beyond anything that
we can possibly experience at first hand. It also helps us to interpret society in terms
of the mainsprings of human action and the dynamics of power shaping our lives.

This inference is supported by a longstanding tradition of research mainly
concerned with the effects of news reporting. For example, one notable study, based
on experimental research, found that when crime and terrorism were reported as
a series of discrete events, it encouraged responsibility to be attributed to the individuals involved.[22] But when crime and terrorism were reported in a contextualised
way, it encouraged attribution to societal causation. The strength of this framing
effect varied across issues and was affected by intervening variables like partisan
orientation. Given this demonstration of the cognitive influence of news reporting,
it would seem likely that the cumulative consumption of fiction over a long period
also influences our understanding of the world.

The way that entertainment depicts reality can have significant political implications. Take, for example, popular American drama concerned with the role of the
American military and security services. There are a very large number of American
war films, extending from *Sands of Iwo Jima* (1949) to *Saving Private Ryan* (1998),
which focus on the self-sacrifice, heroism and nobility of the American armed
forces.[23] There is also a genre of Cold War science fiction film, once very popular,
that features a terrifying menace – such as monsters from the sea, invaders from
another planet or an invisible enemy within (as in *Invasion of the Body Snatchers*
(1956)). These threats – thinly disguised metaphors for the communist menace –
were usually thwarted at the end of the film with the help of the American armed
forces. In the post-Cold War period, this science fiction genre was reworked in
an imperialist form by depicting the American armed forces as saviours of the
world. For example, *Armageddon* (1998) climaxes with two American military shut-
tles called 'Freedom' and 'Independence' (the latter including a Russian cosmonaut)
racing to prevent an asteroid from destroying the planet. The earth is saved, and the
surviving crew of 'Freedom' return as heroes. Similarly, in *Independence Day* (1996),
US armed forces lead the world's remnants of resistance to an alien invasion of
earth. People in different continents pray for the success of the American military
and then greet its heroic triumph with grateful joy.

After the 9/11 attacks in 2001, extraterrestrial threats were supplemented by
ruthless terrorists. The most popular of the terrorist dramas is the long-running

Fox TV series *24*, featuring Jack Bauer, the indestructible hero of the Counter Terrorism Unit. He prevents a succession of terrorist plots: to assassinate a senior politician (2001), blow up Los Angeles with a nuclear bomb (2002), spread a deadly virus (2003), generate carnage at the behest of terrorist mastermind, Habib Marwan (2005), release deadly nerve gas in a shopping mall (2006), explode nuclear devices in suitcases (2007) and control America's energy, water and air-traffic control systems (2008).

Taken together, this vast fictional output underwrites the need for America to be ever vigilant in warding off manifold threats, to spend heavily on its military and intelligence forces and to be grateful for the bravery of its armed forces. This provides implicit support for America's large military budget, something that has not been lost on the Pentagon. It has long given logistical and technical support to Hollywood, providing in effect a hidden subsidy for American war films.[24]

But Hollywood has also produced films that cut across or even challenge the 'national security' theme of patriotic war films. There is a long tradition of critical war dramas from *Red Badge of Courage* (1951) through to *Platoon* (1986) and *Jarhead* (2005). Their most often recurring themes are that war brutalises everyone, exacts a terrible human cost and should be avoided whenever possible. There is a second cluster of critical films, from *Three Days of the Condor* (1975) through to the Bourne franchise (*The Bourne Identity* (2002), *The Bourne Supremacy* (2004) and *The Bourne Ultimatum* (2007)), which feature murderous, corrupt groups of operatives in the CIA. Their implication is that a democracy needs to exercise control over its security forces. Thus, *Three Days of the Condor* ends with the hero (a CIA employee) walking towards the *New York Times* building as a whistleblower, while *The Bourne Ultimatum* features in its conclusion a news report of a US Senate hearing into CIA abuses. There is also a third, small group of popular anti-imperialist films. This includes the remake of *The Quiet American* (2002), which draws attention to an American CIA agent's moral ambiguity, implying that he had been implicated in a massacre in French Indochina; *Rendition* (2007), which depicts the CIA as being involved in the abduction and torture of an innocent engineer, who is induced to 'confess' to terrorism that he never committed; and *Syriana* (2005), which portrays the American state as being hand-in-glove with the oil industry and deploying arms to prevent a moderate Arab from introducing democracy, establishing the rule of law and advancing the position of women in a Gulf emirate. Here, the American state is portrayed as using violence to prevent the promotion of American values of freedom and democracy overseas – the obverse of countless American films.

Thus if many American military films implicitly support a Pentagon perspective, there are also anti-war, CIA conspiracy and anti-imperialist movies. In effect, Hollywood stages an implicit political debate about America's national security state. The spectrum of positions expressed in this debate goes beyond that of conventional politics. The anti-imperialist perspective of *Syriana* falls outside the bi-partisan consensus of Capitol Hill, while the TV series *24* pushed the boundaries by championing state torture.

Drama can also provide a focus for collective debate, a point illustrated by the impact of Jack Bauer on America. Bauer dramatised torture, making it real: something enacted in people's living-rooms. Although Bauer often takes the law into his hands, and acts in an unauthorised way, he invariably saves people's lives. Torture is thus presented as something that has to be done in order to defeat terrorism and to prevent (sometimes literally) a 'ticking bomb' from exploding. However, three things made this justification of state torture a catalyst for national debate. First, the TV series featuring Jack Bauer was so widely viewed that it provided a common basis of experience and shared point of reference. Second, Bauer's use of torture became more frequent and prominent from 2005 onwards (with Bauer reflecting upon and justifying his actions in the series itself). Third, and most importantly, Jack Bauer came to be seen by large numbers of people as representing something more than just fiction. The 'abuses' of Abu Ghraib, revealed in 2004 and the subject of publicised courts martial up to 2006, were widely presented as the actions of pathological individuals. But by 2007, increasing prominence was being given to the claim that the American state was outsourcing torture to other countries through secret renditions and also sanctioning 'high-pressure' interrogation methods by its own agents when dealing with suspected terrorists. Public discussion of Jack Bauer greatly increased in 2007 and focused on his use of torture, partly because it became widely suspected that torture was being deployed by the 'good side' in the battle against terrorism.

In 2007, Jack Bauer came up in a televised presidential debate between Republican presidential candidates, prompting one columnist to call the debate 'a Jack Bauer impersonation contest'.[25] Conservative Supreme Court Justice Antonin Scalia made headlines with a remark, much quoted (and also misquoted): 'Is any jury going to convict Jack Bauer? … I don't think so.'[26] Former President Bill Clinton condemned torture, but commented on Bauer in an elliptical manner that was interpreted in different ways.[27] Brigadier General Patrick Finnegan, dean of the elite West Point Military Academy, urged the producers of the show to eliminate torture scenes in order to prevent a negative influence on young soldiers.[28] Some Protestant evangelical religious leaders took a public stand against torture, in opposition to the Bauer enthusiasts within their community.[29] A satirical cartoon strip in which little Jack Bauer takes after his father and tortures Arab children at a cub scout camp provoked uncomfortable laughter in the blogosphere.[30] A national debate about Bauer and torture was conducted in the media, extending from the *Washington Post* through to Yahoo! chatrooms.[31] Some of this was insubstantial, typified by the claim that the success of *24* was a popular referendum in favour of torture and the counterclaim that a drop in the show's ratings reflected a changing public mood. But at its heart was a serious discussion centred on three contending positions: the Jack Bauer view that the 'means justifies the ends'; its antithesis that torture is always wrong; and a centre ground of worried pragmatism (disapproving of torture but believing that, in certain circumstances, it is necessary, while also registering that overdone torture can produce unreliable information).

Jack Bauer thus provided a catalyst for a national community to engage in a moral-democratic debate about torture, at a time when it was divided and, to some degree, in two minds. A Pew survey in April 2009 found that just 25 per cent said that 'torture to gain important information from suspected terrorists' is never justified. In comparison, 22 per cent said that torture is rarely justified, 34 per cent that it is sometimes and 15 per cent that it was often justified.[32] Although most Americans support torture in certain circumstances,[33] President Obama changed American state policy on interrogations to comply with international law in January 2009.

Entertainment and public norms

The fourth way in which the media impinge on public life is through contributing to a dialogue about public norms. These are the rules, conventions and expectations that guide individual behaviour and the social interaction of society. Public norms generate shared understandings about what actions are appropriate and inappropriate, and also help to define acceptable and unacceptable attitudes.

However, public norms evolve and change over time. They also vary in terms of their force. They can be coercive because they are consensual and enforced by law; and they can also be weak because they are contested and widely breached. Norms can also demarcate very sharply the boundaries of what is acceptable, or leave a wide spectrum of behaviour as a matter of individual and subcultural choice. Despite this variability, public norms are an essential part of the way in which we govern our common social processes.

The media are involved in norm enforcement through pillorying or demonising transgressors (for example, mothers who go abroad on holiday, leaving their children behind unattended – a favourite British tabloid target). But the media can also participate in the weakening, strengthening or revision of norms. This can take the form of opening up public norms to explicit debate, leading to their reaffirmation or modification. Alternatively, revision can be enacted symbolically through changing representations of the 'other' in a way that redraws the boundary between the acceptable and unacceptable. This will be illustrated through a brief account of changing portrayals of sexuality and gender.[34]

In Britain, gay sex used to be a crime, and was discouraged through strong social disapproval. This was reinforced through negative representations of gays and lesbians in films during the first half of the twentieth century. Gay men tended to be depicted as silly and comic or as sinister, predatory and menacing.[35] When attitudes in Britain liberalised during the 1960s, this was accompanied by less hostile film representations (including a notable film, *Victim* (1961), in which the sympathetic hero is a blackmailed gay man), and by the decriminalisation of gay sex in 1967. Screen hostility towards gays and lesbians continued to decrease in the next thirty years, though they long continued to be depicted as 'other' (i.e. not normal), with the most sympathetic portrayals usually being reserved for the 'asexual'. There was a corresponding change in British public attitudes, with those saying that homosexuality is always or mostly wrong decreasing from 70 per cent to 47 per cent between 1985 and 2001.[36] In the early twenty-first century, there was a further liberalising shift. While there continued to be negative screen depictions (fuelling displays of public disapproval and violent 'queer-bashing' by normative vigilantes), almost for the first time, there were also screen portrayals of gays and lesbians as 'ordinary'. A notable landmark was the British TV series *Queer As Folk* (1999–2000), whose narrative, camera gaze and sex scenes normalised being gay.[37] A combination of decreasing hostility and more positive media representation gave a further impetus to legislative change. In 2001–4, same-sex partnerships were legally recognised (with important financial consequences), and the age of sexual consent was made the same for all.

Similarly, the weight of tradition – underpinned by religious interpretation and biological theory, supported by early socialisation, peer-group pressure and popular culture and underwritten by patriarchal authority – projected a clear normative understanding of gender difference in late Victorian Britain. This ordained that the woman's place was *rightfully* in the home (though this was often breached in practice) and that men should be the principal breadwinners and play the principal role in public life. Gender convention also assumed that women were inherently different from men. Thus, it was widely believed that men were naturally ardent, initiating, rational and independent, while women were naturally disposed to be demure, dependent, emotional and nurturing.[38]

This normative inheritance was contested, renegotiated and modified in the subsequent period. The organised women's movement, supported by a significant feminist press,[39] secured major legal reforms, not least, in 1918, the right of women over thirty to vote. Subsequent legislative reform was accompanied by gradual normative revision that was played out in the contemporary media. Thus, most popular newspapers in the 1920s and 1930s depicted women's increased freedom from confining social codes and dress and a greater stress on female athleticism as part of a generational change that was to be welcomed as a way of being 'modern'. Yet, while these papers mostly put their weight behind gender change, their women's pages remained focused on looking good and being a housewife and mother.[40] Similarly, the male ideal in young women's magazine fiction shifted in the 1950s towards a new stress on boyishness and gentleness, though the ideal man was still expected – as in the 1920s – to be 'strong'.[41] This combination of continuity and change is typical of the way in which media support normative adjustment.

From the 1970s onwards, the advance of women in Britain accelerated (though significant gender inequalities remained). This shift was accompanied by changes in the way in which women were depicted in the media. In the period 1945–65, autonomous, independent women tended to be symbolically punished in popular films: they usually came to an unhappy end or were portrayed as unfeminine or unfulfilled.[42] By contrast, popular TV drama from the 1980s onwards featured an increasing number of autonomous heroines who were also successful, fulfilled and feminine.[43] Changing representations of gender were linked to a growing repudiation of the Victorian gender order. Thus, in 1989, only 28 per cent in Britain agreed with the statement that 'a man's job is to earn money; a woman's job is to look after the home and family'. By 2002, this traditionalist minority had shrunk to just 17 per cent.[44] But this repudiation of the past is beset by ambiguity, not least over who does what in the home. The same study also found that in 2002, 48 per cent said that that women should stay at home when there is a child under school age, a figure that is significantly less than the 64 per cent who adopted this position thirteen years before, but still substantial.[45]

This background of changing gender relations partly accounts for the impact of the American TV series *Sex and the City* (1998–2004) in Britain and elsewhere. The series is an improbable fable about four professional women (three in their mid-thirties and the other in her early forties) living the life of the super-rich in

Manhattan, but without the kind of jobs or private incomes that would sustain this. The series has been championed as expressing a new generation's updated feminism[46] and denounced as a return to a reactionary pre-feminist past.[47] Both positions are wrong, because the series stages a *debate* between alternative gender norms.

This debate is sustained in four ways. First, it is expressed in the monologues of the journalist, Carrie, as she writes or thinks about her weekly sex column. One of its recurring themes is the tension between expectations shaped by the popular culture of the past and the reality of her life and that of her friends. A world of celluloid romance and fairy-tale princesses is contrasted with the routines and disappointments of quotidian life. 'No one has "Breakfast at Tiffany's" and no one has "Affairs to Remember"', she comments. 'Instead we have breakfast at 7 a.m., and affairs we try to forget as quickly as possible.'

The second way in which this normative dialogue is sustained is through the contrast represented between the four friends at the heart of the series, each of whom embodies different orientations and expectations. At one end of the spectrum is Charlotte, an art gallery director who yearns for a Tiffany engagement ring, marriage to WASP perfection, a fulfilled life as mother and wife. Her search is unrelenting: 'I've been dating since I was fifteen', she declares. 'I'm exhausted. Where is he?' Samantha, the head of a small public relations company, represents the other end of the spectrum: the female equivalent of a 'laddish' male, who regards the idea of eternal love as an illusion, abhors the notion of marrying and is a confident, initiating libertine. 'I am try-sexual', she explains, meaning that she will try anything. Situated between these two are journalist Carrie, who oscillates between romantic yearning for a perfect man and the sceptical detachment of a journalist-ethnographer, and Miranda, a Harvard-trained lawyer who is focused on her career, does not want a child and makes occasional feminist outbursts. Exasperated by the men-talk of her friends, she exclaims on one occasion: 'How does it happen that four such smart women have nothing to talk about but boyfriends? It's like seventh grade with bank accounts. What about us – what we think, we feel, we know? Christ …'

The third way a dialogue is staged is through the ritual meetings that take place between the four friends, in almost all 94 episodes, in a restaurant, bar, coffee shop or apartment. These meetings become occasions for sharing recent experiences or future plans and generate contrasting reactions. Thus, when Charlotte announces that she intends to give up her job as the head of a fashionable art gallery in order to prepare for her first child, redecorate her flat and help her husband through volunteer fund-raising for his hospital, she gets a strongly disapproving response from her friends. In a subsequent heated phone conversation with one of them, Charlotte defends her gender traditionalism by declaring: 'The women's movement is supposed to be about choice', and she is entitled to make a choice that is right for her.

The fourth device for critically reflecting on contemporary gender norms is that the four women respond in different ways to what happens to them. While Charlotte secures a 'dream husband – a blue-blooded surgeon', the dream turns out to be an illusion, like 'a fake Fendi – just shiny and bright on the outside'. Closer knowledge of her husband reveals him to be deficient in most ways that matter.

The dream's emptiness is underscored when Charlotte poses with her estranged husband in their soon-to-be-sold Park Avenue apartment for a fashionable magazine – generating the sort of image that had nourished her romantic yearning for years. Although Charlotte's home-making ambitions do not change, she becomes more pragmatic and less tied to social convention. Similarly, the fiercely independent Samantha acquires a sense of vulnerability, as a consequence of ageing and getting cancer, and settles for the emotional stability of living with a young, loving actor (whose career she transforms). Carrie secures the romantic, exciting man of her dreams, but not before discovering – from a lonely vigil as a pampered but neglected doll in Paris – that the combination of romance *and* a career is what makes her happy. Miranda has a child that she had not bargained for and settles for a nurturing man who becomes the principal home-maker in a traditional gender-role reversal. Each woman thus opts in effect for different strategies in being a contemporary woman.

Of course, at one level, the series is steeped in convention in that it is based on a man-hunting narrative that ends in all four women getting their men – three of whom could have stepped out of the pages of a Mills & Boon or Harlequin novel. However, the four friends in *Sex and the City* have in a sense everything: they are clever, successful, witty, good-looking, warm, imaginative and in touch with their feelings. This is in marked contrast to most men they meet, who, however promising they first appear, turn out to be sadly inadequate: they are self-obsessed, emotionally immature, unable to commit, have unacceptable character defects or, in the case of the best-drawn male character (Aidan), are just too ordinary. This depiction of underlying inequality between the heroines and the men they encounter is the dynamic that subverts the conventional formula on which the series is based. The women in *Sex and the City* have demand- rather than supply-side problems in finding a man. Although they are sometimes rejected, they more often turn down men as not being good enough. And although they all seem anxious to find a man, each (apart from Charlotte) actually has rather ambivalent feelings. One is centred on her career, another on recreational sex and the third enjoys her freedom and independence and has a panic attack when she tries on a wedding-dress. These are women who have come into their own, who are seeking out new relationships and solutions. So, to see the series as simply a reversion to a patriarchal era in which women yearn to be married, and are only fulfilled through their relationship to a man, is to misunderstand its complexity. It is also to miss the significance of the series as an extended dialogue – notwithstanding its fairy-tale content – between the past, present and future of gender relations.

In brief, entertainment connects to the democratic life of society in four ways. It provides a space for exploring and debating social values, which occupy a central place in contemporary politics. It offers a means of defining and refashioning social identity, something that is inextricably linked to a sense of self-interest. It affords alternative frameworks of understanding, which inform public debate. And it provides a way of assessing, strengthening, weakening and revising public norms that are an integral part of the way we govern ourselves. To continue to view entertainment as something removed from politics, and unrelated to the democratic role of the media, is no longer sustainable.

Globalisation

If one adjustment that needs to be made is to take account of the rise of mass entertainment, another is to register the development of globalisation. When the democratic role of the media was first elaborated, it was taken for granted that the role of the media was to serve national and local publics. The nation and the locality were where democracy was first developed and where newspapers circulated. So theorising was confined within the container of the nation.

But during the course of the twentieth century, the nation state declined.[48] The rise of international, deregulated financial markets, and of transnational corporations able to relocate, with relative ease, production to other countries, reduced the ability of national governments to manage their domestic economies. National governments also became subject to increasing global economic pressure to adopt market-friendly policies (such as low corporate taxation), irrespective of the wishes of their electorates. Governments of nations are still important in a wide area of everyday life (as responses to the 2008 economic crash underlined). But national government power, and that of national electorates, diminished as a consequence of deregulated globalisation.

The democratic system is adjusting to this decline.[49] In addition to national and local government, two new tiers have been introduced. The first new tier comprises continental or subcontinental structures such as the European Union (EU), where national sovereignty is partly pooled, and the Association of Southeast Asian Nations (ASEAN), which facilitates a collective response to political, economic and environmental issues in the region. The second tier is global agencies, of which the three most important are the United Nations (with numerous ancillary organisations), the International Court of Justice and the World Trade Organization. There has also been a growth in the number of quasi-global forums like the G20 country summits designed to support intergovernment initiatives and agreements. The hope informing all these developments is that they will assist the extension of public control in areas like climate change and the global market, where governments acting alone have limited power, and that a system of regulation can be developed in relation to issues like human rights that reflect 'global norms'.

But this project of strengthening public power in a post-Westphalian world is still at a developmental stage. Thus, the EU has a democratic deficit as a consequence of the limited powers of the directly elected European Parliament. Similarly, global regulatory agencies are subject to strong influence by the US and leading nations, and by financial and administrative elites.[50] More generally, there are enormous obstacles in the way of improving 'multilevel governance', though there are also compelling reasons for persisting in this process of democratic renewal.[51]

One difficulty is that 'multilevel governance' is not matched by a comparable, multilevel sense of citizenship. For the last twenty years, the European Commission has attempted to engineer through its competition and 'audio-visual' policies the building of a pan-European media system that fosters a European sense of identity and citizenship, promotes higher levels of European political participation and forges a European public that holds to account European political institutions. But Europe-wide media remain weak and mostly reach small elite or specialised audiences. While national media have made adjustments, these have been modest. Wessler and associates found that although leading newspapers in different European countries gradually increased the amount of attention they gave to EU institutions since 1982, they failed to foster 'discursive integration', that is the linking up of debates and concerns across European nations.[52] *European* citizenship, based on a shared cultural identity and involvement in a common political process, thus remains relatively unsupported by the nation–centred media of Europe.

Similarly, the development of global governance has not been matched by a corresponding sense of global citizenship. However, this is contested by some theorists. They point to the rapid growth of international civil society, reflected in the increased membership and activity of international campaigning organisations and the burgeoning of international NGOs.[53] Some also argue that the rise of the Internet and satellite TV, among other influences, has forged interconnected webs of communication around the world. These different influences are said to have created a new sense of global consciousness and led to the creation of a 'global public sphere' that is allegedly giving rise to a new popular force in the form of 'international public opinion'.[54]

However, this optimistic interpretation fails to grasp just how underdeveloped the world *news* media's system remains. The audiences of leading transnational TV news channels are, in most countries, very small. While the Internet has a growing audience, accounting for about a quarter of the world's population in 2009,[55] this audience is subdivided into language publics. The Internet is also used more as a medium of entertainment than of news. In 2006–7, the Internet was the primary source of news for just 6 per cent of adults in Britain, 6 per cent in Sweden and 12 per cent in Norway, all countries with a high internet–penetration rate.[56]

The principal news medium, in most countries, is still television. Although television draws on global news agencies, it is organised primarily as a national medium, with national news priorities, serving national audiences. As it will be argued in the next chapter, television tends to focus on national news and to cover the world from the perspective of the home nation. The dominant news medium thus supports national rather than global citizenship.

The production and consumption of drama and music is more global than is the case with news, and is perhaps a more important carrier of a sense of global citizenship than journalism. Thus, Hollywood film production has become more internationalised, and its penetration of international markets has steadily increased.[57] There has been a rapid growth in the international buying and selling of television programmes, while the rise of the Internet and MTV have contributed to the globalisation of music. Even so, the equivalent of 'national domestication' is taking place in factual entertainment, with the growth of national variants of reality TV formats.[58] MTV has abandoned its one-planet music policy in favour of tailoring its output to the different musical tastes and cultures of multiple subregions.[59] In general, the world's production of entertainment is multipolar: it is organised around leading production countries like America, Mexico, Brazil, Egypt, India and China, each catering for different language publics.[60]

In short, an attempt is being made to offset the decline of the nation state by developing transnational structures of governance and regulation. But this project is being hindered by the overwhelmingly national nature of television, the dominant news medium. While national television news and current affairs scrutinise national government, they are less active in holding to account international regulatory agencies. While they promote debates within national communities, they are much less concerned about fostering debate between nations. Above all, national television fosters a strong sense of national identity in a form that takes precedence over international and transnational identities. As long as this remains the case, building a better system of governance in a globalised world will be an uphill struggle.

Organised democracy

The third major adjustment that media democratic theory needs to make is to take account of the development of *organised* democracy. When press theory was elaborated in the mid-nineteenth century, it was commonplace to think of the press as the sole intermediary between governed and governed, the latter conceived as an aggregation of individuals. For example, when in 1841 Thomas Carlyle famously dubbed the press the 'Fourth Estate', he made no reference to intermediary agencies between lawmakers and the people apart from the press.[61]

This convention has persisted in a surprising amount of scholarly commentary about journalism, especially in America, where it is not uncommon for a simple image of government, media and the public to be invoked.[62] It is also embedded in the objectivity tradition of journalism, informing its understanding of how the newspaper should be organised. In this canon, impartial news briefs the individual citizen; view-based features provide a forum of debate shaping public opinion; and, in some versions, the editorial represents public opinion to government. The objectivity tradition also holds that the newspaper (and television channel) should sever all connection to sectional groups in order for its news to be impartial, its debate open and free and its allegiance to the general public unqualified. This conception is contrasted with debased forms of journalism, in which reporting is partisan and propagandistic and media discussion is distorted by predetermined agendas. The US, the home of objective journalism, is contrasted with more benighted countries where advocacy journalism prevails and where the media manipulate rather than empower the public.

The trouble with this general view, often promulgated in American journalism schools, is that it is based on an atomistic view of democracy as being constituted by individual citizens. This ignores the central role of collective organisation in the functioning of contemporary democracy. Thus, political parties are central cogs in the working of most political systems (though not the American one). Interest groups, new social movements and the myriad organisations of civil society are also essential components of contemporary democracy. They monitor power-holders, seek to influence public policy and represent different constituencies. They are a key means by which ordinary citizens can advance different – and often contending – agendas, opinions, values and solutions.

These organisations can sometimes emerge from the collective forging of cultural identities supported by minority media (some of which can seem 'non-political'). Thus, in the US, small-scale gay newspapers and magazines – mostly short-lived

– first appeared in the 1940s and early 1950s, at a time when homosexuals were persecuted and tended to seek anonymity. The growth of this press, and of gay theatre, dance, publishing and clubs, helped to build increasingly confident, mutually supportive, openly gay and lesbian subcultures in major American cities. Out of these communities emerged the gay liberation movement, following the 1969 Stonewall riots in New York, which secured important legal reforms as well as confronting homophobic attitudes.[63] Similarly, minority media played a significant part in sustaining the cohesion and intergenerational adaptation of African American communities during the civil rights era,[64] and were central in the development of working–class identity, political consciousness and collective organisation in nineteenth–century Britain.[65] The growth of minority media can thus help to constitute communities and assist them to become politically organised. New technology is currently facilitating this process in authoritarian as well as democratic societies.[66]

This way of viewing contemporary democracy as being organised and underpinned culturally by communal identities invites a different understanding of the role of the media. Media which are the mouthpieces of collective organisations and solidary groups should be viewed as having as much legitimacy as impartial media informing individual citizens. Expressed concretely, this means that media that are partisan, that seek to interpret rather than to report passively the news, that assimilate specialist knowledge in the service of a cause, that facilitate dialogue between an organisation's leadership and rank, that furnish symbols of collective identity supporting the maintenance of a social group or organisation, that identify problems and propose solutions from a sectionalist viewpoint and that proselytise distinctive perspectives of society offer something that is valuable. They support the functioning of collective organisations and of the communities that sustain these: in other words, the infrastructure of democracy.

More generally, by reinforcing political commitment, partisan journalism supports effective involvement in the political process, at a time when public connection with politics is waning in many countries (reflected in falling electoral turnouts, declining trust in public institutions and increased individualism).[67] Activist media also encourage popular participation, something that offers a potential counterweight to corporate and elite dominance of public life.

But if sectionalism is the fuel of politics, it can also have negative consequences. It can encourage fragmentation into separate social enclaves, which are assertive of their own rights and interests, but are unheeding of others. It can promote government, based on a clientelist system of patronage. It can also lead (as in Northern Ireland during the Protestant Unionist ascendancy) to systemic oppression of a minority by the majority in a form that is democratically sanctioned. So, a brake needs to be applied to unchecked sectionalism that goes beyond the necessary checks of judicial independence and constitutional protection of human rights. A way needs to be found of sustaining a public debate concerned with the common good, underpinned by a wider sense of mutuality.

There is thus a need for a media system that both empowers social groups and subgroups within the community and seeks to reconcile them. Fortunately, we do not have to opt for either 'American' or 'European' styles of journalism. An optimal media system is one that includes advocacy media with close links to collective organisations and communities of interest, and a core public-service television sector that reaches out to a more extensive audience, reports the news in a neutral way and sustains debate in a form that is orientated towards the public good. The latter's purpose is to provide disinterested briefing for individual citizens, promote reciprocal dialogue across society and foster a broadly based sense of solidarity. If one part of the media system should energise civil society, another should bring contending groups and individuals into communion with each other.

In brief, a democratic media system should include media serving sectionalist groups as well as society as a whole; speak in the register of grassroots rage as well as evidence-based civility; and sustain civil society, not just individual deliberation. This approach thus entails recognising that *media doing different kinds of journalism can make different contributions to the functioning of democracy*.

Theories of democracy

There are two outstanding issues to address. One has to do with alternative ways of viewing the democratic process and the way in which these lend themselves to different conceptions of how the media should be organised.

Setting aside the chimera of direct democracy, which works well only in small, participatory polities, there are four prominent rival views of democracy.[68] These are really clusters of associated ideas and hover uncertainly between description and prescription. But for the sake of expository clarity they will be presented here as sharply delineated alternatives, each linked to different media regimes.

Occupying one corner is the liberal-pluralist perspective, which sees democracy as a process of competition between diverse interests and multiple power centres.[69] It holds that diverse interests should be free to compete in the media marketplace, just as they do in the political marketplace. If this results in media one-sidedness or excessive concentration, the market provides the potential solution. According to this tradition, freedom of corporate media expression should not be constrained significantly by government intervention, since this threatens media freedom. The only accepted rider to this is that the media market must be potentially 'contestable' through the launch of new media or at least be exposed to the 'disruptive' potential of new technology (conditions which nearly always exist, happily precluding the need for public intervention). This liberal-pluralist perspective is closely associated with the free-for-all market approach to journalism that embraces advocacy and partisanship. It is openly contemptuous of what it sees as the bland worthiness and dull pomposity of American journalism. This is, in essence, the underlying creed legitimating the British approach to print journalism.

In another corner is the 'rational-choice' perspective, which tends to view democracy as a battle between competing teams of elites seeking to win public backing.[70] The team that successfully aggregates most individual preferences wins the prize of elected office for a finite term. In this context, goes the argument, it does not make a great deal of sense for the majority of citizens to become news junkies, because they have very limited chances of influencing public policy. There are also many other more enjoyable and rewarding ways for people to spend their time. Responsibility can be delegated to political representatives and intermediaries, in much the way that one calls in a plumber to fix a faulty boiler rather than do it oneself.

It is sufficient for most people just to scan the news. But the news media have nonetheless certain responsibilities. They should provide a succinct, impartial news briefing, and be ready to sound an alarm if there is a crisis or acute problem that warrants the 'monitorial' citizen's urgent attention. In addition, there need to be quality media, inspired by a sense of professional mission, providing intelligent, extensive news coverage and facilitating informed dialogue between elites. In effect, this approach legitimates (though some within the rational-choice school would say 'realistically accepts the necessity for') America's 'two-nation' media system in which elite papers like the *New York Times* offer extensive news coverage, while the television networks marginalise the news by scheduling it very early in the evening in order to make way for uninterrupted entertainment.

In the opposite corner is the deliberative model of democracy.[71] It argues that the democratic process should be determined not by a periodic aggregation of individual preferences (as in the rational-choice model) or driven by the tug-of-war between special interests (as in the liberal-pluralist model) but through collective deliberation shaped by a sense of civic duty. The central role of the media is to assist the public to reach informed and considered judgements not merely at election time but between elections, and to enable the public to exert a cumulative influence on the direction of society. This approach stresses that public discussion is a learning process that registers complexity, alerts people to other interests and viewpoints, helps to identify different options, leads to positions being modified through reciprocal exchange and encourages compromise through reasoned argument. In order to promote public rationality, the media should provide a full and intelligent news service and also an open forum of debate. Its current affairs coverage and mediated discussion should encourage civility, a shared pursuit of truth and a desire to understand other groups and viewpoints. It should also promote a public interest rather than a 'what's in it for me?' orientation, and (in some versions) urge public recognition that the democratic state can achieve goals that cannot be attained by the individual. This tradition is associated with media systems, especially entrenched in Northern Europe, with well-funded public-service broadcasting organisations and extensively regulated commercial television.

The fourth corner is occupied by radical democracy.[72] This tradition attacks liberal pluralism for downplaying corporate power and ignoring the enormously unequal resources available to different groups in society. It contends that rational-choice theory legitimates public passivity and the perpetuation of inequality. And it views with suspicion the deliberative tradition, claiming that the rhetoric of 'being reasonable' can be deployed by the powerful to exclude what they regard as 'unreasonable', while the pursuit of consensus can obscure irreconcilable conflicts of value and interest in a manipulative form of closure.

Although it is eclectic, the radical democratic tradition has come to stand for certain things. It stresses the need for media to critically scrutinise social and economic power, not just government. It emphasises the role of partisan media to arouse, engage and mobilise disadvantaged groups. In its feminist version, it stresses the power of emotion, the subjective and the personal narrative as a discourse of resistance to patriarchal power. And in nearly all versions, it emphasises the need for the media system to give a powerful voice to the marginalised, excluded and subordinated. This approach usually emphasises the importance of wider social struggle in generating oppositional media. However, its social democratic versions look to the state to provide a helping hand, through the creation of public-service channels committed to promoting the concerns of minority groups or of social market subsidies that support minority voices in imperfect markets. Media regimes that approximate to this blueprint (or parts of it) are in either social democratic countries (like Norway) that deliberately seek to foster media diversity for the health of democracy or societies with polarised political cultures (like Greece).

This ideal typification downplays points of affinity and overlap between the four positions. Baker (working from a different understanding of the relevant literature) sensibly concludes that the best approach is to synthesise different perspectives in what he calls a 'complex' model of democracy.[73] We have followed this logic in that the approach adopted here implicitly seeks to combine the awkward bedfellows of deliberative and radical democracy. Thus, the media model advocated above, which stresses the need to combine a core public-service television sector with sectionalist, advocacy media, seeks in effect to integrate deliberative and radical traditions within one media system.

Entertaining democracy

The second outstanding issue is to reflect on the wider implications of revalorising media entertainment. It has been argued here that media entertainment informs a debate about values, identities, understandings of society and norms that feed into the democratic process. It is very easy to see how this argument can be incorporated into a rational-choice view of media and democracy. Already, this tradition contends that people have cognitive shortcuts – for example, following the cue of a preferred political party – that enable effective democratic judgements to be reached without accumulating detailed knowledge of public affairs. To this can now be added recognition that people can also key into democratic debate through pleasurable entertainment.

However, empirical evidence refutes the rational-choice approach by demonstrating that knowledge of public affairs empowers the citizen. In particular, Delli Carpini and Keeter's classic study demonstrates that in an American context informed citizens are more likely to have stable, meaningful attitudes towards issues, align their attitudes to their interests, participate in politics and vote for political representatives consistent with their attitudes than less informed citizens.[74]

Delli Carpini and Keeter also argue eloquently that informed citizenship should be viewed as a civic duty, not just a lifestyle choice. This presumably applies with particular force if one country visits death on another. Yet, it is clear that large numbers of Americans are remarkably uninformed about the circumstances that led to a war and insurgency in Iraq that led to the death of over 100,000 civilians. In 2006, 41 per cent of Americans said that Iraq had, at the time of the 2003 invasion, weapons of mass destruction or a major programme for developing them. A further

49 per cent believed that 'Iraq was directly involved in carrying out the September 11 attacks' or that 'Iraq gave substantial support to al-Quaeda'.[75] This is not an aberrant result, but consistent with poll findings going back to 2003 revealing a high degree of misperception about the circumstances leading to the Iraq War.[76]

While American war movies may provide a cognitive orientation towards different positions in relation to the American military state, this is no substitute for journalism-based knowledge of what the American state is actually doing. Because the American media system is entertainment-centred, it provides an inadequate basis for knowing what is happening in the real world and gives rise to a citizenry insufficiently aware of what is being done in its name.[77] A healthy democracy needs to be informed as well as entertained.

5   Liberal dreams and the Internet

James Curran and Tamara Witschge

Introduction

The international public sphere is now regularly referred to as something that actually exists.[1] It is invested with almost the same sense of reality as the World Trade Organization and the International Criminal Court. All are supposedly integral parts of the new global polity.

By 'international public sphere', most critical theorists intend more than just a synonym for international civil society in which organised groups seek to exert public influence on a transnational basis (something that dates back to at least the late eighteenth century, when campaigns were mounted in Britain, France and America against the slave trade). What leading critical analysts like Nancy Fraser[2] have in mind when they refer to the international public sphere (though they do not all agree)[3] is something more recent and also less concerted: the bringing together of individual citizens and informal networks through interconnected global webs of public communication and dialogue. This is giving rise, they argue, to the creation of a new popular force in the form of *international public opinion* which is influencing both public and private structures of power.

The international public sphere has supposedly come into being as a consequence of multiple globalising influences, including the growth of international social movements, the expansion of global markets, the increase of migration and foreign tourism, the development of global governance and the communications revolution. This last development tends to be emphasised in particular, because it is thought to be bringing the world closer together and enhancing international communication and understanding. Satellite transmission, global telecommunications networks and cheap air travel, it is argued, reduce both distance and time; international news agencies wholesale the same news across continents; the global integration of media markets is promoting the consumption of the same media; and the rise of the Internet is fostering interactive dialogue between nations.

All these different developments are allegedly forging a new cultural geography. Circuits of communication, patterns of public discourse and the lineaments of imaginary life are all bursting out of the 'container' of the nation, and providing the basis for generating new global solidarities, shared concerns and common positions. These underpin, we are told, the emergence of international public opinion and 'global norms'. In brief, the international public sphere is widely proclaimed to exist. It is said to be the product of globalising tendencies, especially in the realm of communication. And it is bringing into being a powerful constituency of world citizenry.

Wistful projection

Despite its mandarin eloquence, this critical theorising has little connection to empirically grounded reality. The international public sphere does not exist, save in an embryonic – or, at best, nascent – form.

This is partly because communication about public affairs has not been properly 'globalised'. The most important source of news in much of the developed world is still television. Thus, in Britain, 65 per cent said in 2006 that television was their main source of news, compared with just 6 per cent who cited the Internet.[4] Yet, television is orientated primarily towards national and local affairs, even if it also reports events from faraway places. Even in internationalist Finland and Denmark, domestic news accounts for around 70 per cent of their principal TV channels' main news programme content, while in the US it accounts for 80 per cent.[5] The same study found that foreign TV news tends to focus on parts of the world where the home nation has a connection. This is part of a broader process of 'domestication', in which foreign news tends to be interpreted selectively in accordance with the political culture, national interest and collective memory of the country where the news is shown.[6] Understanding of the world is still filtered through a national prism.

It is sometimes claimed that the Internet is overturning this because it transcends place and makes available a vast, shared storehouse of public information. However, the Internet is used primarily for entertainment, correspondence and practical aid rather than for news and political information.[7] The most visited *news* websites, as in Britain and the USA, are the websites of the dominant national news organisations,[8] which tend to have national news priorities. Nationalist cultures can also influence online interactions, as in Trinidad.[9] Above all, the great majority of the world's population do not have access to the Internet.[10]

While global consumption of the same media content is increasing, this trend is very much more pronounced in relation to screen drama and music than it is to news. Transnational satellite news channels like CNN have tiny audiences in most countries, indeed often so small as to be difficult to measure.[11] The trend towards global media convergence is also very uneven. The two most populous countries in the world – China and India – are in media terms still largely 'self-sufficient' (something that they have in common with the US, which also has low media imports).[12] In addition, people in different parts of the world also tend to make sense of the same media content in different ways, as a consequence of the different national cultural and subcultural discourses that they draw upon.[13]

More generally, the world is divided and fragmented in ways that impede the development of global norms and public opinion. While EFL (English as a foreign language) is emerging as the shared language of elites, it is incomprehensible to most people. Chinese, not English, is in fact the language understood by the largest number of people in the world. The development of global consensus is impeded also by divergent cultures, values, economic interests and affiliations. Indeed, empirical research tends to affirm the geographically confined rather than international nature of most people's primary orientation.[14]

Yet if the global public sphere does not yet exist, it is much to be desired. Elected national governments have diminished control over their economies.[15] Global financial markets, transnational corporations and the evolving system of global governance remain insufficiently accountable to the public.[16] A number of responses to this democratic deficit are available.[17] One of these is to develop a communicative space between nations in which international civil society and international opinion become a growing political force, facilitating the reassertion of public influence in a globalised world.

This is why the subject of this chapter – an e-zine (website magazine) called *openDemocracy* – has an interest extending beyond its seeming significance. It is one of a number of new ventures that are using the web as the means of publishing international journalism. In the process, they are contributing to the creation of an international public sphere.

Tufnell Park phoenix

openDemocracy was originally conceived as a networking facility for British activists campaigning for constitutional reform. It then dawned on public intellectual and activist Anthony Barnett that the Internet made possible something more ambitious – the launch of a virtual magazine of politics and culture – with only a limited outlay. He established a launch team of four (only one of whom was paid initially) in his garage in north London's Tufnell Park, created a wider network of volunteers[18] and, with some difficulty, secured small grants from charities and gifts from well-wishers, totalling almost £100,000.

When *openDemocracy* was launched in May 2001 as a 'pilot' project, it got off to a slow start. While it was free, and hosted some good writing, the e-zine remained virtually unknown. It had no promotional budget and gained almost no media attention during its launch. Average weekly visits to its website in May–June 2001 averaged a mere 1,750.[19] The new venture seemed destined to be yet another of the rags-to-bankruptcy failures that feature prominently in the history of alternative media.[20]

An unmistakable watermark of Britishness also permeated *openDemocracy*'s early content. The magazine's office was in London; all its paid employees were British; and their contacts tended to be home-based. However, the magazine aimed from the outset to be international and to cover globalisation issues. It was geared, therefore, to respond to an international event.

The September 11 attacks saved the magazine and altered its editorial trajectory. Todd Gitlin, the volunteer 'North America editor', posted on September 12 an impassioned article in *openDemocracy* urging his country to respond in a restrained way, with 'a focused military response – a precise one, not a revenge spasm'. Citing Hannah Arendt's dictum that 'violence happens when politics fails', he emphasised that the US should not become involved in an indiscriminate jihad.[21] Gitlin's article was accompanied by other instant responses, including contributions from

Muslim Pakistan, commissioned by the home team working on an emergency basis in London.

This orchestration of an immediate, international debate about the implications of September 11 caused the magazine's audience to grow. Weekly visits to its website of around 2,000 before September 11 rose to over 8,000 in September–October and to over 12,000 in November 2001.[22] Many of the magazine's new readers lived outside Britain. Indeed, by April 2002, the magazine's largest national contingent of visitors was American (44 per cent), while continental Europe (excluding the UK) accounted for a further 20 per cent.[23]

In effect, a growing international audience discovered the website. This raised the magazine's status and made sizeable grants, especially from American charitable trusts, much easier to obtain. This in turn increased the magazine's resources, enabling it to attract still more visitors. *openDemocracy* was relaunched, with increased staff and a broader range of content, in November 2002. Its post-launch audience was double that in the aftermath of September 11. Website visits increased still more in 2004, and soared to 441,000 a month in 2005. *openDemocracy*'s audience contracted subsequently as it entered a period of economic crisis. Even so, it was still receiving a respectable 224,000 visits a month in 2008 (see Table 5.1).

A number of influences – which we will consider shortly – shaped the magazine. But it is worth stressing here that a global event, and a global technology, proved to be the making of *openDemocracy*. The magazine won a new audience because its web-based accessibility enabled people from around the world to connect to a global debate about key issues in the aftermath of September 11.

Global conversations

In line with the increasingly international nature of its audience, the magazine's editorial agenda also became more international. By 2002, its three most prominent debates were about the impact of globalisation, the use and abuse of American power around the world and the character of Islam (a discussion that tended to emphasise its pluralism). As the magazine developed, the topics it covered extended across a widening spectrum of international themes from the politics of climate change and the regulation of global markets (long before the crash) to the future of multiculturalism and the impact of migration. The countries featured in the

Table 5.1 Average monthly visits to *openDemocracy*

2001	2002	2003	2004	2005	2006	2007	2008
30,000	60,000	196,000	105,000	441,000	233,000	179,000	224,000

Sources
The magazine's archives were dispersed, and largely discarded, when it moved offices several times during a period of growing financial difficulty. Consequently, figures for monthly visits relate to different months of the year, rather than strictly comparable periods, as follows: September–October 2001 and 2002 (*openDemocracy* board meeting statistics report, 2002); November–December 2003 (*openDemocracy* site statistics since 2001); October–December 2004 and 2005 (*openDemocracy* 2005–6: progress report); July–December 2006, January–December 2007, January–May 2008 (Google analytics).

magazine also widened. In January–July 2008, for example, 69 articles published on three themes – globalisation, democracy and power and conflicts – covered 26 nations.

The magazine also recruited more contributors from outside Britain. In a sample of 134 articles published in January–July 2008, authors came from 33 countries spanning 5 continents. Even well before then, authors were drawn, seemingly, from different backgrounds, persuasions and social networks (including different sectors of civil society). Foreign ministers and Third World activists, famous authors (like John le Carré) and unknown journalists, business leaders and trade union organisers, public officials and poets, accountants and artists mingled, clashed and conciliated on its pages. Contributors also wrote from conservative, liberal, socialist, green and feminist positions. These manifold contributors reached a far-flung audience. In the period from mid-2006 to 2008, visitors to the *openDemocracy* website came from 229 countries and territories, ranging from Albania to Ecuador (this last country generating 1,262 visits during the period).[24]

The e-zine also sought to further mutual understanding by the way in which it developed discussion through commissioned articles. In its early years, *openDemocracy* gave extensive space to set-piece debates from opposed positions on a major issue. These duels (for example, Hirst versus Held over the nature of globalisation)[25] were usually evidence-based and deliberative, and were followed by discussion that generally became less polarised after 'seconds' had packed away their duelling pistols and others joined in the debate. This format gave way increasingly over time to a less confrontational one in which authors offered different interpretations and responses to a common theme, such as the struggle for effective democracy in different parts of the world.[26]

This approach was overlaid in turn by a more event-driven rather than issue-driven format in which authoritatively voiced, 'balanced' contributions were published in relation to topics and places in the news. This placed the reader in the more subaltern position of being briefed, rather than, as before, being tacitly invited to arbitrate between opposed positions. But sometimes, the views of external experts on specific countries were challenged or supplemented by contributions from people in these countries (as in the case of China, Iraq, Kenya, Peru, Turkey, Russia and India) who offered different perspectives and sources of knowledge (as in the case of the Tibet protests in 2008).[27]

The magazine's topical journalism also tended to be interpretative and framed in terms of a wider context, rather than a record of discrete events in the tradition of conventional reporting. Alongside these threads of analytical debate and interpretation there were also articles that invited a sense of solidarity, for example with women working in Asian 'sweatshops'[28] or migrants on an epic journey from Burundi destined for a cold reception in the West.[29] These appeals to solidarity based on empathy were supplemented by those based on affinity, typified by two early evocative articles celebrating a similar love of neighbourhood in Britain and the Czech Republic.[30]

In short, the e-zine appeared to be assisting people of different nations, backgrounds and opinions to come together to discuss issues of common concern and to understand these better through informed debate, while at the same time fostering, at an emotional level, mutual understanding and a sense of togetherness. It thus seemed – at least at first glance – to be in the vanguard of building a better, more enlightened world through the use of the Internet. In the eloquent words of the magazine itself: 'We aim to ensure that marginalised views and voices are heard. We believe facilitating argument and understanding across geographical boundaries is vital to preventing injustice.'[31]

But while this self-conception is partly true, it contains also an element of delusion. In reality, the debate staged by *openDemocracy* was distorted by the external context in which it operated.

Global inequality

In the late 1990s, the richest fifth of the world's population had 86 per cent of the world's GDP, while the poorest fifth had just 1 per cent[32] – an enormous disparity that has broadly persisted.[33] This disparity is reproduced as a structure of access to the Internet, with the world's poor being largely excluded. Their voice is muted, and their participation limited, by poverty. This is illustrated by the fact that the entire continent of Africa hosted fewer websites than London in 2000.[34]

Economic inequality is associated with other forms of inequality, in terms of access to education, the acquisition of knowledge, language and communication skills and links to global social networks. Poverty is associated, in other words, with diminished cultural and social capital. This puts the poor at a disadvantage compared with the affluent, who have greater resources and cultural competences at their disposal. The world's poor tend to be disadvantaged also by linguistic inequality. The population of Marathi-speaking India, for example, greatly exceeds that of Britain, yet an article in Marathi, however eloquent, will be understood by far fewer people in the world than one written in English.

So when *openDemocracy* sought to 'ensure that marginalised views and voices are heard', it set itself an enormously difficult task, especially for a magazine based in London, with limited resources, publishing only in English. How, then, did it respond to this challenge?

Its first strategic decision was to invest minimal resources in translation. Unlike an interesting offshoot, *China Dialogue*, the e-zine translated only a tiny number of articles into languages other than English. It thus excluded, in terms of contributions, most of the non-English-speaking world.

The magazine also raised a further barrier against the 'marginalised' by insisting on a high level of 'quality', usually defined in terms of clarity and eloquence of expression, insight and intelligence and the appropriate marshalling of evidence. The threshold level of quality was high, with novelists like Salman Rushdie[35] turning an elegant phrase and the American philosopher Richard Rorty[36] offering intellectual firepower, and a legion of more frequent contributors from the sharply perceptive academic Paul Rogers[37] to the eloquent journalist Caroline Moorehead[38] setting a consistently high standard. Judged by these standards, the marginalised tended to be found wanting. As one senior *openDemocracy* journalist put it, 'It is hard to find those people – you know, Southern voices – without sounding too bad, writing well.'[39]

Finding globally marginalised voices takes time, the cultivation of an extended network of contacts and sensitive support for inexperienced writers. This did happen, to some extent, especially during *openDemocracy*'s most affluent years (2003–4), when clumsily written articles, in general, were heavily edited and when, on occasion, contributions were ghostwritten on the basis of interviews. However, the e-zine adopted a more topical editorial agenda, and accelerated the cycle of production, in 2005. Severe budget cuts were also made in 2005 and in subsequent years. This had the cumulative effect of speeding up the editorial process, increasing (temporarily) the volume of editorial output and reducing the time and people available. Staff responded by relying on a coping mechanism: turning to predictable sources of good copy that tended not to include 'Southern voices'.

This conjunction of global inequality, knowledge-based and stylistic definitions of editorial quality and limited resources/time had an entirely predictable result: a dialogue about the world in which one part of the world did most of the talking as well as most of the listening (see Table 5.2).

In the first half of 2008, 71 per cent of contributors came from Europe and the Americas. The poverty-stricken continent of Africa contributed a mere 5 per cent, and distant Oceania only 1 per cent, of authors. While *openDemocracy* did host, as it claimed, a dialogue across national frontiers, this primarily took the form of people in the affluent north-western hemisphere talking about the rest of the world. Those whose first language was English also dominated. Americans and Canadians accounted for 90 per cent of article writers from the Americas, while the British constituted 62 per cent of writers from Europe.

The geographical distribution of contributors was broadly similar to that of visitors. The e-zine had an international audience, with the UK generating only 24 per cent of total visits to the website. However, most of the remainder were concentrated in the affluent English- or EFL-speaking part of the northern hemisphere, with North America and Europe accounting for 83 per cent of website visits in 2006–8.

Table 5.2 Geographical distribution of *openDemocracy* authors and audience

Continent	Europe	Americas	Asia	Oceania	Africa	Unidentified
Percentage of total contributors[a]	61	10	16	1	5	6
Visitors (percentages)[b]	46	40	9	4	2	–

Notes
a   Analysis of authors (*n* = 102) is based on a sample of 25 articles on the 3 main themes 'globalisation', 'democracy and power' and 'conflicts', and all articles on the other themes published in *openDemocracy* between January 1 and July 10, 2008 (a total of 134 articles). Biographical details about the authors were derived from the *openDemocracy* website and the World Wide Web.
b   Analysis of visitors is derived from Google analytics and relates to the period June 2006–June 2008 (total number of visits during this time was 4,777,919, with a total of 3,093,096 unique visitors).
All percentages have been rounded off to the nearest whole figure.

Social inequality

If the external context influenced which national citizens wrote for *openDemocracy*, it also affected who *within* nations were invited to write. The disposition of knowledge, communication skills and time is unequal. This encouraged the e-zine to turn to the accredited rather than the marginalised, the expert rather than the ordinary citizen.

The first port of call was academics, because they possessed specialist knowledge, flexible working hours and, as public-salaried workers, would write for free. To use them was to take advantage of a hidden public subsidy. However, they also posed a problem, because many academics have become accustomed to writing for specialist knowledge communities with a shared vocabulary and referential (a typical academic word) understanding and are consequently unused to communicating with a public audience. The e-zine got around this problem in two ways: by investing considerable resources in sub-editing clunking academic prose (sometimes in a broken EFL form) and by developing a repertory of academics who were adept at public writing and who were invited to write frequently. The second group the e-zine turned to were journalists and professional writers, usually with a special area of knowledge. Their attraction was that they tended to write well, and fast: their disadvantage was that they generally expected to be paid. The third group were people from the world of politics, especially public and NGO officials and civil-society activists. However, *openDemocracy* staff – especially more senior ones – tended to be sharply critical of this last group's efforts, complaining that they were inclined to get 'bogged down in detail', to 'fight micro turf wars', to 'fail to see the big picture' and to offer a 'poor journalistic product'.[40] Rival e-zines were also criticised for being ready to publish 'NGO public relations stories'.

This confluence of influences had, again, predictable results. In the first half of 2008, eight out of ten *openDemocracy* authors were academics, journalists or writers. Activists and those employed by civil-society organisations generated only 14 per cent of contributors (see Table 5.3).

There is another significant way in which the external context influenced the editorial content of *openDemocracy*. While gender inequality has lessened, it is still manifested in multiple forms, from the distribution of life chances to pensions.[41] The norms of traditional gender differentiation, ordaining that women should take the primary role in the home and the man the primary role in the economy and public life, have left a residual cultural legacy even though the economic division of labour on which this differentiation was based has been transformed. In Britain, for example, this contributes to a situation where women have long paid less attention to 'public affairs' in newspapers than men,[42] and where women still constitute only 20 per cent of MPs in the UK.[43]

Table 5.3 Occupation of *openDemocracy* authors

Occupation	Academic	Journalist	Writer	Civil-society activist	Politician/ lawyer	Unknown
Percentage of total	48	20	10	14	3	4

Sample = 134 articles published by 103 contributors from January 1 to July 10, 2008.

This gendered inheritance left a strong imprint on *openDemocracy*. Women writers were well represented in sections devoted to 'women and power' and 'arts and culture' but underrepresented in the political sections (see Table 5.4). Feminist pressure within the office led to the establishment of the 50:50 section, 'a series of editorial projects designed to make *openDemocracy* a current affairs forum which is written, read and used equally by women and men'. But in 2008, 72 per cent of the e-zine's contributions were still written by men.

The geographical, class and gender imbalance of article authors might have been redressed through the interactive dynamics of the e-zine. However, discussion forums were developed as a separate space within the website and had a semi-detached relationship to its editorial content. One senior editorial executive confessed to 'rarely' looking at these forums during the period 2005–6. When users' comments were published below articles from 2007 onwards, there were relatively few of them. Even the most discussed article on the site in the first half of 2008 attracted just 36 responses.

In brief, the e-zine aimed to bring into play different perspectives, including marginalised ones, in order to foster international understanding. But in reality, it orchestrated predominantly elite, male contributions from the richest part of the world. Even so, the quality and intelligence of its articles, and its departure from a narrowly national perspective, makes this e-zine especially significant in the field of online journalism.[44]

Cultures of production

If the external context strongly influenced the content of the e-zine, other factors also played a part. Thus, charitable funding exerted an influence, not directly on editorial policy but indirectly on strategy and personnel (with some changes linked to new pitches for grants). Stormy office politics also had an effect, contributing to the introduction of new topics and the exodus of some staff. The social and cultural networks that fed into the e-zine left an imprint: for example, a seminar series on 'Town and Country' at Birkbeck, University of London was a key recruiting ground of *openDemocracy* writers, including two out of its three editors. To focus on the alleged determining influence of new communications technology, as some studies do,[45] is to overlook the range of influences that shape the use to which new technology is put.

Table 5.4 Relative gender distribution of *openDemocracy* articles (as percentage of total per theme, January 1–July 10, 2008)

Theme	Women/ power	Arts/ culture	Globalisation	Democracy/ power	Conflicts	Faith/ ideas	Other	Total
Men	32	42	64	84	92	80	75	72
Women	68	58	36	16	8	20	25	28

Sample = 134 articles.

Because of the limited space available, attention will be focused mainly on one of these influences here – the evolving 'culture of production'. Three distinct cultural regimes can be identified, though in reality each new regime incorporated elements from the past and also had a continued 'life' after it had ended.

The first culture that shaped *openDemocracy* was primarily that of a political magazine but it changed over time by absorbing other inputs. The founding editor, Anthony Barnett (2001–5), was a charismatic man of letters and politics, who had been on the editorial board of the leading radical journal, *New Left Review*, written a number of books (including *Iron Britannia*), directed an influential constitutional reform group, Charter 88, and been a freelance journalist. The people he recruited to establish the e-zine were the founder of an experimental theatre group, a film-maker and a former college lecturer. The enlarged team at *openDemocracy* recruited people from still more diverse backgrounds, including international civil-society activism and corporate business.

This heterogeneity bred innovation, something that was fostered also by the hori-zontal management structure of the organisation, and the early ceding of consid-erable autonomy to different sections ('themes') which were allowed to develop in divergent ways. In 2001, *openDemocracy* was a print magazine in virtual drag: a cross between the *New Statesman* and *Encounter* (a political and literary *belles-lettres* magazine that had died in 1990). It even had numbered issues like a conventional print publication. Over the next four years, *openDemocracy* evolved into something that was original and different. Articles broke free from a common template and came to vary enormously in length (some running to 5,000 words or more). Parts of the e-zine were like entering a university symposium, with academics spar-ring with each other. One part was like entering an art exhibition, with images rendered luminous by the light of the computer screen.[46] Still another resembled the 'comment' section of a broadsheet paper. Yet another was like entering a rowdy political meeting, especially in the run-up to the Iraq War, when an *openDemocracy* discussion forum took off. Other parts of the website synthesised diverse influ-ences, as in the case of a remarkable series of articles on the different significations of hair as a source of beauty and fear, fetish and protest, universalism and localism, accompanied by a collage of visual images and quotations (the latter derived from poems, pop songs, sacred texts, novels and plays).[47] In a quiet corner, there was a quirky series of short articles on untranslatable words, illuminating the interior life of different languages and cultures, from Albanian to Japanese.[48] And all the time, the e-zine was evolving into a more cosmopolitan form, with more inputs from non-British writers. By the end of 2004, *openDemocracy* had ceased to be a replica political weekly and had come to resemble only itself. It was a hybrid, drawing on different cultural forms – print journalism, photo-journalism, art installation, book, academic seminar and political meeting. It was like a caravan procession, laden with goods from different sources, travelling to an unknown destination.

The new editorial regime of Isabel Hilton (2005–7) imposed a culture of broad-sheet newspaper journalism. Hilton was an assured and successful journalist who had been a distinguished foreign correspondent, book author and BBC radio presenter. The talkative, decentralised, experimental and sometimes disorgan-ised nature of the e-zine, in its first manifestation, was utterly different from the routine-driven, streamlined structures of professional journalism. She immediately set about embedding the disciplines, and conventions, of Fleet Street. A centralised structure of control was established, based on daily morning editorial conferences (as in a newspaper office). Staff members were instructed to listen to the radio news and read newspapers before these conferences so that they had something 'useful' to contribute. The editorial agenda of the website shifted from being issue-driven to being news-driven, and became more orientated towards the pre-scheduled events and cycles of the political calendar. Articles were published at a shorter, more consistent length, with few being allowed to exceed 1,200 words, in line with British newspaper convention. Article output rose, shifting from a weekly to daily cycle of production. The composition of contributors also changed, with more professional journalists being used.

What emerged from this reincarnation was something much closer to the traditional Linotype culture of print. The reinvented e-zine had greater quality control (with fewer weak articles). It was better written, more topical and less eclectic. It was less cerebral, making fewer demands on the user. It was also less different from the mainstream media, less quirky and less original. In part, this was a consequence of the steep decline of the arts and culture section, where budget cuts fell with disproportionate severity. But the website also innovated during this period, with the development of podcasts and with the recruitment of good contributors from China and Latin America. Isabel Hilton had a difficult task in taking over a project with a greatly reduced budget. She restabilised the magazine at a time of crisis and reversed a precipitous decline of site visits.

The third reinvention of *openDemocracy* occurred under the editorship of Tony Curzon Price (2007–). He was constrained by further budget cuts and a skeletal (and shrinking) staff. But he brought with him a Californian, communitarian culture that offered potentially a new lease of life for the e-zine. Curzon Price had been a pilgrim to Silicon Valley, where he had worked as an internet entrepreneur during 2001–4. He took charge of an e-zine with a relatively low level of user interaction, and one of his first steps was to symbolically relocate readers' comments beside the relevant article rather than in a separate space. A desire to forge an *openDemocracy* user-generating community not unlike that of *Slashdot*, though of a more diverse kind, led to the imaginative decision to establish an 'Ideas Forum' in 2008. A hundred people were invited – on the basis of their past significant contributions to the magazine – to participate online in proposing and discussing ideas for articles and the selection of suitable authors. This went far beyond the very small group of mostly British external editors that Anthony Barnett recruited in the pilot phase of the magazine. It also went beyond the building up of a team of interns and volunteers (some operating from abroad) who had come to play a significant role in the administration, sub-editing and publishing of the e-zine. In effect, Curzon Price was seeking to use net technology to facilitate editorial commissioning as a collaborative process (while retaining final control to ensure quality). He was thus attempting to harness the network energy to be found in other web-based projects by 'wikifying' a central aspect of *openDemocracy*. Whether this will succeed, it is too early to say. But it represents a departure shaped by a communitarian culture different from the more hierarchical ethos of the previous editorial regime.

Yet even though all three editors drew upon divergent cultures to take the magazine in different directions, they have also in certain respects been similar. All three had elite educational backgrounds (with degrees respectively from Cambridge, Edinburgh and Oxford Universities and, in the case of Tony Curzon Price, a doctorate from the University of London). The people they recruited tended to come from similar backgrounds (the small staff of *openDemocracy* in mid-2008, for example, included people with degrees from Yale and McGill Universities). This shared educational background predisposed the e-zine, under all three regimes, to look for certain kinds of article – critically independent (whether on the right or left), evidence-based and analytical.

Above all, at the very heart of the magazine, there has been a shared commitment to some version of internationalist humanism. All the central figures in the magazine, in its different phases – including the long-serving, influential deputy editor, David Hayes – have believed in the importance of being respectful to other cultures; of getting people in different countries to speak for themselves rather than be spoken for; and of developing a reciprocal exchange based on a relationship of equality. The investment made in improving foreign writers' copy through sub-editing was partly born out of a desire to foster discursive equality between nations. Facilitating international dialogue as a way of promoting greater understanding has been the central *telos* of the magazine in all its incarnations (whatever its limitations in practice).

Technology and money

The economics of *openDemocracy* have also been central to its development. Indeed, its history underlines the point that web publishing – beyond the modest blog – is far from 'free'.

The Internet lowers costs by transferring print and reproduction costs to the user. It opens up market access through bypassing wholesalers and retailers (the last a major obstacle to minority magazines unless their distribution is protected in law, as in France and Greece). The global reach of the Internet also makes new kinds of ventures possible through the aggregation of minority audiences in different countries (producing a situation that is analogous to art-house film production). *openDemocracy* benefited from all of these advantages – lower costs, enhanced market access and global aggregation.

But the e-zine still had to spend money. Its largest outlays were on the salaries of staff to commission, sub-edit and publish (i.e. code, lay out and present) content and to administer its business; payments to contributors; and office overheads. In addition, it had miscellaneous calls on its budget, for example £120,000 on website design and redesign in its first three years (and on the commissioning of a less labour-intensive website in the subsequent period). The e-zine in fact cut a number of corners. It spent little money on promotion and translation, paid its editorial staff low salaries and developed a network of volunteer and intern labour. Even so, in 2001–8 it spent around £4.35 million.[49] Part of this outlay was admittedly misspent, since it was directed towards generating income that failed to materialise. But a significant part of *openDemocracy*'s expenditure was unavoidable, given what it set out to do.

The real obstacle to net publishing lies on the revenue side. The World Wide Web was given as a free gift to the world in order to foster interconnection and the open accessing of knowledge.[50] This legacy was supported by workers within the computer industry,[51] and reluctantly embraced by large media corporations, nearly all of whom now provide free access to their online news sites (partly in a bid to protect their offline business). Users have thus become accustomed to *not* paying for web-based press content.

This made it impossible for *openDemocracy* to charge a website entry fee. Its audience, though substantial, was too small in relative terms to generate substantial advertising. The e-zine's lofty humanism was not like an urgent humanitarian cause or a passionate partisan commitment propelling sympathisers to reach for their credit cards. Yet, the e-zine made an undertaking to the Ford Foundation that it would seek to become self-funding when it received a loan of $1.6 million. *openDemocracy* took on staff to syndicate articles, market archived articles as e-books, sell institutional subscriptions, solicit donations and sell advertising. The new business personnel were expensive and failed to raise significant revenue.

This plunged the magazine, at its peak with 24 employees, into a crisis that almost destroyed it. It received emergency charitable funding that enabled a soft landing in 2005–6. It then lurched into a near-terminal crisis in 2007, after two major funders – Ford and Rockefeller – declined to help further. The magazine even moved for a time, in 2007, into the waiting room of a friendly NGO, after finding itself without an office, before eventually securing better accommodation. Its core staff dwindled to three people in 2008, with others employed in linked projects that contributed to overall overheads.

These projects included one devoted to cultivating an informed and critical dialogue about Russia funded by George Soros' Open Society Institute, and another devoted to British politics (and constitutional reform) financed by the Joseph Rowntree Reform Trust. In effect, this development has come to represent a new funding model: the parcelling out of *openDemocracy*'s website into discrete projects that appeal to different charitable trusts. It also represents a move towards the Balkanisation of the website into more nation-centred enclaves that sits unhappily with the internationalism of the project.

Indeed, perhaps the most significant implication of this study is that the international space between commercial and state-linked media – between CNN and BBC World News, *The Economist* and al-Jazeera – is not sustained by an online revenue stream that will enable new ventures to grow and flourish. There is not a ready-made business model that will support worldwide online journalism of a kind pioneered by *openDemocracy*.

Partly for this reason, the building of an international public sphere is going to be a lot more difficult in practice than its magical realisation has been in critical social theory. And, to judge from this case study, global inequalities of power and resources are likely to distort the international public sphere that will eventually emerge.

Part III

Media and new technology

6　Technology foretold

Introduction

There is a long tradition of millenarian prophecy in relation to new media. It was predicted that the 'facsimile newspaper', dropping 'automatically folded from the home radio receiver', would rejuvenate the monopolistic American press;[1] citizens' band radio, said to be 'taking the US by storm' in 1975, would recreate a sense of community;[2] computer-assisted print technology was destined to subvert the established press;[3] the camcorder would democratise television and empower the people;[4] the CD-rom would transform publishing and 'replace books in classrooms entirely'.[5] All these predictions, mostly American, proved to be wrong.[6]

The case studies that follow look at what was predicted, and what actually happened, in relation to four 'new media' developments during the last thirty years in Britain. While they are British in terms of their specificity, they have more general implications. They underline the need for sceptical caution when assessing seemingly authoritative predictions about the impact of new communications technology. They offer an explanation of why techno-fantasies are constructed, and circulated, that probably has parallels elsewhere. This study also suggests that spurious projections about the future of the media were sometimes used to justify media deregulation, something that clearly happened in some countries, though in complex and variable ways.[7] Thus, while the study is UK-centred, it has a wider resonance for our times.

Cable television

In 1982, few people were better placed to discern the future of the media in Britain than Kenneth Baker, the newly appointed information technology minister. A rising star destined to become a long-serving member of the cabinet,[8] he had been briefed by civil servants and leading industry experts. His considered judgement, delivered in a Commons speech, was that the advent of cable television 'will have more far-reaching effects on our society than the Industrial Revolution 200 years ago'.[9] Not one member of the opposition rose to contradict this confident pronouncement. It was based on the apparently secure premise that 'wide-band' cable television would deliver a popular 'film-on-request' service; a multiplicity of minority channels including some for the deaf, elderly and adults seeking education; and, above all, a range of new *consumer* services that would be delivered through 'off-air television sets'. These last, according to Kenneth Baker, 'could literally change the fabric of society in which we shall be living in the course of the next few years'.[10] Speaking on another occasion, Baker promised that 'by the end of the decade [1980s], multi-channel cable television will be commonplace countrywide', and cable TV 'will be used for armchair shopping, banking, calling emergency and many other services'.[11]

In fact, we now know that cable television did not have a greater impact than the industrial revolution. Cable TV did not even become 'commonplace' by the end of the 1980s: it was adopted by just 1 per cent of homes in 1989,[12] and by only 13 per cent in 2008.[13] Many of cable TV's much-vaunted new services, such as utility-meter reading, opinion polling, home security services, home banking and home visits by the doctor, either never materialised or were short-lived.

Yet, Kenneth Baker was not alone in misreading the runes. Much of the national British press, during the period 1992–4, gave prominence to confident forecasts that cable TV would usher in an entertainment-led revolution, accompanied by information channels and exciting new services that would boost economic growth. Publications differed primarily in terms of what they stressed (with the partial exception of the sometimes sceptical *Financial Times*). Thus, the *Times Educational Supplement* (November 4, 1983) likened the advent of cable TV to the arrival of public libraries, and excitedly predicted that its educational programmes would reach the home-bound, the very young and adults who shunned evening classes. The *Financial Times* (October 13, 1982) in an upbeat moment foresaw cable television as enabling 'direct buying and selling from the home'. The *Sunday Telegraph* (March 26, 1982) reported the expert claim that cable TV would destroy the postal service, apart from 'one postal delivery a week'. Yet, despite all these differences of emphasis, the underlying message was the same: cable television would have a profound impact on British society. Even the normally sober *Economist* (March 6, 1982) declared the cable TV initiative to be 'the most important industrial decision' of the Thatcher administration.

Interactive digital television

However, there were some early cable TV sceptics, and their number grew significantly by the mid-1980s. But if neophytes did not have it all their own way to begin with, they carried all before them in the 1990s. Essentially, the same story that had been told in relation to 'two-way' cable television was retold about 'interactive' digital TV. But this time, the story was repeated at regular intervals from 1994 onwards and encountered little criticism. The technological messiah had at last risen, and the good news was spread to the four corners of Britain, and unto all those who would believe.

It was proclaimed that interactive digital TV (now sometimes called iTV) would be endowed with the same 'killer application' that had been promised for early cable TV. However, 'film-on-request' – now named 'video-on-demand' – was to be even better than anything promised before. According to a report in the *Independent* (January 12, 1996):

Video-on-demand, once fully operational, will allow us to call up almost any film in the world, to watch any TV programmes, and to compile 'dream schedules' – our own perfect evening's viewing.

A heart-warming vision was again invoked of a caring technology: interactive TV, reported the *Sunday Times* (October 4, 1998), would offer a 'glut of new services for the sick, elderly and infirm'. A futuristic fantasy, this time pitched at a new level of extravagance, was projected on to the interactive consumer experience that digital TV would provide. Viewers would shortly be able to have 'elaborate conversations' through their TV sets with travel companies about the kind of holiday they wanted (*Independent*, October 24, 1994); women would be able to try out new clothes on a virtual catwalk (*Times*, November 27, 1994); and viewers would soon be sauntering down a shopping mall, walking into virtual shops and buying whatever they liked, without ever moving from their sofas (*Independent*, October 6, 1994).

As before, it was anticipated that the new technology would have far-reaching effects. 'This futuristic device', it was reported in the *Sunday Times* (April 30, 1995), 'is an "interactive TV", poised to revolutionise the way information, education, media, commerce and entertainment are channelled into the 21st century home.' But the good-news message of interactive digital TV was pitched in a higher register than before by emphasising viewer empowerment. According to the prestige press, viewers will be able to 'vote on key issues' through interactive TV 'within a year' (*Guardian*, June 21, 1994); take control by being able 'to choose the storyline for a drama' and specify 'whether they want a sad or happy ending' (*Independent*, August 16, 1997); and select from hundreds of channels of information overnight 'to report whatever news you are interested in' (*Sunday Times*, November 20, 1994). All this meant that there would be a 'fundamental shift in power from the TV director to the consumer in the home' (*Sunday Times*, April 30, 1995).

In fact, the iTV that was developed in the late 1990s and early 2000s was neither very interactive nor very empowering. Shopping on TV meant choosing between a limited number of heavily promoted products; video-on-demand offered a restricted number of often not very good films; home visits by the doctor amounted in the end to NHS Direct, in effect the accessing of a glorified medical dictionary; NatWest pioneered an interactive TV banking service in 1995, only to close it down in 2003;[14] there was a restricted choice of camera angles for some football games available on certain subscription channels; and iTV provided an alternative way of placing a bet.

Yet, despite the fanfare of press publicity over iTV, viewers remained mostly unimpressed. A mere 20 per cent, in a 2003 Ofcom survey, indicated a willingness to pay in principle for interactive television services.[15] Interactive services accounted for only 36 per cent of British television's *non*-broadcast revenue in 2006,[16] most of which was attributable to premium-rate telephone calls.[17] The most important form of television interactivism was probably mass voting in the *Big Brother* show. However, *Big Brother* discontinued red-button voting in 2004, and SMS voting in 2006, preferring to stick to the interactive technology of the telephone,[18] first developed in the late nineteenth century. This was not what the transformation of 'dumb' television sets into 'intelligent machines' had been intended to achieve.

According to market research, only a minority with red-button facilities actually used them.[19] The number of interactive users even decreased between 2003 and 2006.[20] The epiphany that iTV disciples had been expecting for a quarter of a century failed to materialise.

Local community television

The rise of local community television was another hardy perennial of fallible forecasting. It was authoritatively predicted in the early 1980s that cable TV would give rise to local community TV services and that this would strengthen local communities.[21] This vision of a new tier of local television stations, comparable to local newspapers, captured the imagination of politicians, journalists and activists alike in the 1980s and 1990s. Thus, the television journalist Richard Gregory wrote in 1990 that 'new cable operators have tremendous opportunities' to create through community channels 'a television equivalent of the best of the weekly newspapers', achieving 'a closeness with the community that not even local radio can match'.[22] Some like Graham Allen, Labour's shadow media minister, went further, hoping that local television would regenerate a sense of local community, democratise programme-making and ensure that a plurality of social experiences 'found life on the screen'.[23]

This mixture of prediction and advocacy was repeatedly confounded. The leaden growth of cable TV in the 1980s 'delayed' the anticipated growth of local community television. It was not until the mid-1990s that ambitious local television *news* channels were launched in major urban centres like London, Birmingham and Liverpool. Most of these failed, dampening hopes that new technology would give rise to a renaissance of local journalism.

A different strategy was then embraced, based on the issue of short-term, localised licences for new local TV stations authorised by the 1996 Broadcasting Act. This gave rise to renewed expectations that grassroots television journalism was about to take off (even though it was actually employing 'old' technology). For example, the *Sunday Times* (September 27, 1998) reported lyrically that 'a quiet revolution is taking place in British television', based on the plans of '50 new local companies' to launch new local community channels. The same hyperbolic image of a revolution was invoked by the *Independent* (February 14, 1998) when it reported that 'in a backroom in Oxford this week a small revolution was under way'. A new local channel, the Oxford Channel, had been launched with thirty professional staff, numerous local volunteers and an appealing schedule of local programmes. Its joint managing director aimed, according to the report, to 'get the community involved in programming'.

As it turned out, most of these newly licensed local channels did not have a viable economic model to sustain them. They gained only small audiences, and therefore limited advertising, and had no significant public funding. Fatality among local TV channels was consequently high. Out of 23 local TV channels licensed after 1996, only 13 were still in operation in early 2006.[24] Many of the survivors had only a vestigial connection to the pioneer dream of grassroots, locally produced programming that had so excited sympathetic journalists. Thus, Oxford Channel's employees were sacked in 2000 and replaced with a skeleton crew by its new owners, the chain-owning Milestone Group. Under the new regime, the Oxford Channel transmitted Sky News, pop videos, 'advertisement features', and '*up to*' three hours of new local factual programming each week (emphasis added).[25]

Apart from a few hopeful exceptions, local community television proved to be a failure. In 2007, all local community TV channels combined accounted at most for a mere 0.5 per cent of viewing time in Britain.[26] The 'quiet revolution' had been postponed for another day.

Dotcom bubble

Panglossian predictions about the impact of new communications technology reached their apotheosis in the dotcom bubble during the late 1990s. It was widely reported in the business sections of the press that the Internet was poised to transform buying and selling and was already making fortunes for techno-savvy entrepreneurs. Thus, *The Times* (December 31, 1999), reviewing the year, commented euphorically: 'It should be impossible for 14 men to make £1.1 billion in twelve months out of nothing but a few second-hand ideas, a handful of computers, and some petty cash. Yet that is exactly what happened.' Similarly, the *Independent on Sunday* (July 25, 1999) recorded under the headline 'Web whiz-kids count their cool millions' that 'the precocious and proliferating breed of "dot com" millionaires are fabulously rich and ludicrously young. Their fortunes reduce national Lottery jackpots to peanuts.'

The implication was that readers could also share in this market jackpot, if they joined the dotcom bandwagon. The *Sunday Times* (December 26, 1999) reported that 'the mania for investing, to hitch a ride on the road to wealth, is reflected in the cover of the current *Forbes* magazine, which proclaims that: "Everyone Ought to Be Rich"'. The *Sunday Mirror*'s (October 17, 1999) advice was characteristically more direct: 'Your wealth: get on the net to get ahead.' During this period, wildly overoptimistic forecasts were given prominence. For example, the *Independent* (July 14, 1999) concluded that the good times were still rolling thanks to the 'billion dollar brains behind the net'. Financial analyst Roger McNamee was quoted as saying 'logic would suggest that this market [cycle] would have ended four or five years ago. But anyone following logic would look foolish today. The fools are dancing, but the greater fools are just watching.' His optimism was matched by Silicon Valley venture capitalist Joel Schoendorf, who said: 'I wouldn't be surprised if we saw a 5 per cent increase in investment next year, and every year for the next five to 10 years.'

In fact, the dotcom boom came to an end less than twelve months after this prediction was made. Yet, very few British publications – with the notable exceptions of the *Financial Times* and *The Economist* – foresaw, in unequivocal terms, the bust before it happened (resembling in this respect the no less credulous American press).[27] For the most part, British newspapers were content to chronicle the fortunes being made from dotcom start-ups without investigating whether these were based on secure foundations. They did little to illuminate the enormous differences in the cost reductions, enabled by the Internet, in different retail sectors.

Still more surprisingly, they gave scant attention to one crucial fact made available by the Office of National Statistics. Even in April–June 1999, when the dotcom boom was almost at its height, only 14 per cent of British households had home internet access.[28]

While the Internet has since had a profound impact, this has always been contingent on the wider societal context.[29] In this instance, a large number of dotcom companies in the UK went bankrupt during 2000–2 without ever making a profit. Pension funds were depleted as a result of failed investments, and Britain only narrowly missed following the US into recession.

Dynamics of misjudgement

British journalists are not naturally gullible and trusting. Yet, the mistakes they made in reporting the dotcom boom were not an isolated event but part of a general pattern in which they responded uncritically to the hyping of new communications technology. What, then, accounts for this blind spot?

The principal explanation is that journalists were merely responding to what informed sources were saying to them. They were exposed to mutually reinforcing misjudgement, and merely reproduced it. This conclusion is consistent with a large body of literature which argues that how journalists report the news is strongly influenced by their main news sources.[30]

The principal source of misinformation about new media was, in every instance, the business interests promoting them. Thus, the hyping of cable television in the early 1980s came primarily from electronic consumer, computer and cable television interests.[31] They presented an 'industrial' case for cable television as an engine of economic growth partly in order to outflank the prevailing consensus in favour of public-service broadcasting, based primarily on cultural concerns. Their extravagantly optimistic projections for cable TV growth were designed also to secure deregulation. It was based on the conditional argument that cable TV would triumph, and bring enormous benefits to the community, only if it was allowed to develop unfettered by bureaucratic controls.[32] There was thus a partial 'brief' embedded in their briefing of journalists.

The main sources of iTV hype were interactive TV developers, most notably BSkyB, British Telecom (BT) and Videotron. In each case, they were seeking to drum up consumer interest in new interactive services. To take one specific example, numerous articles were published in 1999 in the national press about the start-up of the Open Channel (a project jointly owned by BSkyB and BT, among others) on Sky digital. The central themes of most of these articles were that television shopping was finally coming of age; it would profoundly change social habits; and Open Channel would make large profits. This hype was especially prominent in Murdoch-owned newspapers, sister companies of the new venture. For instance, *The Times* (April 15, 1999) reported city analysts as valuing the Open Channel at £1.4 billion before it had even started trading. This fanfare of publicity bore little relationship to Open Channel's real significance: it was an ignominious failure, and closed in 2001.

Similarly, the main source of the dotcom hype in Britain was a coalition of dotcom entrepreneurs, venture capitalists and investment analysts who reinforced one another. Senior executives in local community TV start-ups were the principal source for stories about the 'quiet revolution'.

The second influential group contributing to the dynamics of collective misjudgement was senior politicians, both Conservative and Labour. Ever since the early 1980s, successive governments supported the development of the 'new information economy' as a way of offsetting the decline of the manufacturing sector. They also sought to foster the acquisition of information technology skills as a way of assisting the British workforce to compete effectively in the global economy. Rapid conversion from analogue to digital broadcasting also became a bi-partisan objective partly in order to boost public revenue through the sale of spare spectrum. More generally, new communications technology was hymned as a tool of education and citizenship.

This official championship provided a background that was conducive to new media hype. For example, the Labour government proclaimed during the height of the web-based dotcom boom: 'the explosion of information has fuelled a democratic revolution of knowledge and active citizenship. If information is power, power can now be within the grasp of everyone.'[33] Endorsement could also go much further than this generalised cheerleading. Kenneth Baker, information technology minister in the first Thatcher government, became the cable TV industry's most eloquent spokesman because he believed that its success would contribute to the modernisation of the British economy.[34] Tony Blair became a similarly committed and outspoken ambassador for interactive TV. As opposition leader in the mid-1990s, he urged people to have 'your television connected through your phone line to a world of almost limitless opportunities'. He continued, in the style of a salesman: 'you would be able to choose what shops to visit and what items to buy simply by sitting in front of your TV. Because the system is interactive, you will even be able to decide what estate agent or travel shop brochures you want to view.'[35] He persisted in this vein in his early days as prime minister. 'The day is not far off', he declared, 'when interactive TV will give us the convenience of home visits [by the doctor] that can be done through technology.'[36]

The third major source of endorsement was technology and financial experts. The Information Technology Advisory Panel (ITAP), dominated by industry experts at the heart of government (Cabinet Office), produced in 1982 a very flawed report,[37] whose forecasts of cable TV's growth and impact were falsified by events, but which was widely reported and trusted at the time. City experts played a role in the hyping of the dotcom bubble and interactive digital television. The media industry also generated its own gurus such as Emily Bell, who became the *Guardian*'s director of digital content. An ardent apostle of iTV, she kept the faith despite being sorely tested. In 2001, she acknowledged that it was impossible to ignore evidence of some iTV failures, yet insisted that 'iTV is threatening to be the hot platform of tomorrow'.[38] Seven years later, she was still writing enthusiastically about the power of 'red-button interactivism'.[39]

The universities also supplied experts who talked up the impact of new media developments. These included computer scientists eager to promote their prototypes. For example, Steven Gray, professor of communications and computer graphics at Nottingham Trent University, featured in *The Times* (November 27,

1994) because he had developed a way of enabling viewers to 'try on a new dress on your TV screen'. This facilitated, the professor explained, a 'personalized home fashion show, allowing shoppers to see what they will look like in the clothes before buying them'. Little more was heard of this software in the subsequent decade.

The somewhat idiosyncratic selection of academics quoted by the press suggests, however, that journalists were not simply 'victims' passively reproducing a source consensus, but were also making editorial judgements about what was newsworthy and orchestrating stories in ways that made for good 'copy'. A stress on novelty accorded with traditional news values. Articles about how new media will change how people will live (with headlines like 'Are you ready for the future?')[40] were well suited to filling the expanding space devoted to consumer and lifestyle issues. The more extravagant the claim about the impact of new communications technology, the better was the story in terms of grabbing attention.

The US was another source of seemingly disinterested endorsement. It featured in the press in the early 1980s as a country being transformed by advanced cable into a communal, interconnected 'wired society' and, in the later 1990s, as leading the way in developing advanced interactive TV systems and trailblazing the dotcom revolution. The US was also the home of revered prophets. The influential ITAP report already referred to[41] drew heavily on two popular American books on cable television that proved to be misleading.[42] Press reports quoted on a number of occasions the MIT guru Nicholas Negroponte,[43] many of whose confident predictions about the impact of interactive digital television were never realised.[44] The recurring tenets of this tradition of US futurology – that new media will create wealth, rejuvenate the local community and empower the citizen – connect to central themes of the American Dream.

Weak dissent

Although sceptical sources were also available, they tended to be less prominent, less accessible or less 'credible' than those hyping new media applications. Thus, in the early 1980s, cable TV sceptics came from two quarters: senior executives in the BBC and ITV who argued that cheap entertainment programmes, vital for cable TV's success, were not easy to find, and some City analysts who doubted whether cable TV would be profitable in the short term. The former were viewed as rivals opposed to cable TV, with obvious axes to grind. But as senior figures in the broadcasting industry, they were 'accredited' news sources, and their doubts about cable TV's future were sometimes reported.[45] Sceptical City analysts of cable TV's prospects had the ear only of the *Financial Times* during 1982–3, but seemingly contributed to its more critical coverage.

Another potential source of scepticism was insider knowledge. An advanced cable TV experiment (QUBE) had been pioneered by Warner Cable Corporation in Columbus, Ohio in 1977. It offered multiple channels, pay-per-view films, computer games, interactive services and offline services like domestic security and energy conservation systems. A similar, though more civic-orientated, interactive cable television experiment had been developed in Nara, Japan in 1978. Both experiments had yielded disappointing results, showing interactive services to be very costly to develop and eliciting only lukewarm consumer responses. This information had already leaked out and been documented, for instance in an academic study in Italian.[46] However, most British journalists reporting cable TV in the early 1980s were not technology experts and had seemingly little connection with the US or Japanese TV industry. An exception was Brenda Maddox, an American journalist with extensive US media contacts, who had written a good media book.[47] She differed from her peers by attacking the ITAP report. 'Based on wishful and selective reading of American experience by a panel composed of vested interests in computing and cable television', she wrote presciently in 1982, 'it made optimistic and unfounded calculations about the likely popularity of cable services in Britain.'[48] Her hard-earned specialist knowledge gave her the confidence to break free from the press pack.[49]

Similar insider knowledge should have led to the debunking of interactive television. Time Warner launched in 1995–7 a second experimental interactive television service (this time deploying more advanced technology and a wider range of services), called Full Service Network, in Orlando, Florida, only for it to flop.[50] This information was slow to leak out, and did not have the impact it should have done. The nearest equivalent to Brenda Maddox in the 1990s was sceptic Azeem Azhar, who did something unconventional. Instead of relying on selective briefing from BT, he interviewed people who had taken part in a local BT interactive television experiment. His respondents complained about 'totally naff content' and technology that sometimes did not work and delivered little.[51]

New communication hypes collapsed ultimately because the gap between promise and performance became too big to ignore. Thus, the cable TV spell broke by the mid-1980s, when it became clear that the cable TV industry was having difficulty in attracting both investors and customers. Kenneth Baker was pointedly asked why there were no homes with thirty TV channels in 1985, when he had predicted in September 1982 that 'over half the country' could have these within two years. His inspired response was that 'we have shown a capacity bordering upon genius to institutionalize torpor'.[52]

Similarly, the dotcom bubble began in the mid-1990s but only burst in March 2000, when it became apparent that most dotcom companies showed no sign of making a profit. By contrast, the interactive television hype slowly deflated rather than being abruptly punctured, because the hopes invested in it were residually rewarded. The BBC's iPlayer system was not *interactive* in the evangelical sense proclaimed by iTV enthusiasts, nor was it operated through a handset linked to the TV screen. But like other recording devices, it usefully extended the range of programmes available to viewers.

Cultural framing

British reporting was influenced not only by seemingly authoritative sources but also by ways of seeing the world that are embedded in British culture. Most of the time, journalists were predisposed to believe that new communications technology would be transformative because, like pollen, this assumption was carried in the air they breathed.

The belief that science and technology have transformed our world is the foundational theory of modernity. This recalls that scientific advance has created freedom from famine induced by local harvest failure, raised standards of living, brought liberation from unremitting domestic drudgery, enormously expanded intellectual horizons, greatly increased social and geographical mobility, hugely extended lifetimes and brought about dramatically reduced risk.[53] Although some aspects of the Victorian vision of progress have been repudiated, the conception of technology as the midwife of social and economic advance has long retained a powerful hold on social thought.[54]

This was reflected in the way in which some journalists wrote about the introduction of cable, and its 'off-air' services, in the early 1980s. It was presented as a new technology that would build a better world. This millenarian strand is typified by a *Times* editorial (January 11, 1982) on 'the new industrial revolution'. The first revolution, recalled the editorial, 'saw a total change in the means of manufacture', while 'this one is envisaged as seeing a total change in the means of organizing society and its knowledge, overthrowing the old need for centralized units and repetitive labour and substituting a new decentralized society with infinite leisure'. One great advance, the editorial hoped, will be followed by another with the advent of advanced cable-based television and communication.

This millenarian rhetoric persisted in the 1990s, although the vision was sometimes diminished. This could lead to a strange combination of utopian rhetoric and mundane prophecy, exemplified by this opening to a *Sunday Times* feature article (October 4, 1998) entitled 'Your gateway to the world':

> Television has been the 20th century's window on the world. The dawn of the 21st century will mark the first time we will open it. The interactive television which digital broadcasting will make possible will elevate the status of the box in the corner from household icon to a home multiplex cinema, a sports grandstand with an editing suite and a shopping centre to put Oxford Street to shame.

Despite its rhetoric of 'opening the window on the world' through interactive TV, the rest of the article makes no mention of the wider world outside Britain, still less advances claims about increased interaction between nations. Its core message is more limited: switch on, go shopping, you get to choose. Yet, it reveals the power of modernist thought in its opening trope: the window created in the twentieth century will be opened in the twenty-first. Despite the narrowness of the article, it invokes an expansive modernist rhetoric, associating new technology with enlightenment and progress. At such moments, one gains a glimpse into a mindset that embraced uncritically the hyping of new technology.

The second key way in which the culture of British society influenced reporting was to encourage a technology-centred framework of interpretation. This arose from the lack of influence of the social sciences. Their characteristic way of looking at new technology is to place it in context and to emphasise the ways in which wider social and economic processes shape the design, content and use of new technological developments. But this way of viewing technology was not widely disseminated and so was not readily available to most journalists.

Instead, news reports tended to assume that if something was technologically possible, it would 'happen'. That is to say, it would be adopted and its potential would be realised. Journalists' focus was therefore on what the new technology 'could do', since it was assumed that this would determine its impact.

This technology-centred approach tended to inflate the significance of new developments. This can be illustrated by an especially prominent feature of the reporting of both cable and interactive digital TV. Readers of the press were told, at periodic intervals, for a quarter of a century that they would soon have at their fingertips an almost infinite choice of films from an electronic 'library' or digital 'store'. Two-way technology, it was explained, would enable TV viewers to summon up what they wanted.

But while it became technically possible to access through television a vast cornucopia of films, this did not happen, because it was contrary to the interests of the major holders of American film rights. The US-based 'sexopoly', which dominates back catalogue as well as current film rights, had developed a profitable business model based on the careful sequencing of the same product on different platforms – film exhibition, merchandising, the rental of transmission rights to television companies around the world and the marketing of videos and subsequently DVDs – in a way that maximised revenue. The rise of video rental stores had temporarily threatened this business model, prompting Hollywood majors to take control of the dominant Blockbuster video chain. In this way, they shared in its profits and ensured that rented videos supplemented rather than undermined their business.[55] However, the Hollywood majors concluded that video-on-demand represented a more serious threat to their economic interests and declined to collectively back – and adequately stock – its development. This explains why video-on-demand was a relative failure: its repertoire of films was restricted. Thus, what technology 'could do' was blocked by the power of economic oligopoly, underpinned by copyright and an international system of law. Unless circumstances change (as a consequence of global pirating of digitised film), this obstruction is likely to persist. Yet, this point was repeatedly overlooked in the press, because it meant examining not what new technology could do, but what economic power would permit.

Brief reference should also be made to the politics of British newspapers. The dominant national press was very much more rightwing than its readership in terms of party preference in every general election between 1979 and 1992.[56] While there was a realignment behind New Labour for a time after 1996, most national newspapers continued to favour market-friendly politics. A view of *market*-based technological development building a better world – the central theme of much new media reporting for three decades – fitted the general editorial orientation of most of the press and generated no problems in terms of internal office politics.

Retrospect

The British press was caught up in the hype of early cable TV, local community TV, the dotcom bubble and interactive digital television. On each occasion, the press failed to see through the emptiness of the promises that were made.

This failure can be attributed to two main causes. The press reflected the wider collective failure of 'authoritative' sources to foretell adequately the impact of new communications technology. The press also drew upon pervasive cultural scripts, in particular a belief in the power of technology to engender progress and a techno-determinist perspective little influenced by economics and sociology.

But what should not be lost sight of is that the hyping of new media fitted a neo-liberal political agenda, and sometimes originated from sources that favoured media deregulation. Vested business interests dominated the Information Technology Advisory Panel (1982),[57] whose report provided the blueprint and justification for the deregulated development of cable TV. The Conservative government led by Margaret Thatcher was strongly predisposed to accept its advice because it offered the promise of releasing private capital and energy to 'modernise' the economy. 'Margaret Thatcher – very unpopular at the time – immediately saw the potential of this', recalls Lord Baker, 'because it provided a way of tackling unemployment.'[58] The compliant press hype of cable TV smoothed the way towards rupturing the cross-party consensus in favour of public-service broadcasting that had prevailed for over half a century. Cable TV (unlike ITV) was developed broadly outside a public-service framework.

Similarly, the no less misleading prospectus that accompanied the development of interactive digital television came primarily from self-serving corporate interests (prominent among them Murdoch's News Corporation, which controlled BSkyB). Tony Blair also talked up interactive television partly because it fitted his pitch to the electorate as the modernising leader of 'New Labour'. The press followed suit, joining the chorus of approbation for digital TV interactivism and user control.

Of course, new technology did change television, most importantly by enabling an increase in the number of channels. Yet, what was promised in relation to cable TV and interactive digital TV did not, by and large, happen. During the 1980s, cable TV did not inaugurate an economic and social revolution: on the contrary cable TV suffered from underinvestment, lost money and was a relative consumer flop. And during the 1990s and early 2000s, iTV did not place the user in control and reconfigure the television experience: instead, it introduced new facilities that were a welcome but modest improvement.

However, a cumulative impression was cultivated over three decades that television was about to be so transformed that legislative safeguards protecting programme quality and diversity were less called for. During this period, television deregulation took place in Britain on a much greater scale than in most other northern European countries.[59] This was aided by the way in which the future was enlisted to change the present.

7   The future of journalism

The main line adopted by the leaders of the news industry echoes Gloria Gaynor's song 'I will survive', in which she says that initially she was petrified after being deserted. But 'we will survive', declare news industry leaders, without mass advertising. They point to a record of prudent stewardship. News websites have been established in order to retain audiences in the new environment. In most cases, online and offline news rooms have been integrated in order to reduce costs. Some journalists have been made redundant, and their colleagues have partly filled the gap by being more productive. The pagination of newspapers has also declined to save costs.

Further adjustments are on the way. Traditional news organisations are seeking to cut a better deal with content aggregators. Regulatory authorities are being pressed to permit increased cross-media ownership as a way of reducing overheads and enhancing media synergies.[1] The News Corporation (the biggest press group in the world) is experimenting with new ways of 'monetising' their news websites by charging a website entry free. Expect further experiments in which different strategies are explored, including a loss-leader strategy in which some content remains free but a charge is levied for entering the inner sanctum of premium content, and the inclusion of a website subscription as part of a TV or telecommunications package.

News-industry leaders thus proclaim that an effective conservation strategy is in place in order to secure strong journalism. The more difficult the situation becomes, the more reassuring their public pronouncements.[2] Journalism is not in crisis, they insist, but merely undergoing a process of well-managed transition. In brief, *the future of journalism is safe in their hands*.

Crisis of journalism

This is not how it seems to a growing number of their employees. A study in the US found in 2007 that 'financial woes now overshadow all other concerns for journalists'.[3] The migration of advertising to the web, compounded by the 2008–9 recession, led to a rising number of newspaper closures and also contractions in news operations. Between January 2008 and September 2009, 106 local newspapers (mostly freesheets) closed down in Britain,[4] while in America significant newspapers like the *Christian Science Monitor* and *Seattle Post* ceased print publication. The principal commercial television channel in Britain, ITV, wants to disengage from regional and local news reporting, while a growing number of local TV channels in the US have stopped originating local news.[5]

The rise of the Internet has also led to the haemorrhaging of paid jobs in journalism. The Pew Research Center estimates that in 2008 'nearly one out of every five journalists working for newspapers in 2001 is now gone' in the US.[6] In Britain, a major regional chain, Trinity Mirror, reduced its staff by 1,200 in 2008–9;[7] ITV cut around 1,000 jobs during the same period; and Northcliffe Media set a target of shedding 1,000 local press jobs in 2009.[8]

Closures and redundancies are undermining, it is argued, the quality of journalism. 'Local and national democracy is suffering', warns Jeremy Dear, General Secretary of the [UK] National Union of Journalists. 'Councils, courts and public bodies', he claims, 'are no longer being scrutinised.'[9] This general perspective is eloquently presented in a Martin Rowson cartoon, based on the celebrated Tenniel *Dropping the Pilot* cartoon about the sacking of Bismarck.[10] In the Rowson cartoon, the marine pilot stepping down the ladder from a ship is the 'Reporter', with the blindfolded figure of 'Public Understanding' in front of him, stumbling into the sea. On the ship, an accountant is absorbed in a balance sheet, a bearded journalist gazes at Google on his computer and a manic member of the public photographs with his mobile phone the departing 'Reporter'. In the sea, a forlorn 'Citizen Journalist' clings to a life-buoy, with a shark circling nearby. The Rowson cartoon encapsulates a widespread view among journalists: *the current crisis of journalism is weakening public understanding and poses a threat to democracy.*

Purgative

This view is challenged by some radical commentators, who view the mounting financial problems of the press and the sacking of journalists as a cleansing purgative that is removing toxic journalism. The thought that this crisis could be terminal fills them with unmitigated joy. As the American press historian John Nerone comments: 'the biggest thing to lament about the death of the old order [of journalism] is that it is not there for us to piss on any more'.[11]

In a similar vein, the radical environmentalist George Monbiot refuses to shed crocodile tears over newspaper closures. 'For many years', he writes, 'the local press has been one of Britain's most potent threats to democracy, championing the overdog, misrepresenting democratic choices, defending business, the police and local elites from those who seek to challenge them.' While there are in his view a handful of decent local newspapers, in general 'this lot just aren't worth saving', because they 'do more harm than good'.[12]

This group of critics tend to see the crisis of traditional journalism as an opportunity. New openings for progressive initiatives are being created, they believe, that were effectively blocked when leading media conglomerates had a market stranglehold. In the hopeful words of John Nerone, 'journalism will find its future when it finds its audience, and that audience will be many hued, sexually diverse, and composed mostly of workers'.[13] In short, this view can be summarised as: *things are getting better because they are getting worse.*

Renaissance

The view that journalism is in crisis is challenged by a fourth interpretation, which proclaims that, on the contrary, journalism is at the threshold of a glorious renaissance. This position, which tends to be associated with journalism educators, is based on three central arguments.

First, the Internet is said to be enriching the quality of traditional media journalism. Journalists now have instant access to a rich store of public information and diverse news sources. As a consequence, it is claimed, traditional news media are better able to verify stories and to offer a wider range of views and insights.

Second, the Internet is bringing into being, it is argued, an efflorescence of web-based journalism, which is compensating for the decline of traditional news media. In this view, the old order of monopoly journalism was a 'desert of Macworld', now being reclaimed by a legion of bloggers, citizen journalists and proliferating web-based start-ups. This advance is said to be unstoppable. As Steven Berlin Johnson puts it, 'there is going to be more content, not less; more information, more analysis, more precision, a wider range of niches covered'.[14]

Third, the two worlds of old and new journalism are coming together in a protean synergy of 'network journalism'. The crisis of the traditional *economic* model of journalism is giving rise to a new *social* model based on a pro–am (that is, professional–amateur) partnership. While in some projects volunteers are in control, in others they provide a feed chain of news and information, with professionals at the centre. The key to understanding the future, in this view, is to substitute for the word 'journalism' (with its association of vertical, gatekeeper institutions) the phrase 'journalistic activity', based on open-ended, reciprocal, horizontal, collaborative, self-generating and inclusive (the same affirmative adjectives keep being repeated) reporting and comment of a kind never experienced before.[15] Universities have allegedly a vital role to play in facilitating this advance. 'Media studies', solemnly proclaims one academic, 'must become a Networked Journalism thought leadership program.'[16]

These developments constitute supposedly a paradigm shift. Thus, Yochai Benkler argues that we are moving from a monopolistic 'industrial model of journalism' to a pluralistic 'networked model' based on profit and non-profit, individual and organised journalistic practices.[17] Similarly, Guido Fawkes proclaims, in a more unguarded fashion, that 'the days of media conglomerates determining the news in a top-down Fordist fashion are over. ... Big media are going to be disintermediated because the technology has drastically reduced the cost of dissemination.'[18] In short, the cuts and closures taking place in traditional news media are merely the necessary price to be paid for shifting from a top-down to a bottom-up form of journalism.

This approach thus argues that the Internet is extending participation, promoting media diversity and reconstituting the organisation and practice of journalism. Its message is deeply reassuring: *the crisis is leading to the reinvention of journalism in a better form.*

What are we to make of this baffling difference of opinion? Leaders of the news industry proclaim that they are successfully managing a transition; numerous journalists declare that there is a crisis of journalism that is damaging democracy; millenarians look forward to radical renewal; and some liberal educators declare that a journalistic renaissance has already begun. In other words, there is a complete absence of consensus.

In these circumstances, perhaps the best way forward is to consider each position in turn and see who is right.

Ostrich-like denial

The tide is flowing away from traditional news media in one crucial respect. They are losing advertising to the web.

After a slow beginning, the rise of internet advertising has been meteoric. To take one illustrative example, online advertising in Canada grew from $50 million in 1999 to $1.6 billion in 2008.[19] This growth – taking place throughout the Western world – has been at the expense of traditional news media. In 2008, internet advertising overtook television advertising in Denmark; and the same thing happened in Britain in January–June 2009.[20] However, the biggest inroads made by the Internet have been not in the display advertising medium of television but in newspapers that derive substantial revenue from classified advertising. In Britain, the Internet's share of classified expenditure soared from 2 per cent to 45 per cent between 2000 and 2008, while that of the local and regional press declined from 47 per cent to 26 per cent and that of national papers slipped from 14 per cent to 6 per cent in the same period.[21]

Most terrestrial commercial television channels are almost entirely dependent on advertising, and most newspapers derive the greater part of their revenue from advertising. The consequences of this redistribution have been, consequently, devastating.

Yet, there is little prospect of this redistribution being reversed. The Internet has triumphed as an advertising medium for good reason. The Internet is cheap. It has built a large audience. Thus, in Britain, households with internet access grew from 14 per cent to 64 per cent of homes between 1999 and 2008.[22] In 2009, homes with net access accounted for an estimated 64 per cent of homes in the EU.[23] Above all, the Internet is very good at targeting consumers (which is why 'search' advertising is now the largest category of internet advertising in America, Britain and elsewhere).[24]

Indeed, the likelihood is that internet advertising will continue to grow at the expense of traditional news media in the future. The internet audience – currently only about a quarter of the world's population,[25] and still excluding a sizeable section of most economically developed societies – will increase. Advertisers are also exploring new ways of utilising the advertising potential of the Internet.

If the tide in favour of the web seems unstoppable, the sandbags that traditional news media erected to protect themselves are leaking badly. They created satellite-news websites that, in some cases, attracted a substantial number of visitors and were journalistically accomplished. But most of these websites failed in one crucial respect: they did not attract substantial advertising. Thus, American newspapers derive, on average, no more than 10 per cent of their total revenue from their websites.[26]

The uncertain moves towards charging for news websites in 2010 were in effect an admission of failure. The strategy of giving away online content free in order to tap into a new stream of advertising revenue has not worked. But, at the time of writing, it is not at all clear that charging will provide a solution either. Aside from the financial press, its most likely effect will be to decimate the number of visitors to charging websites, because people will look for free alternatives.

The only positive signal is that some newspaper circulation and TV news audiences have held up better than advertising. Indeed, in countries like India and China, circulation is actually rising;[27] and in countries like Belgium and the Netherlands, the TV audience remained stable between 1997 and 2007.[28] But in most developed countries, newspaper circulations and, to a lesser degree, TV news ratings are in steady decline.

In short, most traditional news media controllers are far from being in control. The future offers the prospect of continued decline, almost regardless of what they do.

Millenarian fantasy

However, traditional news media are not faced with an apocalypse. For a start, television remains the dominant news medium. This is true not only in Britain, France, Germany, Italy and Japan where only a minority of Internet users said that the Internet was their primary source of news,[29] but also of the US, where respondents in a Pew survey were allowed to nominate more than one main news source. On this basis, 40 per cent of Americans in 2008 cited the Internet and 70 per cent cited television.[30]

This continued importance of television as a news medium has something to do with how the Internet is used. In Britain, only one traditional media organisation (BBC) featured in the top ten most visited websites in early 2009.[31] This reflected the ascendancy of search engines and of social and shopping sites on the web (and, more generally, the entertainment orientation of web users).

Continuity is reflected not only in the continuing importance of television as a news medium, but also in the continuing dominance of leading news *brands*. Thus, in Britain, two leading TV organisations (BBC News and Sky News) and five leading newspapers (*Guardian*, *Times*, *Telegraph*, *Mail* and *Sun*) accounted in 2008 for seven out of the ten top UK news websites (with the remaining three being aggregators (UK MSN, Yahoo! News, and Google News)).[32] In the US, the situation is broadly similar. Eight of the ten *news* websites with the most unique visitors in 2008 were traditional news media (five leading TV organisations and three leading newspaper organisations): their top spot was shared only with Yahoo! and AOL.[33]

Talk about the death of the old order of journalism is thus premature. Decline is not the same as apocalyptic death and renewal – the millenarian fantasy. We are not experiencing a Schumpeterian purge in which traditional media are being displaced by the new and ground zero has been cleared for green shoots of progressive journalism to rise up unimpeded.

Journalists' protests

So, are protesting journalists right to argue that the crisis of traditional news journalism represents a threat to democracy and public understanding? If one thing is clear, it is that the loss of advertising to the web will especially damage the democratic performance of media that derive substantial revenue from classified advertising. In Britain, this means especially the local daily and weekly press. Already, its editorial standards were dramatically lowered by the freesheet revolution that siphoned off revenue from paid-for local papers in favour of inferior editorial products.[34] The evisceration of the local press is now being increased further by its loss of advertising. This will weaken the role of the local print press in holding to account local government and in sustaining a sense of local community.

Advertising redistribution will also undermine expensive journalism. The big journalism superstores – such as the great metropolitan dailies and TV network news in the US – will have less money for time-consuming investigative journalism and high-cost foreign journalism. This is where major economies have been made already and where more economies will be made in the future, to the impoverishment of democracy.

In general, the quality of traditional, market-based media will probably deteriorate over time. This will be manifested partly in obvious ways: for example, the decline of Washington coverage in the American local daily press that is already under way. But it will also happen almost invisibly. A glimpse into the dynamics involved is provided by a study undertaken by the Goldsmiths Leverhulme Media Research Centre, based on over 150 interviews with journalists and three small news ethnographies.[35] British journalists are under strong pressure to produce more, in less time, as a consequence of newsroom redundancies, and the work generated by websites established by traditional news media, requiring stories to be updated in a twenty-four-hour news cycle. This is fostering 'creative cannibalisation', the mutual lifting of stories from rivals' websites, as a way of increasing output. It is also encouraging journalists to rely on a restricted pool of tried-and-tested news sources as a way of quickly generating more stories. And in general, it is giving rise to a more office-bound, routine, scissors-and-paste form of journalism. While in principle the Internet should be encouraging greater editorial diversity and more extensive use of grassroots sources by leading news media, in practice it seems to be having the opposite effect in Britain.

Yet, before the arguments of protesting journalists are fully accepted, two issues need to be addressed. The difficulty with the claim that the crisis of journalism is undermining public understanding is that journalism can sometimes foster public *misunderstanding*, on topics ranging from weapons of mass destruction to the MMR vaccine.[36] It is not sufficient just to canvass for more journalism as an end itself without making some kind of qualitative judgement about the kind of journalism being done.

This brings us to the second issue – the kind of journalism that the web is enabling. Any assessment of the future of journalism needs to reach a view about the *benefits* of change, not merely its cost. This is an issue about which protesting journalists tend to be reticent.

Renaissance dreams

The rise of the web enables people to answer back: to hold the media to account, to verify or falsify its claims and provide a counterweight to its oligopolistic power. Thus, in the much-cited Trent Lott saga, in 2002 an indignant blogosphere shamed leading American journalists into reassessing a news event – a speech given at a birthday party in which a leading politician, Senator Trent Lott, referred nostalgically to the racial-segregation politics of the past. Although this was largely ignored by the elite press corps at the time, growing protests from bloggers caused prominent news media to give belated, critical coverage to Senator Lott's comments as well as to similar statements he had made on previous occasions. In the ensuing row, Lott was forced to stand down as the Senate majority leader. It marked the moment when bloggers first successfully challenged American news values and in the process redefined what was acceptable and unacceptable in American politics.[37]

The Internet has also helped to facilitate new journalism at different levels. This is typified at an individual level by the way in which bystanders caught on camera the killing of Nada Soltan and the manslaughter of Ian Tomlinson in demonstrations in Tehran and London, in 2009, giving impetus to stories that gained international attention. It is typified at a local level by the *VoiceofSanDiego.org*, a website launched in 2005 and still operating in 2009 with twelve full-time staff, that has undertaken serious investigative journalism winning widespread plaudits.[38] And at a national level, it is typified by the website Politico (with a weekly print edition), which regularly demonstrates that web journalists report as well as comment on the news. Among other things, it revealed in 2008 that vice-presidential candidate Sarah Palin – viewed at the time as a typical ice-hockey mum – had spent $75,062 on just one shopping spree, and had a $150,000 clothes budget donated by the Republican National Committee.[39] And at an international level, it is typified by new e-zines – like the one examined in Chapter 5 – which mediate debates and experiences between nations.[40]

The net has also enabled new collaborative, network projects to take off. One of the most successful is *ProPublica*, an investigative newsroom in New York, funded generously by a rich donor. Its editor-in-chief is Paul Steiger (former editor of the *Wall Street Journal*), with a core of experienced journalists and a growing number of volunteers (according to Steiger, some 5,000).[41] While it has its own website, *ProPublica* gets round the problem of limited visibility and impact by developing stories in conjunction with major media organisations. It is the first online source to win a Pulitzer prize (for a Hurricane Katrina story published in conjunction with the *New York Times*). It has also broken notable local stories, from the way in which unsupervised drilling for gas endangered the water supply (placed in the *Albany Times-Union*) to the failure to take prompt action against nurses who have abused their patients (published in the *Los Angeles Times*), that were followed by changes in public policy.

But all these admirable developments need to be put into perspective. The web has not connected bloggers to a mass audience. In Britain 79 per cent of *internet users* in 2008 had not read a blog during the last three months.[42] To judge from an American study, citizen news sites are relatively rare, and mostly precarious.[43] While the web has provided a low-cost springboard for some significant new publications, these are largely niche publications with relatively small audiences. Thus, the much-cited *VoiceofSanDiego.org* attracted, in 2008, a modest audience of 70,000–80,000 unique visitors a month.[44] Even the handful of new website start-ups in the US that have reached large audiences, notably the *HuffingtonPost*, *Politico* and *Real Clean Politics*, each still obtained in 2008 less than one-seventh of the visits to popular news websites like those of MSNBC and CNN.[45]

There has been also a tendency to mythologise the role of the web in 'mainstreaming' minority journalism. A recent British study found that 'no alternative news sites were returned in the first page of search results' for all five sample news issues on either Google or Yahoo![46] These aggregators in fact tended to privilege the best-known news providers, reproducing their ascendancy. More generally, social network sites are strongly influenced by the news agendas set by dominant media.[47]

However, the single most important point to stress is that new web ventures are no more successful – indeed they are a great deal less successful – in attracting advertising than established media. Bloggers in Britain are mostly hobbyists, dependent on their day job.[48] A 2009 Pew Research Center study found in relation to new, web-based journalistic ventures in the US that 'despite enthusiasm and good work, few if any of these are profitable or even self-financing'.[49] Similarly, a 2009 *Columbia Journalism Review* study concluded that 'it is unlikely that any but the smallest of these [web-based] news organisations can be supported primarily by existing online revenue'.[50] The absence of a strong online revenue stream – in the form of subscriptions, consumer donations and advertising – means that the future growth of independent web-based journalism will be retarded, unless steps are taken to change this.

In brief, the web cavalry riding to the rescue is too small and without sufficient firepower to offset the decline of traditional journalism.

Public reformism

Thus, all four prominent positions that have been considered so far have defects. However, there is waiting in the wings a compelling alternative, which I will call public reformism.

Public reformism seeks to enhance the democratic performance of the media through concerted action. This has led to varied reformist strategies, from the promotion of a public-interest culture among professional journalists as in America, the public ownership and funding of leading broadcasting organisations in numerous democratic countries from Japan to Canada, legislation imposing public-service objectives on commercial broadcasters (well entrenched in northern Europe), the Scandinavian policy of subsidising minority newspapers, through to community, mutual, worker and public-trust media ownership.[51]

In this case, the decline of traditional news media is not being fully offset by the rise of web-based journalism, as a result of the partial decoupling of advertising from news production. A significant number of advertisers have switched not from old to new news media, but to parts of the web (such as craigslist) where there is no journalism. In effect, the commercial subsidy for journalism is contracting.

This raises the question of whether we should accept passively a situation in which a change of advertising strategy, unrelated to consideration of the public good, diminishes the democratic performance of the media. One temporising response has been to suggest that local aristocrats/plutocrats, and their family bequests, should come to the rescue. Just as the aristocracy supported the arts and classical music in times past, so now, it is reasoned, they should support journalism.[52] It is a view much favoured by those who fear the democratic state.

The alternative is for some form of state intervention. There are a range of alternatives on the table, which will be illustrated by two contrasting American reports, one liberal[53] and the other radical.[54] The radical report proposes a costly subsidy scheme that includes paying half the capped salaries of journalists in post-corporate newspapers, a graduated postal subsidy and financial support for high-school journalism and rookie trainees. By contrast, the liberal report advocates low-cost measures, with a stress on voluntarism in which universities play a more active role as centres of community media, charitable foundations are encouraged to fill the void left by advertisers and donations in general are fostered by expanding the legal definition of journalism ventures eligible for tax-deductible gifts.

But both reports also have certain things in common. They stress that public media subsidy is not un-American in terms of what has happened in the past and that foreign experience shows that public subsidy is not incompatible with media freedom. Both call for the enhanced funding and more local orientation of public radio and television (though whether this will have a profound impact may be questioned, since in the US public television (PBS) accounts for less than 2 per cent of viewing time). Both reports also have at their core funding proposals that, despite a big difference in the sums involved, are not fundamentally dissimilar. The radical report proposes that every American adult gets an annual $200 voucher to donate to a news medium (or media) of her choice, providing that it passes a modest threshold of audience demand, takes the form of a non-profit or low-profit venture uncompromised by non-media interests and makes its content freely available on the web. The liberal alternative proposes a National Fund for Local News, which would provide grants for 'advances in local news reporting and innovative ways to support it' in both commercial and not-for-profit media. Both reports also share common ground in that they seek to recycle money from the communications industries and their users to support journalism. The possible (and not necessarily mutually exclusive) mechanisms for doing this mooted in the two reports are: a levy on telecom users; a charge on TV and radio licences; a tax on broadcast spectrum rental or sale; a surcharge on internet service providers; a tax on consumer communication electronic durables or an advertising tax.

Journalism in countries where publicly funded broadcasters are strong has a less serious crisis than that in the US, and perhaps calls for a different response. One battle, largely won in Europe, is to resist commercial media lobbies seeking to prevent public broadcasters from developing an online presence. The web is a new terrain, where public broadcasters can renew their public-service mandate through journalistic innovation. To do this, they need to be adequately funded. This happened in the case of the BBC, which developed a good website, attracting in early 2009 an average of 21 million unique visitors a week – vastly more than any other media organisation in Britain.[55]

However, this public space needs to be defended from future encroachments. Across much of Europe, commercial media lobbies are clamouring for public-service broadcasters to be hobbled. This usually includes a demand for public-broadcaster websites to be reined in. For example, commercial media corporations in Austria are arguing that the website of the public broadcaster should be restricted to programme-related content (as a way of limiting its attraction).[56] In Britain, it is claimed that the BBC has become 'too big', and in the words of Culture Secretary Jeremy Hunt (responding to press lobbying), the BBC website 'needs clearer red lines about what it will and won't do'.[57] This is an old story: the press successfully lobbied to prevent the BBC from developing its own independent news service until 1932 on the grounds that public funding of news reporting (other than use of press agency material) was 'unfair'.[58] The public needs to rally yet again to defend public-service broadcasting against its self-serving rivals.

In Britain, at a time of spending cuts and frozen wages, the opportunities for new initiatives are limited. Priority should be given to supporting local news reporting, because it is the sector in Britain that has been worst hit. This could be done in a form that deliberately encourages pro–am news operations across different news platforms through the establishment of local news hubs, funded by a broadband tax.[59]

Different reformist proposals should be tailored to the needs of different media systems and framed in terms of what is possible within different political cultures. But whichever path is followed, one thing needs to be stressed. It is not enough to predict passively the future of journalism and debate between contrasting Doomsday and Micawberish versions. Instead, we should seek actively to shape the future in order to have a better outcome.

Part IV
Media and history

8 Narratives of media history revisited

Introduction

It was chance that took me to see *Copenhagen*, a play that re-enacts, from different perspectives, fateful interchanges between a Danish and German physicist during the 1930s and 1940s. It gave me the idea of presenting British media history as a series of competing narratives in the opening chapter of my book *Media and Power*.[1] This outline subsequently provided the organising framework for a good collection of essays on media history.[2]

In adopting an unconventional formula for a literature review, I was responding to what seemed to me to be three underlying problems. British media history is highly fragmented, being subdivided by period, medium and interpretative strand. It is often narrowly centred on media institutions and content, leaving the wider setting of society as a shadowy background. And media history has not become as central in media studies as one might have expected, given that it is a grand-parent of the field. So I was looking for a way of integrating *medium* history into general accounts of *media* development, and of connecting these to the 'mainframe' of general history. I was also seeking to convey how media history illuminates the role of the media in society – in the present, as well as the past.

In returning to the subject of my essay some seven years after it was first written, I shall attempt to do two things. I will briefly restate the essay's central themes, though in a new way by concentrating primarily on recent research. I will also suggest, with great diffidence, possible new directions in which media history might develop in the future, including the reclaiming of 'lost narratives'.

Dominant tradition

Any review of British media history must begin with its leading and longest-established interpretation – the liberal narrative. This was first scripted, in its initial form, in the nineteenth century and comes out of the hallowed tradition of 'constitutional' history which examines the development of Britain's political system from Anglo-Saxon times to the present.

Key landmarks in Britain's constitutional evolution are said to be the defeat of absolutist monarchy, the establishment of the rule of law, the strengthening of parliament and the introduction of mass democracy in five, cautious, instalments. It is also claimed that the media acquired a 'constitutional' role by becoming the voice of the people and a popular check on government.

The media's constitutional elevation is usually described in terms of two intertwined narrative themes. The first recounts how the press became free of government control by the mid-nineteenth century, followed by the liberation of film and broadcasting in the mid-twentieth century. The second theme is concerned with how liberated media empowered the people. Recent historical work has focused on the latter, so this is what we shall concentrate upon.

There is broad agreement among liberal media historians that the rise of a more independent press changed the tenor and dynamics of English politics. Newspapers increased their political content during the eighteenth century, and successfully defied during the 1760s the ban on the reporting of parliament. This enabled newspapers to shine a low-wattage light on the previously private world of aristocratic politics. People outside the political system could observe, through the press, factional battles among their rulers. How spectators reacted to these battles began to matter, as increasing references in the later eighteenth century to the wider public testify. In a more general sense, the rise of the press was part of a profound shift in which it came to be accepted that the general public had the right to debate and evaluate the actions of their rulers. Some publications also directly attacked corruption and oligarchy, functioning as pioneer watchdogs monitoring the abuse of official power. In short, the growth of public disclosure through the press rendered the governmental system more open and accountable.[3]

The expansion of the press after the end of licensing in 1694 also contributed, it is argued, to the building of a representative institution. During the eighteenth century, newspapers mushroomed in different parts of the country and expanded their readership. An increased number of newspapers published views as well as news reports, seeking to speak for their readers. By the 1850s, following a period of rapid expansion and enhanced independence, the press allegedly came of age as an empowering agency. Its thunder echoed down the corridors of power.

However, the central unanswered question at the heart of this eloquent liberal narrative is precisely *who* was being represented by this 'empowering' press. A much-favoured answer used to be that the expanding press was speaking primarily for the dynamic forces of the 'new society': that is to say, the expanding middle classes and urban working class brought into being by rapid economic growth in the 'first industrial nation'.[4] This interpretation stressed the progressive nature of the evolving press, the way in which it broke free from the political agenda of the landed elite and supported campaigns to reform the institutions of the British aristocratic state. Indeed, in some versions of this argument, the growing power of the press both reflected the changed balance of social forces in British society and contributed to the building of a new, post-aristocratic political settlement.

This beguiling interpretation has been undermined from two different directions. Revisionist histories of nineteenth-century Britain increasingly emphasise continuity rather than radical change. They point to the embedded nature of the *ancien régime* before the extension of the franchise; the powerful pull of Anglicanism, localism and tradition; the incremental, uneven nature of the industrial revolution; and, above all, the landed elite's continued dominance of political life until late in the nineteenth century.[5] Meanwhile historical studies of the press have drawn attention to the continuing importance of the conservative press (which greatly strengthened in the last quarter of the eighteenth century), the enormous diversity of nineteenth-century newspapers and the tenuous evidence that the press strongly influenced political elites and public policy, save in special circumstances.[6] The thesis that an independent press, representative of a transformed society, helped to forge a new political order is now widely disputed.

So whom did the press represent? The undermining of the claim that the later Hanoverian press represented a progressive social alliance has encouraged a return to a traditionalist Whig view of the press as the voice of an indeterminate 'public'. Typical of this shift is Hannah Barker's now standard textbook, which argues that newspapers gained a larger and more socially diverse readership and came to be shaped primarily by their customers in the absence of strict government censorship. 'The importance of sales to newspaper profits', she writes, 'forced papers to echo the views of their readers in order to thrive.'[7] By 1855, she concludes, 'the newspaper press in England was largely free of government interference and was able – with some justification – to proclaim itself as the fourth estate of the British constitution'.[8] In her view, the press informed and represented public opinion and made it a powerful political force.[9]

However, some liberal historians remain rightly uneasy about viewing the press as the voice of an undefined (and indivisible) public. Jeremy Black, for example, argues that 'the press was at best a limited guide to the opinions of the public' and should be viewed as connecting to 'public opinions rather than public opinion'.[10] This more nuanced view enables him to conclude that 'public culture' (in which the press was central) became less representative of political difference during the post-Chartist era.[11] Other liberal historians point to the growing interpenetration of journalism and politics in the second half of the nineteenth century and early twentieth century, when much of the press became an extension of the party system.[12] Indeed, the liberal historian Stephen Koss concludes that the British press did not become fully independent, and subject to popular control, until the late 1940s and 1950s.[13]

But if the Whig conception of the press as a fourth estate looks vulnerable, there is another interpretation waiting in the wings. In 1982, Brian Harrison wrote an erudite essay assessing the role of the pressure-group periodical in the nineteenth and twentieth centuries. He showed that these modest, and widely overlooked, publications helped to sustain pressure groups 'through three major functions: inspirational, informative and integrating'.[14] They inspired some people to join or support a public-interest group; they armed activists with factual ammunition and strengthened their resolve; and they could build bridges, helping to unify reforming movements. By contributing to the functioning and effectiveness of pressure groups, the minority political press contributed to the development of a maturing democracy.

This is an important line of argument that can now be extended, with the help of more recent research, to the earlier period. The eighteenth-century press provided the oxygen of publicity for political campaigning centred on petitions, addresses, instructions (to MPs), public meetings and concerted demonstrations.[15]

These fostered a 'modern' style of politics based on public discussion and participation, rather than on personal relationships, clientelist networks and social deference. Sections of the press aided this new politics by conferring prominence on leading campaigners, by communicating their arguments and demands and by mobilising public support. They contributed in other words to building a democratic infrastructure of representation based on collective organisations.

In the nineteenth century, radical newspapers contributed to the growth of trade unions; reformist papers sustained a growing multiplicity of interest groups and a new, party-aligned press helped to transform aristocratic factions in parliament into mass political parties. This last development – often attracting disapproval from liberal press historians – represented a crucial contribution to the building of a key institution of democracy. Political parties became key co-ordinating organisations within the British political system: they aggregated social interests, formulated political programmes that distributed costs and redistributed resources across society and defined political choices for the electorate.[16]

A view of the press as an agency contributing to the building of civil society is subtly different from, and more persuasive than, a traditional conception of the press as the representative organ of public opinion. Arguments and evidence supporting this alternative interpretation are to be found in numerous radical[17] as well as liberal accounts.[18] These portray the press as contributing to the development of civil-society organisations *through which different publics were represented.* Implicitly, they also depict civil society rather than the press as the main locus of representation.

Mark Hampton has revised traditional liberal press history in another way. In a notable book, he documents the mid-Victorian elite vision of an educative press that would induct large numbers of people into 'politics by discussion'. This gave way, he shows, to growing disenchantment when newspapers became more commercial and sensational, and large numbers of people turned away from 'liberal' enlightenment. After 1880, the educational ideal was increasingly replaced by a view of the press as a representative institution – something that Hampton, drawing on radical press history, largely rejects.[19]

He has since written an essay that can be read as an account-settling epilogue to his book.[20] In effect, he concludes that the twentieth-century press may not have measured up to the unreal expectations of Victorian visionaries, nor fulfilled the heroic destiny assigned to it in Whig history, yet neither should the press's democratic role be written off as an illusion. There were times during the twentieth century – most notably during the South African War, at the onset of the Cold War in the 1940s and during the 1970s debate about economic management – when the British press offered multiple perspectives. This enriched public debate and manifestly contributed to the functioning of democracy.

Some liberal historians also argue that the educational mission of the press may have faltered, but it was absorbed by radio and television. The rise of public-service broadcasting, it is claimed, diminished the knowledge gap between elites and the general public; aided reciprocal communication between social groups; and fostered the development of a policy-based discourse of rational democratic debate, orientated towards the public good.[21]

One counter-charge to this is that public-service broadcasting was locked into a paternalistic style of journalism, a view that is in effect endorsed by Hugh Chignell.[22] However, his contention is that BBC radio introduced more popular styles of journalism, particularly during the 1960s, in response to social change, competition and the possibilities created by new technology. This popularisation produced a furious reaction from elite critics, who were placated in the 1970s by the development of a more analytical, research-based form of journalism on BBC Radio 4. The implication of this study is that the BBC learned to develop different registers of journalism, which responded to the orientation of different audiences.

Liberal media historians have usually shrugged off criticism by ignoring it. Both Hampton and Chignell signify a change by registering and partly accepting critical arguments originating from outside the canon. In doing so, they are contributing to the development of a more guarded and persuasive liberal interpretation of media history.

Feminist challenge

The dominance of the liberal narrative is now challenged by the rise of feminist media history. This argues that the media did not become fully 'independent' when they became free of government, because they remained under male control. And far from empowering the people, the media contributed to the oppression of half the population. This feminist interpretation is thus not merely different from the liberal one but directly contradicts it.

It comes out of a historical tradition that documents the subordination of women in the early modern period, when wives, without ready access to divorce, could be lawfully beaten and confined by their husbands, and when women did not have the same social standing or legal rights as men. It describes the struggle for women's emancipation and advance as a qualified success story in which women gained new legal protections, greater independence and improved opportunities, but in a context where there is not yet full gender equality. Its account of the development of media history is told as an accompaniment to this narrative.

Feminist media history is now the fastest-growing version of media history. This return visit will thus focus attention on recent work that is revising the pioneer version of feminist media history.

This pioneer version argued that popular media indoctrinated women into accepting a subordinate position in society. It did this primarily by portraying men and women as having different social roles – men as breadwinners and partici-pants in public life and women as mothers and housewives. As the *Ladies' Cabinet*, a leading women's journal, apostrophised in 1847: woman 'is given to man as his better angel ... to make home delightful and life joyous' and serve as a 'mother to make citizens for earth'.[23] This understanding of the proper role of women was justified in terms of the innate ('natural') differences between the sexes and, in the earlier period, by divine providence. During the course of the nineteenth century, this gender discourse was strengthened by being articulated to discourses of class and progress. Images of femininity were linked to those of affluent elegance, while understandings of domestic duty were associated with the moral improvement of society. Traditional gender norms were upheld also by family custom, peer-group pressure and education, and rendered still more coercive by being reproduced in mass entertainment – including media produced specially for women.

This pioneer version also stressed the underlying continuity of patriarchal representations of gender from the nineteenth through to the late twentieth century. The main concerns of women were defined, according to this account, as courtship, marriage, motherhood, home-making and looking good. There were minor shifts of emphasis over the years (for example, a stress on being a professional housewife and mother in the 1930s, 'make do and mend' in the 1940s and 'shop and spend' in the 1950s). But the central media message remained, it is argued, essentially the same. Women's concerns were projected as being primarily romantic and domestic; men and women were depicted as being innately different; and women who transgressed gender norms were generally portrayed in an unfavourable light. The functionalist cast of this argument is typified by Janet Thumim's analysis of post-war film. 'Our exploration of popular films', she concludes, 'shows that screen representations in the period 1945–65 performed a consistently repressive function in respect of women. There are, simply, no depictions of autonomous, independent women either inside or outside the structure of the family, who survive unscathed at the narrative's close.'[24] Popular media, in short, consistently sustained patriarchy.

This stress on continuity is now being challenged within the feminist tradition. First, revisionist research is drawing attention to women's active resistance to patriarchal domination through the creation of their own media.[25] In particular, Michelle Tusan shows in a ground-breaking book that the women's press grew out of women's associations and single-issue campaigns in Victorian Britain. Originating in the 1850s, the women's press confounded Lord Northcliffe's observation that 'women can't write and don't want to read'[26] by gaining a significant readership before the First World War. Its leading publications reported news that was not covered in the mainstream press, developed women-centred political agendas and advanced alternative understandings of society. Even when the women's press was in decline during the 1920s, it still boasted the early *Time and Tide*, a weekly that published a satirical 'Man's Page' and thoughtful commentary by leading feminists from Virginia Woolf to Rebecca West. Eclipsed in the 1930s, the feminist press was reborn in the 1970s.

Second, increasing references are made to the advance of women within media organisations. Thus, David Deacon documents how female journalists, mostly from privileged backgrounds and with influential male patrons, made a breakthrough in the 1930s by breaching a traditional male preserve: the reporting of war. Even so, female journalists were still encouraged to concentrate on the everyday lives of ordinary people and to report war as an extended human-interest story.[27] Yet, by the 2000s, women had risen to positions of increasing prominence within the British media.[28]

Third, revisionist research argues that representations of gender changed in meaningful ways in response to wider changes in society. Thus, Adrian Bingham attacks the standard view that the popular press sought to contain the advance of women during the interwar period.[29] A narrow focus on women's pages, he argues, ignores the diversity of viewpoints that were expressed in the main body of popular daily papers. Although reactionary sentiments were sometimes voiced, the prevailing view expressed in the interwar press was that there should be no going back to the pre-war era. Women's increased freedom from restrictive social codes and dress was generally welcomed; successful women in public and professional life were depicted both prominently and positively; the greater independence, assertiveness and athleticism of 'modern women' was widely presented as being part of a generational change and an inevitable step towards greater gender convergence; there was an increased stress on the need for a companionate marriage and for an appropriate adjustment of traditional male behaviour; and women were invested, in a variety of ways, with greater prestige (not least as newly enfranchised citizens).

However, this scholarly study acknowledges that change was not unidirectional or across the board. Fashion, housewifery and motherhood still dominated women's pages. The women's movement was under-reported; feminism itself was frequently said to be outdated and 'superfluous'; and the Rothermere press opposed votes for women under thirty. Women were more often presented in sexualised ways, which had no counterpart for men. But although Bingham's assessment stresses complexity and diversity, his conclusion is that the interwar popular press adopted, overall, a more enlightened view of gender.

In passing, it should be noted that revisionists are not having it entirely their own way. Thus, Michael Bailey looks at radio's response to 'gender modernisation' during the same era as Bingham but reaches a significantly different conclusion. Like the press, the BBC also encouraged women to be efficient housewives and informed mothers during the interwar period. However, Bailey argues that the BBC's briefing was more than just helpful advice since, implicitly, it was also a way of making women internalise a sense of domestic duty and feel guilty if they fell short of the standards expected of 'modern women'. The BBC's domestic education is thus viewed by him as psychologically coercive and strongly traditionalist in reaffirming women's place in the home.[30]

Fourth, revisionist research has drawn attention to the ambiguity or 'textual tension' of some media representations. This argument is not new and can be found in earlier studies of eighteenth-century ballads,[31] nineteenth-century women's magazines,[32] and twentieth-century women's films[33] – all media, it is argued, which sometimes provided a space in which women could imagine a different gender order or express a veiled form of protest. But while this argument is not original, it has become both more prominent and more explicitly linked to social change. For example, Deborah Philips and Ian Haywood draw attention to popular 1950s women's novels which featured women doctors.[34] These heroines were held up for admiration and were even portrayed as builders of a brave new world represented by the post-1945 welfare state. But they were also presented as being traditionally feminine, and their careers were implicitly viewed as being an extension of women's traditional caring role. These books, according to Philips and Haywood, were pleasurable because they offered a mythological resolution of conflicting impulses, one embracing change and the other harking back to the past.

Deborah Philips extends this argument in a subsequent study.[35] In her account, 1980s 'sex-and-shopping' novels celebrated women's advance, without questioning the structures of power that held back women. The 'Aga-saga' novels of the 1990s reverted to domesticated romance, while expressing unmistakeable dissatisfaction with contemporary men. And some early 2000s 'chick-lit' novels depicted successful women in search of still more successful men. All these novels responded, according to Phillips, to contradictions in contemporary female sensibility.

Fifth, revisionist research points to a different denouement of the feminist narrative. Instead of arguing that media representations of gender remained fundamentally the same, the case is now being made more often that a cumulative sea change took place from the early 1980s onwards. A growing number of TV series – made or shown in Britain – depicted independent women with successful careers as being strong, capable and also appealing, indeed as people to identify with.[36] Teen magazines emerged that expressed female sexuality in new, more open ways.[37] However, some traditionalist representations of gender also persisted.[38] Depictions could also mislead by implying that gender equality had been achieved: indeed, as one analyst wryly notes, women in the fictional world of television have advanced further than women in real life.[39] Some seemingly 'progressive' lifestyle journalism also had conservative undertones, urging women to take control of their lives in individualistic ways rather than seeking to change society through collective action.[40] And some dramas like the cult series *Sex and the City* (1998–2004) expressed conservative consumerist values, while also staging a debate about what women should expect out of life.[41] Its success was emblematic of a more questioning media orientation towards gender relations at the turn of the century, compared with even twenty years before.

This feminist narrative, in its revised form, does not question the historical role of the media in socialising women into the norms of patriarchy. But the contours of this narrative, and its ending, are changing in response to new research. Historical work on the development of masculinity is also developing in a way that shadows, and supports, the feminist narrative.[42] In short, a new way of viewing the media's evolution has come into being that takes account of one of the most important social developments of the last 150 years – the advance of women. It is leading to the rewriting of media history.

Radical challenge

The liberal tradition is also assailed from another direction. Radical media historians attack the same vulnerable point of the liberal narrative as feminist critics: its assumption that the media switched allegiances from government to the people when the media became 'free' of official control. Radical media history argues that, on the contrary, mainstream media remained integrated into the underlying power structure and continued to support the social order.[43]

This version of media history comes primarily out of a historical account that records the rise of an organised working-class movement in the first half of the nineteenth century. This movement became more radical, won increasing support and developed its own popular press, which conferred publicity on working-class institutions and radical causes and encouraged its readers to view society in more critical ways. But early working-class militants, and their heirs, were defeated. And, subsequently, the winning of equal citizenship, through mass enfranchisement, did not lead to the creation of an equal society.[44] Radical media history seeks to shed light on this by focusing on how, in its view, the media were 'tamed' even when they ceased to be government controlled.

In essence, its explanation boils down to three arguments. First, the market developed as a system of control (not as an engine of freedom, as in the liberal narrative). The rise of *mass*-market newspaper entry costs in the period 1850–1918 contributed to the consolidation of unrepresentative, capitalist control of the press (and also of the music hall and later film and television industries). The media's growing dependence on advertising also disadvantaged the left, while the development of media concentration curtailed choice.

Second, elites exerted influence on the media through informal processes. A modern apparatus of news management developed, beginning with the 'introduction' of the lobby system in 1885 and culminating in the enormous expansion of state public relations in the period after 1980. Informal alliances were forged between press controllers and governments, as during the Chamberlain and Thatcher eras. Above all, elites set the parameters of political debate in broadcasting through their ascendancy over state institutions, especially parliament.

Third, dominant groups also influenced the culture of society, and in this way shaped the content of the media. The prevailing ideas of the time – the intensification of nationalism in the eighteenth century, the rise of imperialism in the nineteenth century, the diffusion of anti-communism during the Cold War and the triumphalist neo-liberalism that followed – have tended to uphold, implicitly or explicitly, the prevailing social order.

This narrative has been usefully synthesised in a recent essay.[45] And it continues to be embellished by new research. Examples include a study of the radical press during its triumphant Chartist phase;[46] an illuminating study of the role of the media in the transformation of Queen Victoria into the 'Mother of her People' and symbol of imperial and industrial greatness;[47] and a radical, Foucauldian analysis of how the BBC sought to 'train and reform the unemployed as docile but efficient citizens' during the 1930s.[48]

This historical tradition has unstitched the more vulnerable seams of traditional liberal history. It also makes an insightful contribution to a historical understanding of why socialism was defeated in Britain. But it suffers from one central defect: its failure to acknowledge that the reformist heirs of the early working-class movement succeeded in the twentieth century in changing significantly the social order. Moreover, a progressive alliance did so partly as a consequence of securing an extensive hearing – even support – from part of the media system. Misleading arguments about the 'refeudalisation of society' after 1850, linked to a very simplistic sketch of a subordinated media system, as in Jürgen Habermas' classic radical account,[49] no longer seem satisfactory – even to the author himself.[50] In short, the traditional radical narrative needs to pay more attention to political success rather than to failure and to the media's involvement in progressive change. To this, we shall return.

Populist challenge

The populist interpretation of media history describes the development of the media as a prolonged escape story – not from government but from a cultural elite which once controlled the media and which sought to foist its taste and cultural judgements on the people. It recounts how the public demanded entertainment in place of uplift, and largely prevailed as a consequence of the increasing commercialisation of the media.

This interpretation connects to two themes in the general history of Britain. Its description of a revolt against a cultural elite is part of a more general account of the erosion of deference to authority (whether based on birth, wealth, age, education or occupation). And its celebration of the 'egalitarian' power of the media consumer connects to a more general narrative that describes the rise of a consumer society and the alleged subversion of class authority by consumer power.

The core of this media narrative is provided by specialist studies that record the triumphs of the entertainment-seeking public over high-minded Victorian elites and their heirs: registered for example in the advent of the 'new journalism' in the 1880s, the stocking of light fiction in Edwardian public libraries, the expansion of popular music on 1940s and 1960s radio and the cumulative popularisation of television. This narrative has as a subsidiary theme an historical account of the pleasure people derived from the media.

New studies continue to fill out this narrative. Thus a recent study of the rise of a consumer society in nineteenth-century Britain portrays the growth of popular journalism as part of an efflorescence of 'bright colour, light and entertainment' in which life became more fun, fuller and richer – enhanced by the retail revolution and the rise of football, mass tourism, bestselling books and the music hall.[51]

Similarly, another populist study argues that the expansion of popular music through the gramophone, radio and dance hall immeasurably improved the quality of life in interwar Britain, just as cheap food, electricity and better housing did. The enormous pleasure derived from popular music was allegedly a direct consequence of its commercialisation. 'In an important sense', writes James Nott, 'the application of the profit motive to cultural production was democratic.'[52] It meant that music was directed towards what people wanted, rather than what disapproving – and sometimes snobbish and racist – cultural gatekeepers thought was worthy. Nott also argues that commercial popular music during this period had vitality, affirmed the ordinary, connected to popular romanticism and produced sounds and songs that have lasted.

Likewise, Jeffrey Millard contrasts the patrician and paternalistic sentiments of those who shaped the development of a public-service broadcasting regime (including commercial television) in the 1950s and 1960s with the opportunities for pleasurable fulfilment created by multiple digital television channels and video-on-demand in the twenty-first century.[53] This interpretative strand of media history also continues to generate celebrations of popular media content, as connected to the real, lived experiences of ordinary people.[54]

The populist tradition of media history has limitations, and is not the dynamic force that it was during neo-liberalism's heyday. It does not evaluate how the rise of entertainment impinged on the democratic role of the media. It mistakenly equates consumer and civic equality with social and economic equality. And it fails to engage adequately with issues of cultural quality. Even so, it has illuminated greatly the life-enhancing pleasures generated by the rise of the media.

Nation building

The liberal, feminist, radical and populist traditions belong recognisably to the same intellectual family. They recount media history in relation to different forms of power – political, economic and social/cultural. They also intersect, overlap and confront each other in ways that indicate a troubled relationship of affinity. However, there are three other established narratives which have only a tangential relationship to this core of media history. But what they have to say is important.

The 'anthropological' narrative is inspired by the insight that the nation is partly a cultural construct and explores the role of the media in fostering an imaginary sense of national communion. The UK is in fact a relatively 'new' nation: created formally (though there had been a historical build-up) through the political union of England and Wales with Scotland in 1707 and the constitutional union of Britain and Ireland in 1801 (followed by a messy divorce with most of Ireland in 1921). The emergent media system, it is argued, played a significant part in bonding this conglomerate of nations and forging a sense of being 'British'.

Thus, print media helped to foster a British national identity in the eighteenth century principally through Protestant bigotry and antagonism towards Catholic France (with whom Britain was at war for much of the century).[55] This became overlaid in the nineteenth century by a sense of imperial superiority, expressed in a hubristic view of national character, and in the first half of the twentieth century by widely diffused images of Britain as an Arcadia.[56] However, the decline of Protestantism and the dismantlement of the empire after 1945 undermined the traditional conception of Britishness, while conventional visualisations of Britain as an unchanging Constable painting did not accord with a new stress on modernity. With difficulty, and still in a contested form, a weaker national identity emerged after 1970, a time when the UK joined the EEC (1973) and was exposed to increased globalising influences. This took the form of a multicultural, multi-ethnic, plural understanding of Britishness. Thus, the optimistic claim is that British national identity, forged originally through religious hatred and racist imperialism, evolved to include people of all religions and none and to embrace people of different ethnic backgrounds.

Recent research has extended this relatively new narrative, giving it greater depth and fine-grained detail. For example, James Chapman's examination of British historical films between the 1930s and 1990s argues persuasively that these films say as much about the time they were made as about the past.[57] Among other things, his study draws attention to a deepening sense of national decline during the 1950s. Richard Weight's study of patriotism between 1940 and 2000 is especially illuminating about the attempt, with strong press support, to reverse this sense of national decline during the 1980s through the projection of Britain as a recuperated nation, the victor of the short, exciting Falklands War, and further regenerated through a return to traditional values (with an implied single ethnicity).[58] This failed to capture permanently the national imagination, Weight argues, and gave way by the 1990s to a looser, more inclusive and multiple understanding of Britishness. However, a sense of being British has always been mediated through other identities, such as class, gender, region and membership of the nations of Scotland, Wales and Ulster. As Paul Ward argues, there is an underlying continuity in the fractured and mediated nature of British national identity between 1870 and the present.[59]

But if recent research extends existing lines of argument, it also offers a new twist by giving more critical attention to identification with the 'national regions'. This reorientation has given rise to ground-breaking research into Englishness. Richard Colls argues that a sense of Englishness was buried inside the mythologising of the 'Anglo–British imperial state', and came to be viewed as synonymous with Britishness. But this equation of England and Britain was undermined first by the death of imperialism (a project in which all countries of the UK had a shared investment) and then by political devolution. However, the English found difficulty in expressing their sub-national identity partly because readily available images of England were so outdated. As Richard Colls eloquently puts it, 'island races, garden hearts, industrial landscapes, ecclesiological villages, fixed properties, ordered relationships, native peoples, cultural survivals, northern grit, southern charm, rural redemption, rule Britannia – all these discourses persist, but with less conviction'.[60] This portrait of 'Englishness' as a buried, inarticulate sense of commonality accords with Krishan Kumar's subsequent study, which argues that an English identity was deliberately repressed for the sake of imperial and national unity (with clear parallels to the Austro-Hungarian and Russian empires).[61]

Historical exploration of Englishness has been accompanied by renewed interest in Welsh and Scots national identity (and a boom in good, revisionist books about Irish nationalism that lies outside this review). Especially notable is a study of the media in Wales.[62] The Welsh region of the BBC (radio) was established in 1937; a Welsh ITV company in 1958; a unified Welsh BBC television service in 1964; and the Welsh television channel, Sianel Pedwar Cymru (S4C), in 1982. All these initiatives came about partly as a consequence of Welsh nationalist pressure and helped to sustain a distinctive Welsh identity. S4C played an especially important role in supporting the declining Welsh language (which is now spoken by only 20 per cent of Welsh people).

But these developments should not obscure the extent of national (and predominantly English) domination of Britain's media system. Barlow and associates point out that, in 2002, 85 per cent of daily morning papers bought in Wales came from across the border.[63] In 2003, less than 10 per cent of the output of BBC1 and 2 and ITV1 (HTV) was produced specifically for Welsh consumption, and much of this was accounted for by news.[64] While emphasising the complex factors in play in sustaining rival national identities, this study highlights just how important the national integration of the UK's media system has been in supporting an overarching British national identity.

The increased attention given to 'regional nationalism' is thus an important feature of the way in which the anthropological narrative is developing.[65] This is partly a response to the revival of separatism and the establishment of the Scottish Parliament and Welsh National Assembly in 1999.

Culture wars

The libertarian media narrative arises from different developments in British society. There was a sustained decline of religious belief and observance from the later nineteenth century onwards. The increasing de-Christianisation of Britain, combined with greater individualism fostered by capitalism, contributed to the advance of social liberalism in the 1960s. This was fiercely resisted by traditionalists, who sought to turn the clock back. The battle between social conservatives and social liberals that ensued provides the central theme of the libertarian narrative for the second half of the twentieth century.

The best-documented part of this narrative is provided by research into the social reaction that took place against 1960s social liberalism. This highlights the role of the media in generating moral panics about a succession of deviant groups from the 1960s through to the 1980s. The media presented these groups in stereotypical and exaggerated ways; represented them to be part of a deeper social malaise; mobilised support for authoritarian retribution; and recharged in varied ways social conservatism.[66]

Recent work, within the libertarian narrative, updates this narrative and offers a different provisional ending. Thus, one study examines the emergence of a new kind of left in municipal politics – owing more to the Sixties counter-culture than to Marxism or Methodism – which was symbolically annihilated in the media during the 1980s. Yet, its political agenda and some of its once controversial policies became almost mainstream in the early 2000s, when the Sixties generation gained control of leading public institutions. This outcome 'was because in Britain – unlike America – progressives were winning major battles in an unacknowledged culture war'.[67]

If this study suggests that the tide of social reaction receded after the 1980s (though this did not extend to issues arising from immigration and terrorism during the early 2000s), another survey reappraises the concept of moral panic, the *deus ex machina* of the radical libertarian narrative. Chas Critcher argues that some moral panics were prevented through opposition and expert intervention (as in the 1980s, over AIDS); some were deflected from authoritarian control towards harm minimisation (as in the 1990s, over raves and ecstasy); and some led to ritualistic illusions of effective action (as when the complexities of child abuse were reduced, in the late 1990s and early 2000s, to a hue and cry against 'stranger paedophiles'). The concept of moral panic, concludes Critcher, is an 'ideal type' which, in reality, takes different forms and has different outcomes.[68] This is a significantly different position from the depiction of the moral panic as a mechanism for the reassertion of the 'control culture' that featured in his earlier, co-authored work.[69]

The libertarian narrative exists only in embryonic form and is in need of more work and clearer definition. However, one can obtain a glimpse of how it can be projected back in time through research into media representations of 'out' groups. These helped to establish boundaries delineating what was acceptable.

During the 1880s, the press supported an outcry against gay men (accompanied by the strengthening of penal legislation), followed by a comparable crusade against lesbians in the 1920s. Representations of sexual minorities continued to be strongly hostile until there was a softening of media homophobia in the 1960s (accompanied by the partial decriminalisation of gay sex). Even so, gay people were often presented on British television in the 1970s as being either silly or threatening. The 1980s witnessed a dichotomisation in TV drama: positive portrayals of gay men tended to be confined to those who appeared reassuringly asexual, while the sexualised were more often projected in strongly negative ways. It was only at the turn of the century that gay people were more often featured as 'ordinary'.[70] The symbolic turning point was the British TV series *Queer As Folk* (1999–2000), a soap opera set in Manchester's gay village. It portrayed, in bright primary colours, a young generation of gay men as intelligent, attractive, heterogeneous and 'normal': free of shame or concealment and relatively untouched by the stigmata of traditional celluloid representation. The perspective of the series' narrative, the gaze of its camera, even its sex scenes, normalised rather than pathologised being gay. It marked a milestone of social change, followed by legislation in the early 2000s that ended some forms of continuing discrimination against gays and lesbians.

Another way in which the libertarian narrative can be extended over time is through studies of moral regulation of the media. There was draconian censorship in the first half of the twentieth century (especially in relation to sex, morality and bad language) but this tended to diminish overall during the second half.

Technological determinism

The last of the alternative interpretations of media history, technological determinism, transcends national frontiers and represents a proposed 'master narrative'. Instead of seeing the media as linked to change, it portrays the media – or rather communications technology – as being the origin and fount of change.

There are a number of classic studies advancing this position. Harold Innis argues that each new medium of communication changed the organisation of society by altering dimensions of time and space.[71] Elizabeth Eisenstein maintains that the printing press contributed to cultural advance in early modern Europe by preserving and making more widely available the intellectual achievements of the past.[72] Marshall McLuhan claims that electronic media fostered a 'retribalised', syncretic culture by re-engaging simultaneously the human senses.[73] Joshua Meyrowitz argues that the universality of television changed social relations by demystifying the 'other'.[74]

This tradition is now being renewed through accounts which argue that the Internet is fundamentally changing the world. The Internet, we are told, is 'blowing to bits' traditional business strategy;[75] rejuvenating democracy;[76] empowering the people;[77] inaugurating a new era of global enlightenment;[78] transforming human sensibility;[79] rebuilding community;[80] generating a self-expressive culture;[81] and undermining, with interactive television, established media empires.[82]

There is only sufficient space here to register briefly two points in relation to these studies. A review of the evidence strongly suggests that the offline world influences the online world – in particular its content and use – more than the other way around. However, this should not lead us to accept a social determinist position, the mirror opposite of technological determinism, which is now gaining ground. This last sees the Internet – and by implications all new communications technology – as merely an extension of society reproducing, in a closed loop, its culture and social relations. This misses the point that the specific attributes of internet technology (its international reach, cheapness, interactivity and hypertextuality) make a difference. Social determinism also tends to present society as a simplifying abstraction, instead of investigating the ways in which the architecture, content, use and influence of the Internet have been shaped by interacting and contending forces within society that have evolved and changed over time.[83]

Wider issues in relation to the development of new media continue to be explored. For example, Paddy Scannell makes an eloquent case that communications technology has built a better world, though most of his essay is about technology in general (from the atomic bomb to washing machines) and is therefore utterly irrelevant to a discussion of media development.[84] Graham Murdock and Michael Pickering address one aspect of the modernist thesis, arguing that the telegraph and photography have not automatically promoted communication and understanding through killing distance: in fact, they have been misused to extend control and to impede understanding through objectification.[85] In a similar vein, Menaham Blondheim argues that the starting point of many influential techno-determinist accounts – their view of communications technology as autonomous – is misleading.[86]

Technological determinist media history, based on the argument that new media technologies have transformed society in successive waves, has been highly influential. But it has limitations and is in need of academic revision.

Lost narratives

Where does this leave us? The obvious next step is to construct alternative syntheses of the seven narratives in a battle of meta-narratives. However, rather than recapitulate my own outline version,[87] it is perhaps more useful to reflect upon what has been left out of this review.

I set about writing my original essay, after some initial difficulty, by listing on a sheet of paper key trends in British history and then reflecting upon what the available media-historical literature said in relation to each of these. Some trends I had to omit because there was no relevant media historical research to sustain a 'narrative'. The six trends that survived this winnowing process were: (1) national unification; (2) mass democracy; (3) defeat of socialism; (4) advance of women; (5) rise of consumer society; and (6) decline of religion/moral traditionalism.

But this leaves out important developments in the history of Britain in which the media played a part. It is worth drawing attention to four 'lost narratives', in particular, which failed to make the shortlist. They merit further investigation.

The most glaring omission is the building of the welfare state, linked to a 'reformist' narrative of media development. Adapting rather freely a celebrated essay by the social democratic theorist T. H. Marshall[88] it is possible to see British history as an evolving, collective struggle for securing human rights: civil rights (notably the right to assembly and equal justice), political rights (the right to vote), social rights (including access to free health care and social security) and cultural rights (including access to 'cultural privilege', public-affairs information and symbolic representation). The first of these two struggles had been largely (but not wholly) won by 1918. The period from 1918 to the present marked the intensification of the collective battle for social and cultural entitlements. Late nineteenth- and early twentieth-century advances in social welfare were greatly extended in the 1940s to include state protection 'from the cradle to the grave'. In the cultural sphere, nineteenth-century advances – free elementary schools, public libraries, parks, museums and galleries – were extended in the next century through the expansion of free education, public-service broadcasting, creative arts subsidies and the creation of the *free* World Wide Web.

This historical perspective bears some resemblance to that proposed by Graham Murdock.[89] Ross McKibbin's fine study is a key source for this narrative, showing the way in which a solidaristic working-class culture, supported by popular entertainment, reached its zenith of confidence and influence in the 1940s.[90] Elements of this narrative are to be found in a study by James Curran and Jean Seaton, which dwells, in three chapters, on the 1940s, a time when much of the media system (including a radicalised section of the wartime press) contributed to building a consensus in favour of a consolidated welfare state.[91] This study also differentiates between the positive role of public-service broadcasting (including *regulated* commercial TV) and of the web, and the negative role of a debased press – a theme partly shared with other histories.[92] This critical celebration of public-service broadcasting is supported by other studies documenting the development of innovative public-service TV journalism;[93] the BBC's struggle to defend public-service virtues under siege;[94] public-service TV's extension of symbolic representation in the second half of the twentieth century;[95] and, of course, Asa Briggs' (1961–85) history of the BBC.[96] More generally, there is a strong historical tradition of policy analysis that examines successful and failed attempts to reform the media and to resist neo-liberal transformation (although some of these authors would object vehemently to being characterised as 'reformist' historians).[97] There are rich secondary materials available for the development of a reformist media history, especially in the twentieth century. But these are currently too fragmented, and more importantly their perspectives are too internally divided, for this proto-history to make it into the 'canon' of established media-historical narratives. But there is a gap here that needs to be filled.

The second missing dimension is a narrative that describes the distributional battles between social classes in terms of power, status and material rewards, and describes the evolving role of the media in relation to these. Surveying the last two centuries, there have been two major losers: the aristocracy, which used to rule Britain (but does so no longer), and the working class, which was once a powerful political, economic and cultural force but which has now contracted, subdivided and in important respects lost ground. The great victors have been key sectors of the bourgeoisie best adapted to the globalising economy. A class media narrative can be constructed for the nineteenth century, but – because of the present state of research and shifting fashion – it loses coherence by the later twentieth century. In essence, this would be a more ambitious version of the radical narrative we have now.

The third lost dimension is the rise of the British economy (and associated gains in living standards and job creation) paired with an economic history of the British media. Britain became the 'first industrial nation', was overtaken by the US and then evolved into a service-based economy. This seems to have parallels with the development of British media. Imperial Britain played a key role in the development of telegraph technology and of news agencies. But it was the US, not Britain, which pioneered industrialised, mass journalism, while Hollywood locked horns with, and defeated, the British film industry by 1910. Britain failed also to capitalise on the construction of a pioneer digital computer in 1944 and its prominent role in the development of packet-switching network technology during the 1960s. Yet, Britain became (and remains) the second biggest exporter of TV programmes in the world. Whether there are links between the successes and failures of the British economy and of the British creative industries would be an interesting avenue to explore. Stefan Schwarzkopf has made a pioneer contribution to this potential 'narrative' by examining the American take-over of much of the British advertising industry, at a time when many British agencies were slow to respond to the rise of commercial television.[98]

A fourth theme was half in, and half out of, my review. This featured a techno-logical determinist view of new communications technology in a supranational context. It was not possible to present an alternative version of this perspective in a UK context, given the existing nature of research. Good work has been done in this general area, but primarily limited to researching influences shaping communications technology and mostly in other countries.[99] But it would be interesting to develop a national account of how new communications technology changed British politics, culture and social relations.

Retrospect

In short, what I came up with was necessarily highly selective. It offered only a partial account, dictated by what was available rather than what was needed. But, hopefully, its portrayal of how the media contributed to the making of modern Britain – as a series of competing narratives – will provoke further discussion and serve as an antidote to the narrowness of too much media history.[100]

Of course, specialist studies provide the essential building blocks of all areas of enquiry. But it is also important to advance a tradition of media history that seeks ambitiously to situate historical investigation of the media in a wider societal context. In due course, this approach should widen the context still further through comparative research.[101]

9 Press as an agency of social control

Introduction

The social and political roles of newspapers have been conceptualised by historians in a seemingly infinite variety of ways: as agencies of social reform, forums for the exchange of ideas, purveyors of public information, checks on government abuse, sources of diversion and entertainment, the personal platforms of politician-proprietors, agencies of cultural debasement, and so on. The list is apparently endless, and the above is merely a popular shortlist. Yet conspicuously absent from these conventional historical accounts is a conception of the modern British press as an agency of social control.[1]

The omission is no coincidence. To conceive of the press in these terms would mean contesting the framework of analysis in which the press is conventionally discussed. The press is acknowledged to be an instrument of social control only in authoritarian societies, whereas in the free world it is the institutional embodiment of the democratic principle of freedom of expression. A free press, after all, is partly what makes Western democracies free.

The exclusion is scarcely surprising for another reason. It is generally accepted that the press ceased to be an agency of social control when it was no longer an arm of the state. Thus, according to the conventional wisdom, the historical development of the British press can be subdivided into three phases: in its first phase the press was licensed and functioned to support the state; in its second, transitional phase, the press became increasingly independent of state control; and in its third phase, the press became a fully autonomous institution that served the public.

Historians differ over when these three phases began and ended.[2] Some historians also refuse the implied narrative of unfolding progress, and view the late Victorian period as the golden age of journalism when, allegedly, there was a glorious hiatus between the abandonment of government controls and the consolidation of commercial controls.[3] A number of historians are also critical of the commercialisation of the modern press.[4] But few voices are to be heard challenging the basic premise of historical convention: namely that the transition from state to market control of the press marked the shift from subservience to commercial autonomy, transforming a state apparatus into an independent channel of communication between government and governed.

The only discordant note comes from the people celebrated in this historical legend. The courage of early radical journalists directly involved in the struggle against state repression of the press, and their commitment to a free press, is well documented.[5] It has suffused the nineteenth-century parliamentary campaign against state economic controls of the press with a liberal glow that the much-quoted sentiments of middle-class liberals like Richard Cobden seem merely to echo and corroborate. This has given rise to the belief that the parliamentary campaign against the 'taxes on knowledge' was inspired by liberal ideas grounded in Milton, Locke, Mill and the Enlightenment, albeit laced with a 'low politics' desire to dethrone *The Times*.[6]

But what parliamentary campaigners against the 'taxes on knowledge' actually said bore little relationship, as we shall see, to how they are remembered in liberal history. This must raise questions, in turn, about the validity of the historical drama – the emergence of a free press and public empowerment – in which they have featured so prominently.

Rise of the radical press

Before considering the parliamentary campaign against press taxes, it is worth recalling that the first generation of radical papers, which emerged in the Napoleonic Wars, were viewed as a threat to the social order. Secret Service reports that radical papers were being read by common soldiers, and by servants below stairs in the great houses of England, were the subject of anxious parliamentary discussion, fuelling fears of armed insurrection.[7] While this concern was absurdly alarmist, the rise of radical journalism did pose a long-term threat to the social order, because it encouraged people to question its legitimacy. As one parliamentarian complained in 1819:

> Those infamous publications of the cheap press tended to disorganise the very frame of society … they inflame their [the poor's] passions and awaken their selfishness, contrasting their present condition with what they contend to be their future condition – a condition incompatible with human nature, and with those immutable laws which Providence has established for the regulation of civil society.[8]

Radical papers mercilessly lampooned the dominant ideology of a divinely ordained natural order as a fairy tale invented by the rich to cheat the poor. They regularly affirmed the possibility of changing society through political means, both by proclaiming a mythical past, in which abundance and natural justice had prevailed, and by promising the end or relief of poverty through the elimination of aristocratic exploitation. They systematically reviled the monarchy, aristocracy and clergy as a parasitic 'crew' living off the productive community in a sustained assault on the social prestige of the traditional leaders of society. They directly challenged the legitimacy of state institutions, portraying them as merely the oppressive apparatus of a corrupt regime. And the more radical early papers, like *Twopenny Trash* and *Black Dwarf*, identified the agents of radical change as 'the productive classes' in a view of society that explicitly rejected the traditional conception of a socially harmonious hierarchy of rank and degree.

Yet, while early radical papers were viewed as a threat, they were still contained in both a physical and ideological sense. Their distribution was inadequately organised, and their circulation amongst the working class was limited. Their attack on privilege was often set within the framework of the eighteenth-century liberal critique of 'old corruption'. 'Productive classes' were frequently defined as the non-aristocratic strata, including both working masters and their employees; conflict was defined primarily in political terms as a struggle between democracy and aristocracy; and the main focus of their critique of contemporary society was corruption in high places and regressive direct taxation that allegedly impoverished the productive community. The main thrust of their attack was thus defined in terms that would leave the reward structure of society fundamentally unchanged.

However, when the radical press revived in the 1830s, it developed in a new and more combative form.[9] The more militant papers like the *Poor Man's Guardian* argued that there was an underlying conflict between labour and capital, between the working classes and a coalition of aristocrats, 'millocrats' and 'shopocrats'. Underpinning this analysis was a radical view of society as a system of exploitation that was simultaneously economic and political. Poverty was caused – proclaimed militant papers – primarily by the ownership of property, enabling capitalists to appropriate in profits the wealth created by labour. This system of economic exploitation was legitimised and maintained, in turn, by the law made in a parliament which the 'property people elected', by the law courts, the army and the police which they controlled, the capitalist press which they owned and the Church and charity schools which they directed. In short, the radical press shifted its attack from aristocratic political domination to economic exploitation and the ideological and coercive institutions that maintained this exploitation. While the Charter (demanding the vote) became in due course the immediate goal of the radical press, it was not seen as an end in itself. Changing the political system was viewed as the first step to transforming society.[10]

The new generation of radical papers also helped to develop a novel sense of class identity. The labour theory of value which they promoted hailed the working classes as the makers of the country's wealth: the least in society were projected as its most important part, turning upside-down the traditional status hierarchy of society. Radical papers also published news and views that other papers did not carry, highlighting the common predicament of working people as a class and showing that purely local struggles – whether in setting up a trade union, resisting wage cutting, demanding better working conditions or opposing the new poor law – were part of a wider struggle throughout the country (and, increasingly in their pages, in other countries as well). By building national circulations, the new radical press also helped to combat the localism that stood in the way of forging a national working-class movement. The newspaper became, in the words of the Chartist leader Feargus O'Connor, 'the link that binds the industrious classes together'.[11]

The early radical press was also successful in building a substantial, and growing, audience (increased by the public reading aloud of newspapers and the sharing of copies). The principal unstamped radical papers in the early 1830s broke all previous circulation records for weeklies. They were followed by new radical papers, like the *Northern Star* and *Reynolds's Weekly Newspaper*, which achieved even higher circulations. Each reached at their peak between 1838 and 1856 about half a million readers at a time when the population of England and Wales over the age of fourteen was little over 10 million.[12]

The radical press had a less commanding position in relation to its direct rivals in the early 1850s than it had two decades before. The radical analysis that the more militant papers advanced was sometimes fused with the old liberal critique in an uncertain synthesis. But perhaps the key point is that a section of society – shut out from the political system – controlled its own press. It thus had the institutional resources to develop an alternative understanding of society, support its collective organisations and nourish a radical subculture. It was rightly perceived to represent a challenge, in the long term, to the social order.

Parliamentary opposition to press controls

The authorities relied on two ways of controlling radical journalism. The first was the laws of sedition and blasphemy that made fundamental criticism of the social order a criminal offence. However, their effectiveness had been reduced by Fox's Libel Act of 1792, which made juries the judges of guilt or innocence. Since trials generated circulation-boosting publicity, and juries proved increasingly reluctant to convict, seditious libel prosecutions became a blunt instrument against the radical press.

The authorities relied instead on press taxes as a way of containing radical journalism. Stamp, paper and advertising duties inflated the price of newspapers, with the intention of making newspapers too expensive for ordinary people to buy. Press taxes also raised the costs of publishing, with a view to placing control of the press in the propertied class.

The response of the Conservative government to the initial rise of radical journalism was in 1819–20 to extend the scope of the Stamp Duty (a tax, in effect, on newspaper sales), strengthen seditious libel law and introduce a security system requiring bonds to be placed with the authorities before a newspaper could be legally published. Whig opposition to some of these measures was both weak and at times ambiguous.[13] These measures were not revoked when the Whigs regained office. There was also little parliamentary support for repealing press taxes during the 1820s. Joseph Hume's attempt to repeal the Stamp Duty in 1827 – his third – received only ten votes, some of which were probably cast for purely factional reasons.[14] This lack of support was influenced by the fact that radical journalism had declined sharply and press taxes had seemingly proved to be a bulwark against 'sedition'. As Sir James Scarlett, the Whig attorney general, said in 1827 in defence of the Stamp Duty, 'it had shown itself a useful agent in the preservation of the well-being of the state'.[15]

In the early 1830s, radical journalism resurfaced in the more organised form of an underground press that paid no press taxes and was supported by a network of sellers (with a relief system for their families when they were gaoled). The rise of new radical journals caused growing alarm partly because they outsold their rivals. Yet, seditious libel prosecutions again proved ineffectual because of jury recalcitrance. 'A libeller', a disillusioned attorney general complained in 1832, 'thirsted for nothing more than the valuable advertisement of a public trial in a Court of Justice'.[16] The state system of press control had seemingly broken down.

This led in the early 1830s to a number of parliamentary debates about whether to retain press taxes, framed largely in pragmatic terms of how best to destroy the radical press.[17] Traditionalists argued that the government should step up legal prosecutions of unstamped and seditious papers; that the security system and press taxation helped to keep newspapers under 'the control of men of wealth and character' by inflating the costs of publishing; that the Stamp Duty, however imperfect a barrier against 'atrocious publications', at least restricted their circulation by putting up their retail price; and that what was needed was not a change in the law but its tougher enforcement. Reformers argued that, on the contrary, the law was unenforceable because of organised mass resistance; that it merely put control of the popular press in the hands of 'persons of desperate fortunes' who thought nothing of breaking the law; that the Stamp Duty had given rise to a contraband press filled with 'the most pernicious doctrines' that was selling at less than half the price of its taxed and respectable rivals; and that, while 'cheap dangerous publication was not checked', the Stamp Duty 'suppressed the cheap reply' from responsible quarters. Repeal (or reduction) of press taxation, on the other hand, would promote responsible cheap journalism. It would encourage men of capital to invest in an expanding market, increase the flow of advertising to 'the best papers' and enrol 'more temperate and disinterested friends of the people who would lend themselves to their real instruction'.[18]

The two sides in the debate did not fundamentally differ in terms of the goals they wanted to achieve. Both desired a responsible press that upheld the social order.[19] Indeed, one thing that tended to differentiate reformers from traditionalists — apart from a disagreement over tactics — was that reformers generally had a more confident and optimistic attitude towards the role of the press as an agency that could promote social stability and enlightenment. Whereas some traditional adherents of state controls viewed popular journalism in any form with suspicion, reformers argued that cheap newspapers would restabilise the social order. 'We have made a long and fruitless experiment of the gibbet and the hulks', declared Edward Bulwer-Lytton in a speech against the Stamp Duty. 'Is it not time to consider whether the printer and his types may not provide better for the peace and honour of a free state, than the gaoler and the hangman? Whether in one word, cheap knowledge may not be a better political agent than costly punishment?'[20]

Most opponents of press taxes, in parliamentary circles, were as 'controlling' in their approach as supporters of press taxes. Indeed, one of the reformers' central themes in the 1830s was that cheap newspapers, owned by businesspeople, would pacify workers. Francis Place, the secretary of the Society for the Promotion of the Repeal of the Stamp Duties, told a Parliamentary Select Committee in 1832 that 'there would not have been a single trades union either in England or Scotland' if the Stamp Duty had been repealed some years earlier.[21] Bulwer-Lytton assured the Commons that 'the recent case of the Dorsetshire labourers' [at Tolpuddle] 'would probably never have occurred' if the Stamp Duty had been repealed. 'Instruction', he explained, 'not the strong arm of the law, was the only effective instrument to put them [the unions] down.'[22] George Grote, the indefatigable campaigner for a free press, went even further, arguing that not only 'the evil of the Unions', but also 'a great deal of the bad feeling that was at present abroad amongst the labouring classes on the subject of wages' was due 'to the want of proper instruction, and correct information as to their real interests' caused by restraints upon a free press.[23] Bulwer-Lytton, Place and Grote were all leading organisers of the parliamentary lobby against press taxes. For them, the cause of a deregulated press was synonymous with the defeat of organised labour.

In the event, the Whig government decided that it was too dangerous to repeal press taxes. Instead, they opted in 1836 for new measures that were designed to rejuvenate a failing system of control. The Stamp Duty was reduced from 4d to 1d, as a strategic concession designed to reduce the advantages of evasion. But financial securities for registering papers were greatly increased; search and confiscation powers were strengthened; and the penalties for having an unstamped newspaper were raised. The purpose of these measures was, as Spring Rice, the chancellor of the exchequer, openly stated, to 'put down the unstamped', 'protect the capitalist' and secure 'a press responsible to the country and the King'.[24]

Although these measures were repressive in both intention and effect, they were opposed by few MPs. And because the reforms 'worked', in the sense that the underground press disappeared and radical papers subsequently paid taxes (and charged much higher prices), it proved difficult to muster much enthusiasm for continued parliamentary opposition to press taxes. A half-hearted attempt was made to repeal the Stamp Duty in 1837, after which the parliamentary campaign was in effect called off.

Revived campaign

It was not until 1848, in very different circumstances, that the campaign to repeal press taxes was reconstituted in the form of the People's Charter Union. The indoctrinating orientation of this campaign was made evident from its first public address, which begged for education about the 'natural laws' governing the production and distribution of wealth:

> By the penny stamp ... it is made impossible for men of education and capital to employ themselves in instructing us. ... We require to know the natural laws by which the production and distribution of wealth are guided, in order that we may quietly submit to these laws and resist all others.[25]

The People's Charter Union (which included some working-class activists) became the Newspaper Stamp Abolition Committee in 1849 and subsequently the grander-sounding Association for the Repeal of the Taxes on Knowledge. Its real composition, by the 1850s, was no secret to its organisers: as Cobden wrote privately, 'exclusively almost, we comprise steady, sober middle-class reformers'.[26]

The broad attraction of the repeal campaign was that, if press taxation was cut and newspaper prices halved, there would be an enormous expansion of the press. This opened up new prospects of influence for a wide variety of groups and causes that came together under the umbrella of the repeal campaign. Some local businessmen and politicians hoped that the expansion of the local press would enhance their position of leadership in their local communities;[27] Conservatives like Disraeli saw in the repeal of the Advertisement Duty a means of increasing advertising support for papers that would popularise their party;[28] a number of senior Liberal politicians hoped that repeal would undermine the ascendancy of *The Times* and assist the rise of the regional press;[29] free-trade radicals like Cobden hoped that the new journalism would encourage greater 'exertions' and mobility among the labouring classes;[30] educationalists saw in repeal a means of extending adult education;[31] and senior policemen proclaimed that cheaper journalism would make reporting of crime and punishment more widely available and so deter criminals and assist in the maintenance of law and order.[32]

These different groups thus perceived in an expanded press an opportunity to promote their specific concerns. But while competing for influence, they were also concerned to shore up the social system, in the wake of the violent agitations of the 1830s and 1840s in Britain and the ominous Continental revolutions of 1848. The theme of social control was a central plank of the parliamentary campaign, something that was proclaimed in an explicit way by stalwarts and converts alike.[33] 'The larger we open the field of general instruction', declared Palmerston when advocating the repeal of the Stamp Duty, 'the firmer the foundations on which the order, the loyalty and good conduct of the lower classes will rest.'[34] Repeal the taxes on knowledge, proclaimed the Irish politician John Maguire, and 'you render the people better citizens, more obedient to the laws, more faithful and loyal subjects, and more determined to stand up for the honour of the country'.[35] 'The freedom of the press', argued Gladstone, 'was not merely to be permitted and tolerated, but to be highly prized, for it tended to bring closer together all the national interests and preserve the institutions of the country.'[36]

But while a fundamental objective of the campaign against press taxes was to extend social control, its rhetoric was modified in the 1850s. Whig history was invoked more often to stigmatise supporters of press taxes as enemies of liberty and the heirs of court censorship of the press. Opposition to press taxation was also expressed more frequently in the form of elevating principle. Freedom of expression should not be taxed; the voice of the people should be heard; truth would confound error in open debate; good publications would drive out bad ones in fair and open competition; and even that truth would only emerge through the interplay of the free marketplace of ideas.[37]

How was it possible for campaigners to speak, almost in the same breath, of both liberty and control? The answer is that no tension was perceived to exist between these two concepts within an intellectual framework that acknowledged no conflict of class interest, but merely a conflict between ignorance and enlightenment, and between the individual and the state. Thus, Alexander Andrews, editor of the first journalists' trade magazine, wrote shortly after the repeal of the Stamp Duty that the great mission of the free press was 'to educate and enlighten those classes whose political knowledge has been hitherto so little, and by consequence so dangerous'. The theme of indoctrination was linked unselfconsciously with liberty. 'The list of our public journals', Andrews continued, 'is a proud and noble list – the roll call of an army of liberty, with a rallying point in every town. It is a police of safety, and a sentinel of public morals.'[38] Within this intellectual universe, there were perceived to be two threats: the masses, in want of proper political education, and the over-weening state. It followed therefore that the press *ought* to be both a guard dog shepherding the public, and a watchdog scrutinising government.

Informing the campaign against press-specific taxes was also a growing commitment to free trade. The benefits of free competition had been invoked in the successful campaign against agricultural protection, resulting in the repeal of the Corn Laws in 1846. They were invoked also in the 1850s in attacks on public appointments through social connection that led to a cumulative overhaul of the armed forces and civil service that extended middle-class access to well-remunerated employment. Free trade was thus associated with the legitimation and extension of the interests of the professional and industrial middle class.

In the context of the press, there was an implicit confidence that press deregulation would enable middle-class enlightenment to prevail. This was based partly on the assumption that the press would develop as a top-down system of communication. The growth of a cheap press, explained William Hickson, a leading campaigner, would enrol journalists 'two or three degrees' above the labouring classes to enlighten them.[39] To Gladstone, the principal attraction of repeal was that more men of 'quality' would be deployed in educating the people through the press.[40] 'A perfectly free press is one of the greatest safeguards of peace and order', wryly commented the lawyer J. F. Stephen, because able journalists come from 'the comfortable part of society, and will err rather on the side of making too much of their interests than on that of neglecting them'.[41]

The leaders of the 1850s free-press campaign also grasped more clearly than their predecessors that the free market favoured some more than others. The repeal of press taxes, declared Thomas Milner-Gibson, President of the Association for the Repeal of the Taxes on Knowledge, would create 'a cheap press in the hands of men of good moral character, of respectability, and of capital'.[42] Aware of the high costs of popular newspaper publishing in the US,[43] he stressed, in common with other leading campaigners, that state deregulation would 'give to men of capital and respectability the power of gaining access by newspapers ... to the minds of the working classes'.[44] The free market, argued Sir George Lewis, the Liberal chancellor of the exchequer, would promote papers 'enjoying the preference of the advertising public'.[45] The expanding market press, it was also hoped, would influence demand since 'the appetite grows by what it feeds on'.[46]

But perhaps the key to the success of the campaign against press taxes was a growing sense – absent in the turbulent 1830s – that it was now safe to 'trust' the people. The Chartist movement had peaked in 1848 and fell into sharp decline thereafter. There was, proclaimed one veteran parliamentarian, 'a great increase of intelligence among the people'.[47] Seditious ideas, and the ignorance that had given rise to them, were everywhere on the retreat. It was this diagnosis of the mood of the country that led Whig politicians like Palmerston to accept somewhat reluctantly that there was 'no real danger to the morals or loyalty of the country' in repealing press taxes.[48] Others, like Bright, Roebuck and Thomas Spencer, who were less certain whether the working class would 'become the glory, or might prove greatly dangerous, to the peace of the country', nonetheless stressed the need to take advantage of the breathing space afforded by the increased tranquillity of the people to combat disaffection through a popular press.[49] But, significantly, those convinced that 'the lower and poorer classes' were wedded to 'prejudices' inconsistent with 'the interests of society in general' were hostile to repeal.[50] They included not only conservative traditionalists but also some liberals, like the political economist J. R. McCulloch, strongly in favour of free trade in other areas of life.[51]

It was this rising tide of optimism that led ultimately to the abolition of press taxes. This tide was skilfully harnessed by seasoned campaigners who established and packed a Commons Select Committee (and largely wrote its report), won allies among civil servants, harried sometimes poorly briefed ministers, organised public meetings, petitions and deputations and lobbied newspapers (which were divided over the Stamp Duty).[52] Their virtuosity was rewarded with the abolition of the Advertisement Duty in 1853, the Stamp Duty in 1855, the Paper Duty in 1861 and the security system in 1869.[53]

In short, the respectable campaign for a free press independent of state economic control was never actuated by a commitment to freedom and diversity of expression, in a contemporary sense. On the contrary, the reasons that led parliamentarians to support further economic restrictions on the press in 1819–20, and the crackdown on the radical press in 1836, were fundamentally no different from those that inspired the lifting of controls in the 1850s. Both the proponents and opponents of state control were concerned to ensure that the press provided institutional support for the social order. All that had changed was a growing commitment to positive indoctrination of the lower orders through a cheap press and a growing conviction that free trade and normative controls were a morally preferable and more efficient control system than direct controls administered by the state. Underlying this shift was the growing power and confidence of Victorian middle class reformers who dominated the parliamentary campaign for repeal of press taxes and recognised in the expanding press a powerful agency that would advance their interests.

Change of journalism

In the period after the repeal of press taxes, British journalism was transformed. A number of radical newspapers closed down or were incorporated into the mainstream of liberal journalism. A new generation of local dailies, often controlled by local notables, was established and new national titles – many on the right – were launched. Parliamentary campaigners for the repeal of press taxes were thus entirely right in believing that the free market would be more effective than state controls in conscripting the press to the social order.

Whereas the early militant press had sustained the development of an autonomous working-class movement, and fuelled suspicion of middle-class reformists with a barrage of criticism against 'sham-radical humbugs' and 'the merciful middle class converts to half Chartism at half past the eleventh hour',[54] the new regional daily press that emerged immediately after the lifting of the Stamp Duty was closely affiliated to the two political parties. This new press played an important role in building popular support for these and thus contributed directly to the integration of the activist working class into the political system.

The new regional press was also an important agency of socio-cultural integration in the local community. Radical papers like the *Northern Star* had provided a round-up of local news, focusing upon and amplifying stories of conflict ('to talk of reconciliation between the middle and working classes in Leicester will, henceforth, be a farce'[55] is not untypical of the paper's polarising style). In contrast, its successors tended to block out conflict, minimise economic differences and encourage positive identification with the local community, its traditions and middle-class leadership. A typical story in the *Leeds Mercury* (published in the same city as the *Northern Star*) is a report of local MPs, the mayor and the newspaper proprietor addressing the annual public soirée of the Leeds Mechanics Institute on the subject of 'these popular institutions, sustained by the united efforts of all classes ... thereby to promote the virtue, happiness and peace of the community'.[56]

While it is difficult to generalise about multiple titles, and while it is important to register the fact that there developed significant differences between mainstream papers over key issues like women's rights, union protection and war, yet there was a tendency for radical themes to be effaced or diluted in the post-1856 press. This is perhaps best illustrated by the contrast in the way Queen Victoria was represented. The radical press in the period 1837 to 1855 was aggressively republican: the queen was vilified as politically partisan and reactionary, the head of a system of organised corruption, the mother of a brood of royal 'cadgers' and the friend and relative of royal tyrants in continental Europe. There was a transitional phase when some mainstream newspapers were critical, especially during the queen's extended 'retirement'. But from the mid-1870s onwards, the queen was presented as a dutiful and benign matriarch who symbolised in an almost talismanic way the moral and material progress of her reign. The tenor of this coverage is reflected in *Lloyd's Weekly*, the biggest-circulation paper in Britain at the time, and, as a Liberal paper, on the 'left':

> Looking back over the sixty years Her Majesty has occupied the throne she has seen the growth of this great Empire, the expansion of the colonies, the increase of prosperity and comfort of her people, and the strengthening of the ties that make for the federation of all the English speaking races united with us under the British flag.[57]

Structural transformation of the press

The main cause of this sea change was the political upheaval that took place in Victorian Britain. The collapse of Chartism in the 1850s was followed by the transformation of parliamentary parties into popular movements, franchise extensions, the introduction of progressive social reforms, the development of a more pragmatic union leadership, rising real incomes generated by a successful economy and the growth of popular imperialism.

But the reconfiguration of British journalism also came about as a consequence of the structural transformation of the press industry. Where the state security system had failed, the free market succeeded in regulating ownership of the press. As mentioned earlier, the government had introduced in 1819 a requirement on would–be publishers to deposit bonds, ostensibly to guarantee payment in the event of being found guilty of a libel suit, but in reality, as Lord Castlereagh had openly stated in 1819, to ensure 'that persons exercising the power of the press were men of some respectability and property'.[58] The bonds had been set at £300 for London papers and £200 for provincial papers, sums that some on the opposition benches had protested at the time were too high. These bonds were then increased in 1836 by between 30 per cent and 50 per cent depending on location, again with the objective of vesting press ownership in 'respectable' hands. In practice, they were set too low to prevent the continued growth of the radical press.

However, the costs of publishing were subsequently increased well over a hundredfold by the capitalist development of the press. Expensive technology was developed to feed a mass market, leading to the installation of massive Linotype and web rotary machines. The scale of newspaper operations greatly increased, reflected in higher pagination levels, the employment of more staff and larger overheads. Initial outlay costs could be minimised through employing an independent printer (the strategy adopted by the radical *Daily Herald*, launched in 1912). However, it was the operating costs of publishing that soared, forcing up the circulation threshold that needed to be crossed before a paper broke even. Starting, and more especially establishing, newspapers for the popular market became prohibitively expensive.

The extent of this change can be illustrated by two examples, one at the beginning and the other at the end of the period of press industrialisation.[59] The two examples are, in the context of their time, similar. The *Northern Star*, launched in 1837, became by 1839 the second-biggest-selling weekly newspaper in Britain: the *Sunday Express*, launched in 1918, also subsequently gained the second-largest 'weekly' newspaper circulation in Britain. But there the resemblance ended. The *Northern Star* needed only £690 to be launched, with a further outlay of £400 in its early days: its break-even threshold was about 6,200 copies and it moved into profit within a month.[60] By contrast, the *Sunday Express* required over £2.5 million before it made money: it was still unprofitable with a circulation of well over 250,000 and it took years to move into the black.[61] A modest public subscription, raised mostly in northern towns, with a small supplement from its publisher, Feargus O'Connor, was sufficient to launch and establish the *Northern Star*, but it needed the resources of an international conglomerate headed by Beaverbrook to do the same for the *Sunday Express*.

Whereas it had been possible for people with modest resources to launch a nationally successful paper in the 1830s, this had long been impossible by the 1920s. This shift had profound consequences. Some leading newspapers in the first half of the nineteenth century had been owned by people drawn from the ranks of the working class, or their sympathisers. In the post-Stamp Duty period, the popular press was overwhelmingly owned by wealthy businesspeople.

The second key economic change was that the press became dependent on advertising. The radical press in the period up to 1856 had been able to make profits largely on the proceeds of sales alone.[62] They differed from their rivals, most of whom attracted significant advertising.[63] But in the post-Stamp Duty period, all newspapers charging competitive prices in the popular market required substantial advertising. This was the consequence of two changes: the surge in costs, noted above, and successive reductions in newspaper prices from a modal price of 5d in the early 1850s to ½d in the 1890s, the result not just of the repeal of press taxes but also the rapid growth of press advertising from 1853 onwards.[64] However, radical papers found it difficult to stay afloat in this new financial environment because they encountered strong advertising discrimination.

As I have argued elsewhere, this pattern of discrimination played a critical role in the destruction, containment or incorporation of the early radical press.[65] It had five observable consequences: some radical papers were forced to close down with circulations far larger than those of their rivals; others were contained in small-readership ghettoes, charging high prices, with manageable losses that could be met out of private donations; others moved upmarket and moderated their radicalism as a survival strategy, partly in order to court the more affluent readers that advertisers wanted to reach; and still others (like the early *Daily Herald*) survived by relying upon an alternative source of institutional patronage.

These two key changes in the press industry – the rise in costs and increased dependence on advertising – remoulded the Victorian press. When the left regained momentum in the two decades before the 1914–18 war, the radical press remained relatively weak as a result of these structural constraints.[66] Indeed, when the Labour Party (in effect formed in 1900) won 22 per cent of the vote in the 1918 general election, it lacked the support of a single national daily.[67]

Reformed social system

In 1918, the majority of British adults acquired for the first time the right to vote and to determine their political rulers. This helped the centre-left to build electoral support for an extension of the state in ways that limited people's exposure to risk, provided essential public services and redistributed resources and life opportunities in favour of less advantaged groups. In effect, the social system was modified, with a watershed change taking place in the 1940s.

The press duly adapted to the new political consensus in favour of welfare democracy and contributed to normative integration within its terms. The press linked together socially differentiated and geographically dispersed groups, emphasising collective values (for example, 'the national interest') and collective symbols of identification (for example, British sportspeople). It ritually affirmed the rules under which the political system operated (by giving prominence, for instance, to general elections). Its news reporting also tended to construct reality as a series of more or less discrete events that encouraged the belief that the social and political structure was 'natural' – the way things are.

But the dominant weight of the press was situated, most of the time, to the right rather than the centre or left of this welfarist consensus.[68] This is borne out by comparing the sales of newspapers expressing a preference for a political party and the votes cast in general elections. In every general election between 1945 and 1992, the British press was consistently more Conservative than the British public.[69] The biggest discrepancy occurred in February 1974, a bitterly fought general election occasioned by a long-running strike in which the Conservatives invited the electorate to determine 'who runs Britain?'. The third Royal Commission on the

Press estimated that, in that election, 'the share of newspaper circulation held by papers supporting the Conservative Party was 71% greater than Conservative votes as a percentage of votes cast'.[70] This Conservative preponderance was temporarily ended between 1997 and 2005, as a consequence of a tacit deal between the dominant press controller, Rupert Murdoch, and the New Labour leader, Tony Blair, even though Murdoch's New Labour-supporting papers continued to espouse rightwing politics. The 2010 general election marked a resumption of Conservative one-sidedness.[71]

The rightist orientation of the British press was revealed in other ways. The press stigmatised a succession of groups on the left: conscientious objectors in the First World War, trade unionists in the 1926 General Strike, the Unemployed Workers' Movement in the 1930s, the squatters movement in the 1940s, militant disarmament campaigners in the 1950s, anti-Vietnam War protestors in the 1960s, union militants in the late 1970s and the municipal 'loony left' in the 1980s, among others.[72] These groups tended to be characterised as irrational, unrepresentative and a threat to the majority.

By contrast, the press was more open to rightwing than leftwing ideas. This was especially noticeable in the 1980s, when a large section of the national press supported the Thatcher government's privatisation, anti-union and 'small state' policies, as well as its repudiation of liberal corporatism (the way Britain had been run from 1940 to 1979). But even during this period, the press did not attack the core institutions of the welfare state like the National Health Service. And apart from a brief period in the 1930s, when Lord Rothermere's newspapers supported a British fascist party, the British press was – unlike some of its European counterparts – consistently critical of the anti-democratic right.

Partial adaptation

The right-of-centre preponderance of the national press was an inheritance from the Victorian era. Adaptation was further limited by high publishing costs that sealed off market entry. Between 1914 and 1977, no new national daily was established in Britain, with the marginal exception of the thin, tiny circulation, Communist-controlled *Daily Worker/Morning Star* (launched in 1930). The much-vaunted print revolution of the 1980s bequeathed one new, surviving national daily: the *Independent*, now owned by a Russian oligarch.

Yet, significant changes did take place within the news environment. The market system was not fixed and immutable, and the controls embedded within it were not unchanging. The Victorian legacy was modified in one very significant way. It is to this that we now turn.

10 Advertising as a bounty system

Introduction

In the mid-Victorian era, radical publishers faced a toxic combination of economic and political prejudice.[1] Their publications tended to be rejected by advertisers on the grounds that their readers had limited money to spend on goods and services. As the head of a leading advertising agency wrote in 1856, 'some of the most widely circulated journals in the Empire are the worst possible to advertise in. Their readers are not purchasers, and any money thrown upon them is so much money thrown away.'[2] By contrast, smaller-circulation papers reaching a better class of reader tended to be preferred. As an advertising handbook recommended in 1851, 'A journal that circulates a thousand among the upper or middle classes is a better medium than would be one circulating a hundred thousand among the lower classes.'[3]

Radical publishers also suffered from the partial politicisation of advertising. In 1856, the leading advertising directory detailed the political views of the principal London and local newspapers with the proud boast that 'till this Directory was published, the advertiser had no means of accurately determining which journal *might be best adapted to his views, and most likely to forward his interests*' (emphasis added).[4] The Liberal *Daily News* was boycotted by some advertisers when it embraced Irish Home Rule.[5] Similarly, the Liberal *Pall Mall Gazette* lost substantial advertising when its editor, William Stead, 'procured' a thirteen-year-old girl as part of the paper's campaign against child prostitution.[6] Conservative papers could also encounter discrimination. In 1893, the incoming Liberal home secretary, Herbert Asquith, was told that generally 'it is the custom to transfer advertisements according to the politics of governments'.[7] The leftwing press stood to lose most from this politicisation since few advertisers were on the left.

The early 1920s

This legacy had been modified by the early 1920s. The growth of production for the mass market had encouraged some advertisers to turn to large-circulation newspapers and magazines. Advertising was also much less politicised than it had been in the 1850s. Even so, a Conservative paper like the *Daily Mail* still thought it worthwhile to boast in the late 1920s of its 'fearless advocacy of every measure and movement likely to be of benefit to British commercial enterprise' in its pitch to advertisers.[8]

When advertiser prejudice occurred, it tended to be expressed as a subjective assessment of readership and impact. Subjectivism loomed large in advertising selection in the early 1920s, something that is exemplified by advertising guru Thomas Russell. His many books on advertising were widely read,[9] and he was remembered by a well-known advertising trade journalist as 'the leader of the profession until his death'.[10] Russell's pronouncements combined implausible assertion with whimsical observation. The *Daily Telegraph*, he declared, was 'the unequalled medium' for advertising musical instruments because it has 'a big Jewish circulation, and everyone knows that the Jews are the most musical race in the world'.[11] The sobriety of *The Times*, he argued, disposes readers to order through the tradesman, whereas the style of the *Daily Mail* encourages the reader to respond directly to mail-order advertisements 'because when he reads the *Daily Mail*, he is in a "*Daily Mail*" frame of mind – rather eager, rather excitable, rather energetic, not so dignified and formal'.[12]

In common with others, Russell was working in a fog of uncertainty engendered by the absence of reliable data.[13] Immediately after the war, circulation figures were often unavailable or misleading,[14] and survey-based readership research did not exist. Advertisers had therefore to improvise. As the Pitman's advertising guide explained, 'the class of reader reached by different papers can usually be judged fairly accurately from the general appearance of the paper and the nature of its contents'.[15] This could lead to the inadvertent stereotyping of newspaper readers. 'A stodgy paper', wrote Cecil Freer, a lecturer in advertising, 'is read by stodgy people; the socialist press has a following of people who … cannot persuade the world to share its wealth with them.' This simple projection of the attributes of readers from the editorial content of papers could offer an apparently sound economic justification for excluding downscale publications from advertising schedules. 'You cannot afford', continued Freer, 'to place your advertisement in a paper which is read solely by the down-at-heels who buy it to scan the "Situations Vacant" column.'[16]

This concern to exclude the poor – and publications they read – was reinforced rather than challenged by pioneer market research. When in 1926 a survey for a cereal manufacturer asked, 'Do you believe in light, highly nourishing breakfasts, or making breakfast a very substantial meal?', the report noted uncomfortably that in some northern districts the question was 'very difficult to ask, and in some cases proved to be cruel'.[17] While avoidance of the destitute made commercial sense, early market research tended to underestimate the size of the working-class market as a result of flawed sampling procedures. For example, one major commercial survey represented the middle class as constituting 53 per cent of the British population in 1928.[18] The head of the market research company that conducted this survey thought it sensible to avoid all slums and poor areas.[19]

A modified form of economic and political discrimination by some advertisers thus represented a formidable obstacle to the growth of radical journalism in the 1920s in a context where the press was dependent on advertising. Thus, when the leftwing *Daily Herald* was relaunched as a national daily in 1919, its circulation rose sharply, with calamitous results. Its cover price, set at the same level as its rivals, did not cover costs, yet the paper failed to attract significant advertising. 'The rise in circulation', mourned its editor, George Lansbury, '… brought us nearer to disaster' since the more copies the paper sold, the greater were its losses.[20] The *Daily Herald* then doubled its price, causing its rise in circulation to falter. In 1922, it was acquired by the TUC (Trades Union Congress). This imposed a new form of control in which the *Daily Herald's* former radicalism was partly subdued in response to pressure from moderate trade union leaders.[21]

Advertising discrimination partly explains why the rise of the left in the 1920s was not matched by a corresponding rise of radical journalism. Most workers read a Sunday but not a daily paper, also encouraging journalistic under-representation of the left. The Labour Party won 29.5 per cent of the vote in the 1922 general election.[22] Yet, it had the support of perhaps 4 per cent of national daily circulation.[23]

Cumulative transformation

An intuitive approach to advertising placement gradually gave way to a more objective mode of assessment. This change was uneven and took place over half a century. But the crucial period of transition was the late 1920s and the 1930s, when developments in the process of media selection and market analysis, combined with important market changes, altered the way advertising was allocated.

The key drivers of change were the major advertising agencies during the interwar period. They prospered as a consequence of 'recognition' agreements with publishers that prevented advertisers from buying space on the same preferred basis and undermined agencies that split their commission with clients. Competition through service rather than price promoted the development of increased expertise in advertising selection.

Typical of the leading group of advertising agencies was the London Press Exchange (LPE), founded in 1892. In 1927, it established a research department, mainly concerned with marketing and consumer research, and a statistical department responsible for media data analysis and the preparation of media advertising schedules. Company archives show that it was largely the work of these two departments which transformed LPE's advertising media planning during the late 1920s and early 1930s.

Change was facilitated by the provision of more reliable data. After the First World War, the Association of British Advertising Agents (ABAA) campaigned for the release of circulation data, even establishing its own independent audit.[24] This initiative was consolidated in 1931 with the establishment of the Audit Bureau of Circulation (ABC) with the backing of advertisers, agencies and some publishers. But a number of leading publishers still refused to co-operate with the ABC, and their circulation claims were often highly misleading.[25] By 1936, however, the ABC monitored the circulation of 186 publications, while circulation estimates of varying degrees of reliability were available for most important publications not scrutinised by the ABC.[26] The increasing availability and reliability of circulation data caused cost per 1,000 circulation to become more important as a criterion of media selection. The principal beneficiaries of this shift were papers with cheap advertising rates and significant circulations, regardless of their politics. The records of the London Press Exchange reveal, for instance, that the *Daily Herald* came to be included for the first time in major campaigns aimed at the mass market from 1927 onwards.

The provision of more reliable circulation data was overtaken by a development of still greater importance: the rise of readership research. The first 'official' readership survey (sponsored by the Institute of Incorporated Practitioners in Advertising) was conducted in 1930, though it was preceded by earlier private surveys.[27] This breakthrough was followed, in the next nine years, by numerous readership surveys commissioned by advertising industry bodies, agencies and publishers.[28] Although readership research met with initial mistrust (and the words 'circulation' and 'readership' were sometimes used interchangeably, indicating early confusion), this resistance was increasingly overcome. Readership surveys – especially when sampling methods improved in the mid-1930s – provided statistical information about the social composition of newspaper and magazine readers that was much more reliable than subjective inference from content. The classic advertising textbook of the 1930s advised that 'the first test that must always be applied to a press advertising medium is the cost of placing an advertisement of a given size before a given number of suitable readers'.[29] This precept was not new, but the ability to implement it objectively was, as a consequence of the rise of readership research.

This new input encouraged conventional stereotypes of newspaper readers to be overturned. For example, a London Press Exchange executive advised the manufacturers of Farmers' Glory in 1935 to advertise in the *Daily Herald* because 'though primarily it caters for an artisan and lower middle class market, it also reaches a considerable percentage of the population of slightly higher earning capacity'.[30] This observation was a direct reference to the official readership survey of the previous year.[31]

Innovative business researchers also attempted to develop statistical measures of media influence. Between 1933 and 1939, at least five surveys were conducted – in two instances with samples of over 20,000 respondents – into the levels of attention given to advertisements, in different positions, in national newspapers.[32] Some agencies also undertook major analyses of keyed advertisement responses. While this last was useful only in terms of gauging the mail-order effectiveness of rival media, it was indicative of a new, more scientific approach to advertising placement.

There was also a substantial increase in national advertising expenditure, in response to the growth of the economy and mass consumption.[33] Per capita consumer expenditure at constant (1913) prices rose from £42 in 1921 to £49 in 1930, and to £54 in 1938.[34] This led to a boom in some consumer mass-market products: between 1924 and 1935, for instance, consumer expenditure on electrical appliances rose by 438 per cent, on bicycles by 231 per cent, on cosmetics and perfumes by 138 per cent, with further substantial increases on wooden furniture, radios and gramophones and women's clothing.[35] These increases were due, in part, to rising levels of real income among working people during the Depression, providing they had jobs.[36] In effect, increased consumption by the working class generated increased advertising expenditure on publications reaching working-class consumers.

What mattered was not merely objective change but also the development of tools for understanding this change. The growing influence and sophistication of market research brought home the importance of the working-class market and of the media serving it. Typical of this shift was the radically different advice given by J. Walter Thompson (JWT) to a major client, Sun-Maid Raisins, during the late 1920s. 'Research shows', according to a JWT memo, 'that 91.2% of the families of Great Britain have incomes of under £400 … we should concentrate on reaching the immense D class market to the greatest extent possible.'[37] Recognition of the importance of the working-class consumer caused JWT to recommend a shift from 'superior women's magazines', the backbone of Sun-Maid Raisins' advertising campaigns between 1924 and 1929, to newspapers and periodicals with a mass appeal.

An increased orientation towards the mass market was accompanied by greater understanding of its complexity and size. 'The realisation of the intense concentration of wealth in a few hands', wrote Harrison and Mitchell in the leading marketing handbook, 'has led to serious undervaluation of the importance of the "mass market".' 'Inequalities of consumption', they continued, 'are less than inequalities of income and inequalities of income are less than inequalities of wealth.'[38] The same message was projected less abstractly by Odhams, the publisher of the *Daily Herald*, *John Bull* and other publications with a working-class appeal: 'If the housewives who read John Bull', ran a typical advertisement, 'put their purses together next year, they could buy the Giaconda diamond or Da Vinci's "Mona Lisa" hundreds of times over, then they could spend the change on the richest treasures of Bond Street or the Rue de la Paix.'[39]

Market research also emphasised the importance of women as consumers and, therefore, of advertising media appealing to women. In contrast to Chisholm's pioneering marketing textbook of the 1920s,[40] its best-known successor stressed the pre-eminence of the female consumer, even claiming that 'women purchase 80% of the goods sold in retail shops in the country'.[41] Women were distinguished from men in an official readership survey for the first time in 1934. Publishers increasingly stressed the appeal of their publications to women in the advertising trade press during the 1930s.

All these changes had a profound effect on the potential commercial viability of radical journalism. In the first place, they enabled the breakthrough of the pro-Labour *Daily Herald*. It was relaunched in 1929, when Odhams, a major commercial publisher, went into partnership with the TUC and ploughed £3 million into its relaunch. Carrying twice as many pages as before, equipped with a northern as well as a London printing plant and very heavily promoted, the *Daily Herald* increased its circulation from a little over 300,000 in 1928 to 2 million in 1933.[42] It was still making a loss of between £10,000 and £20,000 a week when it became the Western world's largest-selling daily in 1933.[43] Indeed, it carried on making losses in the later 1930s.[44] In 1936, its display advertising revenue per copy was 0.66d, compared with 1.18d per copy earned by the *Daily Mail*.[45] But unlike before, its rise was not suppressed by an untimely price increase, made necessary by lack of advertising. Indeed, between 1932 and 1936, the *Daily Herald* received the second-highest increase of display advertising among national daily papers.[46] By 1936, it obtained over £1.7 million in gross advertising receipts.[47] It had ceased to be an advertising pariah, an essential precondition of its rise.

The change in the economic environment led also to the makeover of the *Daily Mirror*. In the early 1930s, the *Daily Mirror* was a rightwing newspaper in decline, losing about 70,000 circulation a year. It was also thought, as an 'illustrated' tabloid, to be looked at rather than read. This caused it to receive limited advertising, despite its mainly middle- and upper-class readership.[48] Seemingly anticipating closure, its proprietor Lord Rothermere sold his remaining shares in April 1935.[49] This created the opportunity for change since, in the absence of a dominant shareholder, control passed in effect to senior management.[50]

A conscious decision was taken in 1935 to push the paper downmarket. This was a space that had been neglected by publishers. Yet, growing numbers of working-class households were buying a daily for the first time, and advertisers increasingly wanted to reach them. To fill this space implied a change of editorial direction, something that the mostly leftwing journalists in senior positions, like editorial director Harry Bartholomew and features editor Hugh Cudlipp, favoured anyway. But what they wanted was now reinforced by market logic. As Cecil King, the paper's advertising director, pointed out:

> Our best hope was, therefore, to appeal to young, working-class men and women ... If this was the aim, the politics had to be made to match. In the depression of the thirties, there was no future in preaching right-wing politics to young people in the lowest income bracket.[51]

The makeover was assisted by JWT, which advised on changes, urged its clients to back the relaunched paper and unwittingly supplied two executives, Bill Connor and Basil Nicholson, who were to play an influential role in pushing the paper to the left. The *Daily Mirror's* circulation rose from around 700,000 in 1935 to 1.6 million in 1939.[52] After a difficult beginning, its advertising also rose substantially. The paper proudly boasted that its advertising had increased by 670 columns in 1938–9, at a time when six other London dailies had suffered a decline.[53] But its editorial transformation in the 1930s was, in fact, more cautious than it is some-times remembered to have been.[54] And its pitch to advertisers also reflected its concern not to be identified as a working-class newspaper. Indeed, in 1938, the *Daily Mirror* boasted to advertisers that 'only one of the six popular national papers can claim more "A." [upper-class] readers'.[55]

The *Sunday Pictorial*, a sister of the *Daily Mirror*, responded to the same set of economic opportunities and constraints by tacking cautiously downmarket. The change was piloted by its new editor, Hugh Cudlipp, appointed in 1937, and led to a 100,000 circulation gain by 1939.[56]

The shift in the balance of the press – the rise of a mass Labour daily and the detachment of two commercial papers from Conservative moorings[57] – was partly attributable to a change in the climate of opinion during the Depression. Although the 1930s was a period of Conservative political ascendancy, the Labour Party made major advances in local government during the 1930s and secured 35 per cent of the vote in the 1935 general election.[58] The shifting political gravity of the press was also a response to the editorial success of leftist journalists on the *Daily Mirror* and *Sunday Pictorial*. But the shift of the press in the interwar period was also made possible by the redistribution of advertising, as a consequence of increased working-class affluence and changes in the method of advertising media selection. The boulder blocking popular radical journalism had been rolled back.

Wartime liberation

However, advertising disparities still imposed a constraint on the development of radical journalism by penalising newspapers identified with the working class, compared with midscale papers. It was not until the Second World War that the *Daily Mirror* and *Sunday Pictorial* moved much further to the left. This shift reflected the wartime radicalisation of both the Fleet Street milieu and the wider public. In the case of the *Daily Mirror*, radicalisation came about, according to A. C. H. Smith, partly as a consequence of the growing influence of readers' letters and documentary-style reporting on the demotic style and general outlook of the paper. The *Daily Mirror*, he argues, 'placed itself in a position to hear, and then to articulate (in what must be counted one of the most sustained instances of journalistic ventriloquism ever practised) what its readers were feeling and thinking. Thus, in a sense, it *found itself* supporting Labour when the [1945] election came.'[59] But what this illuminating analysis leaves out of account is that wartime regulation facilitated the development of a radicalising rapport between the *Daily Mirror* and its growing working-class readership.

Newsprint rationing, introduced in 1940, led to the reduction of newspapers to a third of their pre-war size. This was accompanied by a voluntary system of advertising rationing that was made compulsory in 1942. The resulting space famine led to a more equal distribution of advertising expenditure across the popular press. Newsprint rationing also reduced costs, inaugurating a period of unprecedented profitability.[60]

It was only in this very different economic environment that the brakes on the *Daily Mirror's* and *Sunday Pictorial's* editorial transformation were lifted. Both papers were free to build solidly proletarian audiences without fear of the consequences in terms of lost advertising revenue. The *Daily Mirror* changed from being the most classless national daily in Britain in 1939, with a readership closely resembling the social composition of British society, to becoming by 1947 a mainly working-class newspaper.[61] The *Sunday Pictorial* made a still bigger change, evolving from being a paper in 1939 with a disproportionately middle-class readership, to becoming a paper in 1947 with a strongly working-class readership.[62]

The *Daily Mirror's* circulation increased from 1.8 million to 3.5 million between 1940 and 1947, while that of the *Sunday Pictorial* rose still further, from 1.7 million to 4 million in the same period.[63] These two commercial pro-Labour papers joined the ranks of the labour-movement press, constituted by the *Daily Herald*, *Daily Worker* and *Reynolds's News* (acquired by the co-operative movement in the 1920s), with ancillary support from the centre-left weekly *Picture Post*, launched in 1938. Not since the Stamp Duty era had the left press been so strong. Indeed, the pro-Labour daily press accounted for 35 per cent of national daily circulation compared with the Labour Party's 48 per cent share of the vote in the 1945 general election.[64] This watershed election greatly extended the welfare state and perpetuated wartime liberal corporatism as a way of running the country.

Post-war consolidation

The transformation of advertising media selection that began in the late 1920s was consolidated in the post-war period. The Audit Bureau of Circulation gained the full co-operation of nearly all leading publishers. Readership research covering the national press became available on a cheap syndicated basis from 1947 onwards and was accepted as an indispensable aid to media planning.[65] Computerisation of media scheduling in the early 1960s made it much easier to calculate quickly and efficiently the cost of reaching a specified market through alternative combinations of media. Product-media analysis (the classification of media audiences in terms of consumer behaviour), first developed in the post-war period by Odhams, Attwood, BMRB and AMPS, came to be adopted on a widespread basis with the introduction of the Target Group Index in 1968. This enabled media planners to calculate the cost of reaching groups of consumers in terms of categories widely used in marketing. These various developments were helpful to the left press by diminishing the scope for subjective judgement and making quantitative calculations more salient as a basis of media selection.

However, overt political bias against radical journalism did not disappear entirely. A minority of advertising agencies told the 1961–2 Royal Commission on the Press that they boycotted publications of 'extremist outlook',[66] those whose 'political creed' is 'in the eyes of public opinion, and our sense of fair play, against the national interest'[67] or which 'unreasonably' pursue 'an editorial policy inimical to a particular industry'.[68] But these were all minor agencies, with the exception of S. H. Benson Ltd, which identified the editorial policy of the communist *Daily Worker* as being 'so diametrically opposed to those of business as to prejudice the chance of successful advertising'.[69] There was another small group of agencies which said that political prejudice could sometimes come into play, but that it always originated from their clients.[70] The occasional persistence of this kind of overt censorship is corroborated by anecdotal evidence. For example, in 1975, one businessman explained to a PA management consultant why he would never advertise in the short-lived, leftwing *Scottish Daily News*: 'I'm not going to keep alive a newspaper which, the first time I get a strike, will back the strikers.'[71]

When political prejudice came into play, it was usually covert and legitimated by an assessment of impact. Thus, one agency in the late 1940s had an openly declared policy of avoiding publications whose editorial policy 'competes with the appeal of the product to be advertised',[72] while another made a point of always considering 'the suitability of a paper as the carrier of advertisements of certain products and ideas'.[73] The censorious implication of this was underscored in the 1960s by Young and Rubicam, then a top agency, which declared that 'the "atmosphere" of a publication – which may include its political leanings – is always taken into account'.[74]

But political bias had ceased to be a pervasive influence on advertising selection by this time because cost of advertisement exposure to the desired audience had become the principal basis for drawing up advertising schedules. The consolidation of this shift is reflected in official handbooks on advertising, published under the imprimatur of the Institute of Practitioners in Advertising. The first text, written by J. W. Hobson and published in five revised editions between 1955 and 1968, included a short chapter that addressed the 'character and atmosphere' of advertising media, and 'the intangible effects of accompanying editorial and advertising'.[75] Its successor, written by J. R. Adams, was brief and disparaging about this qualitative approach: 'Atmosphere, context and impact. These three words, once so important in media planning, have become less popular, largely because of the difficulty of measuring them', and also because, he argued, they could be extremely misleading.[76]

Reinterpreting the market

The adoption of a less intuitive approach to media planning was accompanied by a rapid expansion of market research during the post-war period. The Market Research Society grew from only 23 members in 1947 to over 2,000 members in 1972.[77] Market research was characterised by growing sophistication, reflected in successive textbooks.[78] Whereas there were bitter complaints from market researchers that their work was dismissed by manufacturers as 'an expensive form of witchcraft' in the early post-war period,[79] this scepticism had been largely overcome by the 1970s.

The growth of market research continued to highlight the importance of the working-class market. As Mark Abrams, the doyen of market researchers, wrote in 1950: 'as far as the distribution of purchasing power is concerned, we have become a much more egalitarian economy based on a solid and substantial block of working-class preferences and resources'.[80] Typical of this shift of opinion, informed by market research, is the following evaluation of the *Daily Mirror*, published in an advertising trade journal:

> As an advertising medium there are inevitably reservations, in spite of its high circulation. ... A section of its readership consists of what used to be called 'the lower classes' ... [However,] they may earn less than £600 a year, but they are apparently so well off that they own ... 55% of all television sets, 49% of all cars, 58% of all washing machines and 72% of all motorcycles in the country.[81]

The development of market research also encouraged a more complex conceptualisation of the mass market that made labels like 'lower classes' increasingly redundant. Even by the 1950s, market researchers were stressing that age cycle and family structure were crucial and neglected influences on the demand pattern for products.[82] With the development of greater market segmentation, social class came to be seen as an increasingly inadequate predictor of consumer behaviour, and even as being positively misleading as an indicator of family disposable income.[83] These changes in market cognitions assisted publications with a strong appeal to women and young people – and provided an increased advertising incentive for publishers to reach these groups.

Above all, the more positive assessment of the markets reached by the left press reflected the growth of working-class affluence. Between 1939 and 1965, expenditure per capita at constant prices increased by 49 per cent.[84] This fed a massive increase in spending on heavily advertised products ranging from cosmetics to cars, canned foods to cleaning products.[85] While this was primarily a consequence of sustained economic growth, it was also assisted by the redistribution of personal income after tax in favour of the working class that took place between 1938/9 and 1973/4.[86] This substantial increase in working-class purchasing power invested working-class publications with additional advertising value.

Impersonal nature of the bounty system

The growth of professionalism in advertising media selection, the rise of market research and the increase of working-class incomes all seemed propitious developments for radical journalism. But in fact advertising expenditure shifted, in relative terms, from downscale papers to midscale papers in response to the end of newsprint rationing in 1956. Thus, both the downscale *Daily Herald* and *Sunday Pictorial* received more advertising revenue per copy than their midscale rivals in 1945; ten years later much less; and twenty years later very much less (see Table 10.1).[87]

Indeed, even by 1955, a very clear hierarchy had been established. How much revenue different papers received was partly a function of their class profile. The more upscale their readership, the more advertising revenue per copy they received. This was because the more money readers had to spend, the higher was the bounty their publishers received for delivering them to advertisers.[88]

This redistribution was a reversion to the pattern of a deregulated market. But the wider context rendered this reversion especially problematic for newspapers whose share of advertising decreased. The rise of television, and the reduction of multiple newspaper purchase, resulted in a sustained fall of national newspaper circulations from 1957/8 onwards.[89] The advent of commercial television in

Table 10.1 Advertising revenue per 1,000 copies of selected national newspapers

	1945 £	1955 £	1965 £	1975 £
Dailies				
upscale: *Times*	10.20	24.40	40.51	90.64
midscale: *Daily Express*	0.38	4.61	10.05	16.25
downscale: *Daily Herald/Sun*	0.52	3.86	4.28	11.81
Sundays				
upscale: *Sunday Times*	4.18	22.83	116.38	232.90
midscale: *Sunday Express*	0.91	7.60	24.77	53.56
downscale: *Sunday Pictorial/Sunday Mirror*	1.14	3.69	9.28	19.92

Note
Advertising revenue figures are supplied from publishers, apart from that for the *Sun* in 1975, which is estimated from information presented in the Royal Commission on the Press Interim Report, *The National Newspaper Industry*, London: HMSO, 1976. The advertising revenue figures relate to the financial year but the circulation figures relate to the calendar year. All circulation figures are derived from the Audit Bureau of Circulation, save for those for the *Daily Herald* and *Sunday Pictorial* in 1945, which are based on publishers' estimates.

1955/6 also caused the press's share of advertising to diminish. Television probably caused national advertising to increase (with total display advertising expenditure rising significantly as a percentage of the Gross Domestic Product between 1956 and 1960), which mitigated the press's loss.[90] Even so, downscale papers suffered most from advertising competition with commercial television, since the latter attracted a disproportionately working-class audience. Above all newspapers, locked into fierce competition after the end of newsprint rationing, spent more than they earned, causing a general deterioration in the industry's cost and revenue structure that persisted into the 1960s.[91]

This multiple squeeze led to the death of downscale newspapers with 'minority' audiences. This cull (which killed off minority working-class Conservative papers)[92] resulted in the closure of the *News Chronicle* (1960), a liberal newspaper that was part of the dissenting centre-left tradition; the *Daily Herald* (1964); and the *Sunday Citizen* (1967), previously titled *Reynolds News*. In their last year of publication, these three papers had an aggregate readership of 9.3 million people.[93] They were 'minority' papers only in the context of the mass-circulation press. Their death weakened the social-democratic subculture they had sustained.

While a number of factors contributed to their demise, loss of advertising was especially significant. This is best illustrated by the *Daily Herald*, which suffered not only from having an overwhelmingly working-class readership, but also one that was disproportionately composed of older men. The paper's advertising and research staff did their best in playing a bad hand: they identified products like cereals, canned beef and preserves on which *Herald* readers were big spenders, and even presented the paper as the way to reach a large number of councillors in control of local government spending. But their efforts met with diminishing success. In 1955, the *Daily Herald* had an 11 per cent share of both national daily circulation and national daily advertising expenditure. By 1964, the paper's circulation share had declined modestly to 8 per cent, but its advertising share had slumped to 3.5 per cent.[94]

An attempt was made to overcome the *Daily Herald*'s advertising problem by courting more affluent readers. This was initiated in 1960 and culminated in the paper's relaunch as the *Sun* in 1964, with the objective of building a coalition of middle-class social radicals and working-class economic radicals. These two groups were very different (something documented by the paper's own research which was ignored). Perhaps predictably, the new hybrid failed both to attract new middle-class readers and to please its existing working-class ones.[95] The paper was then sold cheaply in 1969 to Rupert Murdoch, who transformed it into a successful, rightwing, populist paper.

The *Daily Herald* thus had a sad, lingering death. As late as 1958, it had a circulation of 1,523,000, and the most devoted readership of any popular daily.[96] It was first enfeebled and then transformed into Murdoch's *Sun*, which stood for everything that the *Daily Herald* had opposed.

If advertising redistribution was a major factor in the death of the working-class minority press, it also contributed to the deradicalisation of the *Daily Mirror* and *Sunday Pictorial*. The editorial shift of these two papers was primarily an adaptation to the receding tide of radicalism during the 1950s. It also reflected the political mellowing of its two dominant influences, Hugh Cudlipp and Cecil King. The shift in their politics is borne out by their choice of corporate political advisers in the 1950s, Cecil King's desire in 1968 to replace a Labour government with a coalition administration led by Earl Mountbatten of Burma and Hugh Cudlipp's support for the centrist breakaway Social Democratic Party.

But the discipline of advertising funding also played a part in the editorial reorientation of the *Daily* and *Sunday Mirror*. They responded to their falling advertising share by targeting the younger and female readers that advertisers were keen to reach. Their company's research showed that these target groups were less interested in public affairs than male and older readers. This contributed to a major shift of focus, encouraged also by the lifting of newsprint rationing. News and comment about public affairs in the *Daily Mirror* declined from 25 per cent to 13 per cent between 1946 and 1976, and in the *Sunday Pictorial/Mirror* from 26 per cent to 11 per cent in the same period.[97]

In the early 1960s, the *Daily Mirror* broadened its target group to include young upscale readers, who were recruited with great success. However, this widening of the paper's social base was perceived to impose a constraint on what could be published. As Cecil King, then chairman of the Mirror Group, explained in 1967: 'Today newspaper circulations are vast assemblies of people of all social classes and all varieties of political view. A controller who tried to campaign for causes profoundly distasteful, even to large minorities of his readers, would ... put his business at risk.'[98] This concern to reflect the common denominator of a heterogeneous readership reinforced the paper's drift away from its 1940s social and political roots. The class divisiveness of its 'us and them' view of the world gave way in the 1950s and early 1960s to the rhetoric of the 'young at heart' against the old, the modern against the traditional, 'new ideas' in place of 'tired men'.

Intensified competition for advertising also led to the growth of advertising-related content (defined as editorial items covering the same product or service as advertisements on the same or facing page) in eight out of nine sample national papers between 1945 and 1975 (see Table 10.2). This was a way of organising

Table 10.2 Editorial content linked to advertising as a percentage of total editorial space

	1946	1956	1966	1976
Times	14	18	36	30
Daily Telegraph	3	11	14	22
Daily Mail	6	6	10	11
Daily Express	1	5	8	10
Daily Mirror	2	0	3	5
Sunday Times	18	23	38	33
Observer	13	22	13	24
Sunday Express	2	11	12	9
Sunday Mirror	6	2	5	5

Sample = 336 issues.

readers into concentrated consumer groups that could be packaged and sold to advertisers, facilitated by the increased size of newspapers. This increase was especially pronounced in the midscale and upscale press during the period 1956–66. It primarily took the form of increasing space devoted to travel, beauty/fashion, home-making, gardening, property, motoring, eating/drinking, the arts, pets, medicine and business/finance.

Independent editorial judgements were compromised. The growth of advertising-related content was usually linked to the increasing volume of advertising that it attracted. Often it was not justified, to judge from readership research, by reader interest. Some sponsored areas failed to shake off fully their function as bait for advertising by concentrating on advertising-related topics. For example, in 1976, business and financial sections concentrated on stock prices and performance, linked to financial advertising, and, especially in the prestige press, on management news and features linked to executive job advertising. This left very little space for general economic and financial affairs, which accounted for less than 16 per cent of financial and business sections in seven out of ten sample newspapers. The exceptions resisting this service definition were the *Guardian*, *Sunday Times* and *Sunday Telegraph*.[99]

But perhaps the single most important consequence of advertising funding was its influence on the structure of the national press. There was nothing natural or inevitable about the division of the press into public-affairs-orientated papers for the affluent and entertainment-centred ones for the masses. Publishers' own readership research, over a period of fifty years, showed that there was not a gulf between the preferences of quality and popular newspaper readerships. A major survey in 1933, based on a national quota sample of over 20,000 respondents, revealed that the most-read articles in the quality daily press were reports of court cases and divorce – not very different in character from the most-read stories in the popular daily press of the same period, namely reports of accidents and disasters. The least-read items in both categories of paper were also the same – news about foreign politics and news about industry and commerce.[100] Similarly, a large survey in 1963 of what people read in four popular dailies compared with one quality daily found that the most-read categories of content in all five papers were the same – tragic stories about ordinary people and stories about celebrities. The least-read news categories were also the same – city and financial news, news about international affairs, 'special news' and industrial news.[101] Likewise, a series of investigations into what people read in the *Sunday Times*, *Sunday Telegraph* and *Observer* between 1969 and 1971 showed that the most-read items in the Sunday quality press were human-interest stories about ordinary people and stories about celebrities[102] – precisely the most-read stories in the *Sunday Mirror* and *People* during roughly the same period.[103]

Of course, there were public-affairs-orientated readers of the quality press (who tended to be male and older). But there were also public-affairs-orientated minorities in the general population, typified by a large group among readers of the *Daily Herald*, a paper with an unusually high proportion of public-affairs coverage. These minorities were not insignificant in size: on its closure, the *Daily Herald* had a circulation of 1,265,000 – five times that of *The Times* in 1964.[104]

However, advertising funding fostered polarisation in two ways. Minority newspapers were only financially viable, and able to sustain extensive news coverage, if they were read by the wealthy, thus attracting a large advertising bounty. Minority papers read by low-income groups were not viable, because they did not attract the same commercial subsidy.

Second, advertising exerted economic pressure in a form that widened the gap between prestige and popular papers. Prestige papers had to avoid diluting the class basis of their readership if they were to maintain their advertising value. This was a lesson expensively learnt by *The Times* when it incautiously increased its circulation by 69 per cent in 1965–9. Some of its new readers had low incomes, alienating advertisers, who objected to paying high advertising rates to reach them. So *The Times* set about shedding these unwanted readers in 1969–71 through a price increase and change of promotion and editorial content, in order to safeguard its advertising position.[105] By contrast, the *Daily Mirror* was under economic pressure to attract a less differentiated readership in the 1950s and 1960s, both to boost sales and to optimise advertising.

The consequence of this bifurcation can be seen by the nature of the national daily press in 1973. Just 16 per cent of the national newspaper market (in terms of circulation) sustained four 'quality' dailies; the remaining 84 per cent supported five popular dailies.[106] The elite minority dailies derived 70 per cent of their revenue from advertising; the popular papers just 36 per cent.[107] In other words, the economic inequality of British society was reproduced in the structure of the press through the medium of advertising.

This social division in publishing had political consequences. Elites were served by papers that briefed them effectively as citizens: this gave them additional weight as the opinion-forming 'chattering classes'. Elites were also well represented in public life by newspapers that offered extensive coverage of public affairs structured in terms of their concerns, agendas and interests.

Retrospect

For over a century, a standard argument of the left has been that advertisers control editorial content because they call the shots financially. In this view, advertisers undermine papers they do not like politically by refusing to advertise in them; exert blackmailing pressure to prevent publication of views and news that offend them; and cause journalists to censor themselves in order to avoid giving offence.[108]

These arguments are profoundly misleading in relation to the national press that developed after the First World War. The rise of advertising agencies as mediators between advertisers and the press, and the development of quantified calculations of cost of exposure to the desired audience as the principal basis for selecting advertising media, supported by adequate data, greatly reduced the press's exposure to direct political pressure from advertisers. It should also be borne in mind that journalism developed in a form that was resistant to advertiser intimidation;[109] and that national newspaper publishers were supported by numerous advertisers, making it easier to resist pressure from individual companies which sought to abuse their power.

Yet, advertisers did have a negative influence on the press in ways that have not been adequately understood. This was not the product of malignancy or conspiracy, or even something that advertisers consciously sought. This negative influence arose because some readers had more money or disposition to spend, generated higher advertising bounties and were consequently worth more to publishers. This distorted the structure of the press, its editorial strategies and the allocation of space within newspapers.

Part V

Media and culture

11 Media as custodians of cultural tradition

There is a score-settling tradition in British fiction. It features literary critics as brainless bouncers for the literary establishment, blurb-lifting sots, corrupted snobs, sterile scolds, cuckolded inadequates and heartless vigilantes. The vehemence of this tradition – to which Thomas Hardy, Rudyard Kipling, Henry James, George Gissing, Somerset Maugham, Graham Greene and Martin Amis have contributed[1] – is a reminder that book reviews matter to at least one constituency: the writers of books.

There is another tradition, based in traditional literary studies, which is almost equally critical. 'Concerted and conscienceless misguidance' is F. R. Leavis' verdict on book reviewers in the commercial press.[2] 'An inert and timid coterie reluctant to take up the necessary adversary positions' is J. A. Sutherland's no less acerbic assessment.[3] Similarly, D. J. Taylor rounds on the 'coteries, deference, false standards' of the 'literary Establishment'.[4] The central themes of these critics (their formal use of initials reflects their stern, unbending style) is that book reviewers are corrupted by friendship, write inadequate reviews and fail to exercise literary leadership.

This chapter comes out of a different tradition and reaches a different conclusion. It is not interested (save in passing) in whether book reviews are sufficiently critical or whether they improve literary standards. What it seeks to understand is how literary editors do their job and how their judgements reflect and influence the hierarchy of knowledge in society.[5]

Predestination and contingency

Interviews were conducted with eleven literary editors of national newspapers and weekly periodicals in 1986 and in 1999.[6] The term 'literary editor' has stuck, partly because the alternative title of 'books editor' is easily confused with editors in publishing companies. But, as one broadsheet literary editor pointed out, 'books editor would be better … the whole point about being a literary editor is that you should have this huge range of antennae about all sorts of books'.

A stock response from almost all 22 literary editors who were interviewed was that books 'select', 'elect', 'choose', 'present' or 'speak for' themselves. Literary editors merely respond, it was claimed, to the external world. There are important authors, with established reputations and successful track records. There is also a pre-set agenda shaped by what readers are interested in and what is being talked about. The job of the literary editor is really very straightforward, and calls for only limited intervention.

Beneath the surface of these assured responses, however, were sometimes indications of uncertainty. Some books, it turned out, were easier to select than others. Novels by first-time authors were especially difficult to pick, and in general fiction was thought to pose more problems than non-fiction. Indeed, the more literary editors were pressed to explain their decision-making processes, the more they emphasised contingent considerations: what books were available within an irregular cycle of production; who was free to review; which title lent itself to illustration; what combination of reviews produced the right internal balance; the need to avoid duplication with other parts of the paper; and so on. This second level of explanation emphasised the randomness, complexity and unpredictability of the literary editor's life that defied simple generalisation. 'Half of it happens completely by accident … whoever picks up the phone, what pops into your mind, or even if you are scrolling down the name and address list, whether X comes before Y', explains one literary editor. This is why the very idea that there is a general explanation of what books editors do 'amuses' her and needs to be 'be taken with a pinch of salt'. 'The trouble with sociology', pointedly commented another broadsheet literary editor as he ushered me to the lift, 'is that it pigeonholes and simplifies things that are fluid.'

Literary editors thus gave two bafflingly different accounts of what they did, often in the same interview. One account invoked a theory of predestination in which books were not chosen but chose themselves. The other summoned up an image of improvisation and randomness, of actions governed by instinct and insight, without a clear pattern.

Good intentions

One way of seeking to shed light on this contradiction is to understand the objectives of editors. There was wide agreement about the purpose of book reviews, even among literary editors who worked for very different types of publication. One key objective was thought to be alerting readers to 'books they ought to know about'. Time and again literary editors returned to this theme. Book sections should be a 'notice-board of what is new and important'. They should 'keep people in touch with what is written and thought'. They 'should monitor the intellectual and cultural life that's going on'.

A variety of arguments, from different intellectual traditions, was advanced to justify this conception of book sections as a means of cultural and intellectual surveillance. It fulfilled the press's role as a journal of record. It stretched readers, in a Reithian way, by drawing their attention to important books in all areas of knowledge and literary endeavour. It extended the intellectual range of the press since 'under the guise of book reviews you can cover all sorts of things that would not necessarily pass muster if you had to go into a features conference'. However, the most often cited justification for this approach is that it was what readers wanted. In particular, it was widely believed that 'a lot of reviews are read as a substitute for reading a book', so that book pages provided a way for readers to keep abreast of important developments in different fields. Thus, the conception of book reviews as an intellectual monitor was widely shared and strongly defended by literary editors. It is absolutely central to how they approach their work.

Another key objective of book reviews is to engage and entertain readers. One literary editor talked of constructing his book-review section like a 'good dinner party' with the right mix of people and interests. Another invoked the image of 'intellectual cabaret' with 'a contrast between light and shade, seriousness and a bit of levity'. A third editor talked of 'floating long in a stream of signifiers', yet 'being exciting and playful and splashing around in it'. More pointedly, a tabloid literary editor explained, 'one is often looking for an angle to produce an entertaining review'. Her rival on another tabloid sought to generate reader interest through unlikely conjunctions such as highbrow A. S. Byatt praising Terry Pratchett.

A third objective is to offer a critical impression of a book and evaluate worth. However, this was often conceived as an aspect of the book review as a literary form that could be negotiated, rather than as an overriding objective. There is a subtle but important difference between the orientation of some in the academic literary-studies tradition who expect reviews to discriminate between good and bad, interpret meaning in a contextualised way, guide public understanding and regulate literary standards[7] and the attitude of some literary editors who see books almost as feature articles – as a platform for someone to be interesting and intelligent, using books as a cue. Indeed, there was often more resistance than appeared on the surface to a traditional literary-studies approach. The requirement to be 'bright', to be a good guest at a dinner party, militates against textually supported literary scholarship. And the conception of book sections as radar screens monitoring important new ideas and developments in the world of books is close to a journalist's approach: it is about reporting, rather than regulating through praise and censure.

Actual practice

However, this broad measure of agreement among literary editors about the purpose of book reviews adds to, rather than dispels, confusion about how they work. For what they set out to do does not correspond to what they do in practice.

If one of their objectives is to identify books that are important, they manifestly fail in this. Their radar screens have serious and recurrent faults. Foremost among these is a failure to identify important works in the fields of science and technology. Indeed, science and technology accounted for no more than 2 per cent of book-review space in every national newspaper that was examined (see Table 11.1).[8] It was only a little higher in the weekly press (see Table 11.2).

Other areas that receive relatively little attention are the social sciences (sociology, economics, psychology, anthropology, social administration and politics) and business studies. Most of the books in this category were about politics, written not by political scientists, but by politicians and journalists. If the latter are excluded, the attention given to social science is minimal.

Books judged to be important are concentrated in four areas: biography, literary fiction, history and general humanities (of which the leading category is literary

Table 11.1 Distribution of book-review space in national newspapers (percentages)

Category	Observer		Sunday Times		Sunday Express / Express on Sunday		Guardian		Daily Telegraph		Daily Mail	
	1984	1997	1984	1997	1984	1997	1984	1997	1984	1997	1984	1997
Literary fiction	19	14	17	19	6	21	22	23	14	15	14	11
Popular fiction	4	4	2	4	4	14	3	4	4	6	11	14
Sub-total: all fiction	23	18	19	23	10	35	25	27	18	21	25	25
Biographical	34	28	34	44	41	44	29	25	32	43	28	36
Historical	8	18	14	10	13	6	16	12	19	11	12	9
General humanities	16	15	9	15	1	5	13	18	6	11	4	5
Visual and performing arts	5	7	8	–	3	–	2	4	10	2	3	1
Politics, social science, business	8	8	9	7	6	–	7	7	9	8	10	10
Science, medicine and technology	1	2	1	2	★	–	–	2	2	1	1	–
Children's books	1	–	–	–	–	–	–	2		3		1
General interest	4	2	4	★	25	6	7	3	4	1	17	12
(Audio books)	(–)	(–)	(–)	(1)	(–)	(–)	(–)	(–)	(–)	(–)	(–)	(4)
(Paperbacks)	(–)	(6)	(–)	(7)	(–)	(13)	(–)	(9)	(–)	(6)	(–)	(5)

Note
★ = Less than 1 per cent.
Sample = 180 issues.

Table 11.2 Distribution of book-review space in selected weeklies (percentages)

Category	Spectator		New Statesman		Economist	
	1984	*1997*	*1984*	*1997*	*1984*	*1997*
Literary fiction	19	16	15	16	–	–
Popular fiction	2	3	3	–	1	10
Sub-total: all fiction	21	19	18	16	1	10
Biographical	31	35	28	29	35	24
Historical	14	12	8	27	7	25
General humanities	14	14	18	3	4	15
Visual and performing arts	2	4	4	1	5	–
Politics, social science, business	11	10	19	14	34	21
Science, medicine and technology	–	–	2	7	4	3
Children's books	1	–	★	–	9	–
General interest	6	4	2	4	1	2

Note
★ = Less than 1 per cent.
Sample = 90 issues.

criticism). In 1997, these four genres accounted for between 75 per cent and 90 per cent of review space in sample broadsheet papers and between 61 per cent and 76 per cent in sample tabloid papers.[9]

In general, the book-review agendas of the broadsheet, mid-market tabloids and weekly press are relatively similar. Tabloids found more space for fiction (though still only 30 per cent in 1997), and the weeklies found more space for politics. While changes occurred between 1984 and 1997, these were relatively modest.

The results of this analysis conflict with the claims of some literary editors, made in interviews, that they review 'masses' or 'loads' of science. Subjective impression, however informed, is not as reliable as systematic analysis based on careful measurement. It should also be noted that the pattern of book reviews identified in this analysis is consistent with that revealed by Noble and Noble in the only other major, statistical analysis of book reviews to have been undertaken in Britain.[10]

Self-elective or selective

The books which 'chose' themselves in the eyes of books editors seem even more selective when they are considered in relation to book production and consumption.

The number of new books published in the United Kingdom doubled between 1978 and 1992,[11] and rose still higher thereafter, with an estimated 88,032 new titles being published in 1996.[12] Literary editors thus have a dauntingly wide choice.

The lack of attention given to science and social science books is not due to their scarcity. In 1996 11,198 new titles concerned with science or medicine, and a further 5,275 titles covering the principal social sciences, were published in the

UK.[13] Their production is merely part of a vast flow of books that subdivides, so to speak, into a delta of rivers traversing different subject areas. Books editors take up positions along certain riverbanks, fishing mainly from shoals of history, biography and fiction. Yet, these accounted for a mere 27 per cent of books published in 1996.[14] Some big fish are missed because great stretches of riverbank, vast areas of knowledge, are rarely visited.

If book reviews appear selective in the context of book production, this is even more the case in relation to what people actually read. The public reads mainly paperbacks: yet, hardbacks accounted in 1997 for over 90 per cent of all reviews in national newspapers, with one exception (see Table 11.1).[15] In the most recent, publicly available survey,[16] 66 per cent of book readers were currently reading fiction.[17] Yet, well over two-thirds of review space in 1997 was allocated to non-fiction.

The divergence between reviewing and reading becomes even more marked in relation to novels. Among those currently reading a book, only 5 per cent were reading a 'general novel' and 3 per cent were reading classics, contrasted with 58 per cent reading popular fiction.[18] In other words, people were seven times more likely to be reading popular than literary fiction. However, popular fiction received less space than literary fiction in all but one newspaper in our analysis (see Table 11.1).

Another source of information about public preferences is market expenditure. According to not entirely reliable Euromonitor estimates, science, technical and medical books generated 61 per cent more expenditure than history and biography books in 1992 and were the biggest-selling category of non-fiction.[19] This was similar to the pattern of previous years. Some science expenditure would have been on reference works or funded by institutions rather than consumers. Even so, the high level of spending on science books does not suggest that it is a subject about which the public is phobic. Book-expenditure data also reveal that people distribute their spending across a wide range of fiction and non-fiction books, from food and travel to romance and crime. Preferences are fragmented, in contrast to the narrow focusing of review attention on a limited range of books.

It may be objected that the readers of the broadsheet and middle-market press differ from the general public in being overwhelmingly middle class. This was indeed an argument advanced by a number of literary editors. However, it is misleading on two counts.

First, book reading is strongly associated with higher levels of education and social class.[20] In other words, social background skews the composition of book readers, not just of upscale papers. Second, class influences book reading in complex ways that are different from those imagined by some literary editors. For example, historical fiction has a strong appeal among the higher social-economic groups; romance among the lower ones; while crime, thrillers, war and adventure books have a wide cross-class appeal.[21] Readers of the prestige press, it seems, are not an island of elite culture differentiated from mass preferences.

Thus, the book-review selection in the national press is not so axiomatic that it requires no further explanation. It does not reflect what is published. It does not mirror what is important. And it does not correspond to what is popular. How, then, has it come to be like this?

Cultural values

The initial mystery surrounding books editors is easily dispelled. When they say that books select themselves, what they are actually saying is that they choose books within a framework of values that they see no need to question. When some literary editors talk about the myriad, unpredictable things that determine their actions, they appear not to be fully aware of the routines they have adopted to control their environment or of the interlocking chain of influence that leads them to choose books in a highly patterned, uniform and predictable way.

Literary editors' choice of book is influenced by their cultural values. These are not monolithic or unchanging. But what most literary editors, in both 1986 and 1999, had in common was a perception of literature as a hierarchy. At the peak are works of outstanding literary merit reflected in their quality of writing, originality of vision and depth of insight and observation. At the bottom are various forms of genre fiction whose literary value is undermined by their adherence to repetitive formulae. Romantic fiction was usually identified as being especially impoverished and crime fiction as exhibiting 'some redeeming features'.

This hierarchical view results in different levels of attention being given to popular and literary fiction. Literary works are privileged because these are judged to be important and to generate interesting reviews. Space for books judged to be low grade is rationed because these are thought to be of limited value and to produce dull reviews. It was widely assumed that this system of values is shared by readers of the prestige press. As one Sunday broadsheet literary editor explained, his paper's readers 'may read Jilly Cooper on the beach, perhaps. But they wouldn't want us to devote space to covering her.' It was in deference to his readers' wishes, he insisted, that he would not 'slum intellectually'.

Most literary editors were little affected by the anguished rethinking which has taken place in university English literature departments in response to the rise of postmodernism, feminism and post-colonial theory. This has given rise to multi-centred 'regimes' of value different from the simple model of hierarchy adhered to by most literary editors.[22] In addition, they were little influenced by the positive reassessments of popular culture that have taken place in media and cultural studies departments in new universities in Britain.[23]

Part of the explanation for the intact nature of literary editors' traditional cultural values has to do with their age and education. Literary editors in 1999 were predominantly middle-aged and educated at elite universities, as were their predecessors in 1986 (see Table 11.3). Most were also drawn to literary journalism through a love of literature. Significantly, nearly all those in 1999 who admitted taking pleasure in promoting particular books mentioned works of literary fiction or poetry, not non-fiction.

Arts orientation

A number of literary editors said that they selected books that interested them on the assumption that they were like their readers. But, in fact, they were not at all typical of their readers. Not only had the majority gone to Oxford or Cambridge, they had tended to study just two subjects – English or history. Indeed, out of a

Table 11.3 University education of literary editors (percentages)

University	Oxbridge	Civic	New	Overseas	None; n/a	
1999	64	27	–	–	9	
1986	55	–	–	18	27	

Degree	English	History	Other arts/ humanities	Total arts/ humanities	Social science	Sciences
1999	70	20	10	100	–	–
1986	37	37	19	94	6	

Sample
Twenty-two literary editors, eleven in 1986 and 1999. Non-graduates are excluded from degree distri-
bution calculations. English and philosophy degrees (two) have been tabulated as English, while Oxford
PPE has been classified as half social science, half humanities.

sample of eighteen university graduates, seventeen had studied a humanities/arts
subject (see Table 11.3). None had a science or straight social science background.

The belief that readers were like themselves led some literary editors to take a
hospitable view of some books that were relatively esoteric or difficult, because
these were in areas they had studied or were interested in. For example, a recondite
reception study of Shakespeare in Asian countries was picked as the lead review by
one literary editor of a broadsheet daily on the grounds that 'many people will find
it interesting'. What he found compelling as someone who had previously started
a literary studies PhD may not have been viewed in the same light by his readers.

The same intellectual hospitality was not often extended to demanding or
obscure books outside the arts/humanities family. Indeed, all books in the social
sciences tended to be thought technical, specialist and, in 1999, of diminished
authority. 'Social science is rather boring', explained one Sunday broadsheet editor
who deliberately shunned this general area. 'It's badly written … full of jargon,
full of statistics, rather uninteresting.' The problem, according to another Sunday
broadsheet editor, is not only to find an interesting social science book to review
but to find anyone suitable to review it who does not 'write gobbledegook, such
stodgy, jargony prose that you can't use it'. Social science (with the exception of
economics) is also thought to lack the legitimacy needed to make it relevant to a
general audience. 'Things have to be quite established in the culture before they
appear in this paper', explained a tabloid literary editor who avoided all books in
the social science category, however popular. But perhaps the most telling comment
came from the literary editor of the *New Statesman*, a magazine that took over in
1988 the popular social science weekly, *New Society*. 'What do you mean by social
science?', he asked. When the term was explained, he responded, 'Hasn't it been
subsumed by cultural studies?'[24]

Science was thought to have greater intellectual authority than the social sciences.
There was also a sea change of opinion among literary editors, who were much
more likely to say in 1999 than in 1986 that science books ought to be reviewed.

Back in the 1980s, the familiar complaint had been, in the words of the late Terence Kilmartin (*Observer*), that science books were either 'technical and unintelligible' or 'popular and superficial'. The popular success of a number of critically acclaimed science books in the 1990s modified this prejudice. Yet, as our content analysis shows, a reluctance to review science books persisted. This was based partly on fear of *terra incognita*. Science was viewed as a vast area where it was difficult to distinguish good from bad or know whom to trust. This cultural unease with science was sometimes expressed openly and candidly. For example, one literary editor confessed herself 'daunted by all these books that come in, genes and so forth'. She continued:

> Science I find very difficult … It is easier for us to handle science in a 'featurey' way rather than by reviews, and I think that is probably a weakness on my part because I think that I am not sufficiently clued up in that area. I suspect that our readers may not be either, but then that is all the more reason why one should be informing them. I would find it quite difficult to know how to select reviewers in that area.

There was also a residual suspicion that public interest in science was in reality quite shallow. Consequently, science was best left to other parts of the paper (where to judge from available research it is also neglected).[25]

In short, literary editors are educated in the arts/humanities, within a highly specialised educational system, which disposes them against books outside this tradition. This was reflected in the rule-of-thumb proscription adopted by a minority of literary editors: any book with graphs or tables was judged to be a 'technical' book of no interest to a general readership, and therefore unsuitable for review.

Occupational values

Book reviewing is also shaped by the occupational values of journalism. Only one out of 22 literary editors had not worked as a journalist before appointment. Although they had mostly risen by what Tunstall identifies as an elite track,[26] and were rather untypical journalists (especially in 1986), they had all internalised journalistic norms. These stress immediacy, the overriding importance of up-to-the-minute topicality in what Schlesinger calls the 'stopwatch culture' of journalism.[27] This partly explains the neglect of paperbacks. Hardbacks were associated with what was new, while paperbacks were identified with yesterday's news, an old story warmed up in new covers. Significantly, this prejudice is now weakening, primarily in response to the packaging of more new titles as first-edition paperbacks. A traditional news value lives on, even as it is being modified.

Another journalistic axiom is that 'people are more interesting than things'. This is the key to understanding why biographies are the most reviewed books in the press. They are favoured because they are about people and 'tell a story'. They are also widely thought to generate interesting reviews that are easy to write and illustrate. They are the book-review equivalent of the human-interest story, an editorial category that has won steadily more space in the press because it appeals to a wide cross-section of the market.[28]

However, literary editors are both literary people and journalists, and this duality gives rise to value conflicts. Many literary editors despise formula novels, yet publish reviews which often follow journalistic formulae. They disdain market values in fiction, yet compete in the marketplace. Their first love is generally literature, yet they allocate more space to biography.

Tensions are lessened through emphasising those things that literary and journalistic traditions have in common. One thing both traditions value is good writing, and this tends to be elevated into a fetish. Thus, it is thought logical that not only a review but also the book it assesses should be well written. 'You wouldn't expect us to review books that are badly written', declared one literary editor, adding proudly that his paper 'celebrates good writing'. This reverencing of style has the effect of excluding authors who write badly but have important things to say, like Jürgen Habermas.

Literary editors are also drawn to books that succeed in both literary and journalistic terms. For example, A. N. Wilson's biography of Hilaire Belloc was given in 1984 the lead review position in three broadsheet papers, one tabloid paper and two leading magazines, in addition to being very extensively reviewed elsewhere. This book proved to be neither a bestseller nor a landmark study. But, as a well-written study of a literary figure by a journalist of note, it conformed precisely to what is considered a key book in the literary-journalistic community. Similarly, the three most-reviewed books in 1973, identified by Noble and Noble,[29] were all 'celebrity on celebrity' books with a literary-journalistic dimension.[30]

Pre-selection

The personal preferences and values of literary editors provide only one part of the explanation of the book-review agenda. The 'gatekeeper' strand of media research, initiated by David Manning White, is inclined to overstate the importance of the views and experiences of senior journalists because it tends to pay too little attention to wider cultural and institutional influences.[31] The nature of these wider influences is highlighted by this case study.

Even before a book reaches a literary editor, it has been subjected to a filtering process that influences the attention it receives. In effect, the literary editor's selection is merely the culmination of a complex process of *pre-selection*.

The differential resources available to rival publishers constitute the first filter. Major publishers have, generally, larger budgets and greater prestige than smaller ones. Although some literary editors emphasised that they tried to help small publishers as a matter of principle, there was general agreement that a book from a major, prestige publisher tended to be approached with 'greater hope' than one from an obscure publishing house. This was because top publishers were perceived to offer the highest rewards and attract the best writers, and because some of them had track records which indicated good judgement.

Book covers are the second filter. These are widely thought to reveal much about a book. Why this should be the case remained obscure until one literary editor patiently went through two cupboards of books commenting on each cover. The conventional cues of blurb, endorsements and note about author were not what elicited most comment. It became immediately apparent that there are visual codes denoting a book as belonging to different categories: 'library fodder', run–of–the–mill, genre, specialist–academic or – the ultimate visual signifier that invited further attention – a book on which money and time had been lavished to give it a distinctive, designed appearance. Book covers are 'read' by insiders in a way that is different from the rest of us. They can provide clues about what publishers really think about a book, as distinct from what the book's publicity proclaims.

The third filter is the level of commitment made by a publisher to a book. Publishers respond to the unpredictability of the market by overproducing titles.[32] In this way, they hedge their bets and avoid investing heavily in a few titles that may fail. But they also back their judgement by putting extra effort into those titles which they think will succeed. These internal organisational decisions have a way of being self-fulfilling.

The resources committed to winning reviews vary enormously. On an ascending scale, this can be an inconspicuous announcement in a publisher's catalogue; the routine dispatch of a review copy; a cursory phone call to check that the book has arrived; a personalised note drawing attention to the book's virtues; distribution of free copies not only to literary editors but also to reviewers known to the author or publisher; the dispatch of advance proof copies to selected literary editors; extended praise for a book as a key title in personal meetings with literary editors (usually over lunch or at a party); substantial investment in a planned campaign of TV and radio appearances, press interviews, launch party, serialisation and paid advertising; or the full-scale mobilisation of the literary-journalistic community in a way that will be described in a moment.

Circuits of influence

Literary editors follow certain routines in order to control uncertainty, avoid mistakes and ensure a smooth flow of work. One of these routines is to maintain regular contact with leading publishers. They are the literary editors' equivalent of the 'news beat': their key source of information, gossip and data for planning ahead. As in conventional news beats, information is facilitated by professional intermediaries. Major publishing houses have publicity departments employing up to a dozen or more people, one of whose key tasks is to help and influence literary editors.

It is tempting to see literary editors as an extension of this publicity machine, as mere secondary agents who respond to prior processes of selection within the publishing industry. However, this view is misleading because it fails to take account of the unequal relationship between publicists and literary editors. At the end of the day, publicists make a case, literary editors decide whether to listen. Consequently, publicists have to adapt (to their private irritation, sometimes) to the preferences of literary editors in order to be effective. This results in promotion that generally reinforces rather than challenges these preferences.

For example, publishers print many titles without sending a single review copy to a national newspaper (as distinct from journals and magazines). Among these under-promoted books are large numbers of academic social science books, which is one reason given by literary editors why these books are so rarely reviewed.

However, the reason why review copies are often not sent to national papers in the first place is because publishers have learned from experience that it is usually a waste of time and money to do so. The pattern of promotion thus follows rather than dictates the book-review agenda.

The same logic applies to other aspects of promotion to the national press. Publicists from eleven publishers, with different book lists and experiences, were asked in 1986 to estimate in order (1–4) from a prepared list of categories which types of book were easiest to get reviewed in the national press (see Table 11.4). The choices were then weighted in terms of 4 for first choice, 3 for second, and so on, in a descending scale. What publicists thought would be reviewed closely resembled what actually got reviewed. They knew what worked, and prioritised their efforts accordingly.

But if promotion follows rather than challenges, it can also canalise attention towards particular titles. That is to say, it can influence which books within favoured categories get reviewed. For example, it can affect which first novel is taken seriously, as is illustrated by the publication in 1984 of Iain Banks' first novel, *The Wasp Factory*. Its success began with a rumour spreading in Macmillan's offices that there had been a 'discovery', a brilliant, unsolicited first novel sent in by an unknown solicitor's clerk who worked in an office all day and wrote fiction by night. The story became a full-page feature article in the *London Evening Standard*, under the headline 'A flying leap from the junk pile',[33] six weeks ahead of publication. Copies of the *Standard* article were sent out; the trade was flooded with proof copies of the book; a major feature was inspired in *Publishing News*; and a trade advertising campaign was initiated. By this time, the mythic story of an unknown clerk working by night on a masterpiece had become part of the word-of-mouth buzz of the literary-journalistic community. A literary editor, who had decided not to review *The Wasp Factory* after a negative reaction from a regular reviewer, changed his mind when his editor told him excitedly what he had heard about it on the grapevine. This concerted word-of-mouth promotion resulted in the book being reviewed (though in a mixed way) in ten national newspapers and eight national magazines; obtaining spots on BBC2's *Bookmark*, TVS and prestige radio

Table 11.4 Publicists' assessment of review prospects

Biography	38
Literary novels	25
Literature and criticism	17
History	14
Politics and social science	8
Arts	7
Popular fiction	7
Science and technology	0

Sample
Eleven publishers' public relations executives (1986). The points systems was 4 for first choice; 3 for second choice; 2 for third choice; and 1 for fourth choice. The maximum possible score is 44, i.e. 4 for first choice × 11 executives.

programmes (*Kaleidoscope* and Radio 4's *Midweek*); and generating over 600 standard column centimetres of additional feature articles in the press.[34] The book almost immediately sold out and was reprinted.

In this case, the public relations muscle of a major publisher encouraged attention to be given to an innovative first novel. But the close relationship between literary editors and major publishers also has a conservative aspect in that it tends to freeze out small publishers based overseas. For example, Naguib Mahfouz's key works were widely reviewed when they were published by Doubleday, a Transworld subsidiary, in 1991–3. Yet, they received very little attention when they were originally published in English translation by the American University in Cairo Press.

The one partial qualification to this picture of public relations as an agency of reinforcement and canalisation rather than of change relates to the promotion of science. A number of science books, including one on quantum mechanics,[35] sold well in the mid-1980s. In 1988 a major publisher, Transworld, put its promotional muscle behind Stephen Hawking's *A Brief History of Time*. Encouraged by a favourable trade response, it increased its initial print run from 5,000 to 7,500 copies. This information was then fed to literary editors to persuade them that the book was of interest to a general audience, but, as with *The Wasp Factory*, it was primarily the book as a 'story' – in this case, a masterpiece by a crippled British genius, stricken by motor-neurone disease – that was, in publisher Mark Barty-King's words, 'the trigger for review and feature attention'. The book gained extensive coverage in the national press, and subsequently became a bestseller. But while it became a stalking horse for other best-selling science books, and was important in terms of contributing to an increased psychological acceptance of science books among literary editors, it did not in fact fundamentally shift reviewing practice.

Transworld's assault on established attitudes was unusual. In general public relations executives double-guess literary editors and in the process entrench their prejudices. If literary editors prove unresponsive, publishers bypass them by placing increased reliance on other forms of promotion.

Networks

One key network influencing literary editors is book reviewers. These are a mixture of professional writers, journalists and academics, with particular areas of expertise. Their influence has grown over the years because book reviewing has become more casualised. Broadsheets no longer rely on full-time, professional star reviewers. The tabloids have also stopped using literary editors who do virtually all book reviews themselves.

However, the rise of repertories of reviewers has tended to reinforce a pre-set agenda. Literary editors inherit reviewers and prune or add to them over time. Reviewers are thus an extension both of editorial tradition and of the literary editor's own review orientation. These informal teams have knowledge and competence relevant to the categories of book that are regularly reviewed.

This gives rise to a self-reproducing tradition. Book reviewers sometimes propose books they want to review. They can respond negatively or positively to suggestions from the literary editor. They generate a force field of influence in favour of certain kinds of books – biographies, history, literary novels and literary criticism – because these are the books that most of them specialise in reviewing. The composition of review teams thus skews which books get reviewed.

Another key network of influence is what Tunstall calls 'competitor-colleagues,'[36] that is journalists working in the same positions on rival papers. Literary editors often scan other literary pages to see how they compare with their own (often identifying particular publications as 'the real opposition'). The anxious nature of this tracking is well described by Andrew Curtis, the long-serving literary editor of the *Sunday Telegraph* and *Financial Times*. He projects an imaginary situation in which his paper had led with a review of a biography of an obscure Victorian literary figure called Beddoes. He is the only person to do so and he worries, thinking that 'he has achieved a scoop with it – but was it a scoop worth having?'. Perhaps he will be criticised for failing to lead with another important book. Then, 'two or more weeks later, the lit ed notices to his delight that long reviews of the Beddoes biography are appearing in the other papers in the wake of his'.[37] This fantasy captures the central dynamic of this competitor-colleague relationship: to be both first and the same.

In the mid-1980s this herd-like behaviour was disturbed by one man, William Webb, literary editor of the *Guardian*. He was perceived to be something of a loner by other literary editors, and was criticised for reviewing 'obscure' and 'boring' books. However, he was also acknowledged to have a certain standing in the literary-journalistic world. Webb's sin was to deviate not from the balance of disciplines that he covered (which was similar to that of his rivals) but to give prominence to certain kinds of book that his peers tended to ignore: in particular, fiction from Central Europe and Latin America, radical social history and feminist books. But in 1999 there were no respected outsiders among national-press literary editors: no one who was attacked and resented for doing things differently. The group was supported in its conformism.

Another key network is the literary community. Its core is made up of writers, publishers, literary agents and literary journalists, who are bound together by social ties based on friendship, sexual partnership, work, educational background, club membership or neighbourhood. Thus, at the time of writing, novelist Julian Barnes is godfather to poet Craig Raine's daughter. Craig Raine lives in the same street as novelist Ian McEwan, whose wife is literary editor of the *Financial Times*. The *Financial Times* hired Craig Raine as a reviewer … and so on. Only a sociometric diagram of immense intricacy would be sufficient to document the dense web of interconnections which exist between writers, reviewers and literary editors of the British national press.

The literary world also has an unusual degree of cohesion and reciprocal influence because it is sustained, in a sense, by corporate sponsorship: its members are regularly brought together in book launch parties, paid for by the publishing industry as part of its promotional activity. This is not to ignore the rivalries that exist within the literary community, which can spill over into reviews. But it is united in its commitment to literary values and strongly supports literary editors in defending and upholding these.

This literary-journalistic network is London-based and connects to the related worlds of politics, academe, media and the performing arts. The members of this wider 'community' do not necessarily know each other, but they tend to know about each other and to have friends or acquaintances in common. Its leading members regularly propose each other's books in newspaper round-ups of the year's best publications. This community of status supports, and is supported by, the book pages of the national press.

Cultural tradition

Literary editors are the carriers of a cultural tradition. Their literary values and book preferences are shaped by patterns of thought formed long ago. Striking confirmation of this is provided by the Victorian press. The *Edinburgh Review* and *Blackwoods* of 1870 have little in common with the *New Statesman* and *Spectator* of 1997, yet all four publications reviewed essentially the same kinds of books. Similarly, over half the review space of the *Sunday Times* was given in 1870, as in 1997, to literary fiction, history and biography. The paper's review blind spots were also identical: the Victorian *Sunday Times* was no more interested in science and technology than its modern counterpart. While there are differences between the Victorian and contemporary book-review agendas, the most noticeable thing is how small these are.[38]

This agenda was shaped when there was a settled hierarchy of knowledge, under-pinned by an elite educational and social system. In 1870 the humanities (classics, history, theology, law, modern languages and philosophy) enjoyed an unchallenged ascendancy as subjects suitable for young gentlemen to learn. In addition, a discrimi-nating love of poetry and literary fiction was also accepted as being part of 'humane' culture as a consequence of its endorsement by the cultivated elite.

The press's quarantining of science books and disdain for genre fiction also has roots in the snobberies of this period. The natural and physical sciences came low in the hierarchy of prestige. They were developed and taught in socially inferior insti-tutions: Scottish universities, northern higher education establishments, dissenting academies and some grammar schools. Science was associated with irreligion and identified with commerce and manufacture. In 1870 Cambridge University gradu-ated only twenty scientists a year.[39] Even lower in the scale of value came genre fiction enjoyed by the masses.

But what becomes harder to explain is why book-review conventions estab-lished so long ago should have persisted. After all, the production of knowledge was transformed during the intervening period. The sciences made a breakthrough in Oxford and Cambridge from the 1870s onwards and came to be accepted, though more slowly, in public schools. They also won a prestigious position in the university system as a whole, with the 1940s representing a key 'moment' when the sciences were deliberately given preferential treatment over all other disciplines.[40] The triumph of science was followed by the rise of the social sciences in the 1960s and 1970s, business studies in the 1980s and combined studies in the 1990s. The world of ideas, within a greatly expanded university system, became unrecognisably different from that of high Victorian Britain.

The cultural landscape and power structure of Britain also changed during this period. In 1870s Britain, a landed elite was still dominant, something that had ceased to be true a century later.[41] The culture of society also became more commercialised, pluralistic, individualistic and democratised.[42] It was not just literary editors who threw away their frock-coats in the post-Edwardian era: the whole of British society became less confined by inherited tradition.

One explanation for the surprising continuity of the book-review repertoire has to do with the history of an elite group. One accusatory account sees the contemporary intelligentsia as being shaped decisively by the gentrified values of the upper class in the 1850s and 1860s, and to have been frozen ever since in an anti-science, anti-productivist literary mould with a sentimental attachment to a vanished rural idyll.[43] A second account sees the Victorian intelligentsia as the reformers rather than cultural satellites of the aristocracy, emphasises the ways its successors adapted to the embrace of modern science and celebrates its progressive, moralising influence on society.[44] A third view muddies the waters by emphasising differences within the liberal intelligentsia and the deep roots of some attitudes going back to the early modern period.[45] Without getting caught up in the details of this controversy, it is clear that a literature-humanities-and-politics focus shaped the culture of public intellectuals from Victorian times to the present day and powerfully influenced the agenda of the books pages.[46]

However, part of the explanation of why literary editors did not respond more fully to the transformation of British universities has to do with the shortcomings of the universities themselves. Academic specialisation led not only to the 'two cultures' of science and the arts, lamented by C. P. Snow in the late 1950s, but to a fragmentation of academic cultures, each with their own self-referencing debates, technical vocabularies and demarcated areas of knowledge. Universities as communities of learning ceased to be comprehensible even to their own members (as victims of obscure inaugural lectures will testify), still less to a wider public. In part, this may have been an inevitable product of professional specialisation, but it was also fostered by an erosion of the public role of universities. The reward system within universities encouraged introspection. It revolved around elite academic review of research in a form that paid little attention to whether it was read by the wider public or even by students. Consequently, academics came to write primarily for each other. The succession of big-selling science books in the 1990s, for example, originated not in the main from academic scientists (few of whom were willing to lift their sights above refereed journals) but from talented scientist-journalists like Simon Singh. With notable exceptions, academics chose voluntary internal exile by concentrating almost entirely on publications (whether articles or books) with tiny print runs, for narrow professional publics.

Independence

Does it matter that the books agenda of the national press has largely stood still since Victorian times? Before attempting to answer this in the last section, we will follow two brief digressions, the first touching obliquely on the question of diversity and independence and the second identifying key changes that are taking place.

Although convergence between publications has been stressed, there is some diversity in the book-review pages of the national press, reflecting differences of audience, editorial tradition and personality. For example, the range of books selected in *The Economist* is more cosmopolitan than that of other mainstream weeklies, principally because the majority of its readers live abroad.

Even if there is considerable overlap between the books that are reviewed, evaluations are by no means the same. In 1999, fourteen national newspapers regularly published book reviews,[47] and these were supplemented by leading specialist literary journals, like the *London Review of Books* and *Literary Review*, as well as educational weeklies. This is in stark contrast to a more restricted book-review oligopoly in the US (before the era of the Internet).[48]

If book reviews are influenced by coterie, they are also inspired by the ideal of editorial independence. Literary editors in 1986 insisted that book reviews were not – and should not be – shaped by the editorial line of their papers. This claim was cross-checked through an examination of press reviews of two books about the Falklands War, published in 1982 and 1983, that ran counter to the belligerent, pro-war editorial positions of most national papers.[49] These two books received neutral or positive reviews in twelve out of the thirteen notices that appeared in national newspapers, with in some cases reviewers making explicit their own anti-war or critical stance. These reviews plainly did not follow an editorial house line: they seemed, if anything, to reflect reservations about the Falklands War among the wider liberal intelligentsia.

Literary editors in 1999 again stressed their editorial independence, but this time in a more qualified form. More references were made to the looming presence of the editor, and the internalisation of controls was more freely acknowledged. One tabloid literary editor talked about 'an instinctive restraint' that came 'from knowing the place you work in', adding that she 'wouldn't choose a radical feminist to review a radical feminist book'. Similarly, a literary editor of a weekly said that the 'culture' of her office meant that 'it would be very difficult ... to run a review that praised the elimination of the motorcar or socialism as the way of the future'.

One important reason why literary editors felt more constrained was that they were less well established. The majority of literary editors in 1986 had been long-serving, in some cases for over twenty years. By contrast, only two out of eleven literary editors interviewed in 1999 had held the same job for more than six years. The other reason why they felt exposed to more pressure was because the nature of their job was changing.

Key changes

The picture that has been offered so far has stressed continuity with the past. But the 1980s and 1990s should also be viewed as a period of transition, arising from the conjunction of changes in both book and newspaper publishing.

The introduction of new low-cost print technology in the mid-1980s led to an enormous expansion in the size of newspapers. The mean number of pages of national dailies rose by over two-thirds between 1985 and 1995.[50] Newspapers had to fill a widening maw, and looked around for new sources of cheap copy, particularly in the area of features.

During the 1980s and 1990s, publishers were taken over by international conglomerates. They were transformed from small-scale enterprises which, according to Lane, saw 'their real job as bringing books out, not as selling' into market-focused organisations.[51] For the first time, a large investment was made in the promotion of books and in the employment of people whose job was to secure free publicity for new titles.

Literary editors thus found themselves at the interface of two industries under-going change: the one eager for new raw material, and the other newly geared up to supplying it.[52] Novels were increasingly constructed as 'stories' centring on the author, who was made available for interviews. Non-fiction books were more often filleted as newspaper copy in recognition that book authors are cheap sources of labour. The role of the literary editor began to be redefined, from being concerned only with commissioning and writing book reviews to becoming a broker who recognises or responds to ideas for converting books into features, serials, excerpts, interviews or even news reports. This evolutionary change has taken place unevenly in the national press, with some literary editors representing the old way of doing things and others symbolising the new. Typical of the latter was the literary editor of a daily who compared her office to a 'pork butchery'. 'There is no [non-fiction] book we cannot find a use for', she boasted, 'even if it is a trotter to go into the magazine.'

The book-review pages also began to change in a way that our content analysis, which is confined to book reviews, does not document. In some newspapers, new sorts of article were introduced: interviews with authors, features about authors, heritage articles (i.e. 'the book I have loved'), news about publishing and informa-tion about book sales.

The sort of person who was appointed literary editor also changed. In 1986 the majority of literary editors were authors of published books; in 1999 only one respondent was. In the 1980s literary editors were overwhelmingly recruited from literary journalism; now they have more varied backgrounds, often with a more extensive grounding in mainstream journalism. In the 1980s literary editors were often rather hostile to publicists; now they are more positive (with one, very influential, literary editor claiming to have lunch with a publicist four or five days a week). The defiantly Reithian tone of some tabloid literary editors in 1986 (one compared his job to being a 'ballet teacher in East India Docks') has become subdued. There has been a shift, in short, from the literary editor as 'man' of letters to professional journalist.

A further aspect of this change is that literary editors are no longer overwhelm-ingly men. In 1986 only two out of eleven interviewees were women, compared with just over half in 1999.[53] However, it is not at all clear that this gender shift has made much of a difference. Women tended to attend fewer early evening literary functions than men because they assumed a larger domestic load at home. There were some indications that for this and other reasons, female literary editors were less embedded in the literary world and less influenced by its internal hierarchies. Some women (but only some) were more orientated than men towards women writers and towards issues that are of specific interest to women. However, the book pages are shaped by a long tradition of male gender values which persist despite the gender shift.[54] For example, crime fiction with a strong male following still receives more attention than romantic fiction with a strong female following.

Returning to the central thread of this essay, does it matter which books are reviewed? The conventional response to this question is to consider the influence of book reviews on consumer behaviour. The evidence suggests that reviews can influence book sales, with 24 per cent in one national survey saying that reading a review had influenced their last book purchase.[55] Reviews can also influence which books are stocked and borrowed in public libraries,[56] while anticipated review publicity can apparently affect initial bookshop orders.[57] This said, the importance of book reviews has probably diminished as a consequence of the rise of publishers' public relations and the growth of interviews, features and chat shows featuring authors. Books that are excluded from reviews and this kind of publicity are also promoted in other ways: through publishers' catalogues, mail order, specialist book-shops, inspection copies and advertising.

However, this conventional approach to assessing the influence of book reviews – as an 'effect' on consumer behaviour – does not adequately comprehend their wider cultural importance. Press reviews are a form of peer appraisal in which writers judge other writers in a public process of symbolic grading. As Pierre Bourdieu points out, in the context of late nineteenth-century France, this can influence estimations not only of individual writers and artists but also of rival literary and aesthetic traditions.[58] These can affect in turn the production and public reception of these traditions.

Bourdieu's insight can be extended to areas of knowledge. Book reviews in the national press allocate prestige not only between authors but also between the areas they work in. The act of regular critical appraisal affirms the value of the field in which the appraisal is being made. It is a form of public recognition signifying that the area of knowledge is important and relevant, one which an informed person should be expected to know something about. It also implies that certain competencies necessary for understanding that field (such as knowledge of specialist language, concepts, cultural references and relevant analytical tools) are attributes that a cultivated person should possess. The reverse is also true. Areas of knowledge that are relatively invisible in book pages are symbolically shunted to the margins as technical, difficult or unimportant. They do not belong to the 'need to know' area of public knowledge and the skills needed to understand them are optional.

In making visible the humanities, but rendering relatively invisible the sciences and social sciences, the national book pages are engaging in a public process of valorisation. They are signifying that literature, history, biography, literary studies and politics are at the centre of literate culture. Other subjects are by implication outside the core cultural curriculum of informed society. They are less relevant, important or of general interest. The competencies needed to master these other subjects, such as an ability to read a simple regression analysis, are not essential.

The attachment of social value to certain areas of knowledge imparts status to the holders of this knowledge. The celebration of literary and humanities culture in the books pages underpins the prestige of the largely humanities-educated elite who dominate public life in Britain. It also sustains a 'generalist' culture, with its belief that education for no particular occupation is a preparation for all occupations (at least, at the level of leadership). Conversely, the symbolic marginalisation of science detracts from the cultural status of trained scientists and technologists.

Which books are reviewed – in addition to how they are reviewed – may also have some influence on how books are written. The literary skills of academic history are constantly reinforced by the existence of a non-specialist audience for its work, supported by book reviews in the national press. The reverse, unfortunately, also applies. The knowledge that there is rarely a general audience for, or public appraisal of, academic social science reinforces the self-absorption and needless obscurity of its writing.

However, the single most important consequence of the national press's book agenda is that it narrows access to knowledge. By marginalising social science, the book pages obscure its central insight: that the individual is constrained by structures in ways that run counter to the individual-centred, idealist view of the world advanced by much journalism (and also much biography). And, by downgrading science, literary editors are endorsing an inherited system of classification that elevates some books as 'culture' and sees others as merely technical or useful. In fact, science is as important in making sense of ourselves and of the world, and the relationship between the two, as the study of history or literature. It is no less central to 'cultural' understanding. By shrinking the intellectual horizons of the book pages, literary editors are failing their readers.

In sum, what is reviewed in the press should not be reduced to the issue of how it affects the sales of particular titles. Nor should it be judged only in the terms set out by traditional literary critics, cited at the beginning of this essay. What is reviewed also affects how different areas of knowledge are perceived and accessed.

12 Media and cultural theory in the age of market liberalism

Introduction

Media and cultural studies have developed a distinctive rhetoric. Periodically, it is proclaimed that a new 'turn' is taking place, a new orientation towards a better understanding of the field. Prestigious academics are then cited to assure readers that if they join this new 'turn', they will be travelling in good company to the latest intellectual fashion resort. Those staying behind, it is implied, will remain stuck in old thinking and excluded from the vanguard that is transforming the field.

This rhetoric has led to the faddish adoption of gurus and intellectual positions that can seem dated a few years later. It also assumes mistakenly that intellectual development is driven solely by the inner logic of ideas. A new 'turn' is always presented as a response to awareness of a central flaw or gap in the field, or as an awakening to a fresh insight. Missing from this rhetoric is any sense that ideas are shaped by the contexts and times in which they develop, and that some 'turns' can lead backwards rather forwards.

What, then, is the missing context that is written out of accounts of the development of media and cultural research as an unfolding story of progress? A short, necessarily selective answer, focusing on Britain (with occasional sideways glances elsewhere), is that it has been strongly influenced by four key developments. These have shaped the field's concerns, terms of reference and research agendas.

Four key influences

One key influence was the historic victory of capitalist democracy. In 1989, the Berlin Wall came down. This symbolised the popular rejection of communism in East Germany – and implicitly in the Soviet bloc – by the people it was intended to benefit. In 1991, the Soviet Union disintegrated, and its communist regime was replaced by an authoritarian market democracy. China, the only remaining major communist power, enthusiastically embraced market reforms from the 1980s onwards because, in the words of its reforming leader, Deng Xiaoping, 'poverty is not socialism: to be rich is glorious'.[1] China ceased to be, in an economic sense, a communist society.

These developments consolidated the neo-liberal hegemony of the right. The 1980s were dominated by rightwing governments – Reagan in the US, Thatcher in

Britain and their equivalents in many other parts of the developed world. The fall of communism was presented as the end of history, the final arrival to a permanent terminus.[2] It allegedly showed that the free market was the only viable, productive and efficient way of organising society. Regimes based on publicly owned economies had failed, while their capitalist rivals had triumphed. The market came to be viewed as the anchor of freedom and choice: the foundation of the morally superior system of liberal democracy. Part of the seductive power of this rhetoric stemmed from the spurious way in which deregulated capitalism and democracy were presented as joined-at-the-hip twins.

Yet, social democracy failed – in the view of some – to provide an alternative rallying point, despite its greater electoral successes in the 1990s and early 2000s. The starting point of social democracy is that the state should redistribute resources from rich to poor, and from the fortunate to the unfortunate, in order to create a fairer, more fulfilled society. But in the post-Cold War period, social democratic governments were beset by numerous difficulties: tax revolts, a contraction of their working-class base, the ascendancy of neo-liberal thought and above all the diminished ability of national governments to manage their economies in an era of deregulated global capitalism. Even showcase social democracies – most notably the Nordic and Rhineland models – downplayed redistribution and made increasing accommodations to the logic of the market by the early 2000s.

The post-Cold War era was thus a period of disorientation and disempowerment for the left. This was reinforced in Europe – though much less so in the US – by the left's complex, subjective reactions to the historic defeat of communism. In the 1980s, relatively few radical intellectuals in Western Europe had illusions about the Soviet Union, in contrast to their counterparts in the 1930s. Most welcomed the fall of communism as a victory for democracy. But communism's eclipse also represented the end of a historic experiment based on a desire to build a more equal society. Its pathetic ending seemed, especially among an older, radical generation, to signify the closing down of possibilities, the limiting of what it was realistic to hope for. This is well expressed by the British playwright David Edgar (born in 1948). 'I had never been', he said, 'a communist and I had never felt that the Soviet Union was my team.' Yet, 'when the [Berlin] Wall came down, I did feel that it was the death of ideals that I had a relationship with'.[3]

Another key development that influenced the evolution of media and cultural studies had taken place earlier. Many of its pioneers in Britain had entered adulthood in the 1960s and were profoundly influenced by the cultural revolt of that period. At the heart of this revolt was an assertion of individualism. This was widely interpreted at the time to be progressive, since it took the form of an outspoken rejection of nationalism, racism, social hierarchy, bureaucracy, conformism and sexual repression. But it also registered at the same time a repudiation of the collectivism represented by traditional social democracy. Its political ambiguity became more apparent during the 1980s and 1990s, when individualism became one of the forces harnessed by the right to sustain its ascendancy.[4]

The ambiguities of the Sixties cultural revolt – its progressive rhetoric, its individualism, its anti-statism, its disconnection from parliamentary politics, its idealism – contributed to the ambiguities of British cultural studies as it developed over time. While this tradition clearly came from the left and continued to identify with the left, it travelled during the 1980s and 1990s a considerable political distance from where it started.

The third key development was the rise of women. Structural changes in the economy increased female participation in the paid workforce, at a growing rate in the period after 1970. New legislation in 1970 and 1975 outlawed sex discrimination over a wide area in Britain. Above all the feminist movement mounted from the late 1960s onwards a sustained attack on traditionalist gender norms. While sharp gender disparities persisted in terms of power, responsibilities, income and life chances, they were lessened.

Gradual improvements in the position of women penetrated the academic world. Out of over twenty full-time, permanent academic staff employed in the pioneer media/cultural studies centres at Birmingham, Leeds and Leicester Universities and the Polytechnic of Central London media department in 1976, there were just two women. This grotesque gender imbalance was modified over time. In addition, the large majority of students studying media and cultural studies in Britain were, almost from the outset, women. Media and cultural studies – like Eng. Lit. – was primarily a female option. These interrelated changes in society and in the academy transformed media and cultural studies. Gender became a central concern of the field, in marked contrast to the situation before 1980.

The fourth key influence was the intensification of globalisation. This contributed to a rewriting of media history in which the nation was portrayed as culturally constructed rather than 'given'.[5] It also resulted in globalisation becoming a salient concern in a field previously characterised by a high degree of parochialism.[6]

Four key influences thus shaped the development of media and cultural studies in Britain during the last twenty-five years – the political ascendancy of market liberalism, the social dynamic of increasing individualism, the rise of women and increasing globalisation. It is the first of these influences that we will mainly focus on in this chapter.

Exit strategies

Media and cultural studies in Britain developed in the margins of academic life. Its 'second wave' pioneers in the 1970s tended to be non-conformist in both educational and political terms.[7] Indeed, many of them consciously sought to develop a new subject in Britain in a form that was different from its definition elsewhere, most notably as 'communication research' in the US.

The British version that became established in the mid-1970s drew upon different disciplines and intellectual traditions, among them Marxism. However, this 'marxisant' legacy was discreetly repudiated by many media and cultural studies academics in the 1980s and early 1990s. This was accomplished (sometimes, one suspects, unconsciously) by championing, emasculating and then discarding the work of two maverick radical theorists.

Stuart Hall introduced the work of the Italian Marxist theorist Antonio Gramsci – mostly written in the 1920s and 1930s – in a celebrated essay,[8] with significant subsequent reinterpretations.[9] Gramsci, and those who took up his work, emphasised that the social order is maintained not just through coercion but also through active consent. In hegemonic societies, this consent is secured through the cultural leadership of the dominant social grouping. This results in most people making sense of society within the dominant group's framework of thought. However, this hegemony can be defeated, it was argued, through the creation of a 'popular front' of the mind: through different groups coming together in opposition and developing a coherent alternative understanding of society that connects to people's social experiences and identities and is expressed through different symbolic forms.

This set of arguments provided a way of reconceiving the media as a battleground. It offered a new conceptual map of the sources of conflict and opposition in society. It also resulted in popular culture, from music to fashion, being viewed as an important arena of 'contest'. During the 1980s, a Gramscian perspective became almost a new orthodoxy in British cultural studies research. However, in the process of becoming established and actively reinterpreted, certain themes were demoted and others were introduced. The original emphasis on contested *ascendancy* gave way to a stress just on contest, and the media were re-presented increasingly as open fora (with close similarities to a liberal-pluralist conception of the media). Gender and ethnic groups were foregrounded, while social classes receded from view. Above all – and this represented the decisive break with the original analysis – the link between cultural struggle and a collective strategy for winning political control of the state, stressed by Gramsci himself, virtually disappeared. By 1990, Gramsci had been reinterpreted in a way that bore little resemblance to his work,[10] and by 2000 he had largely ceased to be cited. One moment Gramsci was a much admired guru: the next he was, like yesterday's pop star, rarely mentioned.

Something comparable – though occurring in a less extreme form – happened in relation to the German philosopher and social theorist Jürgen Habermas. Nicholas Garnham introduced his work to the British media studies community, though it had been trailed earlier.[11] Habermas argued that there developed in the eighteenth century a 'public sphere' of rational-critical debate, sustained through the press, coffee-houses and salons of privileged society.[12] This gave rise to independent, reasoned 'public opinion' that influenced government. However, this public sphere was allegedly colonised in the subsequent period by an expanded state and powerful corporate interests. Modern media fell, in Habermas' view, under the sway of public relations, advertising and big business, and offered shallow consumerism, empty political spectacle and pre-packaged convenience thought.

This analysis is a curious hybrid. Its description of the eighteenth-century public sphere owed much to traditional Whig history, whereas its pessimistic account of modern media drew heavily on the work of the Marxist Frankfurt school. Garnham drew selectively on this analysis, projecting Habermas' conception of the eighteenth-century public sphere forward in time, while playing down his Frankfurt pessimism. There is, argued Garnham, a contemporary public sphere that is best conceived as the space between the economy and the state. It should stage a rational, universalistic and inclusive form of public debate – an objective furthered by public-service broadcasting.

Garnham's selective extrapolation from Habermas was extended by others who followed in his wake. While Garnham had portrayed the public sphere as an ideal typification, it came to be discussed as a reality. Whereas Garnham had rightly viewed political parties as central components of the public sphere, the conception that took hold was that of an aggregation of individuals gathered together as a public. What people increasingly took from Habermas was a view of broadcasting as an institution that brought people together in reasoned and reciprocal debate[13] – almost the exact obverse of what Habermas had argued in his seminal work.[14]

References to Habermas, once almost a religious act of observance in some circles, became relatively infrequent by the late 1990s. Surprisingly few people in British media studies even noticed, still less discussed, Habermas' important (radical democratic) reconception of the nature and role of the public sphere in a contemporary context.[15] Intellectual fashion – and the intellectually fashion-conscious – had moved on.

This strange taking up and putting down of two maverick radical theorists, accompanied by very free reinterpretations of their work, was a way of settling past debts. For two different but overlapping groups – one centred in cultural studies (Gramsci) and the other in media studies (Habermas) – it represented a way of responding to the fading light of Marxism in the wider environment of the British left.

Postmodernism

A positive feature of the pioneering radical tradition in Britain was that it sought to relate the mass media and popular culture to the wider context of society. For example, a study of a moral panic about 'mugging' was situated in a synoptic analysis of the British state, politics, economy, culture and social processes over a period of almost two decades.[16] Although this celebrated study was unusually wide-ranging even by the standards of the late 1970s, it came out of a 'holistic' tradition that sought to examine the media's relationship to underlying structures of power and wider processes in society.

A growing number of media and cultural studies researchers abandoned this totalising approach during the late 1980s and early 1990s. This was because they found it increasingly difficult to make sense of the rapidly changing world in which they lived. Some turned their perplexity into an intellectual virtue by trumpeting the merits of postmodernist work (some of which had been published over a decade earlier). Especially influential was the French philosopher Jean-François Lyotard, who emphasised the fragmented nature of the social world, the impossibility of advancing claims to any universal truth and the limitations of all foundational social theories and general interpretations of history (apart from postmodernism).[17] Another revered postmodernist, Jean Baudrillard, proclaimed that the mass circulation of media images had transformed the world into a hall of mirrors and led to an implosion of meaning. 'The medium and the real', Baudrillard wrote, 'now form a single inscrutable nebula' resulting in 'the defusing of polarities, the short-circuiting of the poles of every differential system of meaning, the obliteration of distinctions and oppositions between terms, including the distinction between the medium and the real.'[18]

This swirling mist of postmodernist language was accompanied by 'deconstructive' assaults on traditional radical positions. It left some researchers disorientated and confused. It was hard to make critical sense of society, lamented one Baudrillard apostle, 'when no one is dominating, nothing is being dominated and no ground exists for a principle of liberation from domination'.[19]

If one response was deradicalised bafflement, another was circumspection. It was reasoned that since 'old' thinking, from Marxism to traditional socialist feminism, provided unreliable compass bearings for steering a ship in open seas, it was better to hug the shoreline. 'The dangers of easy categorisation and generalisation', warned one influential essay, 'so characteristic of mainstream traditions in the social sciences (including mass communication theory and research), are greater than the benefits of a consistent particularism' in a context where postmodernism has highlighted 'the irreducible complexity and relentless heterogeneity of social life.'[20] In confusing times, cautious specification seemed safer than imprudent generalisation.

A key figure in this postmodernist moment was the historian and social philosopher Michel Foucault (who vehemently denied being a postmodernist). His powerful influence on media and cultural studies during the 1990s further undermined a totalising approach. Foucault's eclectic historical research into institutions as different as hospitals and prisons suggested that power is constituted by a multiplicity of specific relationships and the discursive contexts in which these operate. The interaction between authority and discourse, he also argued, is both multilayered and dynamic. 'There is no power-relation', wrote Foucault, 'without the correlative constitution of a field of knowledge, nor any knowledge that does not presuppose and constitute at the same time power-relations.'[21] Researchers in the Foucauldian tradition who sought to uncover this complexity were increasingly drawn towards narrowly focused micro-research.

The postmodernist rise peaked in the early 1990s, a *High Noon* moment when many researchers sought refuge in the shadowy doorways of scepticism and particularism. This registered not just an erosion of radical certainty but also a growing sense of powerlessness during a period of rightwing ascendancy. Radical cultural studies research, coming out of the University of Birmingham in the 1970s, had communicated a sense of urgency and commitment. Baudrillard's postmodernism, by contrast, implied that all human endeavour was inspired by illusion, while Foucault's work seemed to suggest that simply unmasking the epistemic foundations of power would lead to human emancipation. The rise of postmodernism in cultural studies represented a significant shift. It is best summed up as a movement from the vanguard to the avant-garde, from collectivist to aesthetic politics.

Loving the market

If one route led towards postmodernism, another led to heart-warming populism. This latter transition is exemplified by a weathervane book written by Paul Willis,[22] a Birmingham cultural studies pioneer and the author of a classic study of working-class youth.[23] His 1990 volume, *Common Culture*, came out of a Gulbenkian research project in which many of the great and the good in critical cultural studies were involved. It is worth looking at briefly since it expresses in characteristic language the central themes of cultural populism.

Its starting point is a celebration of the resourcefulness and autonomy of the people, rooted in the rich inherited cultural resources and social practices of their everyday life. 'There is now', writes Paul Willis, 'a whole social and cultural medium of interwebbing common meaning and identity-making which blunts, deflects, minces up or transforms outside or top–down communication. In particular, elite or "official" culture has lost its dominance.'[24]

Against this background, the market is viewed as liberating. It provides the raw material which audiences work on, and transfigure, as 'active producers of meaning'. Furthermore, 'the anarchic market' opens up new vistas. It is unconstrained by official culture and subverts previous certainties and conventions.[25] It offers 'better and freer materials for building security and coherence' in the search for self-actualisation.[26]

This positive view of the market is contrasted with a more critical view of public provision. 'In general, the public sector cannot do better', writes Paul Willis, 'than the commercial sector in supplying attractive and usable symbolic resources.'[27] Indeed, the market surpasses in his view all alternatives in terms of facilitating self-realisation. 'The coming together of coherence and identity', he tells us, takes place 'in leisure not work, through commodities not political parties, privately not collectively.'[28]

Willis originated from a far-left tradition, contemptuous of social democracy. He was still committed, he assures us, to 'socialism', though in an 'unprefigured' form to be determined by the people in the future. So what prompted his Damascene conversion to the virtues of the free market? One clue is provided by his anti-statist orientation and focus on individual self-realisation – a strand of 1960s radical culture that proved to be politically mobile in the 1980s. Another is his reference to 'the now-tumbling walls, towers, and ideas of the East', an allusion to the fall of the Berlin Wall in the previous year. Yet, in some ways still more revealing is his dismissal of 'many' radical alternatives as elitist and socially irrelevant, and his acknowledgement of the 'inevitability of some of the Thatcherite "reforms" of the last decade'.[29]

Cultural populism

The cultural populist tradition usually took a tacitly favourable view of the market, rather than enthusing explicitly about its virtues in the style of Paul Willis. Its more mainstream exponent in the transitional, dying days of the Cold War period was perhaps John Fiske. The people, Fiske assured us, use 'the products of capitalism while rejecting the ideology they more normally bear'.[30] Audiences routinely redirect the meanings of the media in progressive or recalcitrant ways.[31] Audience power is, in this view, like an immune system protecting people from unwanted ideological bacteria.

Audiences are able to impose their own meaning, it was explained, partly because media content is often accessible to divergent interpretation. Market pressures compel the media to connect to the social experiences and concerns of the people, irrespective of the views of media owners or the dominant discourses of society. This can give rise to contradictions and tensions in 'media texts' that facilitate independent audience interpretation. Above all, audiences respond selectively to the media by drawing upon the social discourses of their everyday world.

This thesis gained a new lease of life in the 1990s by being redeployed in a debate about 'cultural imperialism'. A sophisticated orchestration of it appeared in John Tomlinson's synthesis of existing research.[32] Global capitalism is not promoting a capitalist mono-culture, he argued, because the symbolic meaning of globally distributed cultural goods are transformed through local cultural appropriations. While radical critics view Coca-Cola as a symbol of American capitalism, research shows, according to Tomlinson, that many consumers think that it is a local product. Indeed, people in different countries attribute different magical properties to it (such as anti-wrinkling in Russia, raising the dead in Haiti). Similarly, the same TV programmes are understood in divergent ways in different parts of the globe.

This celebration of popular cultural power, rooted in the divergent traditions of different peoples around the world, was linked to another theme: the dynamism of the global media economy. The notion that the 'media are American' fails to grasp, it is argued, that Hollywood's global domination of TV has been challenged success-fully by new centres of TV production around the world, catering for different language markets.[33] Global conglomerates have also been forced to adapt to the demands of local consumers. For example, MTV-Europe abandoned its attempt to impose a single service on Western Europe, and subdivided into four regional services in order to cater for differences of language and musical taste.[34] The global media market is portrayed, with occasional caveats, as dynamic, competitive and responsive to difference.

The central conclusion of this recycled cultural populism is that globalisation is an overwhelmingly positive development. It is a 'decentred' process that has no *necessary* affinity with the interests of the West.[35] Its most important consequence is to weaken nationalist prejudice and foster a new openness to other ideas and peoples, a 'cosmopolitan disposition'. The implication of this analysis – although Tomlinson himself is rather circumspect – is that old-fashioned 1970s concerns about America's imperial power or about increasing indoctrination into consumer values, expressed for example by Schiller,[36] can now be laid to rest, with a knowing smile.

Happy days

The affirmative tenor of contemporary media and cultural theory has been rein-forced by the view that the world is changing for the better in two other important respects. First, improvements in the position, status and economic power of women are beginning to influence media representations of gender. In the 1970s, radical feminist research tended to argue that the media portrayed women almost entirely negatively and encouraged identification with 'hearth and home'.[37] In the 1980s and early 1990s, feminist media researchers tended to draw attention to ambiguities in media representations of women, arguing that these sometimes afforded vicarious identification with powerful 'bad' women,[38] or implicitly 'call[ed] into question women's anomalous position' or dramatised the 'tension between the conventional positioning of women and the entertainment of opposites'.[39] Women's media could be quietly subversive on the side.

In the more recent period, this 'progress through stealth' thesis has given way to the argument that media representations of women have improved. Thus, a case study of a popular British magazine reported that it offered empowering understandings of what it was to be a contemporary woman;[40] an analysis of a leading American daily concluded that, between 1980 and 1996, most of its coverage of feminist politics had been 'overwhelmingly positive';[41] a wide-ranging overview judged that media portrayals of women were becoming, on balance, more emancipated;[42] while Jane Shattuc claimed that daytime, issue-orientated TV talk shows gave working-class women a new voice and provided 'some of the most radical populist moments' in the history of American TV between 1967 and 1993.[43] A subtheme of much of this work is that the market encouraged the media to respond to changing – and more liberated – subjectivities among women.

Second, the advent of the Internet, web and digital revolution is hailed as emancipatory. New media are expanding the diversity of the media.[44] They are promoting a user-driven, 'pull' culture in which people will no longer accept what is pushed at them by media conglomerates.[45] The web is transferring power to the people and facilitating the construction of emancipated subjectivities.[46] It is fostering global activism and a new form of progressive politics.[47] The Internet has facilitated exciting new experiments in 'electronic democracy'.[48] It has enabled the creation of a 'gay global village', an online haven of emotional and practical support for sexual minorities who are persecuted or shunned around the world.[49] It has facilitated the emergence of a networked world and a dynamic 'new economy'.[50] Not all these accounts are unequivocal – the last, for example, is especially eloquent about unequal global access to the benefits of new communications technology. But the general thrust of this literature leaves no room for doubt that our media system has been wonderfully enriched by the addition of new media.

The field thus shifted from its radical moorings in the 1970s, through free adaptations of Gramsci and Habermas and the rise of postmodernism. New themes – audience power, improved gender representation, the benefits of globalisation and new media – entered centre stage. Even allowing for the debates that have been passed over for the sake of brevity, the general tenor of media and cultural studies in Britain (as in many other countries) became more affirmative, more approving of the world in which we live.

Gains and losses

Were these shifts part of an unfolding story of progress in which researchers responded to the new issues and concerns of a changed world? Or did the field become less critical because it was influenced by the assumptions of a more conservative era? Instead of answering these questions directly (and eliciting predictable polarised responses), perhaps it would be more useful to draw up a brief balance sheet of what was gained and lost in the evolution of British media and cultural research.

On the credit side, the rise of feminism addressed a major blind spot in radical media studies. The emphasis on conflict and audience autonomy (however overdrawn) in 1980s media research usefully undermined the simplifications of radical functionalism. The increased attention given to globalisation in the 1990s, and more recently the emergence of comparative media research, chipped away at the parochialism of much media and cultural theory. The booming literature on new communications technology illuminated as well as mythologised. To this shortlist could be added other gains, most notably major advances in film studies and in ways of analysing meaning.

However, there are also entries on the debit side. These need to be set out at greater length to offset numerous celebratory accounts of the field. The case has already been made that the received wisdom both overstates popular power over the media and understates media influence on the public.[51] It does not need to be repeated here. Instead, we will focus on the way in which the neo-liberal ascendancy has promoted favourable impressions of the market.

The main body of work that subjects the market to critical scrutiny is radical media political economy.[52] It is widely discounted in Britain on the grounds that it is 'reductionist' (meaning that it reduces complex phenomena to simplistic economic explanation). This frequently issued health warning has helped to marginalise this work and discouraged researchers from even addressing the central question it raises: has critical economics anything to contribute to the study of the media and popular culture? The answer given in most of the British cultural studies literature is implicitly 'no'. However, it should really be 'don't know', since most cultural studies researchers in Britain, with occasional illuminating exceptions like Hesmondhalgh,[53] lack an economic dimension to their work.

Partial relief is coming from the US, in an ironic reversal of history. British media studies originally defined itself in opposition to the uncritical nature of American media research.[54] Yet, the US is now the main home of critical, economically informed studies of the media. The growing travails of the Hutchins Commission reform tradition, which sought to implant a public-interest culture in the American media industries, have generated a rising volume of academic protest literature. Its main themes are that 'hypercommercialism' is undermining the decision-making power and autonomy of American journalists; weakening professional standards; undermining editorial quality through cost-cutting; and leading to increasingly inadequate journalism that is failing American society.[55]

Just one illustrative theme from this now extensive literature must suffice. Increasing pressure to realise 'market earnings expectations', in the context of deregulation and increased competition, contributed (among other factors) to a sharp increase in American TV coverage of crime during the 1990s.[56] This was especially pronounced in 1992–3, when there was a threefold increase in crime coverage on American national TV network news.[57] By the mid-1990s, violent crime accounted for two-thirds of all local TV news in 56 US cities.[58] This increased daily dosage of crime, encouraged by the fact that it was both cheap and popular, contributed to a spectacular rise in the proportion of Americans who said that crime was the most serious problem facing the nation, even though crime levels were actually falling.[59] Local TV news tended also to focus on decontextualised acts of violent crime by black perpetrators in ways that strengthened racial hostility and fuelled demands for punitive retribution.[60] This gave further impetus to the traditional right in American society.

An unwillingness to confront market issues also accounts for the one-sided understanding of globalisation that dominates media and cultural research. The prevailing orthodoxy adopts a broad, anthropological understanding of 'culture' as a way of life. Yet, it seldom gives more than passing consideration to the inequitable nature of the global market, even though this profoundly affects people's everyday lives. While global market integration has generated additional wealth, its gains have been distributed very unequally. By the late 1990s, the richest fifth of the world's population possessed 86 per cent of the world's GDP, whereas the poorest fifth had just 1 per cent.[61] The gap between the world's rich and poor grew sharply in the 1990s. Whether this was the culmination of a long-term trend towards the polarisation of wealth within the world, fostered by globalisation, is a hotly contested and complex issue.[62] But what is not seriously disputed is that the number of those living in dire poverty increased during the 1990s, despite the sustained growth of the global economy.[63] The institutions of global governance failed to address adequately global inequality because they were dominated by wealthy nations, adhered to rules and assumptions that favoured these nations, were strongly influenced by Western financial elites and were not democratically accountable.[64]

But is not globalisation releasing new political forces operating on a global basis that are alert to a new politics (environmentalism, human rights, world poverty and peace), connected by new communications technology, transcending the limitations of nationalism, bridging the local and global and forging new bases of common action and social purpose? This is the constantly repeated argument within the field. It is an important argument, for which there is some evidence. But this affirmative view needs also to take account of counter-arguments. First, the rise of deregulated, global financial markets has weakened the economic effectiveness of national governments, and by implication the democratic power of the people.[65] Second, global civil society is currently underdeveloped, subdivided, unrepresentative, with only limited influence on structures of military and economic power.[66] Indeed, it would seem that we are passing through a transitional phase whose outcome is uncertain rather than the assured, positive future foretold by some cultural theorists. One form of democratic power, national government, and one progressive tradition, social democracy, are weakening. Yet new forms of democratic power and a new, progressive politics remain buds that have not yet fully flowered, in the context of greatly strengthened global corporate and financial influence and the rise of the 'informal' American empire. It may be that an evolving, multi-layered system of governance will be rendered more subject to democratic control and will contribute to the welfare of humanity.[67] But this is something that needs to be made concrete and fought for. It is not an automatic corollary of globalisation.

In other words, globalisation has negative features – an inequitable global market and the weakening of democracy – to be set beside its positive features identified in 'cultural globalisation' analysis. In passing, it should be added that a similar one-sidedness prevails in the new media literature, much of which is given over to celebrating its technological possibilities and describing in effusive terms its emancipatory uses. This approach tends to take for granted the open architecture and versatile uses of the Internet, which were shaped historically by the values of academic science, American counter-culture and European public service. This legacy has been renewed by the development of social and co-operative networks during the 2000s. However, this inheritance is being challenged by the increasing assertion of market influences, supported by new technologies of surveillance and by the strengthening of national censorship of the web.[68] The historic nature of this contest could not be more important, since its outcome will shape the future of cyberspace. Yet, it has tended to be ignored until recently because even the idea that the virtual world has a political economy is alien to new media studies.

Negotiating hegemony

The ideological ascendancy of market liberalism also penetrated media and cultural research by influencing the way in which society was understood. Market liberalism sees society primarily as an aggregation of individuals rather than in the abstract terms of social groups. People now live, it is stressed, in open societies free of the rigidities associated with class because the market is an egalitarian force that promotes equality of opportunity in the interests of efficiency. Hard work, talent and enterprise are rewarded within market societies as a way of fostering wealth-creation, in the interests of all.

Some of these themes chimed with a reappraisal that took place in media and cultural research. A traditional Marxist view of conflict between social classes defined by their relationship to the system of production was increasingly rejected, mainly on the grounds that it failed to take account of the more complexly stratified and differentiated nature of contemporary society. Class and the world of work, it was also argued, had become less significant as sources of social identity. This reappraisal often led to a stress on social flux and change: the increasing fragmentation of society, the strengthening of multiple social identities, the reconfiguration of space and mental horizons as a consequence of globalisation, the erosion of tradition. The self-defining individual loomed large within this reconception, as did gender, ethnicity and sexuality, which increasingly replaced class as a way of conceptualising disadvantage. This way of looking at the world echoed neo-liberal themes in stressing individual agency, social fluidity and the increasing redundancy of a class perspective. However, it also incorporated critical themes, derived from feminism and gay theory, which were not part of the liberal market tradition. It thus 'negotiated' rather than reproduced a neo-liberal vision of society.

This reorientation ignored a large accumulation of empirical evidence showing that class still strongly influences the distribution of life chances, experiences and rewards in contemporary advanced societies. OECD countries, including both Britain and the US, are not in fact fluid, open societies. Social mobility – whether defined between generations or within a generation, between social classes or 'income groups' (the definition usually employed by economists) – is restricted.[69] Movement is greater in the middle of society, less so at the bottom and top. Yet, the chances of a middle-class child in Britain staying middle class are about four times greater than those of a working-class child becoming middle class, with some data projecting much higher odds.[70]

The reasons for restricted social mobility are complex. Higher social class is associated with multiple advantages – self-esteem, confidence, expectation, sense of control over one's destiny, use of 'educated' language, cognitive development (reflected in differential test scores), educational attainment, social skills, social networks, access to information and access to money and credit. These influences tend to be mutually reinforcing, creating a dynamic that is discernible very early in a person's life.

The rhetoric of reward in relation to 'hard work, talent and enterprise' is thus enormously misleading because it masks the influence of class. Yet, it is invoked to provide spurious justification for large disparities in the distribution of income and wealth. For example, in the US, the richest 20 per cent earn nine times more than the poorest 20 per cent.[71] Class difference also generates other forms of inequality. In Britain, people in unskilled and semi-skilled jobs are more likely than those in managerial and professional grades to die earlier, lose their job, be the victims of crime and have children who become seriously ill.[72]

Inequalities also increased very rapidly, especially in countries where neo-liberal policies and attitudes became embedded.[73] Thus, income disparities soared during the last quarter of the twentieth century in the US, and even resulted in an absolute real decline in blue-collar wages during the 1980s and part of the 1990s.[74] In Britain, incomes at the 90th percentile were 2.9 times those at the 10th percentile in 1976, but had risen to 4.1 by 2001. In the same period, the number of households with incomes below 40 per cent of the median rose 220 per cent.[75]

In brief, media and cultural studies have been seduced by the discourse of market liberalism into bracketing out class. They have colluded in the perpetuation of myths that mask *inherited* privilege and legitimate inequality. They have also been distracted from investigating adequately the part played by the media in the growth of inequality in market liberal societies.

All market systems generate inequalities. These inequalities are alleviated by redistributions of money and resources authorised by the democratic state. The scale and nature of these 'social transfers' are determined by politics. What part did the media play in the politics of the last thirty years that sanctioned a sharp increase of class inequality? Despite occasional shafts of light, it is very difficult to answer this question in relation to Britain. This is because most media and cultural researchers, with notable exceptions like Murdock[76] and Skeggs,[77] ceased to be interested in class inequality and indeed displayed very limited interest in public policy of any kind. Concern with personal politics superseded interest in organised politics, while social recognition came to be viewed as more important than state redistribution.

Retrospect

Numerous *ad hoc* narratives of the development of media and cultural studies proclaim a new insight, agenda or 'turn'. These narratives are usually self-serving. They tend also to be exclusively accounts of ideas that make no attempt to relate intellectual development to a wider context. Instead, they tell a simple story of progress in which error is confounded by enlightenment.

The contextualisation of media and cultural research offers a more complex picture. On the one hand, changes in society have promoted important new ideas and agendas in the field. Thus, the rise of feminism helped to establish gender as a central concern of media and cultural research. The more effective self-organisation of ethnic and sexual minority groups encouraged a revival of pluralist theory that stressed both the heterogeneity of society and also differences within these minority groups. Intensified globalisation caused Western, parochial definitions of cultural value and media theory to be questioned and promoted a new interest in issues to do with transnationalism, global civil society and the erosion of national identity.

On the other hand, wider changes in society have also revealed blind spots in media and cultural research (a point emphasised in this chapter). During the last thirty years, neo-liberal ideas acquired a greater ascendancy in Britain than at any time since the nineteenth century. This hegemony promoted within media and cultural research a tacitly positive view of the market as a *neutral* mechanism harmonising supply and demand that was simplistic and misleading. It also resulted in class being underestimated as an influence on contemporary society and caused the relationship between deepening class inequality and the media and popular culture to be neglected. Neo-liberalism entered the bloodstream of media and cultural studies, almost without us noticing it.

In short, situating the development of research in relation to wider social and political change tends to undermine simple accounts of accumulated insight and wisdom. Instead, it encourages a greater distance of perspective that registers losses as well as gains. The second thing this historical review has highlighted is the fashion-driven nature of media and cultural studies. A field that prides itself on being innovatory and different emerges as rather conformist. If anything, this tendency to hunt as a pack is becoming even more entrenched. Perhaps the next time a collective 'turn' is proclaimed, fewer people should rush to join the caravanserai travelling to the new, approved destination. It might be better if some people decided to journey in the opposite direction.

Notes

Introduction

1   J. Curran, *Media and Power*, London: Routledge, 2002.
2   The place of original publication of each essay is listed in the Acknowledgements, p. xii, above.
3   R. McChesney, *Rich Media, Poor Democracy*, Urbana: University of Illinois Press, 1999; M. Schudson, *Why Democracies Need an Unlovable Press*, Cambridge: Polity, 2008; P. Dahlgren, *Media and Political Engagement*, Cambridge: Cambridge University Press, 2009; C. Edwin Baker, *Media, Markets and Democracy*, Cambridge: Cambridge University Press, 2002; J. Rowbottom, *Democracy Distorted*, Cambridge: Cambridge University Press, 2010; J. Street, *Mass Media, Politics and Democracy*, Basingstoke: Palgrave, 2001; L. Van Zoonen, *Entertaining the Citizen*, Lanham, MD: Rowman & Littlefield, 2005; H. Gans, *Democracy and the News*, Oxford: Oxford University Press, 2003; N. Couldry, S. Livingstone and T. Markham, *Media Consumption and Public Engagement*, Basingstoke: Palgrave Macmillan, 2007; M. Prior, *Post-Broadcast Democracy*, Cambridge: Cambridge University Press, 2007; J. Keane, *The Media and Democracy*, Cambridge: Polity, 1991; J. Lichtenberg (ed.), *Democracy and the Mass Media*, Cambridge: Cambridge University Press, 1990; H. Milner, *Civic Literacy*, Hanover, NH: Tufts University Press, 2002; J. Alexander, *The Civil Sphere*, Oxford: Oxford University Press, 2006; B. McNair, 'Journalism and democracy' in K. Wahl-Jorgensen and T. Hanitzsch (eds), *The Handbook of Journalism Studies*, Abingdon: Routledge, 2009; C. Christians, T. Glasser, D. McQuail, K. Nordenstreng and R. White, *Normative Theories of the Media: Journalism in Democratic Societies*, Urbana: University of Illinois Press, 2009, among many others.
4   Christians *et al.*, *Normative Theories of the Media*.
5   Curran, *Media and Power*, ch. 1; and J. Curran, 'Media and the making of British society, *c.* 1700–2000', *Media History*, 8(2), 2002: 135–54.
6   This is critically assessed in J. Curran, D. Freedman and N. Fenton, *Misunderstanding the Internet*, London: Routledge, forthcoming.
7   J. Turow, *Breaking Up America*, Chicago: University of Chicago Press, 1997.
8   For examples of cultural economy perspectives, see D. Slater 'Capturing markets from the economists' in P. du Gay and M. Pryke (eds), *Cultural Economy*, London: Sage, 2002; D. Slater and F. Tonkiss, *Market Society*, Cambridge: Polity, 2001; L. Moor, *The Rise of Brands*, Oxford: Berg, 2007; and J. Carrier (ed.), *Meanings of the Market*, Oxford: Berg, 1997.
9   This tradition has deep roots. For example, when researching his *English History, 1914–45* the celebrated historian A. J. P. Taylor wrote to his editor: 'I don't think that I will include science – I don't understand it' (cited in A. Sisman, *A. J. P. Taylor*, London: Sinclair-Stevenson, 1994, p. 321).
10   G. Overholser and K. H. Jamieson (eds), *The Press*, The Institutions of American Democracy Series, New York: Oxford University Press, 2005.

Chapter 1

1   Commission on the Freedom of the Press (Hutchins Commission), *A Free and Responsible Press*, Chicago: University of Chicago Press, 1947. Its enormously eminent members – people like historian Arthur Schlesinger, political sociologist Harold Laswell and philosopher Reinhold Niebuhr – wrote a brilliant report, but this did not stop them from accepting absurd predictions about the future of newspapers advanced by supposed technical experts (see Chapter 6). There is something about communications technology that causes some very clever people to leave their wits behind them.

2   Ibid., p. 80.

3   Ibid., p. 77

4   Ibid., p. 96.

5   D. Nord, *Communities of Journalism*, Urbana: University of Illinois Press, 2001.

6   The report attacked universities for not doing enough to nourish a professional journalism culture, something that the report helped to change.

7   D. Mindich, *Just the Facts*, New York: New York University Press, 1998, p. 142.

8   H. Gans, *Deciding What's News*, London: Constable, 1980, p. 101.

9   Ibid., p. 257

10   Ibid., p. 235.

11   M. Schudson, *Discovering the News*, New York: Basic Books, 1978; D. Schiller, *Objectivity and the News*, Philadelphia: University of Pennsylvania Press, 1981; Mindich, *Just the Facts*.

12   G. Tuchman, *Making the News*, New York: Free Press, 1978; M. Fishman, *The Manufacture of News*, Austin: University of Texas, 1980: P. Kaniss, *Making the News*, Chicago: University of Chicago Press, 1991; M. Schudson, *The Sociology of News*, New York: Norton, 2003; R. Entman, *Projections of Power*, Chicago: University of Chicago Press, 2004; W. Bennett, R. Lawrence and S. Livingstone, *When the Press Fails*, Chicago: University of Chicago Press, 2007.

13   For example, M. Parenti, *Inventing Reality*, 2nd edn, New York: St. Martin's Press, 1993.

14   The classic exposition remains G. and K. Lang, *The Battle for Public Opinion*, New York: Columbia University Press, 1983.

15   This relies heavily on ch. 5 of D. Protess, F. Cox, J. Doppelt, J. Ettema. M. Gordon, D. Leff and P. Miller, *The Journalism of Outrage*, New York; Guilford Press, 1991. This chapter seems to me to contradict, or at least greatly qualify, the conclusion of this admirable book.

16   O. Burkeman, 'Chicago police "tortured black suspects"', *Guardian*, July 21, 2006.

17   *All the President's Men* (Alan J. Pakula/Warner Bros., 1976).

18   P. von Zielbauer, 'As health care goes private, 10 days can be a death sentence', *New York Times*, February 27, 2005; P. von Zielbauer, 'In city's jails, missed signals open way to a season of suicides', *New York Times*, February 28, 2005; and P. von Zielbauer, 'A spotty record of health care in city detention', *New York Times*, March 1, 2005.

19   *New York Times*, Editorial, March 10, 2005 cited in J. James, 'Prison health care: *New York Times* series brings attention', *The Body.Com*, April 8, 2005. Online. Available HTTP: <http://www.thebody.com/content/art31623.html> (accessed January 10, 2010).

20   Democracy Now syndicated broadcast discussion on March 4, 2005 on 'Harsh medicine', the transcript of which is available online at <http://www.democracynow.org/article.pl?sid=05/03/041437213> (accessed June 20, 2006).

21   The paper deployed not merely its enormous financial resources but also its political clout to pursue this investigation. Thus, it successfully exerted pressure through the Mayor's Office to compel Department of Juvenile Justice officials to agree to be interviewed, after they had stonewalled for five months.

22   The paper carried on critically reporting prison health care after this exposé (see, for example, *New York Times*, April 4, 2005; May 11, 2005; June 10, 2005; August 11, 2005; December 26, 2005). The outcome of this, and other reforming pressure from the

judiciary and regulators, would make a good topic for an MA dissertation for a student living in New York.

23 Cited in J. Street, *Mass Media, Politics and Democracy*, Basingstoke: Palgrave, 2001, p. 105.

24 Reporters sans frontières, 'Journalist jailed for having informed Al-jazira of the repression of Ismaelis in the kingdom', February 1, 2003. Online. Available HTTP: <http://arabia.reporters-sans-frontieres.org/article.php3?id_article=4853 2003> (accessed January 13, 2010).

25 D. McCargo, *Media and Politics in Pacific Asia*, London: RoutledgeCurzon, 2003.

26 Open Society Institute (OSI), 'Albania' in *Television across Europe: Regulation, Policy and Independence*, vol. 1, Budapest: OSI, 2005; N. Sakr, *Arab Television Today*, New York: I. B. Tauris, 2007.

27 C. Sparks (with A. Reading), *Communism, Capitalism and the Mass Media*, London: Sage, 1998; OSI, *Television across Europe*, vols 1–3 (vol. 1, Overview and Albania to Estonia; vol. 2, France to Poland; vol. 3, Republic of Macedonia to UK), Budapest: OSI, 2005. However, this indirect form of control is loosening in some East European countries. See K. Jakubowicz and M. Sukosd (eds), *Finding the Right Place on the Map*, Bristol: Intellect, 2008.

28 G. Wacker, 'The Internet and censorship in China' in C. Hughes and G. Wacker (eds), *China and the Internet*, London: Routledge, 2003.

29 Reporters sans frontières, 'Intimidation campaign targets opposition and liberal media', October 24, 2003. Online. Available HTTP: <http://www.rsf.org/Intimidation-campaign-targets.html> (accessed January 13, 2010).

30 Y. Zhao, 'Chinese media, contentious society' in J. Curran (ed.), *Media and Society*, 5th edn, London: Bloomsbury Academic, 2020.

31 S. Waisbord, *Watchdog Journalism in South America*, New York: Columbia University Press, 2000.

32 C. C. Lee, 'State, capital and media: the case of Taiwan' in J. Curran and M. J. Park (eds), *De-Westernizing Media Studies*, London: Routledge, 2000.

33 B.-S. Lee, 'The Media and Economic Crisis in Korea, *c.* 1993–2003', unpublished PhD thesis, Goldsmiths, University of London, 2006.

34 C. Lai, *Media in Hong Kong*, Abingdon: Routledge, 2007.

35 N. Sakr, *Satellite Realms*, London: I. B. Tauris, 2001.

36 H. Miles, *Al-Jazeera*, London: Abacus, 2005.

37 O. Koltsova, *News Media and Power in Russia*, London: Routledge, 2006.

38 R. Worthington, *Governance in Singapore*, London: RoutledgeCurzon, 2003; G. Rodan, *Transparency and Authoritarian Rule in Southeast Asia*, Abingdon: RoutledgeCurzon, 2004.

39 J. Curran, I. Gaber and J. Petley, *Culture Wars*, Edinburgh: Edinburgh University Press, 2005.

40 Cited in N. Cohen, 'Going nowhere fast', *Observer*, October 12, 2003.

41 N. Medic, 'Swan bake: making a meal of a myth' in R. Cookson and M. Jempson (eds), *The RAM Report: Campaigning for Fair and Accurate Coverage of Refugees and Asylum-Seekers*, Bristol: MediaWise, 2005, p. 56.

42 Ibid.

43 Letter from PCC cited in N. Medic, 'Making a meal of a myth' in M. Jempson and R. Cookson (eds), *Satisfaction Guaranteed?: Press Complaints System under Scrutiny*, Bristol: MediaWise, 2004, p. 29.

44 'Journalists speak out – "A grubby exercise in excusing the inexcusable"', MediaWise Refugees, Asylum-Seekers and Media (RAM) project. Online. Available HTTP: <http://www.ramproject.org.uk/bulletins/bulletin.php?story=45882> (accessed June 19, 2006).

45 T. Boyce, *Health, Risk and News*, New York: Lang, 2007.

46 'Journal regrets running MMR study', BBC News Online, February 20, 2004. Online.

Available HTTP: <http://news.bbc.co.uk/1/hi/health/3508167.stm> (accessed July15, 2006).

47   N. Triggle, 'MMR scare doctor "acted unethically", panel finds', BBC News Online, January 28, 2010. Online. Available HTTP: <http://news.bbc.co.uk/1/hi/health/8483865.stm> (accessed February 1, 2010).

48   *MRC Autism Review*, London: Medical Research Council, 2006; *MRC Review of Autism Research: Epidemiology and Causes*, London: Medical Research Council, 2001. Online. Available HTTP: <http://www.mrc.ac.uk/index/public-interest/public-topical_issues/public-autism_main> (accessed July 15, 2006).

49   Seventeen out of the twenty-seven publishing days in January 2001.

50   *Sun*, January 26, 2001.

51   Ibid., January 8, 2001.

52   Table provided by the Health Protection Agency reproduced in Triggle, 'MMR scare doctor'.

53   There were enormous regional and local variations, with continuing low take-up in London. See Boyce, *Health, Risk and News*, p. 207; and 'Rise in measles "very worrying"', BBC News Online, June 2, 2009. Online. Available HTTP: <http://news.bbc.co.uk/1/hi/health/7872541.stm> (accessed March 1, 2010).

54   *Sun*, January 26, 2001.

55   NHS Choices, 'Measles', 2010. Online. Available HTTP: <http://www.nhs.uk/conditions/measles/Pages/Introduction.aspx> (accessed March 1, 2010).

56   J. Curran and J. Seaton, *Power without Responsibility*, 7th edn, London: Routledge, 2010, p. 337.

57   This differs from the examples of authoritarian societies discussed earlier because Italy is a democracy where the freedom to attack government is exercised, on a regular basis, by a well-established political opposition with access to the media.

58   G. Mazzoleni, 'Italy' in B. Ostergaard (ed.), *The Media in Western Europe*, 2nd edn, London: Sage, 1997, table 1, p. 132.

59   D. Lane, *Berlusconi's Shadow*, London: Allen Lane, 2004, p. 149, p. 43.; G. Dallera, M. Vagliasindi and P. Vagliasindi, 'Italy' in D. Goldberg, T. Prosser and S. Verhulst (eds), *Regulating the Changing Media*, Oxford: Clarendon Press, 1998.

60   See P. Anderson, *The New Old World*, London: Verso, 2009.

61   C. Padovani, *A Fatal Attraction: Public Television and Politics in Italy*, Lanham, MD: Rowman & Littlefield, 2005, p. 150. I have translated a Latin phrase differently from the author.

62   P. Ginsborg, *Silvio Berlusconi: Television, Power and Patrimony*, London: Verso, 2004, p. 95.

63   For a useful summary of Italian research on this issue, see in particular Padovani, *Fatal Attraction*, pp. 236–8.

64   Lane, *Berlusconi's Shadow*, p. 79.

65   C. Sammut, *Media and Maltese Society*, Lanham, MD: Lexington, 2007.

66   S. Hughes, *Newsrooms in Conflict*, Pittsburgh: University of Pittsburgh Press, 2006.

67   C. Matos, *Journalism and Political Democracy in Brazil*, Lanham, MD: Lexington, 2009.

68   Waisbord, *Watchdog Journalism*.

69   D. Hallin and P. Mancini, *Comparing Media Systems*, Cambridge: Cambridge University Press, 2004.

70   See, for example, *Rhodes Journalism Review*, founded in 1990.

71   C. Edwin Baker, *Media, Markets and Democracy*, Cambridge: Cambridge University Press, 2002; R. Horwitz, *The Irony of Regulatory Reform*, New York: Oxford University Press, 1989.

72   P. Hirsch and T. Thompson, 'The stock market as audience' in J. Ettema and D. Whitney (eds), *Audiencemaking*, Thousand Oaks, CA: Sage, 1994.

73   J. Squires, *Read All about It: The Corporate Takeover of America's Newspapers*, New York: Random House, 1993.

74   P. Meyer, *The Vanishing Newspaper*, Columbia, MO: University of Missouri Press, 2004.

75 J. Hamilton, 'The market and the media' in G. Overholser and K. Jamieson (eds), *The Press*, The Institutions of American Democracy Series, New York: Oxford University Press, 2005.

76 D. Weaver and G. Wilhoit, *The American Journalist in the 1990s*, Mahwah, NJ: Lawrence Erlbaum, 1996; D. Weaver, R. Roam, B. Brownlee, P. Voakes and G. Wilhoit, *The American Journalist in the 21st Century*, Mahwah, NJ: Erlbaum Associates, 2007.

77 James T. Hamilton, *All the News That's Fit to Sell: How the Market Transforms Information into News*, Princeton: Princeton University Press, 2004, p. 184.

78 D. Hallin, 'Commercialism and professionalism in the American news media' in J. Curran and M. Gurevitch (eds), *Mass Media and Society*, 3rd edn, London: Arnold, 2000, p. 230; M. Schudson and S. Tifft, 'American journalism in historical perspective' in Overholser and Jamieson (eds), *Press*, p. 35.

79 S. Murray, 'The politics of reality TV: an overview of recent research' in J. Curran (ed.), *Mass Media and Society*, London: Bloomsbury Academic, 2010.

80 Hamilton, *All the News*, pp. 176–7.

81 Ibid.

82 J. Shattuc, *The Talking Cure*, New York: Routledge, 1997; and J. Gamson, *Freaks Talk Back*, Chicago: University of Chicago Press, 1998.

83 S. Iyengar and J. McGrady, *Media Politics*, New York: Norton, 2007.

84 M. Rogers, M. Epstein and J. Reeves, 'The Sopranos as HBO equity: the art of commerce in the age of digital reproduction' in D. Lavery (ed.), *This Thing of Ours*, New York: Columbia University Press, 2002. For an influential expression of the argument that the commercialisation of journalism had diverse positive as well negative consequences, see Hallin, 'Commercialism and professionalism'.

85 Hamilton, *All the News*; R. McChesney, *Rich Media, Poor Democracy*, Urbana: University of Illinois Press, 1999; T. Patterson. *Out of Order*. New York: Vintage, 1993; T. Patterson, *How Soft News and Critical Journalism are Shrinking the News Audience and Weakening Democracy*. Cambridge, MA: Shorenstein Center for Press and Politics and Public Policy, Kennedy School of Government, Harvard University (2000); and J. Wittebols, *The Soap Opera Paradigm*, Lanham, MD: Rowman & Littlefield, 2004.

86 N. Chenoweth, *Virtual Murdoch*, London: Secker and Warburg, 2001; B. Page, *The Murdoch Archipelago*, London: Simon & Schuster, 2003; Curran and Seaton, *Power without Responsibility*.

87 S. Bird, *For Enquiring Minds*, Knoxville: University of Tennessee Press, 1992.

88 J. McManus, *Market-Driven Journalism*, Thousand Oaks, CA: Sage, 1994.

89 P. Klite, R. Bardwell and J. Salzman, 'Local TV news: getting away with murder', *Harvard International Journal of Press/Politics*, 2, 1997: 102–12; F. Gilliam and S. Iyengar, 'Prime suspects: the influence of local television news on the viewing public', *American Journal of Political Science*, 44, 2000: 560–73.

90 S. Iyengar and J. McGrady, *Media Politics*, New York: Norton, 2006, p. 66.

91 The Pew Research Center for People and the Press Survey Report, 'News Audiences Increasingly Politicized', June 8, 2004. Online. Available HTTP: <http://people-press.org/report/?pageid=834> (accessed March 31, 2010).

92 Cited in J. Lynch and A. McGoldrick, *Peace Journalism*, Stroud: Hawthorn Press, 2005, p. 3.

93 See, in particular, W. L. Bennett, R. Lawrence and S. Livingston, *When the Press Fails*, Chicago: University of Chicago Press, 2007, ch. 1.

94 D. Hayes and M. Guardino, 'Whose views made the news? Media coverage and the march to war in Iraq', *Political Communication*, 27(1), 2010: 59–87.

95 Ibid., p. 80.

96 Cited in Bennett *et al.*, *When the Press Fails*, p. 37.

97 M. Dowd, 'Woman of mass destruction', *New York Times*, October 22, 2005. Online. Available HTTP: <http://select.nytimes.com/2005/10/22/opinion/22dowd.html?_r=1&pagewanted=print> (accessed April 13, 2010).

98 Lord Hutton, *Report of the Inquiry into the Circumstances Surrounding the Death of Dr. David Kelly C.M.G.*, London: HMSO, 2004, ch. 12, par. 46 (5).

99 Lord Hutton's indictment turned, in part, on whether 'sexed up' meant exaggerated or 'known to be false and unreliable', implying deliberate deception. He opted for the latter understanding, ibid., ch. 12, par. 467 (80).

100 Bennett *et al.*, *When the Press Fails*.

101 BBC News, September 6, 2002.

102 Inferred from the voting record, as recorded in The Public Whip, 'Iraq – case for war not established – rejected – 18 Mar. at 21.15'. Online. Available HTTP: <http://www.publicwhip.org.uk/division.php?date=2003-03-18&number=117> (accessed April 2, 2010).

103 C. Murray, K. Parry, P. Robinson and P. Goddard, 'Reporting dissent in wartime: British press, the anti-war movement and the 2003 Iraq War', *European Journal of Communication*, 23(1), 2008: 7–28.

104 As reported ibid.; Hayes and Guardino, 'Whose views'; and PIPA, 'Americans on Iraq and the UN weapons inspections', 2003. Online. Available HTTP: <http://www.pipa.org/OnlineReports/Iraq/IraqUNInsp1_Jan03/IraqUNInsp1%20Jan03%20rpt.pdf> (accessed April 13, 2010).

105 J. Lewis and R. Brookes, 'How British television represented the case for the war in Iraq' in S. Allan and B. Zelizer (eds), *Reporting War*, London: Routledge, 2004; R. Narasimhan, 'Looking beyond flawed journalism: how national interests, patriotism, and cultural values shaped the coverage of the Iraq War', *Harvard International Journal of Press/Politics*, 10, 2005: 45–62.

106 For a good discussion of this, see B. Zelizer, *Taking Journalism Seriously*, Thousand Oaks, CA: Sage, 2004.

107 This is explored further in Chapter 3.

Chapter 2

1 See Google Scholar, <http://scholar.google.co.uk/scholar?q=hallin+and+mancini&hl=en&btnG=Search&as_sdt=2001&as_sdtp=on> (accessed May 17, 2010).

2 D. Hallin and P. Mancini, *Comparing Media Systems*, Cambridge: Cambridge University Press, 2004, p. xiii.

3 Ibid., p. 14.

4 F. Siebert, T. Peterson and W. Schramm, *Four Theories of the Press*, Urbana: University of Illinois Press, 1954.

5 Hallin and Mancini, *Comparing*, p. 247.

6 Ibid., pp. 247–8.

7 Ibid., p. 251.

8 Ibid., p. 234.

9 S. Perlo-Freeman, C. Perdomo, E. Sköns and P. Stålenheim, 'Armaments, disarmament and international security' in *Stockholm International Peace Research Institute Yearbook 2009*, Oxford: Oxford University Press, 2009, ch. 5. Online. Available HTTP: <http://www.sipri.org/yearbook/2009/05/05/?searchterm=united%20states%20military%20expenditure> (accessed November 29, 2009). These estimates are consistent with the slightly earlier ones reported in C. Lutz, *The Bases of Empire*, New York: New York University Press, 2009.

10 US Department of Defense Base Structure Report: Fiscal Year 2008 Baseline. Online. Available HTTP: <http://www.acq.osd.mil/ie/download/bsr/BSR2008Baseline.pdf> (accessed May 17, 2010).

11 The US was one of seven states to vote against the International Criminal Court Treaty in 1998 and joined China, North Korea and Burma in refusing assent to the 2002 Rome statute. See C. Smith and H. Smith, 'Embedded realpolitik? Reevaluating United

States' opposition to the International Criminal Court' in S. Roach (ed.), *Governance, Order, and the International Criminal Court*, Oxford: Oxford University Press, 2009, p. 29; and S. Roach, 'Courting the rule of law? The International Criminal Court and global terrorism', *Global Governance*, 14(1), 2008: 13–20, p. 15.

12 This argument is presented in two key essays: L. Panitch and S. Gindin, 'Global capitalism and American empire' in L. Panitch and C. Leys (eds), *The New Imperial Challenge*, London: Merlin, 2003; and L. Panitch and S. Gindin, 'Finance and American empire' in L. Panitch and C. Leys (eds), *The Empire Reloaded*, London: Merlin, 2004. I have taken a more favourable view of the Bretton Woods system than the latter does.

13 Empires, or parts of empires, can be loss-making. See N. Ferguson, *Empire*, London: Penguin Books, 2004.

14 Hallin and Mancini, *Comparing*, p. 234.

15 Ibid., pp. 234–5.

16 Ibid., p. 287, cf. pp. 253–4 and p. 288.

17 Ibid., p. 290.

18 Ibid., pp. 287–8.

19 The literature on this is very extensive. We have focused our analysis on the US media and military conflict, drawing on the following (excluding publications specifically cited below): M. Baum, *Soft News Goes to War*, Princeton: Princeton University Press, 2003; S. Allan and B. Zellizer (eds), *Reporting War*, Abingdon: Routledge, 2004; A. Hoskins, *Televising War*, London: Continuum, 2004; B. Nacos, *Terrorism and the Media*, New York: Columbia University Press, 1994; M. Morley (ed.), *Crisis and Confrontation*, Totowa, NJ: Rowman & Littlefield, 1988; E. Herman and N. Chomsky, *Manufacturing Consent* (with new afterword), London: Bodley Head, 2008; R. Denton (ed.), *The Media and the Gulf War*, Westport, CT: Praeger, 1993; E.T. May, 'Echoes of the Cold War: the aftermath of September 11' in M. Dudziak (ed.), *September 11 in History: A Watershed Moment?*, Durham, NC: Duke University Press, 2004; E. Herman, 'The media's role in US foreign policy', *Journal of International Affairs*, 47(1), 1993: 24–45; D. Kellner, *The Persian Gulf TV War*, Boulder, CO: Westview, 1992; A. Calabrese, 'Casus belli: media and the justification for the Iraq War', *Television and New Media*, 6, 2005: 153–75; D. Altheide, 'The mass media and terrorism', *Discourse and Society*, 1(3), 2007: 287–308; J. Zaller and D. Chiu, 'Government's little helper: US press coverage of foreign policy crises, 1945–1991', *Political Communication*, 13, 1990: 385–405, among others.

20 It seems almost indecent to pit Hallin against himself. But Vietnam receives only two passing mentions in *Comparing Media Systems*, of a rather misleading kind. We are happy to draw upon the insights of two excellent books: D. Hallin, *The 'Uncensored War'*, Berkeley: University of California Press, 1989, and D. Hallin, *We Keep America on Top of the World*, London: Routledge, 1994.

21 Hallin, *Uncensored*, p. 193.

22 Ibid., p. 199, table 9, cf. T. Gitlin, *The Whole World is Watching*, Berkeley: University of California Press, 1980.

23 Hallin, *We Keep*, p. 51.

24 B. Nacos, *The Press, Presidents, and Crises*, New York: Columbia University Press, 1990, p. 57, table 2.1.

25 Ibid., pp. 61ff.

26 Ibid., ch. 6.

27 Ibid., p. 179, table 6.12.

28 J. Mermin, *Debating War and Peace*, Princeton: Princeton University Press, 1999, p. 45, table 3.1, p. 50, table 3.3 and p. 51, table 3.5.

29 Ibid., p. 49, table 3.2.

30 Ibid., p. 101, table 5.1.

31 Ibid., pp. 101ff.

32 See note 28, above.

33   Mermin, *Debating*, p. 144.

34   R. Entman, *Projections of Power*, Chicago: University of Chicago Press, 2004, p. 73

35   Ibid.

36   Compare Mermin, *Debating*, p. 68, table 4.1, and p. 73, table 4.2, with Entman, *Projections*, p. 80, table 4.1.

37   Entman, *Projections*, pp. 81ff.

38   Ibid., pp. 89–90.

39   D. Paletz, 'Just deserts?' in W. L. Bennett and D. Paletz (eds), *Taken by Storm*, Chicago: University of Chicago Press, 1994, p. 282.

40   Entman, *Projections*, pp. 107ff.

41   See pp. 23–4.

42   W. L. Bennett, 'Toward a theory of press–state relations in the United States', *Journal of Communication*, 40 (Spring), 1990: 103–27. He has since complexified this theory in W. L. Bennett, *News*, 5th edn, New York: Longman, 2003, and elsewhere.

43   Entman, *Projections*, which sets out his 'cascade activation model'.

44   T. Cook, 'Domesticating a crisis: Washington newsbeats and network news after the Iraq invasion of Kuwait' in Bennett and Paletz (eds), *Taken by Storm*, pp. 105–30.

45   See among others P. Taylor, *War and the Media*, Manchester: Manchester University Press, 1992; P. Seib, *Beyond the Front Lines*, New York: Palgrave Macmillan, 2004; S. Rampton and J. Stauber, *Weapons of Mass Deception*, London: Constable and Robinson, 2003; N. Storman, *War Made Easy*, Hoboken, NJ: Wiley, 2005; and Entman, *Projections*, p. 204 (which makes the important point that governments can generate decoy diplomatic initiatives as a way of managing the news).

46   D. Cannadine, *Making History Now and Then*, Basingstoke: Palgrave Macmillan, 2008, pp. 223–4.

47   A. Dawson and M. Schueller, *Exceptional State*, Durham, NC: Duke University Press, 2007, p. 2.

48   Cited in Panitch and Gindin, 'Global capitalism', p. 2.

49   Ibid., p. 3.

50   Ibid.

51   N. Ferguson, *Colossus*, London: Allen Lane, 2004, p. 294.

52   G. J. Ikenberry, 'America's imperial ambition', *Foreign Affairs*, 81(5), 2002: 43–60.

53   W. L. Bennett, R. Lawrence and S. Livingston, *When the Press Fails*, Chicago: University of Chicago Press, 2007, p. 116.

54   Ibid., pp. 87ff.

55   Ibid., p. 107.

56   *Growing Unequal?: Income Distribution and Poverty in OECD Countries*, Paris: OECD, 2008, ch. 1, figure 1.1. Online. Available HTTP: <http://www.oecd.org/document/53/0,3343,en_2649_33933_41460917_1_1_1_1,00.html#DATA> (accessed September 12, 2008). Cf. N. Kelly, *The Politics of Income Inequality in the United States*, Cambridge: Cambridge University Press, 2009, p. 8.

57   *Growing Unequal?*, 'Country Note: United States'. Online. Available HTTP: <http://www.oecd/els/social/inequality> (accessed September 12, 2008).

58   Ibid.

59   *The Measure of America: The American Human Development Project 2008–9 Report*, New York: Social Science Research Council, 2010. Online. Available HTTP: <http://www.measureofamerica.org/2008-2009-report/about/> (accessed June 5, 2009).

60   A. Brandolini and T. Smeeding, 'Income inequality in richer and OECD countries' in W. Salverda, B. Nolan, and T. Smeeding (eds), *The Oxford Handbook of Economic Inequality*, Oxford: Oxford University Press, 2009.

61   Ibid.

62   OECD, 'Infant Mortality' (November 2009), in *OECD Health Data 2009*. Online. Available HTTP: <http://www.oecd.org/document/16/0,3343,en_2649_34631_2085200_1_1 _1_1,00.html> (accessed January 29, 2010).

63   For a useful discussion and evaluation of different methods of measuring poverty, see 'Poverty using different measures of income', Institute for Research on Poverty, University of Wisconsin-Madison. Online. Available HTTP: <http://www.irp.wisc.edu/faqs/faq3.htm#diff> (accessed 30 April, 2010).

64   M. Nord, M. Andrews and S. Carlson, *Household Food Security in the United States, 2008*, Washington, DC: US Department of Agriculture, 2009, pp. i, iv and v.

65   Ibid., p. 4

66   Ibid., pp. 4–5.

67   Ibid., pp. 5 and 9.

68   Ibid., p. i.

69   M. Rank, 'Rethinking the scope and impact of poverty in the United States', *Connecticut Public Interest Law Journal*, 6(2), 2007: 165–81, pp. 170–1.

70   *Growing Unequal?*.

71   Rank, 'Rethinking'.

72   T. Smeeding, 'Poor people in rich nations: the United States in comparative perspective', *Journal of Economic Perspectives*, 20(1), 2006: 69–90, pp. 79–80.

73   American Human Development Project, 'Factoids', New York: Social Science Research Council, 2010. Online. Available HTTP: <http://www.measureofamerica.org/2008-2009-report/factoids/> (accessed January 31, 2010).

74   *Growing Unequal?*.

75   American Human Development Project, 'Factoids'.

76   S. Iyengar, 'Framing responsibility for political issues: the case of poverty', *Political Behavior*, 12(1), 1990, pp. 19–40, p. 22, table 1.

77   R. Entman and A. Rojecki, *The Black Image in the White Mind*, Chicago: University of Chicago Press, 2001, p. 94. Their definition of poverty stories was very narrow, leading to a small number of stories by comparison with other studies such as Iyengar, 'Framing responsibility', above.

78   M. Gilens, *Why Americans Hate Welfare*, Chicago: University of Chicago Press, 1999, p. 114.

79   R. Clawson and R. Trice, 'Poverty as we know it: media portrayals of the poor', *Public Opinion Quarterly*, 64(1), 2000: 53–64, p. 62.

80   J. Dyck and L. Hussey, 'The end of welfare as we know it', *Public Opinion Quarterly*, 72(4), 2008: 589–618, p. 597.

81   Entman and Rojecki, *Black Image*, p. 96.

82   F. Gilliam, S. Iyengar, A. Simon and O. Wright, 'Crime in black and white: the violent, scary world of local news' in S. Iyengar and R. Reeves (eds), *Do the Media Govern?*, Thousand Oaks, CA: Sage, 1997, p. 292.

83   Entman and Rojecki, *Black Image*, ch. 5.

84   D. Kendall, *Framing Class*, Lanham, MD: Rowman & Littlefield, 2005; D. Belle, 'Contested interpretations of economic inequality following Hurricane Katrina', *Journal of Social Issues*, 6(1), 2006: 1–16, among others.

85   M. Gilens, 'Race and poverty in America: public misperceptions and the American news media', *Public Opinion Quarterly*, 60(4), 1996: 515–41; cf. Gilens, *Why Americans*.

86   This is summarised in H. Bullock, K. Wyche and W. Williams, 'Media images of the poor', *Journal of Social Issues*, 57(2), 2001: 229–46. See also H. Gans, *The War against the Poor*, New York: Basic Books, 1995; Clawson and Trice, 'Poverty'; M. de Goede, 'Ideology in the US welfare debate: neo-liberal representations of poverty', *Discourse and Society*, 7(3), 1996: 317–57.

87   Rank, 'Rethinking'.

88   See note 56, above; Belle, 'Contested interpretations', p. 3.

89 Iyengar, 'Framing responsibility'.

90 H. Bullock, W. Williams and W. Limbert, 'Predicting support for welfare policies: the impact of attributions and beliefs about inequality', *Journal of Poverty*, 7, 2003: 35–56.

91 Gans, *The War*.

92 G. Wilson, 'Toward a revised framework for examining beliefs about the causes of poverty', *Sociological Quarterly*, 37(3), 1996: 413–27. Avoidance of structural explanation did not apply, however, to reporting of migrants and the homeless.

93 H. O'Donnell, *Good Times, Bad Times: Soap Operas and Society in Western Europe*, London: Leicester University Press, 1999.

94 Kendall, *Framing Class*, p. 17.

95 A. McCarthy, 'Reality television: a neo-liberal theater of suffering', *Social Text*, 25(4), 2002: 17–41; L. Ouellette, '"Take responsibility for yourself": Judge Judy and the neoliberal citizen' in S. Murray and L. Ouellette, *Reality TV*, 2nd edn, New York: New York University Press, 2009; L. Ouellette and J. Hay, *Better Living through Reality TV*, New York: Blackwell, 2008. See also p. 82 for further discussion of this theme.

96 S. Murray, 'The politics of reality TV: an overview of recent research' in J. Curran (ed.), *Media and Society*, London: Bloomsbury Academic, 2010.

97 Bennett *et al.*, *When the Press*.

98 Belle, 'Contested interpretations'.

99 Ibid., p. 7.

100 A. Alesina and E. Glaeser, *Fighting Poverty in the US and Europe: A World of Difference*, Oxford: Oxford University Press, 2004, p. 183.

101 Bullock *et al.*, 'Media images'.

102 Hallin and Mancini, *Comparing Media*, p. 245.

103 Ibid., p. 229.

104 G. Sussman, *Global Electioneering*, Lanham, MD: Rowman & Littlefield, 2005, p. 203, table 6.9.

105 Center for Responsive Politics, 'Big picture, the money behind the elections', Washington, DC: Center for Responsive Politics, 2009. Online. Available HTTP: <http://www.opensecrets.org/bigpicture/index.php> (accessed February 1, 2010).

106 C. Holtz-Bacha and L. Kaid, 'Political advertising in international comparison' in L. Kaid and C. Holtz-Bacha (eds), *The Sage Handbook of Political Advertising*, Thousand Oaks, CA: Sage, 2006, pp. 3–14, p. 5.

107 L. Kaid, 'Political advertising in the United States' in Kaid and Holtz-Bacha (eds), *Sage Handbook*, pp. 37–64, p. 49.

108 For a useful summary of research on political advertising effectiveness in the US, see ibid.

109 N. Valentine, V. Hutchings and D. Williams, 'The impact of political advertising on knowledge, Internet information seeking, and candidate preference', *Journal of Communication*, 54(2), 2004: 337–54, among others.

110 L. Kaid and C. Holtz-Bacha, 'Television advertising and democratic systems around the world: a comparison of videostyle content and effects' in Kaid and Holtz-Bacha (eds), *Sage Handbook*, 2006, pp. 445–58.

111 Center for Responsive Politics, 'Big picture, election stats', Washington, DC: Center for Responsive Politics, 2009. Online. Available HTTP: <http://www.opensecrets.org/bigpicture/elec_stats.php?cycle=2008> (accessed February 1, 2010).

112 Sussman, *Global Electioneering*, p. 185.

113 Congressional Research Service Report for Congress, 'Campaign finance in the 2000 federal elections: overview and estimate of the flow of money', March 16, 2001, cited Sussman, *Global Electioneering*, p. 189.

114 Sussman, *Global Electioneering*, p. 189.

115 Ibid., p. 207.

116 Ibid., p. 184.

117 R. DeFigueiredo and G. Edwards, 'Does private money buy public policy? Campaign contributions and regulatory outcomes in telecommunications', *Journal of Economics & Management Strategy*, 16(3), 2007: 547–76; F. Monardi and S. Glantz, 'Are tobacco industry campaign contributions influencing state legislative behavior?', *American Journal of Public Health*, 88, 1998: 918–23, among others.

118 Sussman, *Global Electioneering*, pp. 196–200, and *passim*.

119 A. Abramowitz, B. Alexander and M. Gunning, 'Incumbency, redistricting, and the decline of competition in US House elections', *Journal of Politics*, 68(1), 2006: 75–88.

120 Center for Responsive Politics, 'Big picture'.

121 For a list of major corporate donors for Obama see: 'BarackObama (D) Top Contributors'. Online. Available HTTP: <http://www.opensecrets.org/pres08/contrib.php?cycle=2008&cid=N00009638> (accessed June 20, 2010).

122 Kantar Media, 'Election by the numbers', CMAG: The Advertising Research Newsletter for Politics, Public Affairs and Advocacy Professionals, 2008. Online. Available HTTP: <http://www.tnsmi-cmag.com/Publications/NL_20081218.pdf> (accessed January 31, 2010).

123 Center for Responsive Politics, 'Big picture'.

124 Holtz-Bacha and Kaid, 'Political advertising in international comparison', p. 11.

125 Ibid.

126 Kaid and Holtz-Bacha, 'Television advertising and democratic systems', p. 446.

127 M. Scammell and A. Langer, 'Political advertising in the United Kingdom' in Kaid and Holtz-Bacha (eds), *Sage Handbook*, pp. 65–82.

128 Sussman, *Global Electioneering*, p. 152.

129 Ibid., p. 152.

130 Ibid.

131 Ibid., p. 204.

132 Ibid.

133 J. Curran and J. Seaton, *Power without Responsibility*, 7th edn, London: Routledge, 2010, p. 245, table 16.1; 'About PBS: corporate facts' [2008–9]. Online. Available HTTP: <http://www.pbs.org/aboutpbs/aboutpbs_corp_audience.html> (accessed June 25, 2010).

134 For recent information about Eastern European media systems, see B. Dobek-Ostrowska, M. Glowacki, K. Jakubowicz and M. Sukosd (eds), *Comparative Media Systems*, Budapest: Central European University Press, 2010; and K. Jakubowicz and M. Sukosd (eds), *Finding the Right Place on the Map*, Bristol: Intellect, 2008; B. Klimkiewicz (ed.), *Media Freedom and Pluralism*, Budapest: Central European University Press, 2010.

135 M. Kelly, G. Mazzoleni and D. McQuail (eds), *The Media in Europe*, London: Sage, 2004; P. Iosifidis, *Public Television in the Digital Age*, Basingstoke: Palgrave Macmillan, 2007.

136 Open Society Institute (OSI), *Television across Europe*, 3 vols, Budapest: OSI, 2005.

137 D. Freedman, *The Politics of Media Policy*, Cambridge: Polity, 2008; Kelly *et al.*, *The Media*.

138 D. Held, A. McGrew, D. Goldblatt and J. Perraton, *Global Transformations*, Cambridge: Polity, 1999.

139 M. Kaldor, H. Anheier and M. Glasius (eds), *Global Civil Society 2003*, Oxford: Oxford University Press, 2003.

140 See Chapter 5, below.

141 Cannadine, *Making History*.

142 See Chapter 5, below.

143 A. Lijphart, *Patterns of Democracy*, New Haven: Yale University Press, 1999.

144 Hallin and Mancini, *Comparing*, p. 302.

145 See, for example, R. McChesney, *Rich Media, Poor Democracy*, Urbana: University of Illinois Press, 1999; C. Edwin Baker, *Media, Markets and Democracy*, Cambridge: Cambridge University Press, 2002; J. Hamilton, *All the News That's Fit to Sell: How the Market Transforms Information into News*, Princeton: Princeton University Press, 2004;

D. Thussu, *News As Entertainment*, London: Sage, 2007; J. Hardy, *Western Media Systems*, London: Routledge, 2008; and J. Wieten, G. Murdock and P. Dahlgren (eds), *Television across Europe*, London: Sage, 2000.

146   J. Curran, *Media and Power*, London: Routledge: 2002.

147   Hallin and Mancini, *Comparing*, pp. 279ff.

148   Office of Communications (Ofcom), International Communications Market, London: Ofcom, 2010, figure 3.57 online. Available <http://www.ofcom.org.uk/static/cmr-10/ICMR-3.57.html> (accessed January 24, 2011).

149   T. Aalberg, P. van Aelst and J. Curran, 'Media systems and the political information environment: a cross-national comparison', *International Journal of Press/Politics*, 15(3), 2010: 255–71.

Chapter 3

1   This study was co-funded by the ESRC (UK), the Hoover Institution at Stanford University (USA), the Danish Research Council and the Helsingin Sanomat Foundation (Finland). Our thanks go to Sharon Coen (UK), Gaurav Sood, Daniel Shih and Erica McClain (US), Kirsi Pere and Mirva Viitanen (Finland) and Mia Nyegaard, Kalle Marosi, Henrik Jensen and Vibeke Petersen (Denmark) for their able assistance; and to Paul Messaris for his comments at the beginning of our study.

2   If we follow up this first study, we will of course investigate whether the shift towards an unregulated market as a basis of organising the media has increased media independence from government. To judge from studies of the media in Korea, Taiwan, Hong Kong, Brazil, Mexico, Malta, the Middle East, Eastern Europe and Western Europe, among other places, the role of the market is more complex and ambiguous in terms of promoting media 'freedom' than it is often represented to be. See, for example, B.-S. Lee, 'The Media and the Economic Crisis in Korea c. 1993–2003', unpublished PhD thesis, Goldsmiths, University of London, 2006; C. Lai, *Media in Hong Kong*, Abingdon: Routledge, 2007; C. Matos, *Journalism and Democracy in Brazil*, Lanham, MD: Lexington Books, 2008; S. Waisbord, *Watchdog Journalism in South America*, New York: Columbia University Press, 2000; S. Hughes, Newsrooms in Conflict, Pittsburgh, PA: University of Pittsburgh Press, 2006; C. Sammut, *Media and Maltese Society*, Lanham, MD: Lexington Books, 2007; N. Sakr, *Satellite Realms*, London: I. B. Tauris, 2001; C. Sparks, Communism, Capitalism and the Mass Media, London: Sage, 1998; D. Hallin and P. Mancini, *Comparing Media Systems*, New York: Cambridge University Press, 2004; J. Curran and M.-Y. Park (eds), *De-Westernising Media Studies*, London: Routledge, 2000.

3   S. Iyengar and J. McGrady, *Media Politics*, New York: Norton, 2007.

4   D. Shanor, *News from Abroad*, New York: Columbia University Press, 2003.

5   M. Schudson and S. Tifft, 'American journalism in historical perspective' in G. Overholser and K. H. Jamieson (eds), *The Press*, The Institutions of American Democracy Series, New York: Oxford University Press, 2005, pp. 17–46.

6   L. W. Bennett, *News*, 5th edn, New York: Longman, 2003.

7   M. Dimock and S. Popkin, 'Political knowledge in comparative perspective' in S. Iyengar and R. Reeves (eds), *Do the Media Govern?* Thousand Oaks, CA: Sage, 1997, pp. 217–24; S. Kull, C. Ramsay and E. Lewis, 'Misperceptions, the media, and the Iraq War', *Political Science Quarterly*, 118, 2004: 569–98.

8   E. J. Dionne, *Why Americans Hate Politics*, New York: Simon & Schuster, 1991.

9   A. B. Lund, 'Media markets in Scandinavia: political economy aspects of convergence and divergence', Nordicom Review, 28, 2007: 121–34.

10   T. Sauri, 'Television', *Statistics Finland Joukkoviestimet 2006*, Kulttuuri ja viestinta, Helsinki: Tilastokeskus, 2006, pp. 143–77.

11   TNS/Gallup, TV-Meter Denmark, Copenhagen, 2007.

12   BARB (Broadcasters' Audience Research Board), UK TV Facts. Online. Available HTTP:<http://www.barb.co.uk/tvfacts.cfm?fullstory=true&includepage=share&flag=tvfacts> (accessed July 16, 2007).

13   S. Barnett, and E. Seymour, *A Shrinking Iceberg Travelling South*, London: Campaign for Quality Television, 1999.

14   E. Seymour and S. Barnett, *Bringing the World to the UK: Factual International Programming on UK Public Service TV, 2005*, London: Communication and Media Research Unit, University of Westminster, 2006, p. 6, table 2.

15   Ibid.

16   B. Winston, 'Towards tabloidization? Glasgow revisited, 1975–2001', *Journalism Studies*, 3(1), 2002: 5–20.

17   J. Curran and J. Seaton, *Power without Responsibility*, 6th edn, London: Routledge, 2003.

18   In order to check for potential biases as a result of the political orientation of these papers, we also collected and analysed data from the *Guardian* as a control news source. As we found very little difference between the *Guardian* and *Daily Telegraph* in terms of proportion of hard/soft news and main topics addressed, we dropped the first, smaller-circulation title and retained the latter.

19   The overall inter-coder reliability test yielded 88 per cent agreement in Finland, 82 per cent in Denmark and 84 per cent in the UK, while that in the US ranged between a low of 72 per cent and a high of 91 per cent.

20   The survey was conducted in the eight-day period between May 28 and June 4, in 2007. It was carried out by Polimetrix (PMX) in the US, YouGov in the UK and Zapera in Finland, co-ordinated by PMX, and in Denmark by Catinet.

21   For a more technical discussion of sample matching, see D. Rivers, 'Sample matching: representative sampling from Internet panels', unpublished paper, Department of Political Science, Stanford University, 2005.

22   The fact that our online samples were matched according to a set of demographic characteristics does not imply that the samples are unbiased. All sampling modes are characterised by different forms of bias, and opt-in internet panels are no exception. In the US, systematic comparisons of PMX matched samples with RDD (telephone) samples and face-to-face interviews indicate trivial differences between the telephone and online modes, but substantial divergences from the face-to-face mode (S. Hill, J. Lo, L. Vavreck and J. Zaller, 'The opt-in internet panel: survey mode, sampling methodology and the implications for political research', unpublished paper, Department of Political Science, UCLA, 2007; N. Malhotra and J. Krosnick, 'The effect of survey mode and sampling on inferences about political attitudes and behavior: comparing the 2000 and 2004 ANES to internet surveys with non-probability samples', *Political Analysis*, 15(3), 2007: 286–323). In general, the online samples appear biased in the direction of politically engaged and attentive voters. For instance, in comparison with National Election Study respondents (interviewed face-to-face), PMX online respondents were more likely by 8 percentage points to correctly identify the Vice-President of the US. This would suggest that our online samples are somewhat better informed about public affairs, in all countries, than samples based on personal or telephone interviews. However, the issue of sampling bias must be considered in relation to costs. In the US, national samples based on personal interviews cost $1,000 per respondent, while matched online samples cost approximately $20 per respondent, making possible larger samples and increasing the precision of the sample estimates. And as several analysts have noted (e.g. L. Bartels, 'Alternative misspecifications in simultaneous-equation models', *Political Methodology*, 11, 1985: 181–99), a biased but precise estimator may in fact be preferable to one that is unbiased but imprecise.

In Denmark, the online survey reported in this study was duplicated using a comparable telephone-based sample. There were minor differences between the results, confirming the trend towards higher knowledge scores online noted above. But none of these differences detracts from the conclusions of this chapter. Detailed insights to be derived from comparing the two survey modes will be the subject of a separate methodological essay.

23   Newspapers are a more important source of news in Finland than they are in the three other countries. Daily circulation per 1,000 adults in 2005 was 518 in Finland, compared with 250 in US, 294 in Denmark and 348 in the UK (Anon., *World Press Trends*, Paris: World Association of Newspapers-Zenith Media, 2006).

24   See also M. Dimock and S. Popkin, 'Political knowledge in comparative perspective', in Iyengar and Reeves (eds), *Do the Media Govern?*, pp. 217–24, a clever essay which provided a key stimulus for this study.

25   In a recent comparative study of EU nations, for instance, citizens who reported a preference for public over commercial television programmes were more informed (C. Holtz-Bacha and P. Norris, '"To entertain, inform, and educate": still the role of public television?', *Political Communication*, 118, 2001: 123–40).

26   Pew Research Center, *Trends 2005 – Media: More Voices, Less Credibility*, Washington, DC: Pew Research Center, 2005. Online. Available HTTP: <http://pewresearch.org/assets/files/trends2005-media.pdf> (accessed September 22, 2007).

27   Pew Research Center, *Public Knowledge of Current Affairs Little Changed by News and Information Revolutions: What Americans Know 1989–2007*, Washington, DC: Pew Research Center, 2007. Online. Available HTTP: <http://people-press.org/reports/print.php3?PageID=1137> (accessed September 21, 2007); for similar results see T. Patterson, *Young People and News*, Joan Shorenstein Center on the Press, Politics and Public Policy Report, Harvard University, 2007.

28   For example, the BBC urgently sought, in 2007, to connect to the news concerns of the young and ethnic minorities, following a report concluding that the corporation's television news is losing its appeal to these groups.

29   Curran and Seaton, *Power without Responsibility*; J. Turow, *Breaking Up America*, Chicago: University of Chicago Press, 1997; C. E. Baker, *Advertising and a Democratic Press*, Princeton: Princeton University Press, 1994.

Chapter 4

1   J. Curran and J. Seaton, *Power without Responsibility*, 7th edn, London: Routledge, 2010.

2   M. Hampton, *Visions of the Press in Britain, 1850–1950*, Urbana: University of Illinois Press, 2004.

3   M. Delli Carpini and B. Williams, 'Let us infotain you: politics in the new media environment', in W. L. Bennett and R. Entman (eds), *Mediated Politics*, New York: Cambridge University Press, 2001. This argument is extended in an important essay, B. Williams and M. Delli Carpini, 'Media regimes and democracy' in J. Curran (ed.), *Media and Society*, 5th edn, London: Bloomsbury Academic, 2010.

4   J. Wittebols, *The Soap Opera Paradigm*, Lanham, MD: Rowman &Littlefield, 2004.

5   This chapter is concerned only with the role of media entertainment in terms of the functioning of democracy, not with its wider role in terms of human fulfilment.

6   T. Frank, *What's the Matter with Kansas?*, New York: Metropolitan Books, 2004.

7   World Values Survey (1999–2001). <http://www.worldvaluessurvey.org> (accessed July 10, 2010).

8   H. Milner, *Civic Literacy*, Hanover, NH: University Press of New England, 2002.

9   T. Judt, *Reappraisals*, London: Vintage, 2009.

10   K. O. Morgan, *Britain since 1945*, 2nd edn, Oxford: Oxford University Press, 2001.

11   J. Curran, I. Gaber and J. Petley, *Culture Wars*, Edinburgh: Edinburgh University Press, 2005.

12   A. McCarthy, 'Reality television: a neo-liberal theatre of suffering', *Social Text*, 25(4), 2007: 17–41.

13 Ibid., p. 30.

14 L. Ouellette, "'Take responsibility for yourself'": Judge Judy and the neo-liberal citizen' in S. Murray and L. Ouellette (eds), *Reality TV*, 2nd edn, New York: New York University Press, 2009, pp. 223–42, p. 232.

15 *Casualty*, Season 16, Episode 9, 'Distant Elephants' (transmitted BBC1, November 10, 2001.)

16 C. Hay, *Why We Hate Politics*, Cambridge: Polity, 2007; A. Heath, R. Jowell and J. Curtice, *The Rise of New Labour*, Oxford: Oxford University Press, 2001.

17 K. Gelder, *Subcultures Reader*, 2nd edn, London: Routledge, 2005; J. Fornas, U. Lindberg and O. Sernhede, *In Garageland*, London: Routledge, 1995.

18 D. Hebdige, 'Skinheads and the search for white working class identity', *New Socialist*, 1(1), 1981: 38–41.

19 L. Blackman, "'Inventing the psychological'": lifestyle magazines and the fiction of self-hood' in J. Curran and D. Morley (eds), *Media and Cultural Theory*, London: Routledge, 2005; A. McRobbie, *The Aftermath of Feminism*, London: Sage, 2008.

20 D. Kellner, *Media Culture*, London: Routledge, 1995.

21 E. van Zoonen, *Entertaining the Citizen*, Lanham, MD: Rowman & Littlefield, 2004; J. Steet, *Politics and Popular Culture*, Cambridge: Polity, 1997.

22 S. Iyengar, *Is Anyone Responsible?*, Chicago: University of Chicago Press, 1991.

23 J. D. Slocum (ed.), *Hollywood and War*, New York: Routledge, 2006.

24 J.-M. Valentin, *Hollywood, Pentagon and Washington*, London: Anthem Press, 2005. According to Valentin, the Pentagon usually demanded to see advance information about the film's storyline before providing assistance.

25 R. Brooks, 'Don't tell these guys torture is wrong: the GOP debate was a Jack Bauer impersonation contest', *Los Angeles Times*, May 18, 2007. Online. Available HTTP: <http://www.commondreams.org/archive/2007/05/18/1284> (accessed October 12, 2009).

26 A. Sullivan, 'Scala and torture', *The Daily Dish*, 2007. Online. Available HTTP: <http://andrewsullivan.theatlantic.com/the_daily_dish/2007/06/scalia_and_tort.html> (accessed October 14, 2009).

27 Anon., '24: Bill Clinton OK with Jack Bauer's torture tactics', *Buddy TV*, 2007. Online. Available HTTP: <http://www.buddytv.com/articles/24/24-bill-clinton-ok-with-jack-b-117533.aspx> (accessed October 14, 2009); M. McAuliff, 'Torture like Jack Bauer's would be OK, Bill Clinton says', *NY Daily News.Com*, 2007. Online. Available HTTP: <http://www.nydailynews.com/news/national/2007/10/01/2007-10-01_torture_like_jack_bauers_would_be_ok_bil.html> (accessed October 14, 2009).

28 A. Buncombe, 'US military tells Jack Bauer … cut out the torture scenes … or else!', *Independent*, February 13, 2007. Online. Available HTTP: <http://www.independent.co.uk/news/world/americas/us-military-tells-jack-bauer-cut-out-the-torture-scenes--or-else-436143.html> (accessed October 13, 2009).

29 B. Meyer, 'Jesus vs. Jack Bauer', *Cleveland.com*, 2009. Online. Available HTTP: <http://www.cleveland.com/.../torture_debate_prompts_evangel.html> (accessed October 12, 2009).

30 For example, Anon., 'Andrew Sullivan criticizes Jack Bauer cartoon', *Neveryetmelted.com*, 2007. Online. Available HTTP: <http://neveryetmelted.com/2007/05/03/andrew-sullivan-criticizes-jack-bauer-cartoon-torture/> (accessed October 14, 2009).

31 This debate is played out in the 39,100 items recorded by Google on the subject of Jack Bauer and torture [Jack Bauer=torture], as of October 16, 2009. The most prominent of these are voluminous American media news and feature articles.

32 Pew Research Center, 'Public Remains Divided over Use of Torture', Washington, DC: Pew Research Center, 2009. Online. Available HTTP: <http://people-press.org/report/510/public-remains-divided-over-use-of-torture> (accessed October 14, 2009).

33   There was little sustained movement of attitudes towards torture between November 2007 and April 2009, save for a small increase (4 percentage points) in those who thought that torture was 'sometimes' necessary (ibid.).

34   These two themes will be discussed more fully in Chapter 8. A summary has been retained here because they are integral to this chapter's argument.

35   L. Gross, 'Minorities, majorities and the media' in T. Liebes and J. Curran (eds), *Media, Ritual and Identity*, London: Routledge, 1998.

36   G. Evans, 'In search of tolerance' in A. Park, J. Curtice, K. Thomson, L. Jarvis and C. Bromley (eds), *British Social Attitudes: The 19th Report*, London: Sage, 2002.

37   G. Gleeber, *Serial Television*, London: British Film Institute, 2004.

38   S. K. Kent, *Gender and Power in Britain, 1640–1990*, London: Routledge, 1999; D. Gorham, *The Victorian Girl and the Feminine Ideal*, London: Croom Helm, 1982.

39   M. Tusan, *Women Making News*, Urbana: University of Illinois Press, 2005.

40   A. Bingham, *Gender, Modernity and the Popular Press in Interwar Britain*, Oxford: Clarendon Press, 2004.

41   G. Murphy, 'Media influence on the socialisation of teenage girls' in J. Curran, A. Smith and P. Wingate (eds), *Impacts and Influences*, London: Methuen, 1987, pp. 202–17.

42   J. Thumim, *Celluloid Sisters*, New York: St. Martin's Press, 1992.

43   A. Lotz, *Redesigning Women*, Urbana: University of Illinois Press, 2006.

44   R. Crompton, M. Brockman and R. Wiggins, 'A woman's place … employment and family life for men and women' in A. Park, J. Curtice, K. Thomson, L. Jarvis and C. Bromley (eds), *British Social Attitudes: The 20th Report*, London: Sage, 2003, p. 164.

45   Ibid., pp. 164–5.

46   A. Henry, 'Orgasms and empowerment: *Sex and the City* and the third wave feminism' in K. Akass and J. McCabe (eds), *Reading Sex and the City*, London: I. B. Tauris, 2004, pp. 65–82.

47   A. McRobbie, *The Uses of Cultural Studies*, London: Sage, 2005.

48   E. Hobsbawm, *Age of Extremes*, London: Michael Joseph, 1994; C. Leys, *Market-Driven Politics*, London: Verso, 2001, among others.

49   D. Held and A. McGrew, *Globalization/Anti-Globalization*, Cambridge: Polity, 2007.

50   J. Stiglitz, *Making Globalisation Work*, London: Penguin Books, 2006; L. Sklair, *Globalization*, Oxford: Oxford University Press, 2002.

51   D. Held, *Global Covenant*, Cambridge: Polity, 2004; Held and McGrew, *Globalization/Anti-Globalization*.

52   H. Wessler, B. Peters, M. Bruggemann, K. K.-v. Konigslow and S. Sift, *The Transnationalization of Public Spheres*, Basingstoke: Palgrave Macmillan, 2008.

53   M. Albrow, H. Anheier, M. Glasius, M. E. Price and M. Kaldor (eds), *Global Civil Society 2007/8*, London: Sage, 2008.

54   N. Fraser, 'Transnationalizing the public sphere: on the legitimacy and efficacy of public opinion in a post-Westphalian world', *Theory, Culture and Society*, 24(4), 2007: 7–30.

55   Internetworld.stats. Online. Available HTTP: <http://www.internetworldstats.com> (accessed August 20, 2009).

56   The British data are derived from Office of Communications (Ofcom), *New News, Future News*, London: Ofcom, 2007. My thanks go to Toril Aalberg for supplying comparable survey data for Sweden and Norway. Since then, the proportion of people using the Internet as their main source of news has significantly increased, but they remain in a minority even in economically developed societies. See page 115.

57   T. Miller, N. Govil, J. McMurria, R. Maxwell and T. Wang, *Global Hollywood 2*, London: British Film Institute, 2005.

58   J. Steemers, *Selling Television*, London: British Film Institute, 2004.

59   K. Hafez, *The Myth of Media Globalization*, Cambridge: Polity, 2007.

60   J. Tunstall, *The Media Were American: U.S. Mass Media in Decline*, New York: Oxford University Press, 2008.

61   T. Carlyle, *On Heroes, Hero-Worship and the Heroic in History*, London, 1841. Online. Available HTTP: <http://www.gutenberg.org/files/1091/1091-h/1091-h.htm> (accessed July 19, 2010).

62   For example G. Overholser and K. H. Jamieson (eds), *The Press*, The Institutions of American Democracy Series, New York: Oxford University Press, 2005; J. Lichtenberg, *Democracy and the Mass Media*, New York: Cambridge University Press, 1990.

63   L. Gross and J. Woods (eds), *The Columbia Reader on Lesbians and Gay Men in Media, Society and Politics*, New York: Columbia University Press, 1999.

64   S. Strohm, 'The black press and the black community: the *Los Angeles Sentinel*'s coverage of the Watts riots' in M. Mander (ed.), *Framing Friction*, Urbana: University of Illinois Press, 1999, pp. 58–88.

65   Curran and Seaton, *Power without Responsibility*, ch. 2.

66   See, for example E. Friedman, 'Lesbians in (cyber)space: the politics of the Internet in Latin-American on- and off-line communities', *Media, Culture and Society*, 29(5), 2007: 790–811; T. Kern and S.-H. Nan, 'The making of a social movement: citizen journalism in Korea', *Current Sociology*, 57(6), 2009: 637–66; Y. Song, 'Internet news media and issue development: a case study in the roles of independent online news services as agenda-builders in South Korea', *New Media and Society*, 2007, 9(1), 2007:71–92; M. Aouagh, 'Everyday resistance on the Internet: the Palestinian context', *Journal of Arab and Muslim Media Research*, 1(2), 2008: 109–30, among many others.

67   P. Dahlgren, *Media and Political Engagement*, Cambridge: Cambridge University Press, 2009; Hay, *Why We Hate Politics*; N. Couldry, S. Livingstone and T. Markham, *Media Consumption and Public Engagement*, Basingstoke: Palgrave Macmillan, 2007.

68   There are numerous summary maps of this literature. These include D. Held, *Models of Democracy*, 3rd edn, Cambridge: Polity, 2006; J. Fishkin, *When the People Speak*, Oxford: Oxford University Press, 2009; P. Starr, 'Democratic theory and the history of communications' in B. Zelizer (ed.), *Explorations in Communication and History*, London: Routledge, 2008, pp. 35–45; C. Edwin Baker, *Media, Markets and Democracy*, Cambridge: Cambridge University Press, 2002; C. Christians, T. Glasser, D. McQuail, K. Nordenstreng and R. White, *Normative Theories of the Media*, Urbana: University of Illinois Press, 2009; P. Dahlgren, *Media and Political Engagement*, New York: Cambridge University Press, 2009; and M. Ferree, W. Gamson, J. Gerhards and D. Rucht, *Shaping Abortion Discourse*, Cambridge: Cambridge University Press, 2002. There is a surprising degree of difference in their maps, registering an absence of consensus. My thanks to Katharina Hemmer and Frank Esser for pointing out the relevance of this last source.

69   See R. Dahl, *On Democracy*, New Haven: Yale University Press, 2007, for the classic version; and for a populist media statement, R. Murdoch, *Freedom in Broadcasting*, London: News International, 1989.

70   The key presentation of this approach is A. Downs, *An Economic Theory of Democracy*, New York: Harper, 1957. Influential versions of a rational-choice approach, with a focus on the media, are M. Schudson, *The Good Citizen*, New York: Simon & Schuster, 1998; and J. Zaller, 'A new standard of news quality: burglar alarms for the monitorial citizen', *Political Communication*, 20, 2003: 109–30.

71   The key text is J. Habermas, *The Theory of Communicative Action*, Boston: Beacon Press, 2004. For accounts centred on the media, see S. Chambers and A. Costain (eds), *Deliberation, Democracy, and the Media*, Lanham, MD: Rowman & Littlefield, 2000.

72   A very influential general text is N. Fraser, *Unruly Practices*, Minneapolis: University of Minnesota Press, 1989. For publications with a greater media focus, see J. Curran, 'Rethinking the media as a public sphere' in P. Dahlgren and C. Sparks (eds), *Communication and Citizenship*, London: Routledge, 1991, pp. 27–56; R. McChesney,

Communication Revolution, New York: New Press, 2007; and by implication, N. Fraser, 'Rethinking the public sphere: a contribution to the critique of actually existing democracy' in C. Calhoun (ed.), *Habermas and the Public Sphere*, Cambridge, MA: MIT Press, 1992.

73   Baker, *Media, Markets and Democracy*.

74   M. Delli Carpini and S. Keeter, *What Americans Know about Politics and Why It Matters*, New Haven: Yale University Press, 1996.

75   S. Kull, with C. Ramsay, A. Stephens, S. Weber, E. Lewis and J. Hadfield, 'Americans on Iraq: three years on', March 15, 2006, The WorldPublicOpinion.org/Knowledge Networks poll. Online. Available HTTP: <http://www.worldpublicopinion.org/pipa/pdf/mar06/USIraq_Mar06_rpt.pdf> (accessed June 13, 2010).

76   M. Castells, *Communication Power*, Oxford: Oxford University Press, 2009, pp. 166–7.

77   This is the central conclusion of Chapter 3. In this case, misperceptions arose not only from the low level of public-affairs knowledge among Americans, but also from misinformation both before and after the Iraq War.

Chapter 5

1   For example, I. Volkmer, 'The global network society and the global public sphere', *Development*, 46(1), 2003: 9–16; J. Bohman, 'Expanding dialogue: the Internet, the public sphere and prospects for transnational democracy', *Sociological Review*, 52(S1), 2004: 131–55; C. Calhoun, 'Information technology and the international public sphere' in D. Schuler and P. Day (eds), *Shaping the Network Society: The New Role of Civil Society in Cyberspace*, Cambridge, MA: MIT Press, 2004, pp. 229–51. Other synonyms for the international public sphere are the 'transnational public sphere' and 'global public sphere'.

2   N. Fraser, 'Transnationalizing the public sphere: on the legitimacy and efficacy of public opinion in a post-Westphalian world', *Theory, Culture and Society*, 24(4), 2007: 7–30.

3   For divergent socialist, radical democratic and liberal interpretations, see respectively O. Ugarteche, 'Transnationalizing the public sphere: a critique of Fraser', *Theory, Culture and Society*, 24(4), 2007: 65–9; Fraser, 'Transnationalizing the public sphere'; and Volkmer, 'The global network society'.

4   Office of Communications (Ofcom), *New News, Future News*, London: Ofcom, 2007, p. 17.

5   See Chapter 3.

6   K. Hafez, *The Myth of Media Globalization*, Cambridge: Polity, 2007; C. Lee, J. Chan, Z. Pan and C. So, 'National prisms of a global "media event"' in J. Curran and M. Gurevitch (eds), *Mass Media and Society*, 4th edn, London: Hodder Arnold, 2005.

7   Office of Communications (Ofcom), *Annexes to New News, Future News: Research and Evidence Base*, London: Ofcom, 2007, p. 90; K. A. Hill and J. E. Hughes, *Cyberpolitics: Citizen Activism in the Age of Internet*, Lanham, MD: Rowman & Littlefield, 1998.

8   Ofcom, *New News, Future News*; R. W. McChesney, *The Political Economy of Media: Enduring Issues, Emerging Dilemmas*, New York: Monthly Review Press, 2008.

9   D. Miller and D. Slater, *The Internet: An Ethnographic Approach*, Oxford: Berg, 2000.

10   J. Van Dijk, *The Deepening Divide*, Thousand Oaks, CA: Sage, 2005.

11   J. Tunstall, *The Media Were American: U.S. Mass Media in Decline*, New York: Oxford University Press, 2008.

12   Ibid.

13   J. Tomlinson, *Globalization and Culture*, Cambridge: Polity Press, 1999.

14   For example, N. Couldry, S.M. Livingstone and T. Markham, *Media Consumption and Public Engagement*, Basingstoke: Palgrave Macmillan, 2007.

15 L. Panitch and C. Leys (eds), *Global Capitalism versus Democracy* [Socialist Register 1999], Rendlesham: Merlin, 1999.

16 L. Sklair, *Globalization*, 3rd edn, Oxford: Oxford University Press, 2002; J. Stiglitz, *Globalization and Its Discontents*, London: Penguin Books, 2002.

17 For an especially illuminating discussion, see D. Held, A. McGrew, D. Goldblatt and J. Perraton, *Global Transformations*, Cambridge: Polity, 1999, and D. Held, *The Global Covenant*, Cambridge: Polity, 2004, which argue that a more democratically accountable, multilayered system of governance is the best way to reassert public power.

18 Both authors declare a personal interest: James Curran as an early volunteer, external 'media' co-editor with David Elstein and Todd Gitlin, and Tamara Witschge, who is currently involved in the e-zine's strategic discussions. Both authors have sought to maintain, however, academic detachment in writing this essay.

19 *openDemocracy* board meeting statistical report, July 2001.

20 N. Fountain, *Underground: The London Alternative Press 1966–74*, London: Routledge, 1988; J. Downing, *Radical Media*, Thousand Oaks, CA: Sage, 2001; K. Coyer, T. Dowmunt and A. Fountain, *The Alternative Media Handbook*, London: Routledge, 2007.

21 T. Gitlin, 'Is this our fate?', *openDemocracy*, 11September, 2001. Online. Available HTTP: <http://www.opendemocracy.net/conflict-us911/article_213.jsp> (accessed October 10, 2008).

22 *openDemocracy* board meeting statistical reports, August 2001; November 2001; December 2001.

23 *openDemocracy* board meeting statistical report, May 2002.

24 Google analytics.

25 P. Hirst and D. Held, 'Globalisation: the argument of our time', *openDemocracy*, January 22, 2002. Online. Available HTTP: <http://www.opendemocracy.net/globalization-institutions_government/article_637.jsp> (accessed October 10, 2010).

26 For example, J. McGirk, 'Thailand's king and that democracy jazz', *openDemocracy*, 11 June, 2006. Online. Available HTTP: <http://www.opendemocracy.net/democracy-protest/thailand_king_3633.jsp> (accessed October 12, 2008); N. Alavi, 'Iran's circle of power', *openDemocracy*, October 23, 2007. Online. Available HTTP: <http://www.open-democracy.net/article/democracy_power/irans_circle_of_power> (accessed October 12, 2008).

27 S. Brownell, 'The Olympics' "civilising" legacy: St Louis to Beijing', *openDemocracy*, May 23, 2008. Online. Available HTTP: <http://www.opendemocracy. net/editorial_tags/tibet_2008> (accessed October 13, 2008).

28 F. Khan, 'Getting real about globalisation in Bangladesh', *openDemocracy*, April 14, 2004. Online. Available HTTP: <http://www.opendemocracy.net/globalization-trade_economy_justice/article_1851.jsp> (accessed October 10, 2008).

29 C. Moorehead, 'Burundi: a life in fear', *openDemocracy*, October 5, 2003. Online. Available HTTP: <http://www.opendemocracy.net/people-migrationeurope/article_1524.jsp> (accessed October 12, 2008).

30 N. Baird, 'On street safari', *openDemocracy*, November 29, 2001. Online. Available HTTP: <http://www.opendemocracy.net/ecology-climate_change_debate/article_461.jsp>; M. Pospisil, 'Holidays at home: The Czech enthusiasm for weekend cottages and allotments', *openDemocracy*, December 12, 2001. Online. Available HTTP: <http://www.opendemocracy.net/node/440> (accessed October 14, 2008).

31 'About *openDemocracy*', *openDemocracy*, n.d. Online. Available HTTP: <http://www.opendemocracy.net/about> (accessed October 9, 2008).

32 United Nations Development Programme, 'Patterns of global inequality' in D. Held and A. McGrew (eds), *The Global Transformations Reader*, 2nd edn, Cambridge: Polity, 2003, p. 425.

33   United Nations, *World Economic and Social Survey 2006: Diverging Growth and Development*, 2006. Online. Available HTTP: <http://www.un.org/esa/policy/wess/wess2006files/wess2006.pdf> (accessed November 12, 2008).

34   M. Castells, *The Internet Galaxy*, Oxford: Oxford University Press, 2001, p. 264.

35   For example, S. Rushdie, 'Defend the right to be offended', *openDemocracy*, February 7, 2005. Online. Available HTTP: <http://www.opendemocracy.net/faith-europe_islam/article_2331.jsp> (accessed October 16, 2008).

36   R. Rorty, 'America's dreaming', *openDemocracy*, June 10, 2004. Online. Available HTTP: <http://www.opendemocracy.net/democracy-letterstoamericans/article_2067.jsp> (accessed October 14, 2008).

37   For example, P. Rogers, 'The countdown to war', *openDemocracy*, April 5, 2006. Online. Available HTTP: <http://www.opendemocracy.net/conflict/countdown_3426.jsp> (accessed October 14, 2008).

38   For example, Moorehead, 'Burundi'.

39   Interviews were conducted with nine *openDemocracy* editorial employees, past and present. These included the e-zine's three editors and its long-serving deputy editor, as well as junior staff. Past and present staff have not been differentiated, in order to preserve anonymity.

40   These quotations are derived from interviews with senior *openDemocracy* staff.

41   For example, K. Strauss, *Gender Inequality, Risk and European Pensions*, University of Oxford, Department of Geography and the Environment, Working Papers in Employment, Work and Finance, 06-13, 2006. Online. Available HTTP: <http://www.geog.ox.ac.uk/research/transformations/wpapers/wpg06-13.html> (accessed November 12, 2008).

42   J. Curran and J. Seaton, *Power without Responsibility*, 7th edn, London: Routledge, 2010.

43   Fawcett Society, 'Record number of women MPs', 2005. Online. Available HTTP: <http://www.fawcettsociety.org.uk/documents/Women_MPs_May05.pdf> (accessed January 8, 2008).

44   J. Redden and T. Witschge, 'A new news order? Online news content examined' in N. Fenton (ed.), *New Media, Old News*, London: Sage, 2010.

45   For example, J. Stratton, 'Cyberspace and the globalisation of culture' in D. Porter (ed.), *Internet Culture*, New York: Routledge, 1997.

46   For example, N. Robins, 'The East offering its riches to Britannia', *openDemocracy*, January 22, 2003. Online. Available HTTP: <http://www.opendemocracy.net/node/916> (accessed December 14, 2010)

47   For example, S. Ossman, 'Hair goes global: the view from the salons of Casablanca, Cairo and Paris', *openDemocracy*, December 19, 2002. Online. Available HTTP: <http://www.opendemocracy.net/arts-hair/article_857.jsp> (accessed December 4, 2008); E. Dikötter, 'Bring out the beast: body hair in China', *openDemocracy*, December 4, 2002. Online. Available HTTP: <http://www.opendemocracy.net/arts-china/article_811.jsp> (accessed December 4, 2008).

48   For example, A. Kushova, 'Besa', *openDemocracy*, July 21, 2004. Online. Available HTTP: <http://www.opendemocracy.net/arts/article_2114.jsp> (accessed October 12, 2008); M. Kamouchi, 'Sakura', *openDemocracy*, March 27, 2004. Online. Available HTTP: <http://www.opendemocracy.net/arts/article_2123.jsp> (accessed October 12, 2008).

49   This estimate is derived from information provided by two *openDemocracy* editors.

50   T. Berners-Lee, *Weaving the Web*, London: Orion, 2000.

51   S. Weber, *The Success of Open Source*, Cambridge, MA and London: Harvard University Press, 2004.

Chapter 6

1   Commission on the Freedom of the Press (Hutchins Commission), *A Free and Responsible Press*, Chicago: University of Chicago Press, 1947, pp. 34–5.

2   *US News and World Report*, September 29, 1975; *Washington Post*, June 5, 1978.
3   This view was championed by a number of senior British journalists in the mid-1980s (J. Curran and J. Seaton, *Power without Responsibility*, 6th edn, Abingdon: Routledge, 2003, p. 98).
4   *New York Times*, June 26, 1989.
5   Industry expert Tom Laster, reported in the *Boston Globe*, November 7, 1993.
6   See V. Mosco, *The Digital Sublime*, Cambridge, MA: MIT Press, 2005, for examples of Canadian and other false prophecies.
7   H. Galperin, *New Television, Old Politics*, Cambridge: Cambridge University Press, 2004; J. Hart, *Technology, Television and Competition*, Cambridge: Cambridge University Press, 2007; Mosco, *Digital Sublime*; R. Horwitz, *The Irony of Regulatory Reform*, New York: Oxford University Press, 1989.
8   Kenneth Baker (now Lord Baker) entered the cabinet as environment minister (1985–6), and held a succession of cabinet posts as education minister (1986–9), Chancellor of the Duchy of Lancaster (1989–90) and Home Secretary (1990–2).
9   Kenneth Baker, 'Parliamentary Debates', *Satellite and Cable Broadcasting*, 6th series, 22, London: Hansard, p. 230.
10 Ibid.
11 Cited in P. Goodwin, *Television under the Tories*, London: British Film Institute, 1998, p. 68.
12 Cited in D. Goldberg, T. Prosser and S. Verhurst, 'Regulating the changing media' in D. Goldberg, T. Prosser and S. Verhurst (eds), *Regulating the Changing Media*, Oxford: Clarendon Press, 1998, p. 10. This figure is so low that it was double-checked and found to be correct, on the basis of the number of cable TV homes in 1989 reported by the Cable Authority, *Annual Report and Accounts*, London: Cable Authority, 1990, p. 283, and the total number of TV homes in 1989, as recorded by the Broadcasters' Audience Research Board (BARB), 'Television ownership in private domestic households 1956–2009'. Online. Available HTTP: <http://www.barb.co.uk/tvfacts.cfm?fullstory=true&includepage=ownership&flag=tvfacts> (accessed on November 10, 2008).
13 Office of Communications (Ofcom), *The Communications Market 2008*, London: Ofcom, 2008, p. 211. Online. Available HTTP: <http://www.ofcom.org.uk/research/cm/cmr08/tv/tv.pdf> (accessed November 21, 2008).
14 Information derived from *Daily Telegraph*, September 6, 1995; and NatWest Customer Services.
15 Ofcom, *The Communications Market 2004 – Television Appendix: The Public's View Survey Results*, London: Ofcom, 2004, p. 4. Online. Available HTTP: <http://www.ofcom.org.uk/research/cm/cmpdf/cmr04_print/tele_apndx.pdf> (accessed November 21, 2008).
16 Ofcom, *The Communications Market 2007*, London: Ofcom, 2007, p. 120. Online. Available HTTP: <http://www.ofcom.org.uk/research/cm/cmr07/tv/tv.pdf> (accessed November 21, 2008). Revenue from TV shopping has been added to that for 'interactive services', as recorded in ibid., p. 120, figure 2.16.
17 Information derived from interview with senior research executive, Office of Communications, 2008.
18 Information provided by Nikki O'Shea, Factual Entertainment, Channel 4.
19 *New Media Age*, April 27, 2006.
20 *Precision Marketing*, March 9, 2007; cf. *New Media Age*, April 6, 2006.
21 Information Technology Advisory Panel (ITAP), *Cable Systems*, London: Cabinet Office, HMSO, 1982.
22 *Guardian*, August 6, 1990.
23 *Times*, May 24, 1995.
24 Office of Communication (Ofcom), *Digital Local Options for the Future of Local Video Content and Interactive Services*, London: Ofcom, January 19, 2006. Online. Available

HTTP: <http://www.ofcom.org.uk/tv/psb_review/digital_local.pdf> (accessed August 12, 2008).

25 Ibid., Annex A.
26 This estimate is derived from an Ofcom survey conducted in 2007 and is based on an internal extrapolation made by its research team. Local community TV audiences are too small to be measured reliably with standard national samples.
27 J. Cassidy, *Dot.Con*, London: Penguin Books, 2003.
28 Derived from Office of National Statistics (ONS), 'Internet access: households and individuals', London: ONS, 2 July, 2002, p. 1. Its data show that home internet access took off at the end of the dotcom boom and shortly afterwards. By January–March 2000, home internet access had risen to 25 per cent of households, and by January–March 2002, to 40 per cent. The low figure for April–June 1999 was made available in September 1999. Online retailing only became a commercial force in some market sectors when internet penetration had risen far above the level in the dotcom bubble.
29 S. Livingstone, 'Critical debates in internet studies: Reflections on an emerging field' in J. Curran and M. Gurevitch (eds), *Mass Media and Society*, 4th edn, London: Hodder Arnold, 2005; among others.
30 For example, P. Schlesinger, 'Rethinking the sociology of journalism: source strategies and the limits of media centrism' in M. Ferguson (ed.), *Public Communication*, London: Sage, 1990; P. Manning, *News and News Sources*, London: Sage, 2001; J. Curran, I. Gaber and J. Petley, *Culture Wars*, Edinburgh: Edinburgh University Press, 2005; N. Davies, *Flat Earth News*, London: Chatto and Windus, 2008.
31 J. Howkins, *New Technologies, New Policies*, London: British Film Institute, 1982; W. Dutton and J. Blumler, 'The faltering development of cable television in Britain', *International Political Science Review*, 9(4), 1988: 279–303; Goodwin, *Television under the Tories*.
32 ITAP, *Cable Systems*; ITAP, *Report of the Inquiry into Cable Expansion and Broadcasting Policy* (Hunt Report), London: HMSO, 1982.
33 *A New Future for Communications*, London: Stationery Office, 2000, p. 8.
34 Conversation with the author in June 2008.
35 *Daily Mirror*, October 4, 1995.
36 *Guardian*, July 3, 1998.
37 ITAP, *Cable Systems*.
38 *Guardian*, May 7, 2001.
39 Ibid., November 24, 2008.
40 *Sunday Times*, November 20, 1994.
41 ITAP, *Cable Systems*.
42 J. Martin, *The Wired Society*, Englewood Cliffs, NJ: Prentice-Hall, 1978; R. L. Smith, *The Wired Nation*, New York: Harper Colophon Books, 1972.
43 For example, *Economist*, August 19, 2000.
44 N. Negroponte, *Being Digital*, London: Coronet, 1996.
45 For instance, *Times*, December 9, 1982.
46 G. Richieri, *L'universo telematico*, Bari: De Donato, 1982.
47 B. Maddox, *Beyond Babel*, London: André Deutsch, 1972.
48 *Times*, June 10, 1982
49 Brenda Maddox subsequently left full-time journalism and wrote a number of acclaimed biographies (including a perceptive study of the scientist Rosalind Franklin).
50 G. Richieri, 'The history of interactive TV' in F. Colombo (ed.), *TV and Interactivity in Europe*, Milan: Vita e Pensiero, 2004.
51 *Guardian*, January 18, 1996.
52 Ibid., February 19, 1985.
53 K. Kumar, *Prophecy and Progress*, Harmondsworth: Penguin Books, 1978.

54   For a recent example of this modernist perspective, see Paddy Scannell, 'The question of technology' in M. Bailey (ed.), *Narrating Media History*, London: Routledge, 2009.

55   E. Epstein, *The Big Picture*, New York: Random House, 2005.

56   J. Curran and J. Seaton, *Power without Responsibility*, 7th edn, London: Routledge, 2010.

57   They made up the entire membership of the panel apart from one computer services academic.

58   Conversation with the author in June 2008.

59   P. Iosifidis, *Public Television in the Digital Age*, Basingstoke: Palgrave Macmillan, 2007; M. Kelly, G. Mazzoleni and D. McQuail (eds), *The Media in Europe*, 3rd edn, London: Sage; Open Society Institute (OSI), *Television across Europe*, 3 vols, Budapest: OSI, 2005.

Chapter 7

1   British media companies made this argument to the Office of Fair Trading, only for it to be rejected. See Office of Fair Trading, *Review of the Local and Regional Media Merger Regime*, June 2009. Online. Available HTTP: <http://www.oft.gov.uk/news/press/2009/71-09> (accessed December 23, 2009).

2   See, among others, P. Preston, 'Reasons to be cheerful, part 1: recession didn't stop the press', *Observer*, December 27, 2009.

3   'Financial woes now overshadow all other concerns for journalists', Pew Charitable Trust Report, March 17, 2008. Online. Available HTTP: <http://www.pewtrusts.org/our_work_report_detail.aspx?id=36600> (accessed July 1, 2009).

4   Information supplied by the Newspaper Society.

5   L. Downie and M. Schudson, 'The reconstruction of American journalism', *Columbia Journalism Review*, 2010. Online. Available HTTP: <http://www.cjr.org/reconstruction/the_reconstruction_of_american.php> (accessed January 10, 2010).

6   Pew Project for Excellence in Journalism, *State of the News Media 2009*, Washington, DC: Pew Research Center Publications, March 16, 2009. Online. Available HTTP: <http://www.stateofthemedia.org/2009/narrative_overview_intro.php?cat=0&media=1> (accessed December 10, 2009).

7   C. Tryhorn, 'Trinity Mirror sheds 1,200 jobs in 14 months', *Guardian*, February 26, 2009.

8   C. McNally, 'Northcliffe takes job cut target to 1,000 as revenue falls', *Press Gazette*, March 23, 2009.

9   J. Dear, 'The media are failing democracy. Politicians are failing the media', paper presented to the Media for All? The Challenge of Convergence conference, Campaign for Press and Broadcasting Freedom, October 31, 2009. Online. Available HTTP: <http://www.cpbf.org.uk/index_conf.html> (accessed December 21, 2009).

10 One of a series of wonderful Rowson covers, it was commissioned by Routledge for J. Curran and J. Seaton, *Power without Responsibility*, 7th edn, London: Routledge, 2010.

11 J. Nerone, 'The death (and rebirth?) of working-class journalism', *Journalism*, 10(3), 2009: 353–5, p. 355.

12 G. Monbiot, 'I, too, mourn good local newspapers, but this lot just aren't worth saving', *Guardian*, November 9, 2009. Online. Available HTTP: <http://www.guardian.co.uk/commentisfree/2009/nov/09/local-newspapers-democracy> (accessed December 14, 2009).

13 Nerone, 'Death (and rebirth?)'.

14 S. B. Johnson, 'Old growth media and the future of news', 2009. Online. Available HTTP: <http://www.stevenberlinjohnson.com/2009/03/the-following-is-a-speech-i-gave-yesterday-at-the-south-by-southwest-interactive-festival-in-austiniif-you-happened-to-being.html> (accessed February 4, 2009).

15 A substantial number of articles in *The Future of Journalism* special issue of *Journalism*, 10(3), 2009, veer towards this position, prompting me to label it the 'liberal educator' approach.

16 C. Beckett, *Supermedia*, Oxford: Blackwell, 2008, p. 170.

17 Cited R. McChesney and J. Nichols, *The Death and Life of American Journalism*, New York: Nation Books, 2010, p. 77.

18 Cited in Beckett, *Supermedia*, p. 108.

19 Interactive Advertising Bureau of Canada, 'Canadian online advertising revenue survey 2009'. Online. Available HTTP: <http://www.iabcanada.com/newsletters/072709.shtml> (accessed July 23, 2010).

20 Internet Advertising Bureau (IAB), *Fact Sheet: Online Adspend – H1 2009*, London: IAB, 2009.

21 Office of Fair Trading, *Review*.

22 Curran and Seaton, *Power without Responsibility*, p. 242.

23 Internet World Stats. Online. Available HTTP: <http://www.internetworldstats.com/Europa2.htm> (accessed December 1, 2009).

24 See the reports of the Internet Advertising Bureau (US), Internet Advertising Bureau (UK), IREP (France) and Interactive Advertising Bureau of Canada, among others.

25 According to Internet World Stats. Online. Available HTTP: <http://internet.world.stats.com> (accessed July 23, 2010).

26 Pew Project for Excellence in Journalism, *State of the News Media*.

27 R. Benson, 'Future of the news: international considerations and future reflections' in Natalie Fenton (ed.), *New Media, Old News*, London: Sage, 2010.

28 T. Aalberg, P. van Aelst and J. Curran, 'Media systems and the political information environment: a cross-national comparison', *International Journal of Press/Politics*, 15(3), 2010: 255–71.

29 See p. 215n148.

30 Pew Research Center for the People and the Press, 'Internet overtakes newspapers as news outlet'. Washington, DC: Pew Research Center, December 23, 2008. Online. Available HTTP: <http://people-press.org/report/479/internet-overtakes-newspapers-as-news-source> (accessed December 1, 2009).

31 Nielsen NetRatings Website Ranking, January 2009. My thanks to David Cowling (BBC) for supplying this information.

32 'Reach and percentage growth for UK news websites' (table derived from Nielsen, September 2008). BBC News Online, '2008's highlights'. My thanks again to David Cowling.

33 Pew Project for Excellence in Journalism, *State of the News Media*.

34 B. Franklin and D. Murphy (eds), *Making the Local News*, London: Routledge, 1998.

35 Fenton (ed.), *New Media, Old News*.

36 See Chapter 1.

37 E. Scott, '"Big media" meets the "bloggers": coverage of Trent Lott's remarks at Strom Thurmond's birthday party', Kennedy School of Government Case Study C14-04-1731.0. Cambridge, MA: John Kennedy School of Government, Harvard University, 2004.

38 D. Smillie, 'San Diego news shoot-out', *Forbes.com*, June 8, 2009. Online. Available HTTP: <http://www.forbes.com/2009/06/05/internet-advertising-newspapers-business-media-san-diego.html> (accessed December 21, 2009); Pew Project for Excellence in Journalism, Special Report, *Citizen-Based Media*, Washington, DC: Pew Research Center, 2009. Online. Available HTTP: <http://www.stateofthemedia.org/2009/narrative_special_citzenbasedmedia.php?media=12&cat=0> (accessed December 28, 2009).

39 J. Cummings, 'RNC shells out $150k for Palin fashion', *Politico*, October 21, 2008. Online. Available HTTP: <http://www.politico.com/news/stories/1008/14805.html> (accessed December 19, 2009).

40 See also M. Garcelon, 'The "Indymedia" experiment', *Convergence*, 12(1), 2006: 55–82, among others.

41   Paul Steiger, 'US investigative reporting in the internet age', paper presented to the Axess Future of Journalism conference, London, July 9, 2010.

42   Office of National Statistics (ONS), *Internet Access 2008: Households and Individuals*, London: ONS, 2008.

43   Pew Project for Excellence in Journalism, *Citizen-Based Media*.

44   Pew Project for Excellence in Journalism, Special Report, *New Ventures*, Washington, DC: Pew Research Center, 2009. Online. Available HTTP: <http://www.stateofthemedia. org/2009/narrative_special_newventures.php?media=12&cat=2> (accessed December 21, 2009).

45   Pew Project for Excellence in Journalism, *State of the News Media*.

46   J. Redden and T. Witschge, 'A new news order? Online news content examined' in Fenton (ed.), *New Media, Old News*. This matters because, as they point out, most internet users in Europe and the US do not go beyond the first page.

47   Ibid.

48   N. Couldry, 'New online sources and writer-gatherers' in Fenton (ed.), *New Media, Old News*.

49   Pew Project for Excellence in Journalism, *State of the News Media*.

50   Downie and Schudson, 'Reconstruction'.

51   J. Curran, *Media and Power*, London: Routledge, 2002.

52   Steiger, 'US investigative reporting'.

53   Downie and Schudson, 'Reconstruction'.

54   McChesney and Nichols, *Death and Life*.

55   Nielsen NetRatings Website Ranking, January 2009.

56   Information derived from Ina Zwerger at Österreichischer Rundfunk.

57   *Guardian*, July 26, 2010.

58   For a detailed account of the BBC's struggle, in the face of press opposition, to report the news, see A. Briggs, *The Golden Age of the Wireless*, London: Oxford University Press, 1965, pp. 152–5.

59   For a description and justification of publicly funded local news hubs, see N. Fenton, M. Metykova, J. Schlosberg and D. Freedman, *Local News Hubs: Meeting the News Needs of Local Communities*, Goldsmiths Leverhulme Media Research Centre/Media Trust Report, London: Media Trust, 2010.

Chapter 8

1   J. Curran, *Media and Power*, London: Routledge, 2002. See also J. Curran, 'Media and the making of British society, *c.* 1700–2000', *Media History*, 8(2), 2002: 134–54.

2   M. Bailey (ed.), *Narrating Media History*, London: Routledge, 2009.

3   See in particular B. Harris, *Politics and the Rise of the Press: Britain and France 1620–1800*, London: Routledge, 1996; and H. Barker, *Newspapers, Politics and English Society, 1695–1855*, Edinburgh: Longman, 2000.

4   For example, D. Read, *Press and People, 1790–1850*, London: Arnold, 1961; H. Perkin, *The Origins of Modern English Society, 1780–1880*, London: Routledge and Kegan Paul, 1969; J. Brewer, *Party Ideology and Popular Politics at the Accession of George III*, Cambridge: Cambridge University Press, 1976; and a more recent airing of this argument, P. Brett, 'Early nineteenth-century reform newspapers in the provinces: the *Newcastle Chronicle* and *Bristol Mercury*' in M. Harris and T. O'Malley (eds), *Newspaper and Periodical Annual 1995*, Westport, CT: Greenwood, 1997.

5   Among others, J. C. D. Clark, *English Society 1688–1832*, Cambridge: Cambridge University Press, 1985; R. Price, *British Society, 1680–1880*, Cambridge: Cambridge University Press, 1999; D. Cannadine, *History in Our Time*, London: Penguin Books, 2000.

6   J. Black, *The English Press 1621–1861*, Stroud: Sutton, 2001.

7   Barker, *Newspapers, Politics and English Society*, p. 4.

8   Ibid., p. 222.

9   Ibid., p. 5.

10 Black, *English Press*, p. 107.

11 Ibid., p. 192.

12 C. Seymour-Ure, 'National daily papers and the party system' in *Studies on the Press*, Royal Commission on the Press Working Paper no. 3, London: HMSO, 1977; G. Boyce, 'The fourth estate: the reappraisal of a concept' in G. Boyce and P. Wingate (eds), *Newspaper History*, London: Constable, 1978.

13 S. Koss, *The Rise and Fall of the Political Press in Britain*, vol. 2, London: Hamish Hamilton, 1984.

14 B. Harrison, 'Press and pressure group in modern Britain' in J. Shattock and M. Wolff (eds), *The Victorian Periodical Press: Samplings and Soundings*, Leicester: Leicester University Press, 1982, p. 282.

15 J. Black, 'The press and politics in the eighteenth century', *Media History*, 8(2), 2002: 175–82; Brewer, *Party Ideology*; Harris, *Politics and the Rise of the Press*.

16 Political theorists differ in where they locate political parties within their conceptual maps. Parties are perhaps best viewed as being half in and half out of civil society: indeed, ideally, conduits between civil society and the state.

17 For example P. Hollis, *The Pauper Press*, Oxford: Oxford University Press, 1970.

18 Black, 'The press and politics'.

19 M. Hampton, *Visions of the Press in Britain, 1850–1950*, Urbana: University of Illinois Press, 2004.

20 M. Hampton, 'Renewing the liberal tradition: the press and public discussion in twentieth-century Britain' in Bailey (ed.), *Narrating Media History*.

21 The classic exposition of this interpretation is provided by P. Scannell, 'Public service broadcasting and public life' in P. Scannell, P. Schlesinger and C. Sparks (eds), *Culture and Power*, London: Sage, 1992.

22 H. Chignell, 'Change and reaction in BBC current affairs radio, 1928–1970' in Bailey (ed.), *Narrating Media History*.

23 Cited in C. White, *Women's Magazines, 1693–1968*, London: Michael Joseph, 1970, p. 42.

24 J. Thumim, *Celluloid Sisters*, New York: St. Martin's Press, 1992, p. 210.

25 This is the key point made in M. DiCenzo, 'Feminist media and history: a response to James Curran', *Media History*, 10(1), 2004: 43–9.

26 Cited in M. Tusan, *Women Making News*, Urbana and Chicago: University of Illinois Press, 2005, p. 99.

27 D. Deacon, '"Going to Spain with the boys": Women correspondents and the Spanish Civil War' in Bailey (ed.), *Narrating Media History*.

28 See for example Chapter 11, below, which also raises the question of whether changes in the gender composition of the media workforce made a difference.

29 A. Bingham, *Gender, Modernity and the Popular Press in Interwar Britain*, Oxford: Clarendon Press, 2004.

30 M. Bailey, 'The angel in the ether: early radio and the constitution of the household' in Bailey (ed.), *Narrating Media History*.

31 D. Dugaw, *Warrior Women and Popular Balladry, 1650–1850*, Cambridge: Cambridge University Press, 1989.

32 M. Beetham, *A Magazine of Her Own?*, London: Routledge, 1996.

33 M. Landy, *British Genres: Cinema and Society, 1930–1960*, Princeton: Princeton University Press, 1991.

34 D. Philips and I. Haywood, *Brave New Causes*, London and Washington: Leicester University Press, 1998.

35   D. Philips, *Women's Fiction 1945–2005*, London: Continuum, 2006.

36   A. Lotz, *Redesigning Women*, Urbana and Chicago: University of Illinois Press, 2006; L. Cooke, *British Television Drama: A History*, London: British Film Institute, 2003.

37   A. McRobbie, '*More!*: new sexualities in girls' and women's magazines' in J. Curran, D. Morley and V. Walkerdine (eds), *Cultural Studies and Communications*, London: Arnold, 1996.

38   M. Macdonald, *Representing Women*, London: Arnold, 1995.

39   K. Boyle, 'Feminism without men: feminist media studies in a post-feminist age' in J. Curran and M. Gurevitch (eds), *Mass Media and Society*, 4th edn, London: Hodder Arnold, 2005.

40   L. Blackman, '"Inventing the psychological": lifestyle magazines and the fiction of autonomous selfhood' in J. Curran and D. Morley (eds), *Media and Cultural Theory*, London: Routledge, 2005.

41   See Chapter 4 for more detailed discussion of *Sex and the City*.

42   See, for example, the pioneering study by J. Tosh, *A Man's Place*, New Haven: Yale University Press, 1999.

43   While space does not permit a full exposition of this and subsequent narratives outlined in this chapter, they are presented more fully in Curran, *Media and Power*.

44   S. Hall, 'Popular power and the state' in T. Bennett, C. Mercer and J. Woollacott (eds), *Popular Culture and Social Relations*, Milton Keynes: Open University Press, 1986.

45   J. Petley, 'What fourth estate?' in Bailey (ed.), *Narrating Media History*.

46   J. Allen and O. Rushton (eds), *Papers for the People*, London: Merlin, 2005.

47   J. Plunkett, *Queen Victoria: First Media Monarch*, Oxford: Oxford University Press, 2003.

48   M. Bailey, 'Broadcasting and the problem of enforced leisure during the 1930s', *Leisure Studies*, 26(4), 2007: 463–77, p. 464.

49   J. Habermas, *The Structural Transformation of the Public Sphere*, Cambridge: Polity, 1989 (first German edition 1962).

50   J. Habermas, 'Concluding remarks' in C. Calhoun (ed.), *Habermas and the Public Sphere*, Cambridge, MA: MIT Press, 1992.

51   J. Flanders, *Consuming Passions*, London: Harper Press, 2006, p. xvii.

52   J. Nott, *Music for the People*, Oxford: Oxford University Press, 2002, p. 227.

53   J. Milland, 'The Pilkington Report: the triumph of paternalism?' in Bailey (ed.), *Narrating Media History*.

54   For example, S. Wilson, 'Real people with real problems? Public service broadcasting, commercialism and *Trisha*', and M. Hills, 'Who wants to be a fan of *Who Wants to be a Millionaire?*' both in C. Johnson and R. Turrock (eds), *ITV Cultures*, Maidenhead: Open University Press, 2005.

55   L. Colley, *Britons: Forging the Nation, 1707–1837*, London: Pimlico, 1992.

56   J. Mackenzie, *Propaganda and Empire*, Manchester: Manchester University Press, 1984; J. Richards, *Films and British National Identity: From Dickens to Dad's Army*, Manchester: Manchester University Press, 1997.

57   J. Chapman, *Past and Present*, London: I. B. Tauris, 2005.

58   R. Weight, *Patriots*, London: Pan, 2003.

59   P. Ward, *Britishness since 1870*, London: Routledge, 2004.

60   R. Colls, *Identity of England*, Oxford: Oxford University Press, 2002, p. 380.

61   K. Kumar, *The Making of English National Identity*, Cambridge: Cambridge University Press, 2003.

62   D. Barlow, P. Mitchell and T. O'Malley, *The Media in Wales*, Cardiff: University of Wales Press, 2005.

63   Ibid., p. 47.

64   Ibid., p. 144, table 6.2.

65   See for example, J. Medhurst, 'Television in Wales, *c.* 1950–70', and D. Day, '"Nation shall speak peace unto nation": the BBC and the projection of a new Britain, 1967–82' both in Bailey (ed.), *Narrating Media History*.

66   S. Cohen, *Folk Devils and Moral Panics*, 2nd edn, Oxford: Martin Robertson, 1980; S. Hall, C. Critcher, T. Jefferson, J. Clarke and B. Robert, *Policing the Crisis: Mugging, the State, and Law and Order*, London: Macmillan, 1978; P. Golding and S. Middleton, *Images of Welfare*, Oxford: Martin Robertson, 1982.

67   J. Curran, I. Gaber and J. Petley, *Culture Wars*, Edinburgh: Edinburgh University Press, 2005.

68   C. Critcher, *Moral Panics and the Media*, Buckingham: Open University Press, 2003.

69   Hall *et al.*, *Policing the Crisis*.

70   G. Creeber, *Serial Television*, London: British Film Institute, 2004; L. Cooke, *British Television Drama*, London: British Film Institute, 2003.

71   H. Innis, *The Bias of Communication*, Toronto: Toronto University Press, 1951.

72   E. Eisenstein, *The Printing Press as an Agent of Change*, 2 vols, Cambridge: Cambridge University Press, 1979.

73   M. McLuhan, *Understanding Media*, London: Routledge and Kegan Paul, 1964.

74   J. Meyrowitz, *No Sense of Place*, New York: Oxford University Press, 1985.

75   P. Evans and T. Wurster, *Blown to Bits*, Boston, MA: Harvard Business School Press, 2000.

76   R. Tsagarousianou, D. Tambini and C. Bryan (eds), *Cyberdemocracy*, London: Routledge, 1998.

77   M. Poster, *The Second Media Age*, Cambridge: Polity, 1995.

78   J. Stratton, 'Cyberspace and the globalisation of culture' in D. Porter (ed.), *Internet Culture*, New York: Routledge, 1997.

79   S. Turkle, *Life on the Screen*, New York: Simon & Schuster, 1997.

80   H. Rheingold, *The Virtual Community*, rev. edn, Cambridge, MA: MIT Press, 2000.

81   C. Anderson, *The Long Tail*, London: Random House Business Books, 2006.

82   N. Negroponte, *Being Digital*, London: Hodder and Stoughton, 1996.

83   These themes are being developed in a companion book, J. Curran, D. Freedman and N. Fenton (eds), *Misunderstanding the Internet*, London: Routledge (forthcoming).

84   P. Scannell, 'The question of technology' in Bailey (ed.), *Narrating Media History*.

85   G. Murdock and M. Pickering, 'The birth of distance: communication and changing conceptions of elsewhere' in Bailey (ed.), *Narrating Media History*.

86   M. Blondheim, 'Narrating the history of media technologies: pitfalls and prospects' in Bailey (ed.), *Narrating Media History*.

87   Curran, *Media and Power*.

88   T. Marshall, *Citizenship and Social Class and Other Essays*, Cambridge: Cambridge University Press, 1950.

89   G. Murdock, 'Citizens, consumers and public culture' in M. Skovmand and K. Schroder (eds), *Media Cultures*, London: Routledge, 1992; and G. Murdock, 'Rights and representations: public discourse and cultural citizenship' in J. Gripsrud (ed.), *Television and Common Knowledge*, London: Routledge, 1999.

90   R. McKibbin, *Classes and Cultures*, Oxford: Oxford University Press, 1998.

91   J. Curran and J. Seaton, *Power without Responsibility*, 7th edn, London: Routledge, 2010.

92   K. Williams, *Get Me a Murder a Day!*, London: Arnold, 1998; J. Eldridge, J. Kitzinger and K. Williams, *The Mass Media and Power in Modern Britain*, Oxford: Oxford University Press, 1997.

93   P. Holland, *The Angry Buzz*, London: I. B. Tauris, 2006; J. Curran, 'Television and the public sphere: television journalism' in P. Holland, *Television Handbook*, London: Routledge, 1997; and M. Tracey, *In the Culture of the Eye*, London: Hutchinson, 1983.

94   S. Barnett, and A. Curry, *The Battle for the BBC*, London: Aurum, 1994.

95   J. Williams, *Entertaining the Nation*, Stroud: Sutton, 2004.

96   A. Briggs, *The History of British Broadcasting in the United Kingdom*, vols 1–4, Oxford: Oxford University Press, 1961–95.

97 P. Goodwin, *Television under the Tories*, London: British Film Institute, 1998; D. Freedman, *Television Politics of the Labour Party 1951–2001*, London: Cass, 2003; T. O'Malley and C. Soley, *Regulating the Press*, London: Pluto, 2000: S. Tunney, *Labour and the Press*, Eastbourne: Sussex Academic Press, 2007.

98 S. Schwarzkopf, "'A moment of triumph in the history of the free mind'? British and American advertising agencies' responses to the introduction of commercial television in the United Kingdom' in Bailey (ed.), *Narrating Media History*.

99 P. Flichy, 'New media history' in L. Lievrouw and S. Livingstone (eds), *The Handbook of New Media*, London: Sage, 2002; F. Turner, *From Counterculture to Cyberculture*, Chicago: University of Chicago Press, 2006; J. Abbate, *Inventing the Internet*, Cambridge, MA: MIT Press, 2000; C. Marvyn, *When Old Technologies were New*, New York: Oxford University Press, 1990; B. Winston, *Media Technology and Society*, London: Routledge, 1998.

100 This essay was the focus of a round-table debate by leading media historians in *Media History*, 16(2), 2010: 233–52.

101 For pioneer comparative media histories, see A. Briggs and P. Burke, *A Social History of the Media*, Cambridge: Polity, 2002; and J. Chapman, *Comparative Media History*, Cambridge: Polity, 2005. The case for media history to catch up with the rest of media studies by developing a comparative dimension is made in J. Curran, 'Communication and history' in B. Zelizer (ed.), *Explorations in Communication and History*, New York: Routledge, 2008.

Chapter 9

1 This is an updated, revised version of an essay (see Acknowledgements, p. xii, above) which I have shrunk by over a third.

2 Contrast for example, S. Koss, *The Rise and Fall of the Political Press in Britain*, vols 1 and 2, London: Hamish Hamilton, 1981 and 1984, with H. Barker, *Newspapers, Politics and English Society, 1695–1855*, Edinburgh: Longman, 2000.

3 A. Lee, *The Origins of the Popular Press 1855–1914*, London: Croom Helm, 1976; R. C. K. Ensor, *England 1817–1914*, Oxford: Clarendon Press, 1936.

4 M. Hampton, *Visions of the Press in Britain, 1850–1950*, Urbana: University of Illinois Press, 2001; C. J. Hambro, *Newspaper Lords in British Politics*, London: Macdonald, 1958.

5 P. Hollis, *The Pauper Press*, Oxford: Oxford University Press, 1970; J. Wiener, *The War of the Unstamped*, Ithaca, NY: Cornell University Press, 1969; W. H. Wickwar, *The Struggle for the Freedom of the Press, 1819–1832*, London: Allen & Unwin, 1928; and E. P. Thompson, *The Making of the English Working Class*, London: Gollancz, 1963.

6 F. S. Siebert, T. Peterson and W. Schramm, *Four Theories of the Press*, New York: Books of Libraries Press, 1973; F. Williams, *Dangerous Estate*, London: Grey Arrow, 1959; R. Marx, 'Abolition des "impôts sur le savoir" et liberté de la presse', *Revue Française de Civilisation Britannique*, 5(4), 1990: 7–22; Anon., *The History of The Times*, vol. 2, London: The Times Publishing Co., 1939, among many others. Outliers in the consensus include J. Chalaby, *The Invention of Journalism*, Basingstoke: Macmillan, 1998, which emphasises a revenge on the *Times* theme, and J. Steel, 'The "radical" narrative, political thought and praxis', *Media History*, 15(2), 2009: 221–38, which stresses idealism, understood in the context of contemporary utilitarian thought.

7 Dr Phillimore, *Parliamentary Debates*, xci, 1819, col. 1363, London: Hansard, 1819.

8 Wilmot, *Parl. Deb.*, xci, 1819, col. 1357.

9 Hollis, *The Pauper Press*.

10 J. Epstein, *The Lion of Freedom*, Beckenham: Croom Helm, 1982.

11 *Northern Star*, January 16, 1841. The reference was to this paper in particular.

12   This is based on an estimate of ten readers per copy, a conservative estimate in view of the evidence marshalled by Hollis, *The Pauper Press* and Wiener, *The War of the Unstamped*.

13   For example, Brougham, *Parl. Deb.*, xli, 1819, col. 1507.

14   Lord Howick's support for Hume's motion was probably due to the Grey family's opposition to the coalition ministry. Pelham's vote for the motion is also puzzling, since he was a steadfast supporter of the Stamp Duties Act: see, for instance, his explosive intervention in *Parl. Deb.*, xi, 1832, cols 491–2.

15   Scarlett, *Parl. Deb.*, 2nd series, xvii, 1827, col. 1067.

16   Cited Wiener, *The War of the Unstamped*, p. 94.

17   The other focal point of debate was whether, and by how much, reduction or repeal of the Stamp Duty would result in loss of government revenue.

18   These arguments were stated repeatedly by the two opposing sides in the great parliamentary debates of the 1830s. See, for instance, *Parl. Deb.*, xiii, 1832, cols 619–48; *Parl. Deb.*, xxiii, 1834, cols 1193–222; *Parl. Deb.*, xxx, 1835, cols 835–62; *Parl. Deb.*, xxiv, 1836, cols 627ff.; *Parl. Deb.*, xxxv, 1836, cols 566ff.; and *Parl. Deb.*, xxxvi, 1837, cols 1164–84. For typical examples of contemporary polemics on the subject see J. Crawfurd, *Taxes on Knowledge: A Financial and Historical View of the Taxes which Impede the Education of the People*, London: Charles Ely, 1836, and – for the opposing view – C. M. Westmacott, *The Stamp Duties: Serious Considerations on the Proposed Alteration of the Stamp Duty on Newspapers*, London: The Age Office, Catherine Street, 1836. In point of fact, the radical unstamped press was not given a 'clear field': but was consistently persecuted, unlike 'respectable' unstamped papers, in the early 1830s.

19   This did not include a small number of radical MPs like Wakley and Perronet Thompson.

20   Bulwer-Lytton, *Parl. Deb.*, xiii, 1832, col. 634.

21   Report of the Select Committee on Drunkenness, *Parliamentary Papers*, viii, 1834, quo. 2054.

22   Bulwer-Lytton, *Parl. Deb.*, xxiii, 1834, cols 1208–9.

23   Grote, *Parl. Deb.*, xxiii, 1834, col. 1221.

24   Spring Rice, *Parl. Deb.*, xxxiv, 1836, col. 634; and Spring Rice, *Parl. Deb.*, xxxvii, 1837, col. 1165.

25   C. D. Collet, *History of the Taxes on Knowledge*, London: T. Fisher Unwin, 1899, vol. 1, p. 84.

26   Ibid., p. 207.

27   Alderman Heywood, Report of the Select Committee on Newspaper Stamps, *Parliamentary Papers*, xvii, 1851, pp. 658ff.

28   Disraeli, *Parl Deb.*, cxxv, 1853, col. 1178; cf. Bulwer-Lytton, *Parl. Deb.*, cxxxvii, 1855, col. 1128.

29   Collet, *History of the Taxes on Knowledge*, pp. 193–215.

30   Cobden, *Parl. Deb.*, cxx, 1852, col. 1022.

31   Ewart, *Parl. Deb.*, cxxv, 1853, col. 1145.

32   Michael Whitty (Chief Constable of Liverpool), Report of the Select Committee on Newspaper Stamps, p. 688.

33   See *Parl. Deb.*, cx, 1850, cols 378ff. and 1237ff.; *Parl. Deb.*, cxx, 1852, cols 992ff.; *Parl. Deb.*, cxxi, 1852, cols 594ff.; *Parl. Deb.*, cxxv, 1853, cols 1119ff.; *Parl. Deb.*, cxxxviii, 1855, cols 448ff.; *Parl. Deb.*, cli, 1858, cols 98ff.; *Parl. Deb.*, clvii, 1860, cols 375ff.; and *Parl. Deb.*, clviii, 1860, cols 1434ff.

34   Palmerston, *Parl. Deb.*, cxxxvii, 1854, col. 459

35   Maguire, *Parl. Deb.*, clvii, 1860, col. 383.

36   Gladstone, cited in J. Grant, *The Newspaper Press: Its Origins, Progress and Present Position*, vol. 2, London: Tinsley Bros, 1871.

37   See, for instance, Bright, *Parl. Deb*, cxxv, 1853, col. 1160; Milner-Gibson, *Parl. Deb*, cxxv, 1853, cols 1131–2; Bulwer-Lytton, *Parl. Deb.*, cxxxvii, 1855, col. 1120; Marquess of Clanricarde, *Parl. Deb.*, clviii, 1860, col. 1495, among others.

38   A. Andrews, *The History of British Journalism to 1855*, London: Richard Bentley, 1859, vol. 2, p. 347.

39   Hickson, Report of the Select Committee on Newspaper Stamps, para. 3169.

40   Gladstone, *Parl. Deb.*, cxxxvii, 1855, col. 794. See also P. Magnus, *Gladstone*, London: John Murray, 1963, p. 152.

41   J. F. Stephen, 'Journalism', *Cornhill Magazine*, 6, 1862, pp. 57–8.

42   Milner-Gibson, *Parl. Deb.*, cxxvii, 1854, col. 434.

43   Milner-Gibson, like Cobden and Ewart, was well aware that newspaper publishing for the mass market would be capital-intensive. Among other things, they cross-examined Horace Greeley, the American pioneer of mass-market newspaper publishing, about publishing costs. See Report of the Select Committee on Newspaper Stamps, paras 2647ff.

44   Milner-Gibson, *Parl. Deb.*, cx, 1850, col. 378; cf. Hume, *Parl. Deb.*, cxxvii, 1854, col. 460.

45   Sir George Lewis, *Parl. Deb.*, cxxxvii, 1855, col. 786.

46   Michael Whitty, Report of the Select Committee on Newspaper Stamps, para. 600.

47   Bulwer-Lytton, *Parl. Deb.*, cxxxvii, 1855, col. 1118; cf. Lewis, *Parl. Deb.*, cxxxvii, 1855, col. 782; Ingram, *Parl. Deb.*, cli, 1858, col. 112; Digby Seymour, *Parl. Deb.*, cxxv, 1853, col. 1166.

48   Palmerston, *Parl. Deb.*, cxxxvii, 1855, col. 1163: cf. Cockburn, *Parl. Deb.*, cxxxvii, 1855, col. 1132.

49   Bright, *Parl. Deb.*, cxxvii, 1853, col. 118; Roebuck, *Parl. Deb.*, cx, 1850, col. 407; Spencer, Report of the Select Committee on Newspaper Stamps, para. 2369.

50   J. R. McCulloch, *Dictionary of Commerce and Commercial Navigation*, London: Longman, Brown and Green, 1854, p. 893.

51   Ibid.

52   While strongly against the Advertisement Duty, publishers in London and the English regions and – to a lesser extent – in Scotland were sharply split over the Stamp Duty. Many press proprietors believed that their enterprises would be undermined by cheap competition if the Stamp Duty were repealed.

53   This is well described in Collet, *History of the Taxes on Knowledge*.

54   *Northern Star*, February 26, 1842, and *Northern Star*, June 11, 1842.

55   *Northern Star*, May 7, 1842.

56   *Leeds Mercury*, June 14, 1851.

57   *Lloyd's Weekly Newspaper*, June 20, 1897.

58   Lord Castlereagh, *Parl. Deb.*, xci, 1819, col. 1177.

59   For an account of rising publishing costs, reflected in new launches between 1855 and 1912, see J. Curran, 'Capitalism and control of the press, 1800–1975' in J. Curran, M. Gurevitch and J. Woollacott (eds), *Mass Communication and Society*, London: Arnold, 1977, reprinted in J. Curran, *Media and Power*, London: Routledge, 2002.

60   D. Read, *Press and People, 1790–1850*, London: Arnold, 1961, p. 101; J. Epstein, 'Feargus O'Connor and the Northern Star', *International Review of Social History*, 21(1), 1976: 51–97, pp. 56–7.

61   A. J. P. Taylor, *Beaverbrook*, London: Hamish Hamilton, 1972, p. 175. Circulation estimate derived from W. Belson, *The British Press*, London: London Press Exchange, 1959, part 3, p. 14.

62   Curran, *Media and Power*.

63   Most commercial newspapers were dependent on advertising as early as the eighteenth century. See G. Cranfield, *The Development of the Provincial Newspaper, 1700–1760*, Oxford: Clarendon Press, 1962.

64   The shift to advertising dependency, even in the case of a large-circulation radical paper like *Reynolds's Newspaper*, occurred as early as the 1850s. See V. S. Berridge, 'Popular Journalism and Working-Class Attitudes, 1854–86: A Study of *Reynolds's Newspaper*, *Lloyd's Weekly Newspaper* and the *Weekly Times*', unpublished PhD thesis, University of London, 1976.

65   Curran, *Media and Power*.

66   A. Lee, 'The radical press' in A. Morris (ed.), *Edwardian Radicalism, 1900–1914*, London: Routledge and Kegan Paul, 1974.

67   The *Daily Herald* was still a weekly in 1918, having converted from a daily in order to avoid closing down.

68   J. Thomas, *Popular Newspapers, the Labour Party and British Politics*, London: Routledge, 2005.

69   D. Butler and G. Butler, *Twentieth-Century British Political Facts 1900–2000*, 8th edn, Basingstoke: Macmillan, 2000, pp. 536–7. This builds on an analysis pioneered by Colin Seymour-Ure.

70   *Royal Commission on the Press, Final Report* (Cmnd. 6810), London: HMSO, 1977, p. 98.

71   D. Kavanagh and P. Cowley, *The British General Election of 2001*, Basingstoke, Palgrave Macmillan, 2010.

72   For the way the last group was stigmatised, drawing on imagery derived from the past, see J. Curran, I. Gaber and J. Petley, *Culture Wars*, Edinburgh: Edinburgh University Press, 2005.

Chapter 10

1   This is an adapted version of an earlier essay (see Acknowledgements, p. xii, above) which I have shrunk by about a third. My thanks go to the Advertising Association for a small grant from its educational fund; and to J. Walter Thompson, Leo Burnett and the International Publishing Corporation for access to their archives and those of companies that they incorporated.

2   *Mitchell's Press Directory*, 5th edn, London: Mitchell, 1856, p. 7.

3   Anon., *Guide to Advertisers*, London, 1851.

4   *Mitchell's Press Directory*. Mitchell himself cautioned against political bias.

5   L. Brown, *Victorian News and Newspapers*, Oxford: Clarendon Press, 1985, p. 23.

6   Ibid.

7   Cited ibid., p. 57.

8   *How Much Shall We Spend in the Daily Mail?*, London: Associated Newspapers, n.d. [1928?], p. 8.

9   J. Murray Allison, *First Essays on Advertising*, London: Cecil Palmer, 1926, pp. 166ff., for his survey of what advertising publications were read.

10   E. Field, *Advertising: The Forgotten Years*, London: Bain, 1956, p. 118.

11   T. Russell, *Commercial Advertising*, Putnam, London, 1919, p. 1. His observations had been first presented in a course of lectures at the London School of Economics, which he perhaps unwisely reproduced as this book.

12   Ibid., p. 195.

13   T. Russell, *Advertising and Advertisements*, London: Modern Business Institute, 1924; T. Russell, *A Working Textbook of Advertising*, London: Russell Hart, 1925; C. Higham, *Advertising*, London: Williams and Norgate, 1925; and T. B. Lawrence (ed.), *What I Know about Advertising*, London: Spottiswoode, Ballantyre and Co., 1921, among others.

14   Thomas Russell estimated in 1919 that only 5 per cent of publications in Britain made their circulation figures available. See Russell, *Commercial Advertising*, p. 24.

15   N. Hunter, *Advertising through the Press*, London: Pitman, 1925, p. 52.

16   C. Freer, *The Inner Side of Advertising*, London: Library Press, 1921, p. 203.

17 London Press Exchange, 'Report of an investigation made in relation to the consumption of breakfast cereals in general and Grape Nuts in particular in the British Isles', LPE Ltd, company records, London, 1926.

18 *Press Circulations Analysed*, London: London Research Bureau, 1928.

19 A. G. Lyall, *Market Research: A Practical Handbook*, London: London Research Bureau, 1933.

20 G. Lansbury, *Miracle of Fleet Street*, London: Victoria House, 1925, p. 161.

21 This is well documented in H. Richards, *The Bloody Circus*, London: Pluto, 1997.

22 D. Butler and G. Butler, *Twentieth-Century British Political Facts 1900–2000*, Basingstoke: Macmillan, 2000, p. 234.

23 Only some national newspaper circulation figures are available for this year. This very approximate estimate is derived from W. Belson, *The British Press*, London: London Press Exchange, 1959, part 3, pp. 12–13, table 1.

24 *T. B. Browne Advertisers' ABC*, London: Browne, 1921.

25 P. Redmayne and H. Weeks, *Market Research*, London: Butterworth, 1931; H. W. Eley: *Advertising Media*, London: Butterworth, 1932.

26 Anon., 'Flash-backs – 1935', *Statistical Review of Press Advertising*, 4(1), 1936.

27 London Research Bureau's first readership survey was published by Associated Newspapers in *The Nation's Newspaper* (1924), which I have been unable to locate. It was followed by a syndicated survey in 1928 (*Press Circulations Analysed*) and by a 1930 survey sponsored by the IIPA.

28 These include surveys sponsored by the IIPA or the Incorporated Society of British Advertisers (ISBA) in 1931, 1932, 1934, 1936 and 1939; by national surveys conducted by the London Press Exchange (1934, 1938 and 1939), J. Walter Thompson (1936), Crawfords (1934), Repfords (1932 and 1937); and readership surveys commissioned by individual publishers (*Bolton Evening News*, Associated Newspapers, *John Bull*, *Morning Post*, *Daily Sketch*, among others) also during the 1930s.

29 Eley, *Advertising Media*, p. 172.

30 London Press Exchange, 'Farmer's Glory: memorandum on an advertising policy', LPE Ltd, company records, London, 1935.

31 Institute of Incorporated Practitioners in Advertising, *An Analysis of Press Circulations*, London: IIPA, 1934, p. 128.

32 N. Kaldor and R. Silverman, *A Statistical Analysis of Advertising Expenditure and of the Revenue of the Press*, Cambridge: Cambridge University Press, 1948.

33 These were conducted for the *Daily Sketch* (1933), *Daily Herald* (1933), *News Chronicle* (1934), *Daily Herald* (1936) and London Press Exchange (1938).

34 C. H. Feinstein, *Statistical Tables of National Income, Expenditure and Output of the U.K. 1855–65*, Cambridge: Cambridge University Press, 1976, p. 42.

35 R. Stone and D. A. Rowe, *The Measurement of Consumers' Expenditure and Behaviour in the United Kingdom 1920–38*, Cambridge: Cambridge University Press, 1966, pp. 8, 12, 17, 21 and 58.

36 G. Harrison and F. C. Mitchell, *The Home Market: A Handbook of Statistics*, London: Allen & Unwin, 1936; M. Abrams, *The Home Market*, London: Allen & Unwin, 1939.

37 'Sun-Maid plan 1929–30', J. Walter Thompson archives, 1929, p. 6.

38 Harrison and Mitchell, *Home Market*, p. 6.

39 *John Bull*, 'Each week the shopping bills of "John Bull" families exceed three million pounds' [advertisement], *Statistical Review of Press Advertising*, 1935, p. 2.

40 C. Chisholm, *Marketing and Merchandising*, London: Modern Business Institute, 1924.

41 Redmayne and Weeks, *Market Research*, p. 163.

42 Belson, *British Press*.

43 R. J. Minney, *Viscount Southwood*, London: Odhams, 1954, p. 243.

44 Ibid., pp. 286 and 291.

45   London Press Exchange, 'A statistical survey of press advertising during 1936', LPE Ltd, company records, London, 1937, p. 19.

46   Ibid. p. 12. The London Press Exchange estimates are based on applying ordinary position rates to the total volume of advertising published in the publications it monitored. It made no allowance for agency commission, and its definition of 'display' advertising includes some advertisements, notably financial notices, not normally classified as 'display' advertising.

47   Ibid.

48   Despite its middle-class readership, the *Daily Mirror* (like the tabloid *Daily Sketch*) received less advertising revenue per copy than the *Daily Herald* in 1935. See ibid., p. 12.

49   B. Hagerty, *Read All about It!*, London: First Stone Publishing, 2003, p. 36.

50   During the war, the government ordered a search of the *Daily Mirror*'s shareholding in a bid to gag the paper, only to discover that there was no dominant shareholder or small group of shareholders to nobble.

51   C. King, *Strictly Personal*, London: Times Newspapers, 1969, p. 101.

52   Belson, *British Press*, p. 12

53   *Statistical Review of Press Advertising*, 1939, p. 9 [advertisement].

54   Compare H. Cudlipp, *Publish and Be Damned*, London: Dakers, 1953, with M. Edelman, *The Mirror: A Political History*, London: Hamish Hamilton, 1966.

55   *Statistical Review of Press Advertising*, 1938, p. 35 [advertisement].

56   Belson, *British Press*, p. 14.

57   The change was gradual: the *Daily Mirror* supported the Conservatives in the November 1935 general election.

58   Butler and Butler, *Twentieth-Century British Political Facts*, p. 235.

59   A. C. H. Smith (with E. Immirzi and T. Blackwell), *Paper Voices: The Popular Press and Social Change 1935–65*, London: Chatto and Windus, 1975, p. 241.

60   J. Gerald, *The British Press under Government Economic Controls*, Minneapolis, University of Minnesota Press, 1956; *Royal Commission on the Press 1947–9 Report* (Cmnd. 7700), London: HMSO, 1949.

61   Institute of Incorporated Practitioners in Advertising (IIPA), *Survey of Press Readership*, London: IIPA, 1939; P. Kimble, *Newspaper Reading in the Third Year of the War*, London: Allen & Unwin, 1942; *Hulton Readership Survey*, London: Hulton, 1947.

62   IIPA, *Survey of Press Readership*; *Hulton Readership Survey*.

63   Belson, *British Press*, pp. 12 and 14.

64   Butler and Butler, *Twentieth-Century British Political Facts*, p. 537.

65   The Hulton Readership Surveys extended from 1947 to 1956, and were superseded by the Institute of Practitioners in Advertising (IPA) National Readership Surveys between 1957 and 1967 and by the Joint Industry Committee for National Readership (JICNAR) Surveys from 1968 to the present.

66   Central News Ltd, evidence to the *Royal Commission on the Press 1961–2, Documentary Evidence*, London: HMSO, 1962, vol. 5, p. 15.

67   Notley Advertising Ltd, ibid., p. 100.

68   Service Advertising Ltd, ibid., p. 113.

69   Benson Ltd, ibid., p. 10.

70   Hobson Bates and Partners Ltd, ibid., p. 45; cf. Hirst Ltd, ibid., p. 41.

71   Cited in R. McKay and B. Barr, *The Story of the Scottish Daily News*, Edinburgh: Cannongate, 1976, p. 108.

72   Samson Jackson and Co. Ltd, evidence to the *Royal Commission on the Press 1947–9, Memoranda of Evidence*, vol. 5, London: HMSO, 1949.

73   Pritchard Wood and Partners Ltd, ibid.

74   Young and Rubicam Ltd, evidence to the *Royal Commission on the Press 1961–2, Documentary Evidence*, London: HMSO, 1962, vol. 5, p. 136.

75 J. Hobson, *The Selection of Advertising Media*, London: Business Publications, 1959, pp. 20–31; cf. rev. edn, 1968, pp. 10–22.

76 J. Adams: *Media Planning*, London: Business Books, 1971, p. 69.

77 Henry Durant, 'The Market Research Society's early days', *Journal of the Market Research Society*, 14(2), 1972.

78 R. Wadsworth and B. Copland, *Market Research*, London: Butterworth, 1951; A. Davies and O. Palmer, *Market Research and Scientific Distribution*, London: Blandford Press, 1957; R. Worcester, *Consumer Market Research Handbook*, Maidenhead: McGraw Hill, 1972.

79 Wadsworth and Copland, *Market Research*, p. 2.

80 M. Abrams, *The Home Market*, rev. edn, London, Allen & Unwin, 1950, p. 7.

81 R. Elvin, 'The Daily Mirror', *Advertising Review*, 1, 1954.

82 D. Wheeler, 'A New Classification of Households', British Market Research Bureau, June 1955.

83 Brian Allt, 'Money or class: new light on household spending', *Advertising Quarterly*, 1975.

84 Feinstein, *Statistical Tables*, pp. 42–3.

85 Ibid., pp. 151–69.

86 *Royal Commission on the Distribution of Income and Wealth: Report No. 4*, London: HMSO, 1976, pp. 101–9.

87 Quality newspapers maintained their advertising ascendancy during newsprint rationing because they secured good newsprint deals.

88 F. Hirsch and D. Gordon, *Newspaper Money*, London: Hutchinson, 1975.

89 The decline of multiple household purchase of newspapers gave rise to the initial decline in circulation. See J. Curran, 'The impact of TV on the audience for national newspapers, 1945–68' in J. Tunstall (ed.), *Media Sociology*, London: Constable, 1970.

90 *Royal Commission on the Press 1974–7, Final Report*, London: HMSO, 1979, p. 37, table 5.3.

91 Ibid.; *Survey of the National Newspaper Industry*, London: Economist Intelligence Unit, 1966.

92 The most significant of these were the *Empire News* (1960) and *Daily Sketch* (1971).

93 *National Readership Survey*, Reports January–December, 1960; July 1963–June 1964; and January–December 1966, London: Institute of Practitioners in Advertising.

94 Odhams Research and Development Services Dept, company records, London, 1964.

95 'Report of an investigation into the transition from the *Daily Herald* to the *Sun*', International Publishing Corporation, company records, 1968.

96 'Report of a survey to study attitudes to daily newspapers', Odhams Ltd, company records, London, 1958.

97 J. Curran, A. Douglas and G. Whannel, 'The political economy of the human-interest story' in A. Smith (ed.), *Newspapers and Democracy*, Cambridge, MA: MIT Press, 1980, p. 328, table 13.10.

98 C. King, *The Future of the Press*, London: MacGibbon and Kee, 1967.

99 J. Curran, 'Advertising and the press' in J. Curran (ed.), *The British Press*, Basingstoke: Macmillan, 1978, p. 242, table 11.3.

100 'A survey of the reader interest in the national morning and London evening press 1934', London Press Exchange Ltd, 1935 (undertaken for the *News Chronicle*).

101 'Feature readership in national dailies', Odhams Research and Development Services Dept, D. H. 77, London, 1964.

102 Readership surveys, Sunday Times Research Dept, 1969–71.

103 Readership surveys, IPC Marketing Research and Development Services Dept, 1969–70.

104 Audit Bureau of Circulation, 1964.

105 Hirsch and Gordon, *Newspaper Money*.

106 *Royal Commission on the Press Interim Report: The National Newspaper Industry*, London: HMSO, 1976, Appendix E, p. 92, table E.1.

107 Ibid., p. 98, table E.7.

108 For examples of this general argument, see N. Angell, *The Press and the Organisation of Society*, London: Labour Publishing Company, 1922; G. Lansbury, *Miracle of Fleet Street*; H. Wickham Steed, *The Press*, London: Penguin Books, 1938; G. Orwell: 'London letter to Partisan Review', April 15, 1941, reprinted in S. Orwell and I. Angus (eds), *The Collected Essays, Journalism and Letters of George Orwell*, vol. 2, Harmondsworth: Penguin Books, 1970; Labour Research Department, *The Millionaire Press*, London: LRD, 1946, Daily Worker Co-operative Society, evidence to the *Royal Commission on the Press 1961–2, Documentary Evidence*, vol. 1, London: HMSO, 1962, P. Hoch, *The Newspaper Game*, London: Calder and Boyars, 1974, among many others. Advertising influence has continued to be conceptualised as a direct and deliberate form of pressure, even by those who reject the notion of advertising influence. See, for example, J. Bird, 'Remember, advertisers guarantee press freedom', *Big Issue*, August 10–16, 2009.

109 J. Tunstall, *Journalists at Work*, London: Constable, 1971.

Chapter 11

1   A. Curtis, *Lit Ed*, Manchester: Carcanet, 1998.

2   F. R. Leavis, *Nor Shall My Sword*, London: Chatto and Windus, 1972, p. 221.

3   J. Sutherland, *Fiction and the Fiction Industry*, London: Athlone, 1978.

4   D. J. Taylor, *A Vain Conceit*, London: Bloomsbury, 1989.

5   My thanks go to Keith Negus and Herbert Pimlott for their invaluable contributions to this essay, and to Goldsmiths College for providing a £600 research grant. Keith Negus (then an undergraduate on research placement) undertook the content analysis for 1984 and undertook a number of interviews with publicists. Herbert Pimlott did the content analysis for 1997. Both also identified data on book production and consumption and made important contributions to the ideas contained in this essay.

6   The eleven literary editors interviewed in 1996 were divided between broadsheets (four), tabloids (three) and weeklies (four). Those interviewed in 1999 were again divided between these three sectors: broadsheets (six), tabloids (three) and weeklies (two). Fewer weekly literary editors were interviewed the second time around because the decline of the weeklies' influence had by then become fully apparent. All interviews were recorded. The overwhelming majority of comments that are quoted are taken from the more recent batch of interviews. In addition, background interviews were conducted with publishing executives and publicists in 1986 and 1999.

7   Sutherland, *Fiction and the Fiction Industry*.

8   The content analysis was based on 270 issues of the nine titles, in 1984 and 1997 (the latest year for which copies were available in the Colindale Newspaper Library), selected to be representative of the annual output of each publication. The most problematic category, popular fiction, was defined largely in terms of genre fiction. A code–recode test of 398 items revealed a 91 per cent agreement in their classification.

9   A study of lead or joint-lead reviews in 1984 produced results that resembled the overall distribution of space between categories of book, though it tended to emphasise still more the prominence given to biography.

10 D. H. Noble and E. M. Noble, *A Survey of Book Reviews, October–December 1973*, London: Noble and Beck, 1974.

11 Euromonitor, *The Book Report*, London: Euromonitor Publications, 1993, table 8.1.

12 UNESCO, *Statistical Yearbook 1996*, Paris: UNESCO, 1997.

13 Ibid., table 7.59.

14 Ibid.

15   The paperbacks tabulated in the content analysis are those that are explicitly identified as such. Although some paperbacks would not have been detected through this method, their number is not large.

16   This was the most recent publicly available information deposited and classified in the British Library. More recent information was available online, but proved to be too expensive to access.

17   Euromonitor, *Book Report*, table 9.5.

18   Ibid., table 9.6.

19   Ibid., table 8.3.

20   P. Mann, *Books: Buyers and Borrowers*, London: André Deutsch, 1971; Publishers Association (PA), *The Book Trade Yearbook*, London: PA, 1985.

21   Ibid., table 7.7.

22   S. Connor, *Theory and Cultural Value*, Oxford: Blackwell, 1992; J. Frow, *Cultural Studies and Cultural Value*, Oxford: Oxford University Press, 1995.

23   For example, T. Modleski, *Loving with a Vengeance*, Hamden, CT: Archon Books, 1982; J. Radway, *Reading the Romance*, London: Verso, 1987; E. Geraghty, *Women and Soap Opera*, Cambridge: Polity, 1991; and M. Landy, 'Melodrama and femininity in World War Two British cinema' in R. Murphy (ed.), *The British Cinema Book*, London: British Film Institute, 1997.

24   The publication is identified because it is relevant in terms of what was said, and also because this interview was conducted on the record.

25   D. McQuail, *Analysis of Newspaper Content*, London: HMSO, 1977; J. Curran, and J. Seaton, *Power without Responsibility*, 5th edn, London: Routledge, 1997.

26   J. Tunstall, *Newspaper Power*, Oxford: Oxford University Press, 1996.

27   P. Schlesinger, *Putting 'Reality' Together*, London: Constable, 1978.

28   J. Curran, A. Douglas and G. Whannel, 'The political economy of the human-interest story' in A. Smith (ed.), *Newspapers and Democracy*, Cambridge, MA: MIT Press, 1980.

29   Noble and Noble, *Survey of Book Reviews*.

30   They were a biography of Nye Bevan by the politician and former editor Michael Foot; a study of his author parents, Harold Nicolson and Vita Sackville-West, by the author, journalist and former politician Nigel Nicolson; and a biography of Marilyn Monroe by the novelist and journalist Norman Mailer.

31   D. White, 'The "gate keeper": a case study in the selection of news' [1952], in D. Berkowitz (ed.), *Social Meanings of News*, London: Sage, 1997.

32   P. M. Hirsch, 'Processing fads and fashions: an organisational analysis of cultural industry systems', *American Journal of Sociology*, 77(4), 1972: 639–59.

33   *Evening Standard*, December 30, 1993.

34   Our thanks to Marion Milne and Macmillan for making available office records.

35   J. Gribbin, *In Search of Schrödinger's Cat*, London: Bantam, 1984.

36   J. Tunstall, *Journalists at Work*, London: Constable, 1971.

37   Curtis, *Lit Ed*, p. 21.

38   In 1870 the range of books reviewed in the national press was more eclectic and covered topics from fables to stomach disorders, reflecting a time when knowledge was less standardised by the university system. Classical learning received more attention than now and genre novels even less. The printed versions of plays and issues of periodicals were also sometimes reviewed as books, during a period when the book review had not fully stabilised as a literary form.

39   M. Sanderson, *Education, Economic Change and Society in England 1780–1870*, London: Macmillan, 1983.

40   R. McKibbin, *Classes and Cultures*, Oxford: Oxford University Press, 1998.

41   A. Reid, *Social Classes and Social Relations in Britain, 1850–1914*, London: Macmillan, 1992; P. Clarke, *Hope and Glory*, London: Penguin Books, 1997; D. Cannadine, *Class in Britain*, New Haven: Yale University Press, 1998.

42   D. L. LeMahieu, *A Culture for Democracy*, Oxford: Clarendon Press, 1988; R. Hewison, *Culture and Consensus*, London: Methuen, 1995; McGibbin, *Classes and Cultures*; K. Gelder and S. Thornton (eds), *The Subcultures Reader*, London: Routledge, 1997.

43   M. Wiener, *English Culture and the Decline of the Industrial Spirit 1850–1980*, Harmondsworth: Penguin Books, 1985.

44   H. Perkin, *The Rise of Professional Society*, London: Routledge, 1989.

45   N. McKendrick, "'Gentlemen and players" revisited: the gentlemanly ideal, the business ideal and the professional ideal in English literary culture' in N. McKendrick and R. Outhwaite (eds), *Business Life and Public Policy*, Cambridge: Cambridge University Press, 1986.

46   S. Collini, *Absent Minds*, Oxford: Oxford University Press, 2006 (which focuses on the period after 1918).

47   The *Sunday Mirror* dropped book reviews in 1998, but the *Daily Mirror* revived them in the same year.

48   L. Coser, C. Kadushin and U. W. Powe, *Books*, New York: Basic Books, 1982.

49   The two books were David Tinker, *Message from the Falklands* (Penguin Books) and Robert Harris, *Gotcha!* (Faber). The fact that both were critical of official manipulation rather than overtly opposed to the war probably made them more acceptable. *Iron Britannia* (Anthony Barnett), an overtly anti-war book, would have provided a stronger test of independence but its publisher, Allison and Busby, had a very incomplete set of reviews.

50   Tunstall, *Newspaper Power*, p. 32.

51   M. Lane, *Books and Publishers*, Toronto: D. E. Heath, 1982, p. 27.

52   A similar conjunction took place in the same period between TV and publishing, in a process that awaits investigation.

53   This gender shift reflected that of the entire population of literary editors working for the national press. See Women in Publishing, *Reviewing the Reviews*, London: Journeyman Press, 1987; and Media Information, *Editors' Media Directories*, vol. 1, London: Media Information, 1998.

54   Women in Publishing, *Reviewing the Reviews*.

55   Mintel, *Leisure Industry Report (8)*, London: Mintel, 1984.

56   M. Ward, *Readers and Library Users*, London: Library Association, 1977.

57   Women in Publishing, *Reviewing the Reviews*.

58   P. Bourdieu, *The Field of Cultural Production*, Cambridge: Polity, 1993.

Chapter 12

1   Anon., 'Deng Xiaoping quotes and quotations', 2004. Online. Available HTTP: <http://www.brainyquote.com/quotes/authors/d/deng-xiaoping.html>.

2   F. Fukuyama, *The End of History and the Last Man*, Harmondsworth: Penguin Books, 1993.

3   J. O'Mahony, 'David Edgar', *Guardian* (review section), March 20, 2004, p. 23.

4   S. Hall, *The Hard Road to Renewal*, London: Verso, 1988.

5   See Chapter 9.

6   J. Curran, *Media and Power*, London: Routledge, 2002, ch. 6.

7   Many of the 1960s and early 1970s pioneers in Britain – such as Tunstall, McQuail, Blumler, Himmelweit and Halloran – negotiated the American communications tradition by advancing centre-left versions of it. They were followed by a more radical, and more humanities-based, tradition in the 1970s that provides the starting point of this chapter. For an account of one grouping within this second wave of media researchers, see J. Curran, 'The rise of the Westminster school' in A. Calabrese and C. Sparks (eds), *Toward a Political Economy of Culture*, Lanham, MD: Rowman & Littlefield, 2004, and for

the early development of British cultural studies, see G. Turner, *British Cultural Studies*, 3rd edn, London: Routledge, 2002.

8   S. Hall, 'Culture, the media and the "ideological effect"' in J. Curran, M. Gurevitch and J. Woollacott (eds), *Mass Communication and Society*, London: Edward Arnold, 1977.

9   S. Hall, 'The rediscovery of "ideology": the return of the repressed in media studies' in M. Gurevitch, T. Bennett, J. Curran and J. Woollacott (eds), *Culture, Society and the Media*, London: Methuen, 1982; S. Hall, 'Signification, representation, ideology: Althusser and the poststructuralist debates', *Critical Studies in Mass Communication*, 2(2), 1985: 91–114.

10 This said, Gramsci was assimilated *from the outset* in media and cultural studies in a way that was significantly *different from* the understanding of his fragmentary work in political studies (typified by D. Forgacs, 'Gramsci and Marxism in Britain', *New Left Review*, 176, 1989: 70–88).

11 N. Garnham, 'The media and the public sphere' in P. Golding, G. Murdock and P. Schlesinger (eds), *Communicating Politics*, Leicester: Leicester University Press, 1986; revised in N. Garnham, *Capitalism and Communication*, London: Sage, 1990.

12 J. Habermas, *The Structural Transformation of the Public Sphere*, Cambridge: Polity, 1989 (first German edition 1962).

13 For example, P. Scannell, 'Public service broadcasting and modern public life', *Media, Culture and Society*, 11(2), 1989: 135–66.

14 Habermas, *Structural Transformation*, p. 171.

15 J. Habermas, *Between Facts and Norms*, Cambridge: Polity, 1996 (first German edition 1992).

16 S. Hall, C. Critcher, T. Jefferson, J. Clarke and B. Roberts, *Policing the Crisis*, Basingstoke: Macmillan Education, 1978.

17 J.-F. Lyotard, *The Postmodern Condition*, Manchester: Manchester University Press, 1984.

18 J. Baudrillard, 'The implosion of meaning in the media and the implosion of the social in the masses' in K. Woodward (ed.), *The Myths of Information*, London: Routledge and Kegan Paul, 1980, p. 142.

19 M. Poster, 'Introduction' in M. Poster (ed.), *Baudrillard: Selected Writings*, Stanford, CA: Stanford University Press, 1988, p. 6.

20 I. Ang and J. Hermes, 'Gender and/in media consumption' in J. Curran and M. Gurevitch (eds), *Mass Media and Society*, London: Arnold, 1991, p. 323.

21 M. Foucault, *Discipline and Punishment*, Harmondsworth: Penguin Books, 1979, p. 27.

22 P. Willis, *Common Culture*, Milton Keynes: Open University Press, 1990.

23 P. Willis, *Learning to Labour*, London: Saxon House, 1977.

24 Willis, *Common Culture*, p. 128.

25 Ibid., pp. 129–30 and 138.

26 Ibid., p. 158.

27 Ibid., p. 131.

28 Ibid., p. 159.

29 Ibid., pp. 158–60.

30 J. Fiske, *Television Culture*, London: Routledge, 1987, pp. 261–2.

31 Ibid.; and J. Fiske, 'Postmodernism and television' in Curran and Gurevitch (eds), *Mass Media and Society*.

32 J. Tomlinson, *Globalization and Culture*, London: Routledge, 1999.

33 J. Sinclair, E. Jacka and S. Cunningham (eds), *New Patterns in Global Television*, Oxford: Oxford University Press, 1996.

34 K. Roe and G. de Meyer, 'Music Television: MTV-Europe' in J. Wieten, G. Murdock and P. Dahlgren (eds), *Television across Europe*, London: Sage, 2000.

35 Tomlinson, *Globalization and Culture*, p. 94.

36 H. Schiller, *Communication and Cultural Domination*, White Plains, NY: Sharpe, 1976.

37   G. Tuchman, 'Introduction: the symbolic annihilation of women by the mass media' in G. Tuchman, A. Kaplan and J. Benet (eds), *Hearth and Home*, New York: Oxford University Press, 1978.

38   T. Modleski, *Loving with a Vengeance*, Hamden, CT: Archon Books, 1982.

39   M. Landy, *British Genres*, Princeton: Princeton University Press, 1991, pp. 17 and 485.

40   A. McRobbie, '*More!*: New sexualities in girls' and women's magazines' in J. Curran, D. Morley and V. Walkerdine (eds), *Cultural Studies and Communications*, London: Routledge, 1996.

41   A. Costain and H. Fraizer, 'Media portrayal of "second wave" feminist groups' in S. Chambers and A. Costain (eds), *Deliberation, Democracy and the Media*, Lanham, MD: Rowman & Littlefield, 2000, p. 173.

42   M. Macdonald, *Representing Women*, London: Arnold, 1995.

43   J. Shattuc, *The Talking Cure*, New York: Routledge, 1997, p. 2.

44   B. Compaine and D. Gomery, *Who Owns the Media?*, 3rd edn, Mahwah, NJ: Lawrence Erlbaum, 2000.

45   N. Negroponte, *Being Digital*, London: Hodder and Stoughton, 1995.

46   M. Poster, *What's the Matter with the Internet?*, Minneapolis: University of Minnesota Press, 2001.

47   W. Donk, B. Loader, P. Nihon and D. Rucht, *Cyberprotest*, London: Routledge, 2004.

48   R. Tsagarousianou, D. Tambini, and C. Bryan (eds), *Cyberdemocracy*, London: Routledge, 1998.

49   L. Gross, 'The gay global village in cyberspace' in N. Couldry and J. Curran (eds), *Contesting Media Power*, Lanham, MD: Rowman & Littlefield, 2003.

50   M. Castells, *The Internet Galaxy*, Oxford: Oxford University Press, 2001.

51   Curran, *Media and Power*.

52   Good studies in the media political economy tradition include Garnham, *Capitalism and Communication*; T. Gitlin, *Inside Prime Time*, rev. edn, London: Routledge, 1994; P. Golding and G. Murdock, *Political Economy of the Media*, vols 1 and 2, Cheltenham: Edward Elgar, 1997; P. Golding and G. Murdock, 'Culture, communication and political economy' in J. Curran and M. Gurevitch (eds), *Mass Media and Society*, 4th edn, London: Hodder Arnold, 2005; R. McChesney, *Rich Media, Poor Democracy*, Urbana: University of Illinois Press, 1999; C. Leys, *Market-Driven Politics*, London: Verso, 2001; and J. Hardy, 'The contribution of critical political economy' in J. Curran (ed.), *Media and Society*, 5th edn, London: Bloomsbury Academic, 2010. Useful introductions to media economics are provided by R. Picard, *The Economics and Financing of Media Companies*, New York: Fordham University Press, 2002; G. Doyle, *Understanding Media Economics*, London: Sage, 2002; and A. Albarran, *Media Economics*, Ames, IA: Iowa University Press, 1996.

53   D. Hesmondhalgh, *The Cultural Industries*, London: Sage, 2002.

54   Curran *et al.* (eds), *Mass Communication and Society*.

55   Recent publications in this tradition that are illuminating include C. Edwin Baker, *Media, Markets and Democracy*, Cambridge: Cambridge University Press, 2002; James T. Hamilton, *All the News that's Fit to Sell: How the Market Transforms Information into News*, Princeton: Princeton University Press, 2004; W. L. Bennett, *News*, 5th edn, New York, Longman, 2003; D. Shannor, *News from Abroad*, New York, Columbia University Press, 2003; B. Kovach and T. Rosenstiel, *The Elements of Journalism*, London: Atlantic Books, 2003; P. Seib, *Going Live*, Lanham, MD: Rowman & Littlefield, 2002; D. Croteau and W. Hoynes, *The Business of Media*, Thousand Oaks, CA: Pine Forge, 2001; L. Sabato, M. Stencel and S. Lichter, *Peep Show*, Lanham, MD: Rowman & Littlefield, 2000; T. Glasser (ed.), *The Idea of Public Journalism*, New York: Guilford, 1999; McChesney, *Rich Media, Poor Democracy*; and B. Kovach and T. Rosenstiel, *Warp Speed*, New York: Century Foundation, 1999.

56 F. Gilliam, S. Iyengar, A. Simon and O. Wright, 'Crime in black and white: the violent, scary world of local news' in S. Iyengar and R. Reeves (eds), *Do the Media Govern?*, Thousand Oaks, CA: Sage, 1997

57 T. Patterson, *The Vanishing Voter*, New York: Vintage, 2003, p. 89.

58 P. Klite, R. Bardwell and J. Salzman, 'Local TV news: getting away with murder', *Harvard International Journal of Press/Politics*, 2(2), 1997: 102–12.

59 T. Patterson, 'The search for a standard: markets and media', *Political Communication*, 20(2), 2003: 139–43; D. Lowry, T. Ching, J. Nio and D. Leitner, 'Setting the public fear agenda: a longitudinal analysis of network TV crime reporting, public perceptions of crime, and FBI crime statistics', *Journal of Communication*, 53(1), 2003: 61–73.

60 S. Iyengar, 'Media effects: paradigms for the analysis of local television news' in Chambers and Costain (eds), *Deliberation, Democracy and the Media*.

61 United Nations Development Programme, 'Patterns of global inequality' [Human Development Report 1999] in D. Held and A. McGrew (eds), *The Global Transformations Reader*, 2nd edn, Cambridge: Polity, 2003, p. 425.

62 The rise of the Southeast Asian economies, notably Taiwan and South Korea, followed by rapid growth in China and also India, goes against simplistic versions of the global 'polarisation' thesis. What view is taken depends partly on what categories are used, over what time span and also crucially on what can be attributed to globalisation as distinct from other influences. For an illuminating debate, see R. Wade and M. Wolf, 'Are global poverty and inequality getting worse?' in Held and McGrew (eds), *Global Transformations Reader*.

63 J. Stiglitz, *Globalization and Its Discontents*, London: Penguin Books, 2002; United Nations Development Programme, 'Patterns of global inequality'; Wade and Wolf, 'Global poverty', among others. It is also argued that the issue of global inequality is not simply a geographical one: social groups within affluent areas, as well as impoverished areas, have been bypassed by the flows of wealth produced by globalisation (M. Castells, *End of Millennium*, 2nd edn, Oxford: Blackwell, 2000). There is, however, a significant difference in the absolute levels of poverty between poor groups in rich and impoverished countries.

64 Stiglitz, *Globalization and Its Discontents*; L. Sklair, *Globalization*, 3rd edn, Oxford: Oxford University Press, 2002; W. Hutton, *The World We're In*, rev. edn, London: Abacus, 2003.

65 Leys, *Market-Driven Politics*; L. Panitch and C. Leys (eds), *Global Capitalism Versus Democracy* [Socialist Register 1999], Rendlesham: Merlin, 1999; S. Strange, *The Retreat of the State*, Cambridge: Cambridge University Press, 1996.

66 J. Keane, *Global Civil Society?*, Cambridge: Cambridge University Press, 2003; Sklair, *Globalization*.

67 For an optimistic interpretation, arguing that there has been an evolution from a system based on national government to a multi-layered system of governance eliciting a corresponding political and democratic adjustment, see D. Held, A. McGrew, D. Goldblatt and J. Perraton, *Global Transformations*, Cambridge: Polity, 1999.

68 See, among others, D. Schiller, *Digital Capitalism*, Cambridge, MA: MIT Press, 2000; McChesney, *Rich Media, Poor Democracy*; L. Lessig, *Code and Other Laws of Cyberspace*, New York: Basic Books, 1999; L. Lessig, *The Future of Ideas*, New York: Random House, 2001; J. Curran and J. Seaton, *Power without Responsibility*, 6th edn, London: Routledge, 2003.

69 F. Devine and M. Waters (eds), *Social Inequalities in Comparative Perspective*, Oxford: Blackwell, 2004; A. Heath and C. Payne, 'Social mobility' in A. H. Halsey with J. Webb (eds), *Twentieth-Century British Social Trends*, Basingstoke: Macmillan, 2000; M. Savage and M. Egerton, 'Social mobility, individual ability and the inheritance of class inequality', *Sociology*, 31(4), 1997: 645–72, among others.

70 K. Roberts, *Class in Modern Britain*, Basingstoke: Palgrave, 2001, p. 194.

71   Hutton, *The World We're In*, p. 187.
72   S. Aldridge, 'Life chances and social mobility: an overview of the evidence', London: Prime Minister's Strategy Unit, Cabinet Office, March 30, 2004, p. 24. Online. Available HTTP: <http://www.strategy.gov.uk/files/pdf/lifechances-socialmobility.pdf 2004> (accessed November 6, 2004).
73   Castells, *End of Millennium*; J. Kelsey, *The New Zealand Experiment*, Auckland: Auckland University Press, 1995.
74   Hutton, *The World We're In*, p. 188.
75   Aldridge, 'Life chances', p. 6.
76   G. Murdock, 'Reconstructing the ruined tower: contemporary communications and questions of class' in J. Curran and M. Gurevitch (eds), *Mass Media and Society*, 3rd edn, London: Arnold, 2000.
77   B. Skeggs, *Formation of Class and Gender*, London: Sage, 1997.

Index

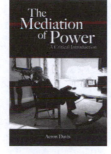